MW00559011

The Verdict of Battle

The Verdict of Battle

THE LAW OF VICTORY AND THE
MAKING OF MODERN WAR

James Q. Whitman

Harvard University Press

Cambridge, Massachusetts

London, England

2012

Library of Congress Cataloging-in-Publication Data

Whitman, James Q., 1957–
   The verdict of battle : the law of victory and the making of modern war /
James Q. Whitman.
      p. cm.
   Includes bibliographical references and index.
   ISBN 978-0-674-06714-1 (alk. paper)
   1. War—Moral and ethical aspects.   2. Combat—Moral and ethical aspects.
3. Battles—Europe—History—18th century.   4. Military art and science—
Europe—History—18th century.   5. War (International law).   6. Military
ethics—History—18th century.   7. Military history—Europe—18th century.
I. Title.
   U22.W55 2012
   172'.42—dc23   2012022176

Contents

A Note to the Reader

The bulk of this book is about the wars of the eighteenth century. Those wars fell into two broad classes: the land wars of the European continent and the wars fought elsewhere on the globe. This book discusses only the great continental wars. It also has nothing to say about naval warfare. This is something to regret, but a single book can do only so much.

All translations are my own, unless otherwise indicated. Citations to classical texts are given to the Loeb Classical Library editions.

The Verdict of Battle

Introduction

TWO ARMED GROUPS MEET IN PITCHED BATTLE. There is a chaotic struggle. Many of the combatants are killed. At the end of a conflict lasting a few hours or perhaps an entire day, one group flees, or perhaps both do. One group, usually the one that manages to hold its ground amid the terror and killing, is deemed the victor.

How should we think about such an event? From the point of view of a pacifist, it can only be regarded as a senseless collective slaughter, a descent into irrational barbarism, a horror. Consider a seventeenth-century painting, *The Aftermath of a Battle*, by Sebastian Vrancx and Jan Brueghel the Younger: as the defeated army flees in the background, the victors brutally finish off survivors and strip corpses of their few valuables.[1] The scene is a study in savagery. Or consider the famous description of the aftermath of the Battle of Solferino in 1859, published by Henri Dunant, the founder of the Red Cross. Here is what Dunant witnessed once the battle was over:

> The poor wounded men that were being picked up all day long were
> ghastly pale and exhausted. Some, who had been the most badly
> hurt, had a stupefied look as though they could not grasp what was
> said to them . . . Some, who had gaping wounds already beginning

to show infection were almost crazed with suffering. They begged to be put out of their misery, and writhed with faces distorted in the grip of the death-struggle. . . .

Anyone crossing the vast theatre of the previous day's fighting could see at every step, in the midst of chaotic disorder, despair unspeakable and misery of every kind. . . .

Some of the soldiers who lay dead had a calm expression, those who had been killed outright. But many were disfigured by the torments of the death-struggle, their limbs stiffened, their bodies blotched with ghastly spots, their hands clawing at the ground, their eyes staring widely, their moustaches bristling above clenched teeth that were bared in a sinister convulsive grin . . .

. . . [B]odies lay in thousands on hills and earthworks, on the tops of mounds, strewn in groves and woods.[2]

What, the pacifist must ask, could possibly justify so much promiscuous death and suffering? How can a pitched battle be regarded as anything other than a frightening exercise in barbarism?

But of course pacifists have been few in human history. Most human beings, in most times and places, have found pitched battles anything but senseless or pointless. Quite the contrary: most human beings, in most times and places, have invested these deadly events with supreme significance. To be slaughtered in pitched battle has often counted as making a profoundly meaningful sacrifice. Victory in battle too has been full of significance, redrawing borders and overthrowing kings and governments.

In particular, in past centuries, a pitched battle was often described as a momentous kind of trial or legal proceeding, a lawful way for two contending parties to settle their differences through a day of deliberate, staged collective violence. During the Middle Ages, for example, a pitched battle was regarded as a judgment of God. Staging a pitched battle was akin to staging an ordeal. Battles and ordeals alike were legal proceedings, ways of summoning the Lord to act as judge in cases where humans could not succeed in settling their disputes themselves.

Later centuries continued to view pitched battles as a kind of legal proceeding. In the eyes of eighteenth-century lawyers, for example, a pitched battle was a settlement procedure fought under a "tacit contract of chance," by which two contending countries agreed to allow their dispute to be resolved by "the chance of arms."[3] As late as the nineteenth century, lawyers still deemed a battle to be a species of contractual settlement procedure. The idea that a pitched battle was a legal procedure, a lawful means of deciding international disputes through consensual collective violence, a kind of trial with a kind of verdict, was a commonplace for centuries.

In the modern world, by contrast, the idea that a pitched battle could be regarded as a form of trial has come to seem bizarre. Resolving matters through law means *eschewing* violence; the proposition that a legal question could be resolved through a deliberate act of large-scale violence seems a contradiction in terms. Certainly we find it hard to accept the idea that it is appropriate for two countries to agree to resolve a dispute by staging a mutual mass slaughter of young men. Nevertheless our ancestors routinely staged pitched battles as a way of settling a dispute, and to understand the history of the law of war we must recognize that they had deep reasons for doing so.

Despite its horror and savagery, a pitched battle is what social scientists call a "conflict resolution mechanism." It is a contained and economical way of resolving a dispute between two warring groups or countries. It may be true that the direct participants in a battle are exposed to a form of nightmarish violence, but the fact remains that the result of fighting a pitched battle is to limit violence in the community at large: if a conflict can be decided by a day of concentrated killing on the battlefield, then violence can be prevented from spilling over to the rest of society. Staging a pitched battle, savage though it is, is a way of limiting war, of sparing society the horrors of worse forms of warfare.

And other forms of warfare, let us not forget, are far worse than pitched battles. The alternative to staging a formal battle, after all, is some form of total war or "hard" war. There have been many such forms in the history of human warfare: the siege; the *chevauchée,* in which medieval horsemen terrorized a countryside; the Muslim *ghazw* or *razzia,* much like the chevauchée; the systematic pillaging in such conflicts as the Thirty Years War; campaigns of devastation like Sherman's March to the Sea; the guerrilla war; the terrorist campaign; or the modern bombing raid.

These are all much more indiscriminately violent than pitched battle, much more dramatic and uncontrolled descents into general killing.

Compared to these other forms of war, a pitched battle is a blessing, an institution that by its very nature contains the violence of war. Indeed in its classic form, as it existed before the late nineteenth century, a pitched battle was supposed to be a beautifully contained event. Like an Aristotelian drama, the classic pitched battle was strictly limited in time and place. Fought on a defined field, it was supposed to last one day and no more, beginning in tension at dawn, ending in exhaustion at dusk, and so (in the best of circumstances) terminating the war by the time night fell. A limited, circumscribed engagement, it was supposed to leave the rest of society untouched.

Ancient authors sometimes described pitched battles as astoundingly contained events. For example, a Greek traveler in ancient India gave this report: "Even when battle is raging nearby, farmers are undisturbed by any sense of danger, for while the combatants on either side make carnage of each other, they allow those engaged in husbandry to remain quite unmolested."[4] Such a description is hard to take entirely at face value, but there is no doubt that contained pitched battles really did take place in the human past. In fact they were still taking place as late as the mid-nineteenth century. Solferino, the battle that horrified Henri Dunant, was just such a classic single-day battle, limited to one battlefield—the "vast theater" through which Dunant walked aghast—on June 24, 1859. In that single day of concentrated killing, Solferino resolved its war, producing a momentous historic verdict: the unification of Italy.

Similar things can be said of the most famous of nineteenth-century pitched battles, Waterloo. Waterloo began and ended on June 18, 1815, starting with maneuvering at dawn, continuing with direct engagement at 11:30, and finishing when the victorious Prussian and British commanders sat down to produce their accounts of the event in the late dusk of summer. The suffering was surely no less than the suffering at Solferino, but once the day of battle had ended, the issue was decided: Napoleon had lost, the war was over, and the course of history had changed.[5] There was no ensuing total war, no pillaging of the French countryside, no besieging of French towns, no March to the Sea. The battle had succeeded in ending its war without breaching its Aristotelian limits.

A true battle, a classic pitched battle, is by no means an unambiguous descent into horror. It is a ritualized means of focusing, and therefore containing, the violence of war—a means, in the words of anthropologists, of "limiting the engagement, and thus the losses."[6]

To be sure, not all pitched battles succeed in ending their wars. In the eighteenth century, for example, many battles were fought, but few proved instantly decisive, and wars dragged on for years. Yet it is important to see that even inconclusive battle warfare is a blessing; it is a very good thing for society when commanders limit themselves to fighting pitched battles, even indecisive ones, rather than allowing their troops to maraud through the country at large. Battle warfare may drag on, just as litigation may drag on. Nevertheless societies that manage to contain the horror of war to the arena of defined battlefields are societies that enjoy an important kind of broader peace—a kind of rule of law.

A pitched battle *is* something like a trial, and warfare that is limited to battles, even when it is inconclusive, represents a kind of rule of law. Confining warfare to a field of battle is like confining disputes to the legal system. If two private parties can be induced to submit their dispute to the judicial process, they will be spared a worse danger: that the conflict between them will degenerate into violence. A trial can be a difficult and embittering experience, and sometimes litigation, like war, may drag on; but deciding disputes through litigation is more civilized than settling them through private vengeance. In much the same way, battle warfare is a more peaceable way of settling international disputes than more savage forms of war.

In fact far from being wholly barbaric, classic battle warfare, of the kind that was fought at Dunant's Solferino, was arguably a more valuable means of civilizing war than anything we can offer in our modern law of war. When modern lawyers try to moderate the horrors of warfare, they appeal to the *jus ad bellum* and the *jus in bello*. The jus ad bellum is the law determining when nations are permitted to go to war, restricting war to cases of self-defense and the like. The modern jus ad bellum strictly forbids parties from agreeing to resolve their disputes through a consensual pitched battle; modern lawyers hold that wars should be fought only in cases where there is an extreme necessity to fend off imminent aggression or prevent an imminent act of gross evil. The jus in bello is the body of rules on how nations must conduct themselves when they are at war, such as rules of engagement, or the definitions distinguishing combatants from noncombatants. The modern jus in bello strictly forbids the kind of conduct painted by Vrancx and Brueghel, the casual murder of the wounded and the plundering of their goods. Acts like that are what modern lawyers call "war crimes" and they are condemned by what modern lawyers call "International Humanitarian Law." These days lawyers also like to talk about a *jus post bellum*, a law for the just treatment of the defeated.[7]

The great aim of the lawyers who have developed all this modern law is to ameliorate and humanize warfare by subjecting it to the most demanding standards of high moral conduct. Undoubtedly their efforts have some impact. But might we not do more to limit the horror of war if we could stage contained pitched battles? Might it not be a blessing if we could agree to resolve our conflicts through contained deadly engagements, begun at dawn, finished at dusk, claiming only military personnel for their victims and leaving the rest of society unscathed?

Of course, no such thing is possible. It is part of the modern condition that we have lost the capacity to limit the conflict of war to pitched battle.

In the societies of the past, the contained pitched battle was probably a universal human institution. To be sure, battles were generally rare events in the past; most wars, in most times and places, have degenerated into uncontainable savagery, spreading far off the field of battle. Battle warfare has been the exception in human history. Nevertheless in all premodern periods our ancestors succeeded in coming together from time to time to stage contained, formal pitched battles. Certain periods in particular are remembered as classic ages of battles. Classical Greece is one example of a culture famous for its pitched battles; another is eighteenth-century Europe and America. Indeed the eighteenth century survives in modern memory as a kind of golden age of battle warfare, an era when war was successfully limited to single-day pitched battles and orderly sieges at famous sites such as Malplaquet, Leuthen, Fontenoy,

and Yorktown. Pitched battles continued to dominate warfare during
the first part of the nineteenth century; even after warfare began to take
on more fearsome forms in the Napoleonic period, European wars were
still largely being conducted through great single-day pitched battles
such as Marengo, Austerlitz, Jena, Leipzig, and Waterloo. Great pitched
battles such as Solferino and Königgrätz (1866) were still deciding wars
as late as the 1860s.

Since the 1860s, however, it has become clear that we no longer have
any hope of confining warfare to the battlefield. The two wars that marked
the unmistakable turning point were the American Civil War and the
Franco-Prussian War. In those great mid-nineteenth-century conflicts,
even pitched battles that wore all the trappings of decisiveness failed to
decide the issue, and the conflict spread far from the field of battle. Gettysburg (July 1–3, 1863), to take the most familiar example, did not settle
the American Civil War any more than the other famous battles of the
conflict did. The war could not be limited to battle at all, as matters degenerated into guerrilla warfare and eventually into Sherman's March to the
Sea. The conflict could be ended only by an uncontainable war of general
devastation.

The Battle of Sedan, the Franco-Prussian battle fought on the momentous day of September 1, 1870, is perhaps an even more striking example, if one less familiar to Americans. On the surface, Sedan closely
paralleled the battle of Waterloo fifty-five years earlier. It was a classic
day-long pitched battle, which produced the facially decisive defeat of
Napoleon III. Newspaper reports described it as one of the most clearly
decisive defeats in all of human history. Eighty thousand French soldiers
were taken prisoner, and the French emperor ceremoniously offered his
sword to the king of Prussia and entered into a formal capitulation, an
act that technically ended the war according to the international law of
the day.

Yet the French populace did not accept the seemingly decisive verdict
of Sedan. The Franco-Prussian War dragged on over months of horror,
as the cities of France were reduced in bloody sieges one by one, while
the French population mounted a bitter guerrilla campaign against the
Germans, just as the Confederates of the American South had done a
few years earlier. The war ended only when Helmuth von Moltke, the

Prussian general, had finally marched all the way to the sea, as it were, just as Sherman had done five years earlier. Again a war of devastation, spilling far off the battlefield, was necessary to secure victory.

As these examples suggest, in the mid-nineteenth century the possibility of containing war within the limits of the battlefield definitively vanished. The "era of decisive battle," as John Keegan writes, had "draw[n] to a close."[8] To be sure, the idea that wars involve battles did not die after 1870. The idea of battle remained gripping enough that twentieth-century wars were still described as fought in battles. But the battles of World War I and World War II had little in common with the classic, Aristotelian, single-day ritualized contests of earlier periods, holding out the possibility of decisive verdicts. Instead they were multi-week or multi-month monstrosities like the "Battle" of Stalingrad and the "Battle" of Verdun—sinks of horror that did nothing to restrain the eruption of violence into society at large, events in uncontrollable wars that ended only in the utter destruction of one side. More recently the Battle of Baghdad in 2003 certainly resulted in the utter defeat of Iraqi forces. In the classic language of Carl von Clausewitz, it was a successful *Vernichtungsschlacht*, a successful "battle of annihilation," which means that, according to Clausewitzian theory, it should have succeeded in deciding the issue. But the Battle of Baghdad did not bring a settled peace to Iraq, as, once again, the war spilled far off anything that could be called a battlefield.

Why was it ever possible to limit warfare to the concentrated collective violence of pitched battle? Why did the classic pitched battle go into decline in the age of the American Civil War and the Franco-Prussian War? Is there anything we can still learn from the battle warfare of the past?

These are the questions this book addresses. As I aim to show, the collapse of pitched battle in the 1860s and 1870s had to do with a breakdown in the *law* of war. The classic pitched battle, of the kind that was still being fought at Solferino in 1859, functioned as a kind of formal legal proceeding, akin to a trial—a form of large-scale trial by combat. The experience of such a battle was typically nightmarish for the immediate participants, but the event served to keep war within the confines of the field of battle. Battles were certainly not always fully decisive, but commanders had strong incentives to abide by the legal rules, seeking victory through pitched battle rather than through wars of general devastation. Indeed strange though it may sound, there was a kind of rule of law in the premodern practice of battle warfare—a shaky rule of law, a perpetually uncertain rule of law, but a rule of law nevertheless. The tale of the making of modern warfare is the tale of how that rule of law functioned, especially in the golden age of the eighteenth century, and how it collapsed in the era of Gettysburg and Sedan.

Some of what I have to say will be familiar to military historians and strategists. Much of it will be alien, though; military writers are not accustomed to thinking of battles as legal procedures. It is one of my purposes to show that military historians have sometimes failed to do full justice to military history, because they have sometimes been slow to recognize that the pitched battles of the past were legal events as well as military ones—that they were fought in line with legal rules, not just in line with tactical considerations.

But military historians are not my only targets, or even my main ones. It is above all the lawyers who have failed to reckon with their past. Modern lawyers have not grasped how the battle warfare of the past functioned. As a result, they have misunderstood much of the drama, and much of the tragedy, of the history of the law of war.

The battle warfare of the past rested on a conception of the law of war that is very different from the modern conception, and very difficult for modern lawyers to accept. For modern lawyers, the law of war is at base a humanitarian enterprise, often close in spirit to criminal law. Its principal business is to prohibit evil acts and punish evil actors. That is why it revolves around the *jus ad bellum* and the *jus in bello*, the law of the just causes of war and the law of the humanitarian restraints on its conduct.[9] Its aim is to guarantee that wars are fought only for the noblest and most urgent of reasons and in the spirit of the most scrupulous respect for human life. Of course, modern lawyers recognize that the necessities of war may force combatants to make some hard choices and ugly compromises.[10] But at the end of the day, they think of their job as keeping the demons of war penned up.

This is a conception of the law of war that follows naturally from the way modern lawyers perceive war itself. When modern lawyers look upon war, they see it the way Dunant did, wandering among the dead and wounded on the battlefield of Solferino. They see the horror, the "unspeakable despair and misery," the "writhing," and the "faces distorted in the grip of the death-struggle."[11] Or else they see war in the way the Nuremberg Tribunal saw it, confronting the crimes of the Nazi regime: as "essentially an evil thing."[12] They see war as one of the Four Horsemen of the Book of Revelation's Apocalypse: as War, the companion of Pestilence, Famine, and Death. Seeing war in this apocalyptic way, modern lawyers arrive naturally at the notion that their role is something like the role of the Red Cross nurses created by Dunant or of the prosecutors assembled at Nuremberg. Their task must be to palliate the suffering and prohibit the evil by every means possible.

Yet our pre-nineteenth-century ancestors perceived war differently, and in consequence they had a different conception of the task of the law of war. They were not blind to the horror of war, and they too sometimes adopted the humanitarian perspective. But when they talked about the law of pitched battle, they adopted an alternative way of thinking, according to which war was not a plague on mankind but a legitimate means of settling disputes and resolving legal questions through violence. Under this alternative view, the law of war, instead of focusing on the jus ad bellum and the jus in bello, concerned itself with what I call the *jus victoriae*, the law of victory.[13] The jus victoriae assumed that war was not a last resort to be used in self-defense and comparably dire circumstances, but a kind of acceptable legal procedure. Correspondingly it aimed to answer two technical legal questions, both very different from the questions asked by the modern jus ad bellum and jus in bello and both often quite difficult to resolve: first, *how do we know who won?* and second, *what do you win by winning?* or, to put it a bit differently, *what rights can the victor claim by virtue of victory?*

This older conception of the law of war is, for all practical purposes, dead today. Modern specialists can no longer accept the proposition that deliberate collective killing could be employed as a lawful way of settling disputes,[14] and they are dismayed by any conception of the law of war that sanctions "victor's justice" rather than pursuing higher ends.[15] In this they follow the teachings of one of the pioneers of the humanitarian approach, Immanuel Kant. Kant sternly rejected the old law of victory, which still dominated in his time. "Reason," he wrote in 1795, "flatly condemns the idea that war could be a legal procedure." It was, he insisted, a piece of plain barbarism to think that "victory" and "force" should decide disputes between states.[16] International disputes should be resolved not through violence, but by some institution like the United Nations, and the law of war should be based on the jus ad bellum and the jus in bello, whose differing roles Kant was the first to articulate clearly.[17] Modern specialists in the law of war wholeheartedly agree. War, for them, is not an appropriate procedure for resolving disputes. War is a man-made disaster, a barbarity, frequently a crime, and it is to be resorted to only in the face of desperate necessity.[18]

Viewing war in this way, modern lawyers will inevitably find the attitudes of the old law of victory disturbing and more than a little repellant. Instead of calling on lawyers to fight the evil of war, the old law of victory seems to make them mere referees or, worse, mere hirelings of the warriors, and this is something that modern international lawyers do not want. Modern lawyers do not think it is their job to grease the wheels of war or play enforcer for the victors. Because of the death of the old attitude toward the law of war, the modern law of war gives essentially no answer to the two questions posed by the jus victoriae. There is no law that allows us to determine who won, and there is virtually no law that specifies what rights the victor may enjoy.

But the pre-Kantian past was different, and in important ways, I want to insist, the pre-Kantian past was wiser. Until the early twentieth century, lawyers understood that it was part of their job to analyze war as a legitimate legal procedure, to determine who had won once the fighting was over, and to specify what rights the victor was entitled to enjoy. And while making those sorts of determinations may seem like coldblooded hireling work to modern specialists in the humanitarian law of war, the truth is that the law of victory contributed powerfully to the amelioration of the horrors of war. Warfare whose ground rules are relatively clear is war that can be conducted in a more limited way, and lawyers who set ground rules can do a great deal of good. The law of victory was about ground rules, and when it worked (which it certainly did not always do), it worked to limit war.

It is essential that we reflect on how this old law of victory worked; for the rise of modern humanitarian law has not succeeded in ending the evil of warfare. Lawyers have grown more and more committed to humanitarianism over the past century and a half, but wars have only gotten worse.[19] The truth is that eighteenth-century wars, wars fought under the chill star of the law of victory, were *more* contained and civilized than the wars that have been fought since 1860, not less. It is an error to write the history of the law of war as a triumphant history of the rise of modern humanitarianism. That history is a history of tragedy, and the tragedy is, in large measure, the tragedy of the death of the law of victory.

To understand the tragedy of the death of the law of victory, we must understand a great deal about the law of war in antiquity and the Middle Ages. But we must focus our attention on the eighteenth century.

The eighteenth century—or, a bit more narrowly, the ninety years or so before the outbreak of the French Revolution—does indeed count as the golden age of war for modern authors, the last age of civilized battle warfare before the disasters of modern war took hold. This was an age, as the standard literature tells us, when Europeans, moved by "revulsion from the horrors of the Thirty Years War, where fanaticism and moral indignation had multiplied the number of atrocities," dedicated themselves to civilizing warfare. "Devastation and unnecessary bloodshed were kept in check by strict adherence to the rules, customs and laws of war, the accepted code of the eighteenth-century war game."[20]

As a result, it was "an era of limited war" by comparison "with almost any other era."[21] As historian David Bell recently put it in his book *The First Total War*, it was a rare interlude in human history when war became "relatively easy to control and to restrain" and consequently a moment whose conflicts "ranked among the least horrific in European history."[22]

It has been common ever since the horrors of World War I to yearn for a return to the battle warfare of the eighteenth century. "The limited warfare of the eighteenth century," as the *International Review of the Red Cross* declared in 1931, was "the last and most beautiful creation of the old civilization destroyed by the French Revolution."[23] Many authors have tried to explain the rise of modern warfare by explaining the collapse of the "beautiful . . . old civilization" of eighteenth-century war. This is true of Bell and other historians just as it is true of international lawyers such as Carl Schmitt, the brilliant interwar legal theorist and sometime Nazi. For all of these scholars, the tragedy of the rise of modern war is the tragedy of the death of the martial civilization of the eighteenth century, and the great questions of military history are the questions of how and why eighteenth-century battle warfare maintained its control and restraint and how and why that control and restraint were lost. That mystery is my subject as well, but the answers I give are different from the answer that is conventionally given.

The conventional explanation is conceived in the spirit of the modern humanitarian law of war: it attributes the high standard of civilization in eighteenth-century warfare to the eighteenth-century jus in bello and jus ad bellum. Thus the conventional explanation begins by insisting that the eighteenth century benefited from a jus in bello that was infused with the values of chivalry. The battle warfare of the old civilization of the eighteenth century, scholars argue, was *aristocratic* warfare—a form, more particularly, of aristocratic dueling. Schmitt gave a famous statement of this standard view: "[T]he contained war of classical European international law, proceeding by recognized rules, [was] little more than a duel between men of honor seeking satisfaction."[24] Contained pitched battles, fought out on a defined field and subject to norms of honorable conduct, were in essence grand duels, conducted in accordance with what Henry Stimson, the American secretary of state, called "the punctilios of the duelists' code."[25] "What governed the experience of warfare for Europe's ruling classes and kept it functioning as a system," as Bell formulates the claim, "was aristocratic culture."[26] In particular, authors often argue, eighteenth-century battle warfare was the product of a revival of medieval noble chivalry. "[T]he chivalric constraints developed during the later Middle Ages," Michael Howard explains, "became generalized."[27] "During the maturity of the Enlightenment," writes Geoffrey Best, "chivalry, honour, discipline, and self-restraint . . . entered into the common discourse of the ruling élites of the whole European states-system."[28] Orderly, contained battle warfare dominated in the civilized eighteenth century, scholars thus argue, because the eighteenth century, with its smartly costumed, studiously polite aristocratic officers, was the age of the duel and renascent medieval chivalry, the high era of chivalric jus in bello constraints.

That is only part of the standard story, though. Scholars also assert that the aristocratic eighteenth century managed to civilize warfare because it abandoned the dangerous moralizing of the jus ad bellum theorizing of the medieval just war tradition. Stephen Neff, the author of the leading English-language text on the history of the law of war, offers a fine statement of the conventional understanding of how the eighteenth-century law of war departed from the just war tradition. The medieval jus ad bellum declared that it was just to go to war only in "a case of right and wrong, of crime and punishment." The eighteenth-century dueling view, by contrast, permitted a less charged, "strikingly amoral" understanding of war.[29] Eighteenth-century law embraced the "bilateral" theory of the jus ad bellum, according to which both sides could be regarded as having just cause;[30] if neither side had to be in the wrong, neither side had any reason to regard itself as punishing the other. The polished aristocrats who faced each other on the battlefield could regard each other with respect, as equals. As Bell puts it, the eighteenth-century law of war "fell into line with aristocratic cultural ideals," which is why jurists abandoned just war approaches in favor of "treat[ing] war as something like a formal duel."[31]

The golden age of the eighteenth century, the conventional account goes, thus embraced a courteous, chivalric jus in bello while wisely discarding the overly moralistic Christian jus ad bellum of previous centuries. None of the many authors who contribute to this conventional account cite Friedrich Nietzsche. Nevertheless the narrative does indeed have a Nietzschean flavor. It is a tale in which eighteenth-century war became a healthier affair because it passed beyond good and evil, becoming the province of a warrior nobility untroubled by traditional Christian morality.

Needless to say, scholars are not alone in thinking of the classic pitched battle as a kind of amoral, chivalric duel, whose jus in bello norms were

founded in aristocratic politesse. Very early on, cinema too picked up on
the aristocratic interpretation of classic warfare, which appears not only
in familiar classics like Jean Renoir's *Grand Illusion*, with its monocles
and aristocratic manners, but also in forgotten films of the 1920s like the
Weimar *Tannenberg*.[32] This image of classic warfare is undoubtedly reinforced among English speakers by their reading of the most famous of
military authors, Clausewitz, who began *On War* by describing war as a
kind of *Zweikampf*, which his eminent translators Michael Howard and
Peter Paret render as "duel."[33] No doubt it is also reinforced by the conviction among some military officers that they are the heirs of a great
aristocratic tradition.

From this widely embraced picture of classic eighteenth-century warfare, two conclusions seem obvious. First, the success of the eighteenth
century in limiting warfare to contained pitched battle had nothing to
do with the law. It was the product of social conventions, "conventions
that reflected the mores of the aristocratic officer class," in the words of a
military historian.[34] It was a state of affairs perhaps best described in the
language of Marxism: it was warfare conditioned by a particular form of
class domination and class consciousness. Second, if aristocratic class
domination was the great force at work, then contained battle warfare
must have gone into decline because aristocratic class domination itself
went into decline. This is the standard interpretation of the transition to
the warfare of the nineteenth century. It is once again Schmitt who offered the most famous version of this claim; he explained that classic
warfare collapsed in the nineteenth century because populist nationalism put an end to the dominance of the aristocracy.[35] Few other scholars
disagree. By the nineteenth century, nationalist, populist ideologies had
begun to take over; by 1918 at the latest, aristocrats had lost their purchase and just war theory, with its dangerous moralizing, once again
came to dominate in the law of war, as the horrors of the age of the wars
of religion returned.

Such is the standard interpretation of the decline of the eighteenth-century
golden age and the rise of the horrors of modern war. It may sound compelling and clearly correct. *Of course*, one might think: a classic pitched

battle was a kind of duel. *Of course* eighteenth-century warfare was civilized because it succeeded in overcoming the moralistic religiosity of previous eras. *Of course* modern warfare emerged when aristocratic class domination collapsed. Nevertheless it is my aim in this book to show that this familiar Nietzschean narrative, this oft-told tale of the decline of the Christian just war jus ad bellum and the triumph of an amoral aristocratic jus in bello, is deeply misconceived. It has nothing to do with the way that war was understood by eighteenth-century jurists; it misses the deep truth about the civilization of eighteenth-century battle warfare; and it stands in the way of our learning the real lessons of the eighteenth-century golden age.

To understand how the eighteenth-century law of war really worked, we must begin by reading what eighteenth-century jurists themselves had to say about it. Their view was not the view of the modern humanitarian. They did not attribute the high standard of civilization in their age to the triumph of an aristocratic jus in bello. Quite the contrary. As they saw it, what mattered most about the war of their time was precisely that it was *not* dominated by aristocrats. As we shall see, the idea that classic battle warfare was aristocratic and chivalric took hold only in the 1830s. It is an invention of the Romantic era, a fantasy of the age of Sir Walter Scott and other enthusiasts for medieval knighthood. As for the idea that the eighteenth century overcame the moralistic jus ad bellum of medieval just war theory, it is false on two counts. Medieval just war theory was not moralistic in the way scholars suppose, and it was by no means abandoned in the eighteenth century.

If the civilized battle warfare of the eighteenth century was not the product of an amoral, chivalric, aristocratic dueling culture, what was it? In fact it had to do with a very different historical phenomenon: it was founded on the political success of monarchical power, a success that came emphatically at the *expense* of the aristocracy. It was founded on a monarchical monopolization of legitimate military violence. The eighteenth-century civilization of warfare was not the product of a chivalric jus in bello or a transformation of the jus ad bellum. It was the product of a jus victoriae that was intimately associated with monarchical supremacy and legitimacy and that was far from humanitarian

The triumph of public war over private war

in spirit. The tale of the law of war, as eighteenth-century jurists themselves told it, was the tale of the triumph of *public war* over *private war*;
it was the tale of how sovereigns, and especially monarchs, had acquired the exclusive privilege of pursuing their rights through victory
in war. In particular, it was the tale of how monarchs had crushed the
cherished historic right of nobles to mount private wars of their own.

Nobles were indeed very much the villains in the standard eighteenth-
century account. Jurists of the eighteenth-century golden age did not
regard war as a form of aristocratic dueling; on the contrary, they made a
sharp distinction between war and what Emer de Vattel, the preeminent
international lawyer of the century, called "the frenzy of dueling."[36] War
was a wholly lawful activity, a kind of formal legal procedure used exclusively by sovereigns to claim rights through victory. Dueling, by contrast,
was a shadowy, illegal activity, a last refuge of recalcitrant nobles who
were still resisting the sovereign monopoly of legitimate violence.

As this suggests, eighteenth-century pitched battles, which were institutions of "public" war, were anything but aristocratic duels. From
the legal point of view, they were princely trials by combat. And while
the distinction may seem slight to modern readers, in premodern law it
carried immense significance. Trials by combat were lawful procedures; duels were outlawed. Trials by combat were governed by a traditional *jus victoriae*, which addressed the critical *jus victoriae* questions:
which of the two contestants counted as the victor, and what rights the
victor acquired by virtue of his victory. Only sovereigns were permitted
to use the deadly trial by combat that was war in order to resolve their
disputes; correspondingly it was a matter of fundamental symbolic importance that eighteenth-century wars were *not* aristocratic duels.

In fact, to call the pitched battles of the eighteenth century aristocratic
duels is to obscure the most important truth about the law of the age: the
law of war of the eighteenth century, which emphatically permitted only
sovereigns to prove their legal claims through "the chance of arms,"
symbolized the triumph of monarchical legitimacy. The very fact that
monarchs had the power to send troops into battle to die declared to the
world that they were sovereign, just as their sole power to inflict the
death penalty declared to the world that they were sovereign. Such was

Sovereignty

the symbolism of the law, and the symbolism of the law matters. Wars are not simply paroxysms of collective killing to be controlled, if at all, through a humanitarian jus in bello. Nor are they simply theaters of violence in which chivalric officers have the opportunity to display their courage and their courtesy. They are legal events with legal meaning, and if we misconstrue their legal meaning we will not grasp their nature.

The claim that the eighteenth-century law of war was the product of an aristocratic jus in bello is thoroughly misconceived, and so is the claim that it represented a rejection of medieval just war jus ad bellum obsessed with the punishment of evil. Strange though it may sound, medieval just war theory was not in fact all about the punishment of evil. It is true that some medieval theologians did sometimes talk in such terms; but that does not mean that just war theory was humanitarian. Much medieval just war theory was jus victoriae, and it bore little resemblance to the modern humanitarian law of war. The surprising truth is that medieval just war theorists generally treated war not as a means of punishing crime, but as a means of acquiring property. War was primarily a form of civil litigation, a way of settling property disputes. Victory was a "legitimate mode" or "natural means" of acquisition,[37] which conferred enforceable property rights on the victor: rights to territory for commanders, and rights to booty for ordinary soldiers. Just war theory was largely property law.

Because just war theory regarded war as a means of acquiring property, it tolerated practices that seem appalling to modern humanitarians. For example, far from treating the sort of corpse stripping portrayed by Vrancx and Brueghel as a war crime, it deemed such booty taking to be a wholly legitimate goal of just war. Moreover the teachings of medieval just war theory were by no means abandoned in the eighteenth century. Eighteenth-century sovereign princes and their advisors continued to regard war as a legitimate means of acquiring property, and they always claimed to be obeying classic just war norms. In fact, theirs was much less an aristocratic, honor-obsessed mentality than an acquisitive, profit-oriented, grasping mentality: eighteenth-century princely warfare was about taking calculated risks in the pursuit of territorial gain, and for the most part it fit perfectly comfortably within the classic norms of just war theory.

Eighteenth-century wars were public wars, fought exclusively by sovereigns as a just means of the acquisition of property (and incidentally permitting soldiers to enrich themselves through booty), and war-making was a glorious activity symbolizing the sole legitimacy of princely governments that had succeeded in crushing the historic pretensions of the nobility. The eighteenth-century law of war was founded not on the jus in bello but on a profound and nearly unconditional deference to the legitimacy of sovereign states. There were certainly jus in bello norms to be found in the law, but they were incidental to the main story: wars were orderly legal procedures. They could be kept within limits because they were fought according to rules established by a well-understood jus victoriae used to resolve conflicts between legitimate sovereigns.

Eighteenth-century warfare was not civilized warfare because aristocrats dominated it; they did not. Nor was it civilized because it rejected just war theory; it did not. Nor was it civilized because the law imposed humanitarian norms of conduct; it did not. It was civilized because the eighteenth century marked the high point of the monarchical monopolization of legitimate military violence used for the lawful pursuit of gain. The best guide to understanding eighteenth-century warfare is not to be found in the thought of Friedrich Nietzsche, the theorist of warrior aristocracy, but in the thought of Max Weber, the theorist of sovereign power.

Because the eighteenth-century law of war systematically deferred to the war-making prerogatives of sovereign rulers, it tolerated many acts that modern lawyers would regard as manifestly criminal. Yet it managed to maintain standards of restraint that we have admired ever since. Therein lies the paradox of the eighteenth-century golden age.

To explore that paradox, this book focuses on one very famous, and routinely misinterpreted, historical example: the seizure of Silesia by Frederick the Great in 1740–1742. This was the military action by which the young Frederick, who had just ascended to the throne, lifted Prussia

into the ranks of the Great Powers and embarked on his career as the
most admired commander of the century. Frederick's seizure of Silesia
is an act that modern historians and lawyers describe as a criminal act
of aggression, and Frederick is portrayed as an unscrupulous oppor-
tunist who had nothing but contempt for the law. Indeed he is sometimes portrayed as the pioneer of a German style of lawless aggression
that eventually culminated in the criminal war-making of 1914 and 1939.

The tale of Frederick's supposedly lawless seizure of Silesia is frequently repeated. Yet it is false. It is based on a thorough misreading of
eighteenth-century law. There was nothing lawless about the seizure of
Silesia. If the eighteenth-century law of war had been humanitarian law
of the modern kind, it certainly would have condemned Frederick's actions. But it was not. Eighteenth-century law was largely law of victory,
and it maintained a very indulgent attitude toward sovereigns who went
to war in order to claim territory.

This book uses the misunderstood case of Frederick's seizure of Silesia to illustrate the critical topics in the eighteenth-century law of victory.
I begin with the most basic juristic analysis of pitched battle found in the
law of war from the sixteenth century through the early nineteenth. According to this analysis, a pitched battle was a form of gambling, subject
to a "contract of chance." It was an enforceable *wager*, by which both
sides agreed to be bound by the result, product of luck though it might be,
of a day of combat. The conceptualization of wars as wagers served an
important civilizing function, helping to keep warfare contained. Wagers
are inherently limited procedures: they rest on a kind of instinct that allows parties to resolve their disputes quickly through a bet. Sovereigns
had every right to enter into such combat wagers, as long as they could lay
claim to some minimally plausible set of territorial rights. As Rousseau
explained, a sovereign prince had the right to "submit his cause to the
chance of war."[38] Frederick had a cause, and as a sovereign he was fully
entitled to submit it to the "chance of war." In invading Silesia, he embarked upon a bold but wholly lawful sovereign gamble.

His cause, moreover, had an entirely plausible claim to be just. Just
war theory had always treated war as a means of settling property disputes, and the seizure of Silesia was not an unjust acquisition in the eyes

of eighteenth-century law. Frederick looks like a criminal brigand to us, but in his own time he simply looked like an unusually bold sovereign who was prepared to submit his fate to the risks of a princely trial by combat. And while our first instinct may be to find this attitude shocking, shock is by no means clearly the right response. As we shall see, though the invasion of Silesia was a fearsome gamble, in the end Frederick fought his war in a civilized way. Monstrous though the eighteenth-century jus victoriae may seem to the modern lawyer, it succeeded in inculcating a culture of contained warfare—a culture that managed to civilize even so bold a commander as Frederick the Great. That is a fact that should give us pause when we insist that the law of war must pursue only humanitarian ends. Humanitarian rules are not the only sorts of rules that can limit warfare.

For Frederick did indeed fight according to the rules. It is one of my principal purposes to show that eighteenth-century warfare was fought according to rules. Some very fine scholars, most prominent among them the Dutch medievalist and social theorist Johan Huizinga, have argued that the pitched battles of the past were rule-bound game-playing activities—activities, as Huizinga famously put it, of *Homo Ludens*, "man the game-player."[39] Others have rejected any such claim, insisting that there were many occasions when warriors denied that they were bound by rules at all. War, these scholars say, was not a game. It was improvisatory butchery. This book aims to settle this long-standing debate. There *were* meaningful rules of battle in the premodern Western juristic tradition, but we must think of them as rules of *law*, not as rules of a *game*. The difference is fundamental. Games require perfect obedience to the rules; law does not. The law is a system of *incentives*; it works when it gives people, in general, good reasons to follow its rules, and it does not cease to be the law simply because some people, whether wisely or not, decline to follow its commands. The rules of eighteenth-century warfare were rules of law in that sense.

To show how eighteenth-century rule of law worked, I trace the history of a rule that gave an answer to the fundamental jus victoriae question, *How do we know who won?* Western law generally endorsed what I call *the retreat rule*, according to which the victor was the party who forced the other side to flee, thus gaining possession of the field of battle and the corpses strewn over it. The history of the retreat rule reaches far back into antiquity and the Middle Ages. The rule remained dominant in the warfare of the eighteenth century in ways that have puzzled military historians, but that are entirely comprehensible from the point of view of the law. Commanders like Frederick the Great certainly had no obligation to follow the retreat rule, but they had good reason to do so, and they almost always did follow it. Victory by the legal rules in pitched battle carried diplomatic, legal, and propaganda benefits, of which eighteenth-century commanders were quite conscious. The rules did not bind them, as the rules of a game would do. But the rules did guide them in their conduct, and that is what matters.

Finally, I turn to the decline of the legal culture of battle in the age of the American Civil War and the Franco-Prussian War. Some military historians have argued that battle warfare broke down because of technological change. Yet the technological advances of the nineteenth century did not make it impossible to stage pitched battles. On the contrary, pitched battles continued to be staged deep into the century. The issues were not technological but political: when nineteenth-century emperors and kings went to war, they continued to fight pitched battles just as their eighteenth-century predecessors had done. Both Napoleon I and Napoleon III continued to stage battles; Solferino is a prime example. As late as 1866, a classic decisive pitched battle could still be fought between the king of Prussia and the emperor of Austria-Hungary at Königgrätz. As long as war-making could be regarded as the glorious business of legitimate monarchs, it could continue to take the form of battle warfare.

By contrast, when nineteenth-century republics fought wars, those wars spun out of control. This was true of the Mexican-American War, of the American Civil War, and it proved true once again with the emergence of the French Third Republic in 1870. Contained battle warfare was a business for legitimate monarchs. Once new republican forms began to shoulder monarchy off the stage, once war ceased to be a means of the acquisition of (dynastic) property and became a means of spreading new forms of government through the world, war ex-

ploded beyond the confines of the classic battlefield. Once war-making
ceased to be a symbolic expression of settled sovereign legitimacy and
became instead a means of contesting legitimacy, it spiraled out of
control.

At the same time, ominously, the historic understanding of battle as
a "tacit contract of chance" vanished. Eighteenth-century law treated
battles as wagers, which meant that commanders and lawyers alike accepted the proposition that great questions of state could be decided,
in some measure, by chance or Fortune. This willingness to accept
decision by chance broke down dramatically in the nineteenth century.
Battle ceased to be the kind of legal wager eighteenth-century Europeans had conceived it to be. Instead observers began to think of battle
increasingly in millenarian terms, as a way of making history. Battle
became the subject of a kind of Great Event theory of history, close in
spirit to the Great Man theories that also swept European culture in
the early decades of the nineteenth century. Instead of serving as a
procedure to settle conflicts between dynastic monarchs, it began to
represent something much grander and much more dangerous: the verdict of history. War ceased to belong to the realm of Fortune and entered the perilous realm of Destiny. The shift in the nature of war was
thus in part the consequence of a shift in the prevailing philosophy of
history.

Wars are horrific ways of making decisions, but they *are* ways of making
decisions; and for that reason they can be thought of as a form of legal
procedure. After all, law is nothing other than the science of making
decisions. In the eighteenth century, war, for all the suffering on its battlefields, was, within the limits of the possible, an orderly and lawful way
of making decisions.

This book is not the tale that historians of the law of war (and undoubtedly most military officers) like to tell; it is not the faintly wistful
tale of the fall of military chivalry and the decline of the aristocratic officer corps. Instead it is the tale of the decline of monarchical legitimacy,
founded on the glorious right to make war, and of a jus victoriae that
once helped keep war in check. It is the tale of the decline of a tradition

The decline of a comparatively restrained warfare in which was war
understood to yield a verdict of law and the rise of a tradition
of unbridled warfare in which war war understood to yield
the verdict of history.   24 ∽ *Introduction*

of comparatively restrained warfare in which war was understood to
yield a verdict of law and of the rise of a tradition of unbridled warfare in
which war was understood to yield the verdict of history. It is the tale of
the displacement of the rule of law by the rule of force. And, I will argue,
it is a tale of loss.

et ... The tale of the displacement of the rule of law
by the rule of force.

CHAPTER 1

Why Battles Matter

Through the fateful outcome of open martial violence comes the
plenitude of victory.

—Vegetius, *Epitoma rei militaris*

*Many contemporary
specialists like to insist
that pitch battles were in
fact exceedingly rare -
so rare that
they cannot be considered
the most significant
moments.*

THIS IS A BOOK ABOUT PITCHED BATTLES, about the sorts of
events that Vegetius, the ancient military writer, called "a fateful
day of open confrontation" between armed groups. Many contemporary
specialists in military history deny that the pitched battles of the past
were really events of much military importance. It is important to begin
by challenging what these specialists say, explaining why pitched battles
really do matter.

Ordinary people generally think of pitched battles, these "fateful days"
with their high drama, as the natural climax of war. Famous battles like
Marathon, Hastings, and Waterloo were the classic topic for traditional
military history, and there remain eminent and brilliant military historians who continue to write about them, figures like John Keegan, John
Lynn, and Victor Davis Hanson. Nevertheless sophisticated contemporary specialists like to insist that pitched battles, dramatic and glamorous
though they may have been, were in fact exceedingly rare events in most
periods—so rare that they cannot be considered, in the words of one such
specialist, "the most significant moments."[1] However much ordinary
people may think of battles when they think of war, however much premodern military authors like Vegetius may have dwelt on them, the reality of warfare, these specialists say, lies elsewhere.

Specialists identify three principal forms of premodern land warfare: the pitched battle, the siege, and the raid. Modern scholars unanimously conclude that raids are the most common, while pitched battles have been by far the least common.

26 ∾ *Why Battles Matter*

✳ If not pitched battles, what? Specialists identify three principal forms of premodern land warfare: the pitched battle, the siege, and the raid.[2] We speak of a battle when armed men directly confront other armed men. Sieges and raids are different, since both involve violence visited by armed men on unarmed victims. Sieges do typically involve the confrontation of two armed groups, one inside the fortifications, one outside, and to that extent they resemble battles. Nevertheless sieges always also target the unarmed general population of the besieged place to some extent. Indeed when sieges end in sacks they carry some of the most awful consequences that unarmed victims can suffer. Raids are defined as events that pit the armed against the unarmed, or at least the unwarned. As scholars use the term, the raid is a broad category, covering any military action in which armed men prey upon unarmed or surprised victims. Raids thus include surprise nighttime attacks on unfortified villages, the sweep of predatory horsemen through the countryside, slaving expeditions, and the widest variety of other forms of violent depredation as well.

✳ All three forms of land warfare are well attested in history. But of the three, modern scholars unanimously conclude that raids are the most common by a very wide margin, while pitched battles have been by far the least common: "For long periods military events could best be described in terms of raids which were far more characteristic of the war than formal battles ever were."[3] The reality is that the vast majority of human warfare has involved not the riveting high drama of pitched battle but the sudden brutality of armed men descending upon unarmed victims, whether in slaving expeditions, the sweep of horsemen through undefended countryside, or the nighttime surprise attack on vulnerable villages. The reality is that human warfare has mostly corresponded to the definition given to war by Aristotle two and a half millennia ago. In the opening of his *Politics*, he defined war as a form of hunting, the hunt for human rather than animal prey.[4] When we survey the history of human warfare with a careful professional eye, that is indeed what we overwhelmingly discover: not heroic confrontations between armed warriors in a "fateful day" of pitched battle but the brutal hunt for human prey, in which armed men turn their weapons on defenseless members of their own species.

That being the case, specialists ask, why should hardheaded scholars ⅄ focus on formal battles, which were not "the most significant moments," rather than on the predatory realities of the warfare of the past? Isn't ▽ there something starstruck and ultimately unserious in writing about the occasional famous battle? Isn't traditional military history, with its focus on great battles, outdated and quaint in much the way that traditional political history, with its focus on high politics, is outdated and quaint? If war, to take a standard social scientific definition, is "a series of acts of ▽ violence, usually involving killing, committed by members of two . . . politically unrelated groups,"[5] then surely a rigorous scholar ought to concentrate on the "acts of violence" that are most common, and those are demonstrably not pitched battles.

Such arguments are made by scholars of many periods. For example, the ⅄ recent anthropological literature on warfare in pre-state societies, what is usually called "primitive warfare," insists that pitched battles were never the predominant form of warfare. Most primitive warfare, past and ▽ present, has involved unbridled, ruthless, and predatory raiding.

Our thinking about primitive warfare has changed over the past genera- ⅄ tion. For a long time, postwar anthropologists promoted the Rousseauian (or sometimes Marxist) view that primitive humans were peaceable crea- tures.[6] However, the powerful drift of recent studies, especially since the ▽ early 1970s, has been to reject that notion. For better or for worse, hu- mans are violent animals, and pre-state human societies were generally in a Hobbesian state. In fact the anthropologist Napoleon Chagnon, ▽ charmingly, adopted Hobbes's spelling *warre* to describe the state of af- fairs among his subjects, the Yanomamo.[7] Our best guess is that some measure of Hobbesian warre was ubiquitous among the humans of pre- state societies, who (like other primates) regularly engaged in deadly raids and the killing of their fellow human beings. As the pioneering ▽ German anthropologist Leo Frobenius concluded more than a century ago, early human warfare was largely just what Aristotle said it was: the *Menschenjagd*, the hunt for human prey.[8]

As contemporary anthropologists present it, this hunt for human prey ⅄ in primitive warfare made particularly heavy use of ambushes and murderous surprise attacks, the kind of raiding warfare that American popular culture associates with the Indians of the old West. Recent scholarship has argued that raids of one kind or another have been by far the predominant form of land warfare over the long course of human history. "[T]he most lethal and common form of warfare," writes Azar Gat, "was the raid, using surprise and taking place mostly at night."[9] Lawrence Keeley gives a similar summary of the findings of the literature in his fine book *War before Civilization*:

> [T]he most common form of combat employed in primitive warfare . . . has been small raids or ambushes. These usually involve having a handful of men sneak into enemy territory to kill one or a few people on an encounter basis or by means of some more elaborate ambush. Women and children have commonly been killed in such raids. . . . [The] proportion of violent deaths is quite high. For example, the homicide rate of the prehistoric Illinois villagers would have been 1400 times that of modern Britain or about 700 times that of the United States in 1980. . . . [A] gradual scalar transition in primitive warfare leads from a small raid to massacres. The latter are larger surprise attacks whose purpose is to annihilate an enemy social unit. The simplest form involves surrounding or infiltrating an enemy village and, when the signal is given, attempting to kill everyone within reach. Such killing has usually been indiscriminate, although women and children evidently escaped in the confusion more often than adult males.[10]

This vicious form of warfare is massively documented in pre-state societies, whose fatality rates far dwarfed those of even such modern conflicts as World War II.[11]

That does not mean, however, that pitched battles never took place in pre-state societies. On the contrary, the great mystery presented by the literature is that almost all documented pre-state cultures have occasionally been able to resolve conflict through pitched battles, and indeed through remarkably limited pitched battles. As Frobenius observed, if the hunt for human prey dominates, there is always also the occasional

Zweikampf, the formal trial by combat.[12] Primitive pitched battles are described by Keeley as follows:

> Many primitive battles were arranged—that is, a challenge or warn-
> ing was issued to the enemy, and the battle site was named or
> understood. . . . Usually . . . the warriors are painted and dressed
> in special decorative or nonfunctional paraphernalia: warpaint,
> headdresses, armbands, and so on. Such battles are typically pre-
> ceded and accompanied by considerable taunting and exchanging
> of insults. Many primitive battles consist of little more than two
> lines of warriors armed with throwing spears or bows, firing at one
> another at about the maximum effective range of their weapons. . . .
> Throughout the world, primitive battles—whether they last a few
> hours or a few days—are commonly terminated by agreement after
> each side has suffered a few serious casualties. These various fea-
> tures of prearrangement, elaborate dress, catcalling, long-distance
> skirmishing, and low casualties give primitive battles their ritual-
> ized allure.[13]

Primitive humans typically mounted raids against each other and perished in raids in great numbers. Yet at the same time the low-casualty
pitched battle was a universal means of "limiting the engagement, and
thus the losses."[14] If pitched battles were a ubiquitous phenomenon, however, Keeley and other contemporary scholars emphasize that they were
also a sporadic one at best—an exceptional event in a world of endemic
raiding.

Anthropologists are not alone in arguing that pitched battle was a rare
occurrence in the past while raiding predominated. Recent scholarship
paints a very similar picture of the complex premodern societies of antiquity and the Middle Ages. In particular, scholars paint a similar picture of three periods of premodern warfare that are of prime importance
for the development of the Western law of war: the warfare of ancient
Greece, of ancient Rome, and of the Western European Middle Ages.

⚹ Certainly we have evidence from many parts of the ancient world suggesting that pitched battle continued to be widespread, and that it perpetuated much of the "ritualized allure" we find in pre-state societies. For example, there is evidence for ritual practice in battle in the literature of the Warring States period in China, examined in Mark Lewis's *Sanctioned Violence in Early China*. In China, as in the West, we find the standard marks of the trial by combat, the naming of the day and place for the clash: "When an enemy force was encountered in the field, the day and place of battle would be formally fixed by the two parties. . . . The battle proper was . . . preceded by a series of religious rituals. . . . A victorious army would often use the corpses of the defeated to erect a monument to its victory, like the Greek *tropaion*. . . . When the army returned to their own state after the battle, they performed the ceremony of 'calling the army to order' and then the ceremonial drinking to mark the conclusion of the campaign." All of this took place, Lewis argues, within a culture of aggressive aristocratic honor, in which "combat was a ceremonial trial of strength."[15] Classical Indian literature is also rich in ritual prescriptions for the conduct of such battles.[16] Looking further afield, we can find similar evidence of ritualized battle in pre-Columbian Mesoamerica, for example.[17] Participants in the battles of these societies undoubtedly died at far higher rates than participants in pre-state battles. Nevertheless the ritualized battles of the ancient world are recognizably variants on a very old human type.

⚹ Yet if the institution of ritualized battle was widespread in the ancient world, it is wise to assume that it was still used only sporadically, at least to judge by the most thoroughly studied cases, those of classical Greece and classical Rome. Studies of the Greek warfare of the classical period— roughly from 480 to 338 BCE—give an account much like the account that anthropologists give of primitive warfare. It is commonplace among historians that the Greek world remained a world of warre, in which hostility was the normal state of affairs and peace the exception. As Arnaldo Momigliano famously observed, war was such an ordinary state of affairs among the ancient Greeks that no one ever bothered to ask what the ultimate cause of war was. It was "a natural fact like birth and death about which nothing could be done."[18] And within the Greek world of warre, leading specialists insist, pitched battle was neither a frequent event nor in the end the most important form of conflict. What dominated was raiding.

To be sure, Greek authors wrote regularly and avidly about formal pitched battles, and nobody doubts that they sometimes fought them. The Greeks of the fifth century BCE, like their Chinese contemporaries, treated combat as a "competition for prestige" that featured pitched battles as their iconic events.[19] Ancient Greek authors prided themselves on the orderly and ritualized character of their battles, insisting that Greeks "fought wars according to rules and openly."[20] Those rules were, in theory, much like the rules of pre-state war, classical Indian war, or the Chinese war of the Warring States period. According to Polybius, Greek battle, like classical Chinese battle, was always preceded by a formal challenge, naming the time and place of the encounter. The battles that ensued involved the same taunting (and elaborate dress) that characterize pre-state societies: "Before engaging, the forces might remain and camp opposite one another for a few days, or even a week. They might try to sting the enemy into action by sending out cavalry to taunt them: 'women!' (Herodotus 9.20)."[21] These battles were governed by rituals both religious and military, including prebattle sacrifices as well as the famous practice of requiring the victor to prove its victory by erecting a "trophy" to mark the turning point at which the defeated side took flight.

In particular the Greek sources mention an institution of notable interest: the formally arranged battle as a means of resolving disputes. Thus Thucydides reports an agreement between the Spartans and the Argives to settle future territorial conflicts by prearranged battle: the two sides agreed in advance that in case of disputes they would simply "fight it out" using pitched battle as a formal settlement procedure.[22] An author like Polybius could treat all formal battles as effectively battles "by agreement," fought when both sides consented to fight.[23] Other similar passages, all of which would be read eagerly by early modern jurists, suggest strongly that there was a shared culture, at least among the Greek city-states on the plains, that permitted dispute resolution through pitched battle. Some classical passages mention possibilities of settlement through battle that were so ritualized as to be almost comical: Herodotus, for example, casually mentions one conflict that was to be resolved by three arranged trials by combat, one involving a man against a man, a second involving a horse against a horse, and the third a dog against a dog.[24]

✳ Probably no one has ever taken that passage entirely seriously. Nevertheless many historians of ancient Greece, especially French scholars, have portrayed classical Greece as a culture whose warfare was primarily a thing of formal pitched battles. As Jacqueline de Romilly put it, "War between the city states was, in effect, a background reality but not an uncontrolled one. Conceived as a kind of tournament, it had its rituals and its limits."[25]

✳ Yet recent scholarship, especially in the Anglo-American world, has turned strongly against this view. Sophisticated historians have argued forcefully that ritualized battle, however much the Greek literature may have celebrated it, was in fact an exceptional event in ancient Greece, just as it was in the pre-state societies studied by Keeley. "[T]hroughout the history of Greek warfare," as Hans van Wees, one of the most important of these revisionist historians, has written, "agricultural devastation, assaults on settlements, ambushes, and surprise attacks were at least as common as pitched battles, and far more common than pitched battles of the most ritualized kind." Nor was warfare by any means routinely limited: "[With] startling regularity . . . the victor insisted on the complete elimination of the defeated community, massacring all adult men, enslaving their dependents, and annihilating the town."[26] If the law of war is a humanitarian enterprise aimed at limiting the horror of warfare, then it is clear that the law of war did not have much impact in classical Greece. Whatever they may have claimed, the Greeks in practice often avoided "decisive battle in an open plain," writes Peter Krentz, preferring "ambushes and surprise attacks."[27] What Keeley says of pre-state societies thus seems also to have been true of ancient Greece: "[D]eadly raids, ambushes, and surprise attacks on settlements were the forms of combat preferred."[28] Ancient Greek authors, like ancient Chinese and Indian authors, loved describing the beauties of ritual battle, and it was the beauties of ritual battle that their poets celebrated. But the reality of most of their conflict, revisionist scholars argue, was the far uglier one of surprise raids, massacres, and enslavements.

Similar stories can be told about many other periods, in particular about Rome and the European Middle Ages. Like Greek authors, Roman authors spun many fine tales of pitched battles, including arranged ones, and those tales were eagerly absorbed by early modern jurists. Nevertheless it is commonplace among careful historians that the reality of Roman warfare was much nastier. The Romans displayed exceptional ferocity, practicing forms of warfare that relied heavily on ruthless slaughters, mass enslavements, and mass rapes.[29] Once again it is hard to avoid the conclusion that the law of war had little impact on Roman practice, at least if we think of the law of war as humanitarian law of the modern kind. The Romans seem to have devoted themselves primarily to something that looks much more like the hunt for human prey.

We get much the same picture from the literature of another heavily studied topic, European medieval military history. Medieval authors, like their ancient Greek, Roman, Indian, and Chinese counterparts, described battles lovingly, and we have plenty of evidence that battles did take place. Like their predecessors, these battles involved "naming a certain day,"[30] taunting, garish dress, and formal challenges. Indeed medieval historians have shown that the practice of the challenge to battle on a certain day at a certain field was quite elaborate.[31] Victors were expected, at least in theory, to follow a long-established demonstrative ritual, camping on the battlefield for three days in order to prove themselves victorious.[32] Many battles were fought, among them such famous "fateful days" as Hastings, Bouvines, Agincourt, Tagliacozzo, Mühlberg, and Nancy.

Moreover there was a great deal of developed law surrounding medieval battle—so much so that it is a commonplace among at least some medieval historians that battles were legal events.[33] In particular, they were legal events with a distinctly religious significance: medieval jurists held that a pitched battle was a *judicium dei*, a judgment of God. There were three kinds of judgments of God: ordeals, trials by combat, and battles. All three were ways of inducing God to intervene in human affairs by putting possibly innocent persons at such risk that He would feel obliged to aid them miraculously. All three were ways of "tempting" God into intervening, as the medieval analysis had it. In the words of Dante, a pitched battle was an event to be staged when "ordinary human justice fails . . . and there is no judge to preside, so that we must have recourse to Him who loved justice so much that he gave his own dying blood to supply it."[34] According to this view, essentially universal in the developed medieval tradition, a battle was a religiojuridical procedure that became necessary when no human jurisdiction was capable of resolving the matter—an evil, in the words of Saint Augustine, but a necessary one.[35] Correspondingly medieval pitched battle was surrounded with religious ritual, such as the formal blessing of swords, and throughout the Middle Ages battles frequently took place on a Sunday or other holy day.[36] This was in flagrant violation of the law of the Church, but it presumably contributed to the sense that battle was an event tinged with religious significance.

The medieval battle tradition, like the ancient Greek (and Roman) traditions, also included examples of arranged battles. This was a very old practice, reaching as far back as the battle of Fontenoy-en-Puisaye, fought between the rival claimants to the mantle of Charlemagne on June 25, 841, "so that their case could be examined by the judgment of God."[37] The history of later medieval arranged battles included some encounters that would be much discussed among early modern jurists, in particular a thirteenth-century battle between a hundred knights on either side, arranged between two princely rivals for control of Sicily "in order that the matter should be settled and the losses kept to a minimum," and the famous Combat of the Thirty of the Hundred Years War.[38]

Yet if medieval chroniclers celebrated the ritualized pitched battle, if medieval lawyers described battle as a kind of judgment of God, if arranged battles were possible, battles remained the exception. Modern historians of medieval warfare, like modern anthropologists and modern historians of ancient Greece and Rome, unanimously conclude that pitched battles were rare events in medieval warfare.[39] The tenor of the modern historiography of medieval war is summarized by Christopher Allmand, in a passage to which I have already referred:

[B]attles, although well known by name, were by no means the . . . most significant moments. For long periods military events could best be described in terms of raids which were far more characteristic of the war than formal battles ever were. Battles involved soldiers fighting soldiers. Raids (or *chevauchées* as they were termed) were an entirely different matter. . . . The tactic was scarcely a new one. . . . Shepherds and their flocks on mountain pastures . . . were an easy target for groups of marauding soldiers. . . . Such acts of seemingly wanton destruction . . . led to entirely predictable results. . . . [N]ormally rich agricultural areas . . . became unproductive wasteland.[40]

Far more common than formal battle, such medieval raids, as Justine Firnhaber-Baker shows in archival work on late medieval France, "invariably involved surprise, the violence of armed men (usually nobles) against unarmed people (usually non-nobles), and the destruction or appropriation of productive resources. Again and again the sources tell of sudden, unadvertised attacks . . . of peasants murdered or mutilated in their fields, of women raped, of vines and trees cut down, of tools destroyed or taken, and of livestock stolen."[41] The picture, in short, differs little or not at all from the picture scholars draw of primitive or classical warfare. Most warfare was fought without the slightest regard for humanitarian restrictions. Most warfare was at base a form of the hunt for human prey.

The story that scholars tell is much the same for all of these pre-eighteenth-century periods. Every once in a long while, in all of these societies, armed men would issue a formal challenge, decorate themselves with paint or feathers, shout insults, and meet other armed men in the "open confrontation" of formal battle. Sometimes we even have reliable reports of prearranged battles used to resolve conflicts. But most warfare involved hunting down unarmed enemies, slaughtering the men and raping the women, or perhaps enslaving both men and women. Ambush, pillage, and wanton destruction were the norm.

Nor is the large predominance of raiding surprising, as Gat observes in his analytic study of the literature, *War in Human Civilization*. The issue, as he forcefully puts it, is simply the calculation of risks. Gat makes the point by invoking evolutionary theory, painting a contrast between humans and other animals. Humans, he observes, have peculiar evolutionary reasons to rely on surprise raids in the closely related practices of both war and hunting:

> Not only is it more difficult among most animal species to get close to a rival without being noticed, because of more acute sense, but also it is above all more difficult to finish off a conspecific in one stroke even if surprise is achieved. . . . [A]nimals are more strongly built because their bodies are their weapons; furthermore, their weapons are "on them" and, therefore, are constantly ready for use. By contrast, if humans can be caught unarmed, they are at a tremendous disadvantage and are extremely vulnerable. Humans thus became quintessential first-strike creatures. As with other animal species, they normally did not seriously fight conspecifics on the open battlefield for fear of being hurt themselves. However, unlike other animal species, they were able to kill adult conspecifics by surprise, when their adversaries were unarmed and vulnerable.[42]

Whether the enemy is an animal or another human, a lethal raid, maximizing surprise, is the least risky way of both hunting and making war. It is entirely unsurprising that warriors in most periods should have opted for raiding when possible. All of the incentives, seen from the sort of evolutionary perspective Gat adopts, seem to argue for raids and against battles.

So if most human warfare involves raiding, if pitched battles have in fact been extraordinarily rare events, if the predominant reality of almost all war is the reality of the hunt for human prey, what can justify studying battles? Even those military historians who do devote themselves to the study of battles do not agree on the answer.

Most modern military historians who choose to write about pitched battles write about them in the spirit of Carl von Clausewitz, the celebrated Prussian father of modern strategy. Clausewitz was a veteran of the

Napoleonic wars, and Napoleon was a general with an appetite for pitched battles and a brilliant capacity to stage great victories. Pondering the Napoleonic experience once the wars had ended, Clausewitz argued that victory in war should be attained through the *Vernichtungsschlacht*, the "battle of annihilation." In preaching the battle of annihilation, he was rejecting the law of war of his time. Early nineteenth-century lawyers condemned annihilation as an uncivilized practice, to be used only against savages and never against fellow Europeans.[43] Clausewitz by contrast insisted that annihilation was the only approach that could lead to true victory, even in wars between "civilized" powers: the road to success was to concentrate the armed forces of the enemy and destroy them.

The Clausewitzian "dogma of the battle of annihilation," as one well-known book describes it,[44] proved immensely influential on strategists, especially in Germany, and it has been immensely influential on military historians as well. We shall see, for example, that our historiography of eighteenth-century warfare has been thoroughly shaped—I shall argue, mistakenly shaped—by the teachings of Clausewitz. Some of the best-known contemporary military historians write in the vein of Clausewitz, most notably Victor Davis Hanson, who has argued that the success of the West has reflected a greater occidental propensity to fight battles of annihilation, a greater willingness to launch its forces, without blanching, into unbridled violence against the armed forces of the other side.[45] The theory of Clausewitz gives one answer to why battles, rare though they may have been, mattered more than raids: raiding may be a profitable and comparatively riskless form of war, according to Clausewitzian teaching, but only fighting pitched battles brings ultimate strategic victory.

Clausewitz is not the only nineteenth-century thinker to influence the military history of battles. Military historians have also sometimes adopted a different tone, following the lead of Edward Creasy, who published his *Fifteen Decisive Battles of the World: From Marathon to Waterloo* in 1851. Creasy, unlike Clausewitz, was not a student of military strategy. He was a contemporary of Karl Marx, and like Marx he was determined to divine the secret forces driving human history. Inspired by a footnote in a survey of medieval history,[46] Creasy experienced a kind of revelation typical of mid-nineteenth-century students of history: truly great battles did not simply win wars; they were the very motor of human historical development. Battles "give an impulse which will sway the fortunes of successive generations of mankind."[47] History was driven not by the struggle of classes, but by the struggle of armies; events like Marathon, Tours, and Waterloo were historic turning points, pivotal moments when human history took one of two divergent paths.

Creasy's notion of the historically decisive battle was taken seriously throughout the nineteenth century, not only by military writers but also by some of the most eminent historians and philosophers. (The battle of Marathon in particular became the conventional example of a battle that had decisively shaped human history, permitting the ultimate triumph of a Western civilization that otherwise would have faded.)[48] Followers of Hegel were particularly excited by the proposition that great battles gave the decisive impetus to human history. Even today books about the great decisive battles of history continue to be published and certainly continue to sell.[49]

It is not surprising that such books sell. Works written in the tradition of Creasy paint stirring pictures of the course of human history. "Had the Moslems been victorious in the battle near Tours," we are told, "it is difficult to suppose what population in Europe could have organized to resist them."[50] Europe, that is, would today be simply a corner of Islam, if Charles Martel's Frankish Square had not held firm against the blows of Abd al-Rahman's cavalry on one cold October afternoon in 732 CE. "Because of the battle of Bouvines (1214)," we read in a similar passage, "France had the basis of an absolute monarchy that lasted until the French Revolution in 1789; England saw its monarch similarly restricted in his power; and Germany saw itself without nationhood or monarch for more than six centuries."[51] Thus victory in one thirteenth-century battle set the course of all of European history for half a millennium. This is stuff that makes for gripping reading; these books really do make it sound as though historical questions of the greatest magnitude can be settled by the clash of armed groups on a single day of battle.

Nevertheless the idea that single battles have such extraordinary consequences is a bit hard to accept, and thoughtful contemporary military historians do not write Creasy-style books. Already in the eighteenth century Montesquieu made the case against the idea of the "world-historical battle" in his analysis of the fall of the Roman Empire: "There are general causes, whether moral or physical, that operate in every monarchy, raising it up, maintaining it in power, or dashing it to the ground; all seeming 'accidents' are the result of deeper causes, and if the chance of a battle, that is to say of a particular cause, has been known to ruin a state, there has always been a general cause that meant that that state *had* to perish in a single battle."[52]

Contemporary military historians have found other ways of explaining why pitched battles deserve attention. J. F. Verbruggen, while acknowledging that medieval battles were rare events, nevertheless insists that it is in battle that "the strength and weakness of a knightly army are revealed."[53] The *real* test of medieval knights, he implies, came in battle, not in the predatory raiding that occupied most of their time, and that is why battles are worth writing about. The dean of ancien régime military history, John Lynn, has used the history of pitched battle as a way of sounding out cultural differences in the practices of war over the centuries—and of questioning the truth of Hanson's argument about the distinctiveness of the West.[54]

Perhaps the most subtle and stimulating contemporary claim comes from John Keegan in *The Face of Battle*:

> Battle history . . . deserves a . . . primacy over all other branches of military historiography. It is in fact the oldest historical form, its subject matter is of a commanding importance, and its treatment demands the most scrupulous historical care. For it is not through what armies *are* but by what they *do* that the lives of nations and of individuals are changed. . . . [T]he engine of change is . . . the infliction of human suffering through violence. And the right to inflict suffering must always be purchased by, or at the risk of, combat—ultimately of combat *corps à corps*.[55]

Like Clausewitz, Keegan thinks of war as a test of wills that must be made *corps à corps*. But unlike Clausewitz, he is interested in the logic of rights as much as the logic of violence: he thinks that the risk of battle confers the "right to inflict suffering"—a strange and striking phrase to which we will return.

That said, the ultimate implication of Keegan's work is the same as the implication of Clausewitz's: pillage is not how true warfare happens. Human suffering may occur outside the realm of battle; there may be raids and sieges; villages may burn; armed men may embark on the hunt for human prey. But raids, however prevalent they may be in the history of human warfare, involve few risks for the warriors involved, and so they do not inflict human suffering *by right*. It is victory in battle, through direct struggle between armed men, that purchases the right to change "the lives of nations and of individuals." If Keegan, Creasy, and Clausewitz agree that pitched battles matter, though, it has to be said that their explanations for why are so different as to be ultimately impossible to reconcile.

What I have to say in this book resembles in some ways what Keegan says, since I too talk a great deal about taking risks and acquiring rights. What I have to say sounds a bit like what Creasy says as well, since I too talk about the perception that battles are great historical events. But for the most part, the justification that I have to offer for studying pitched battles is different from the justifications offered by military historians—and especially sharply different from the justifications offered by Clausewitz and his followers.

Why indeed should we study pitched battles? In what sense was there ever more to war than the hunt for human prey? To give a fully convincing answer to this question we must pass beyond the limits of standard military history. The pitched battles of the past were not just moves in a strategic chess game, to be analyzed by students of Clausewitz. Nor were they just barbaric descents into violence, to be described by social historians of war (and deplored by humanitarian lawyers). They were *momentous* events, events that were perceived as having great significance for society at large. We must understand the momentousness of battle, and that means that we must focus not just on the conduct of war, but on the interpretation of war—on how society at large perceives the significance of what happened at those rare times when a "fateful day" of open confrontation took place on the battlefield.

The question of how society at large perceives pitched battles may seem a matter of wholly secondary interest, an example of the kind of postmodern fluff that military historians understandably despise, but it is nothing of the kind. The great conservative philosopher Joseph de

Maistre, writing shortly after Waterloo, famously said that battles are won and lost in the imagination, not on the battlefield.[56] This was a bon mot, not a scholarly argument, but it captures a manifest truth that matters immensely for the law of war: the consequences of victory must be interpreted after the fact.

After all, once the battle is over, much interpretation is required. Military historians sometimes write as though the events of battle speak for themselves, as though no subsequent interpretation were needed. Hanson, for example, declares, "[T]here is an inherent truth in battle. It is hard to disguise the verdict of the battlefield."[57] But is the verdict really so easy to read? There are many questions that the mere spectacle of death on the field cannot resolve. First, how do we know who won? The problem is by no means necessarily easy to solve. To begin with, our answer to the question of *who won* will differ depending on what rule of victory we apply: Is the victor the side that held its ground longest, or is it the side that sustained fewer deaths? As we shall see later, there have been battles of immense historic importance in which these two different rules gave two different answers. Moreover there have been many battles in which there was no easy answer under any rule. If hundreds or even thousands of dead lie piled on both sides, and both sides have retired in shock, which side is the victor? Such was the case, to take a famous example, at the battle of Eylau (February 7–8, 1807), a horrifically bloody encounter at the end of which both sides simply abandoned the field. Who was the victor of this reciprocal slaughter? The answer may come partly from the participants in the battle, but theirs are not the only views that matter. Society at large must be persuaded; after Eylau Napoleon put great propaganda effort into asserting that he was the victor. The law too has often aimed to provide answers.

Even when there is a clear victor, the problem of interpretation is not at an end. We must also, and most especially, determine the significance of the victory. Battles and wars establish new legal rights and extinguish legal claims. The conclusion of a battle, like the conclusion of a trial, has legal ramifications, which can sometimes be far-reaching. But how do we know what those ramifications are? Even if it is clear that the victor has won, how do we know *what* the victor has won, what kind of award the verdict confers upon him?

After all, the legal ramifications of victory can vary immensely. The victor may receive something relatively minor, like a border adjustment. But he may receive far more substantial spoils than that—for example, the right to kingship in the defeated country. That was the right that King Henry V claimed for his house after his victory over France in the highly controversial battle of Agincourt (October 25, 1415). This was a considerable claim, and one that the defeated French eventually resisted strongly. The same was true of Fontenoy-en-Puisaye; as a result of that battle, three separate legal entities emerged in continental Europe: the West Frankish Realm, the East Frankish Realm, and the middle kingdom of Lotharingia. How can a single day of battle have such momentous legal consequences? Yet momentous legal consequences are not rare: classic battles frequently yielded historic verdicts, ousting dynasties and redrawing borders. As Frederick the Great declared, echoing Vegetius and many other authors of the Middle Ages and early modern period, "[B]attles decide the fortune of states."[58] This is more than a stirring martial platitude; it is a statement of a historical truth, and a very mysterious one. *How* can battles "decide the fortune of states"? Why do people believe that the outcome of a day's slaughter between a few hundred or a few thousand armed men can shape the history of a country for centuries? Why is a decisive battle of world history perceived as so profoundly decisive? What is the source of the *meaning* of victory?

War is not just about the killing on the battlefield. It is about the subsequent debates over what rights the victor has acquired. Nor have these questions vanished in the world of modern warfare. Quite the contrary. We no longer have decisive battles, but we do have momentous verdicts and momentous interpretative debates about the consequences of victory. Indeed modern wars often claim to have ramifications even more profound than the decisive battles of the past. In particular, the victor in a successful modern war may lay claim to the right that modern Americans have claimed under the doctrine of unconditional surrender: the right to change the very form of government and the everyday institutions of the defeated power. This was the sort of total verdict that Americans claimed in Germany and Japan after World War II and tried again to claim after the Battle of Baghdad in 2003: the legal authority to reorder the defeated society from the ground up, imposing not only new rulers but new constitutions and new bodies of law.[59] For that matter, it was the kind of total verdict that both fascists and communists typically claimed in the mid-twentieth century. Let us not kid ourselves. This is an astounding claim. It is one thing to insist that the victor in war may displace the government of a defeated foe. It is something far grander to insist that the victor acquires the legal authority to transform the defeated country's very social order. Yet Americans, communists, and fascists alike have believed that their twentieth-century victories could have such ramifications. How can mere victory in war confer such far-reaching power on the victor?

Military history cannot give us the answers to these questions. Military historians focus on events on the battlefield itself. They can give us brilliant answers to the question posed by Clausewitz and Antoine-Henri Jomini in the nineteenth century: *How do you win battles?* They can also give us brilliant social history. But what may seem the inherent truth told by corpses on the battlefield can yet be the subject of complex and bitter struggles thereafter. The English clearly won at Agincourt, but the French still do not agree that the English won the right to rule France. Military historians, magnificent as their work often is, cannot answer the question implicitly posed by those after-the-fact debates. *Suppose you have won.* What *have you won?* Yet the history of warfare is incomplete if we cannot explain what you win by winning. Pitched battles do not simply win wars. Pitched battles create rights. Pitched battles make history. To fully understand human warfare, we must understand how they do so—and that means we must move beyond the study of the battlefield itself and into the world of de Maistre's "imagination."

Pitched battles are perceived as "fateful days" with momentous meaning. To understand how they come to mean what they mean, we must focus on how they are narrated.

The history of particular pitched battles almost always comes down to us in the form of a narrative with a kind of plot. There is a paradox in this that deserves emphasis. It is a commonplace that a pitched battle is in reality a sink of unconquerable confusion for the immediate participants, about which no reliable narrative could ever be given. Keegan is the most recent author to emphasize this truth, in *The Face of Battle*. Participating in a pitched battle, as Keegan shows, is an experience of overwhelming chaos—so much so that the participants, generally desperate simply to emerge alive, have little hope of understanding what is happening around them.[60] Even commanders have little secure ability to determine how a battle is unfolding. Others have made the same point too, most famously Stendhal, whose Fabrice del Dongo wanders through the Battle of Waterloo ironically unable to follow its famous events. If battle is by its nature incomprehensible, how can we narrate it?

Yet the chaos of the experience of battle does not prevent us from creating a narrative that gives it drama and meaning. It is true that the ordinary soldier cannot comprehend the course of a battle. As a result, it is true that the military historian can never be sure of accurately reconstructing the course of events. Nevertheless the fact remains that we can always compose a narrative of the battle once it is all over—a narrative that tells who is the victor and who is the vanquished. A battle is an event to which a kind of plot can be assigned, if only after the fact, and one to which a plot always *is* assigned.

In fact, accounts of pitched battles are typically immensely (and often implausibly) detailed hour-by-hour narratives of vicissitudes, of events, of surprises and tactical maneuvers—of Pickett's charge and the like. These narratives have an air, once again, of Aristotelian drama. When we read a battle narrative, we watch the building suspense from the morning hours of the battle, follow the turns and *peripateiai*, and reach the conclusion of the day in resignation or (as the case may be) joy.

The observation that dramatic plots are assigned to battles may seem yet another piece of postmodern academic fluff. But it is nothing of the kind, as we can see from the way victorious commanders themselves behave. There is a long tradition of commanders constructing the definitive narrative of the battle in its immediate wake. This was famously done by Caesar in his battle dispatches from the Gallic Wars. It was done by the victorious commanders at Waterloo, whose first act at the end of their "fateful day" was to construct an account of what had happened. Napoleon himself was famously a master at reporting the events of his battles in such a way as to make them seem decisive. Hervé Drévillon's interesting book *Batailles* traces Napoleon's gift for turning the inevitably uncertain results of early nineteenth-century battles into dispatches that describe decisive engagements.[61] Very great generals put very great effort into narrating their battles, and that in itself is enough to show that the narration of battles matters.

To emphasize that the events of pitched battles must be narrated is of course not to say that they did not take place in Caesar's Gaul, at Austerlitz, at Waterloo, or anywhere else. The battle dispatches of commanders are surely not pure invention. The point is a different one: commanders must address themselves to society at large, and the social perception of a battle depends in some way on the tale that can be told about it. It may be that the events of battle are *true*, but they are not *meaningful* until we narrate them, and the meaning has something to do with the vicissitudes of the narrative. Commanders communicate with the public by making dramas out of their triumphs. Indeed it is striking that the accounts that commanders give are typically full of dramatic suspense: "Thus, was the contest long and vigorously carried on with doubtful success," to take a typical phrase from the *Gallic Wars*.[62] Caesar did not present himself as a commander applying overwhelming annihilative brute force against a hopelessly inferior and doomed enemy but as a commander riding the waves of uncertainty. This gave his battle accounts more power, not less, and the same is true of the accounts produced by Frederick the Great and Napoleon.

Battles are presented and perceived as fateful dramas. This is a large part of why, *pace* Clausewitz, they cannot be understood simply as exercises in brute force. Our ancestors did not imagine a pitched battle as pure annihilation, in the way a natural disaster represents annihilation. A pitched battle did not resemble an avalanche or a tsunami. It was an event with human meaning because it was an event to which a kind of dramatic plot could be assigned, if only after the fact.

The fateful drama of battles helps us to answer a crucial question about them: why society at large ever accepted their verdicts. The question is a fundamental one in the sociology of pitched battle, and it is no different from the fundamental problem in the sociology of trial. When it comes to trial, we ask, *Why is it that people accept the verdict?* Why do people submit to the decision rendered by the court, cease struggling, pay the damages they are ordered to pay, and move on in life? Why does trial *work*? Why, in the words of the sociologist Tom Tyler, do we obey the law?[63]

The dramatic forms of the narration of battle offer at least part of the answer. Whatever really happened on the battlefields of the past—and we will generally never know—a pitched battle is remembered after the fact as a drama that exposed its contestants to the play of fate. A battle has fateful vicissitudes, and this gives a sense of satisfying meaningfulness to the fact that one side emerged the victor. When we think of a battle as such a fateful drama it is easy for us to believe that the hand of God or the hand of Chance has reached down to raise up one of the contestants over the other. Conversely, if we did not perceive it as a drama, a pitched battle might well seem what it seems to a modern humanitarian: simply a senseless collective slaughter, a horror. If it had no plot, it would have no claim to larger meaning. But precisely because we understand a pitched battle as a human drama, we can see meaning in it. We can see it as a judgment of God (as medieval observers did) or as a legal wager over the "chance of arms" (as eighteenth-century observers did). We can see it as a meaningful event with a meaningful verdict.

As I will argue in the chapters that follow, Westerners have ascribed two kinds of larger meaning to victory and defeat in pitched battle, each in some tension with each other, what I call *millenarian significance* and *legal significance*. The millenarian significance of pitched battles is the kind of significance that Creasy assigned them; it is the idea of battles as moments that shaped the course of history. This is a conception of battle that had a long history before Creasy wrote; it was already to be found in the Greco-Roman tradition. "By nightfall tomorrow," as Livy's Scipio put it in a typical passage, "we shall know whether it is Rome or Carthage that shall give laws to the world!"[64] It has played a particularly fundamental role in Jewish, Christian, and Islamic religious traditions. The battles of Joshua and Gideon, recounted in the Books of Joshua and Judges, have always been interpreted as pivotal moments in sacred history. In the Christian tradition, it is the Battle of Milvian Bridge that has featured most prominently. Milvian Bridge is the battle that brought Constantine to power in Rome, interpreted as an instance of divine intervention almost from the moment it was fought; it was the moment when God reached down to install Christianity in Rome. Similar sacred interpretations surround Christian events like the Battle of Clavijo, legendarily dated to July 25, 844, the battle in which Saint James Matamoros descended from the heavens to lead the knights of Christendom against the Moors of Iberia and so begin the *Reconquista*. As for Islam, the interpretation of the Battle of Siffin, to take only the most important example, is fundamental to its early conflicts.

Our instinct may be to sneer at the legends that have grown up around such battles, but this idea, that pitched battles are pivotal turning points in history, *does* deserve our attention. The fact remains that human beings of the past *did* perceive pitched battles as great historical events. This too belongs to their meaning, this too has a history, and this too cannot be neglected if we are to understand the history of war.

Pitched battles were also assigned another kind of larger significance by our ancestors: they were often regarded as legal proceedings. In law we establish rights by performing meaningful legal acts, and for many centuries fighting and winning a pitched battle was the paradigmatic meaningful legal act in Western warfare. Much of the law of war of the past was devoted to defining and analyzing the meaning of victory in battle. In the standard view of the Western jurists of the past, the acquisition of rights through war was always best founded on what Vegetius called "the plenitude of victory"; and as Vegetius declared, the plenitude of victory came properly through "the outcome of open martial violence" between armed groups—that is to say through battle, and sometimes through siege, but not through raiding.

As a result, victory in pitched battle played a fundamental role in shaping the legal order of the West for centuries. In particular, as we shall see shortly, it played a fundamental role in the golden age of civilized warfare in the eighteenth century.

Neither the legal nor the millenarian significance of premodern battles is comprehensible from the point of view of either a Clausewitz or a modern social historian. No analysis of the tactics at a battle like Austerlitz, for example, can explain how lawyers and diplomats determined that

Napoleon's victory there meant that the Holy Roman Empire had come to the end after a thousand years of legal existence. No evocation of the violence at the Battle of Denain, however gripping, can explain how lawyers and diplomats determined after long negotiations that French victory there meant that there would be a Bourbon king in Spain. Victory has legal implications that are often both subtle and momentous, and that participants on the ground are commonly in no position to comprehend. Understanding those implications requires something different from what military history has to offer.

Battles *are* "the most significant moments." When revisionist historians deny this, they are taking an impoverished view of the nature of war. They are assuming the truth of the standard social scientific definition of war simply as "a series of acts of violence, usually involving killing."[65] Like Clausewitz, they assume that war is simply about the dynamic of mass violence and not about larger social meanings. And it is true that if war were simply a "series of acts of violence," the revisionists would be right. It would indeed make little sense to focus on the rare occasions when those acts of violence took their most glamorous forms. The hardheaded scientific approach would simply be to tote up all the killings; it would be the mark of the amateur to take an interest in pitched battles. For that matter, if war were simply a "series of acts of violence" the law of war would appropriately consist in International Humanitarian Law, dedicated to the task of tamping down and punishing that violence.

But there is more to war than "a series of acts of violence." The meaning of victory in battle is its meaning for society at large. It is its meaning for ordinary people—and that means that by definition ordinary people are not wrong to think of battles as "the most significant moments." To try to explain how war works as a human institution by looking only at the mechanics of violence on the ground is, if I may be permitted a garish comparison, something like trying to explain how sex works as a human institution by looking only at the mechanics of coupling. Sex operates within a web of larger social relations and human desires. To write only about sex acts without describing their place in a larger world of human relations is to write pornography. Military history of war that lacks any larger account of the social significance of pitched battles too easily degenerates into a kind of pornography too, offering its readers the thrill of a description of violence but making too little effort to ponder what the violence ultimately signifies within the web of human relations.

It is true that the pitched battles of the past happened only sporadically. It is true, as Gat argues, that the logic of evolution would suggest that rational armed men would never take the risk of confronting other armed men. Yet no specialist, no matter how aggressively revisionist, has ever suggested that pitched battles never took place at all. If we are to understand them, we must be able to explain why they were fought when they were fought. Eighteenth-century pitched battles in particular were what raids could never be: a meaningful, lawful means of establishing rights and settling disputes. And when battle warfare broke down in the mid-nineteenth century, it was because its eighteenth-century legal meaning had been lost.

CHAPTER 2

Accepting the Wager of Battle

Sovereigns believe that they are answerable only to God for their
actions, and they recognize no arbiter of their quarrels except the
chance of arms.

—Marquis de Mauvillon, *Histoire de la dernière guerre de Bohème*

IT IS EXCEEDINGLY DIFFICULT for modern readers to understand how
anyone could think of a battle as a formal legal procedure. The first
reaction of any sensitive modern person to the sight of a battlefield is
likely to be a humanitarian one: extreme revulsion and horror, mixed
with shock at the evident senselessness of the loss of life. Michael Howard describes how this modern attitude has grown up since the mid-
nineteenth century:

> Before 1850 few people outside the military profession knew what a
> battlefield was really like; though it is arguable that pain, disease,
> mutilation, and sudden death were so much part of the everyday life
> before the nineteenth century that they would not have been too
> upset if they had. But the dispatches of William Howard Russell
> from the Crimea, and the photographs of Roger Fenton and his col-
> leagues in the American Civil War brought the realities of mass mili-
> tary slaughter to the attention of a generation that hoped and be-
> lieved that mankind was emancipating itself from such barbarities.[1]

The photography of the 1850s, and the descriptions of writers like Henri
Dunant (and poets like Baudelaire),[2] gave the general public a vivid

sense of the horror of battle; since that time battlefields have come to seem almost unbearably appalling scenes of carnage. Accordingly when we read accounts or see pictures of battlefields, we find it easy to understand why people of goodwill would grasp at any chance to eliminate war or at least to embark on humanitarian programs like Dunant's Red Cross. By contrast, we find it hard to conceive how any humane lawyer could believe that deliberately staging a day of battlefield slaughter could qualify as an appropriate way of resolving an international dispute.

But it is not just the awful carnage of pitched battles that puts them outside the pale of modern law. It is also their arbitrariness. As we shall see in this chapter, every premodern observer regarded victory in battle as the result of luck. Pitched battles involve what was proverbially called the "chance of arms," and the universal pre-modern view was that the outcome of a pitched battle was inevitably the product of chance, of circumstances that no human commander could ever fully anticipate or control. Luck determines the winner of a day of battle, at least in large measure; a pitched battle is something of a crap shoot. How can you permit a major international dispute to be settled by the inevitably arbitrary results of a day of battle rather than by some more orderly and carefully reasoned proceeding?

A pitched battle is a ghastly mutual mass slaughter, and victory in battle is the arbitrary gift of luck. Yet early modern lawyers did indeed regard staging pitched battles as wholly appropriate means of settling international disputes. They had no difficulty taking a workmanlike attitude toward the legal significance of even the most arbitrary slaughters. As Howard suggests, this may reflect in part the fact that they were less horrified by violence than we are. Historians believe that our sensitivity to violence has grown dramatically since the end of the eighteenth century. As Robert Darnton famously argued in his essay "The Great Cat Massacre," our ancestors relished displays of cruelty to animals that we would find frightening and revolting.[3] What is more they took some of the same delight in witnessing cruelty toward humans; people used to love gathering around to gawk at a public beating or an execution, for example.[4] Pre-nineteenth-century lawyers were certainly conscious of what were proverbially called the "calamities of war."[5] Nevertheless it may well be the case that they were able to think of battles as acceptable ways of resolving disputes because they were better able to stomach the carnage of a battlefield than we are.

In any case, the fact is that premodern jurists expressed much less interest in the carnage of the event than we do. Instead, what interested them most was the arbitrariness. They found it striking and provocative that luck determined the winner of a pitched battle, and their standard analysis reflected that fact: they based their legal analysis on the legitimacy of luck. For centuries lawyers held that going into battle was a form of gambling, a bet on which of the two sides would win. This wager was founded, according to the law, on a "tacit contract of chance," by which the parties had consented to be bound by the results, and the fruits of victory were treated in law as gambling winnings.[6]

This was a juristic analysis that reached back into the early Middle Ages.[7] The same analysis remained alive into the 1840s, when the standard text still explained that in battle "the warring parties enter, as it were, into a mutual agreement by which they put up [their possessions] as stakes in a game of war."[8] The leading eighteenth-century legal text formulated it this way: "Anybody who has refused to come to a peaceful accommodation with his enemy is deemed to have agreed to allow the decision about their dispute to be settled by the chance of arms."[9] In the eyes of the law, a pitched battle was a lethal game of war, a tacit contract to accept the chance of arms, whose results were just as enforceable as the results of any licit dice game. Eighteenth-century commentators on political affairs used the same language: "Sovereigns recognize no arbiter of their quarrels except the chance of arms."[10] This was a doctrine that corresponded to the realities of war. To be sure, commanders did not literally lay bets before going into battle. The wager doctrine was a legal fiction. Nevertheless when eighteenth-century commanders agreed, in the military parlance of the day, to "risk the hazard of a general affair,"[11] they were taking a well-understood gamble, and they recognized that the stakes in that gamble were legal benefits and detriments.

Understanding this eighteenth-century culture of battle gambles can help us to settle a number of difficult questions. First, it can help us to explain how eighteenth-century warfare was kept within limits. A wager is a naturally contained way of making a decision, with deep roots in a kind of human gambling instinct. Most wagers lead to very quick decisions, and precisely because they include an element of irrational chance, it is extremely difficult for the loser to challenge the results: there is no intelligible way to call into question the outcome of a game of chance. In that sense, wagers are admirably decisive. If the combatants are willing to regard their battle as a kind of bet, the event can be brought to rapid conclusion, and the loser cannot easily contest the results. As we shall see, early modern authors were well aware of this: Machiavelli, Guicciardini, Grotius, and others all recognized that warfare by battle wager was inherently limited warfare. For them, allowing chance to play a part in decision making was a prime means of keeping warfare within bounds.

Second, understanding the eighteenth-century culture of battle gambles can help us to explain the transformation of war that came in the nineteenth century; the great changes of that period occurred partly because military men, and the general public, gradually lost their willingness to allow luck to govern human affairs. Instead of accepting the "chance of arms," some strategists began to insist that victory could be achieved through scientifically guaranteed techniques. At the same time, nineteenth-century Europeans more generally began to insist that it was not the luck of battle, but some sort of momentous historical destiny that determined the outcome of wars. They began to think of battles not as legally enforceable gambles but as millenarian events, as great turning points in history. This inevitably undermined the eighteenth-century gambling culture—and brought with it much more destructive forms of war.

Third, understanding the eighteenth-century culture of battle gambles can help us to resolve the mystery of why pitched battles were ever fought at all in human history. As we saw earlier, contemporary revisionist historians conclude that battles happened so rarely that they could not have been "the most significant moments." Azar Gat summarized the conclusions of the literature by arguing that battle was simply too risky for most armed men to engage in. As he sharply put it, humans "normally [do] not seriously fight conspecifics on the open battlefield for fear of being hurt themselves."[12] Battle, the open confrontation of armed men by other armed men, is much more dangerous than raiding—so much so that is seems difficult to explain why battles ever took place. The risk of death is simply so high that no rational armed man would take it, given the option of simply preying on the unarmed. This left us with an unsatisfying evolutionary puzzle: If battle is so risky, why would human beings ever engage in it?

Once we appreciate the wager doctrine, we can understand some of the attraction that pitched battle exercised for early modern commanders. While the risk of battle was high, the early modern law of victory set the prospect of gain high as well. As the seminal sixteenth-century lawyer and political theorist Jean Bodin put it, a battle was an act by which sovereigns agreed to "wager the Kingdom."[13] Indeed kingdoms were sometimes literally at stake, and when they were not, wealthy territories often were. Rousseau gave a fine statement of the eighteenth-century sensibility in 1756: "A prince who submits his cause to the chance of war is not unaware that he runs a risk; but he is less struck by that than by the advantages that he promises himself."[14] Evolutionary theory can never fully capture the calculations of such a prince. Humans, unlike other animals, have law. They have ambitions to claim rights, and the logic of rights is incomprehensible in the language of Darwin. The premodern law of victory promised potentially rich legal winnings for those who were willing to gamble; if it had not promised such rich winnings, it would indeed be difficult to explain why anyone ever took the risk of battle.

This chapter begins by describing warfare in the eighteenth century, a period widely admired as an unusual interlude of comparatively civilized, limited warfare. The eighteenth century—or perhaps better, the long eighteenth century, beginning around 1660 and continuing until around 1790—was indeed in many ways more civilized than the ages that preceded or followed it, and in that sense it marked a departure. Nevertheless pitched battle, always exceedingly risky, remained a rare event.

I then present the wager theory of battle, focusing on a particular eighteenth-century example, a famous case of supposed lawlessness: Frederick the Great's seizure of Silesia in 1740–1742. This was an event of immense importance in European history, since it propelled Prussia into the ranks of the Great Powers. It was also an event of great importance for the history of the law of war: the seizure of Silesia is typically regarded as a classic example of a species of criminal event condemned by the Tribunal at Nuremberg, the "initiation or waging of a war of aggression."[15] Yet the seizure of Silesia was in fact not a lawless event at all under eighteenth-century law of war. It was an entirely licit, and successful, legal gamble—an enforceable wager that Frederick the Great won through battlefield victories.

We saw that pitched battle was a rare event in those periods of premodern human history that have been carefully studied. For millennia, it was not formal battle, but raiding—Aristotle's hunt for human prey—that predominated in warfare. We turn now to the eighteenth century, a period well remembered in the literature of both military history and international law as a kind of golden age of civilized, enlightened warfare and one often described as a classic age of battles. Were things different in this enlightened age of battles from what they had been in previous millennia? Yes and no. It is true that in the eighteenth century the raiding that dominated human warfare for thousands of years seems to have gone into an almost astonishing decline. But it is important to recognize that pitched battle remained a rare event, for much the same reasons that it always had been a rare event.

The civilization of warfare in the eighteenth century has been a source of fascination for lawyers and military historians both. This was the century of "war in form," as Emer de Vattel, the leading international lawyer of the Enlightenment, called it. Almost all scholars present it as a period of remarkable restraint, when the misery of the raids and sieges of the past gave way to a tamer practice of warfare, an age of reform motivated by a "revulsion from the horrors of the Thirty Years War, where fanaticism and moral indignation had multiplied the number of atrocities."[16] Tired of religious strife, Europeans refused to accept the use of military force as, in Edward Gibbon's words, a "blind and irresistible instrument of oppression."[17] "There was," writes a leading international relations scholar, "a general repugnance toward uncontrolled violence and cruelty. Etiquette and strict rules of warfare replaced the butcheries of the first half of the seventeenth century."[18] "Though there were great wars," wrote the fine American historian Eric Robson, "devastation and unnecessary bloodshed were kept in check by strict adherence to the rules, customs and laws of war, the accepted code of the eighteenth-century war game."[19] Those "rules, customs and laws" centered, in particular, on a highly formalized practice of pitched battle, alongside a highly formalized practice of siege.

To be sure, there *were* great wars. In fact two wars of the period, the War of the Spanish Succession and the Seven Years War, can plausibly be called the first world wars. Wars remained an incessant fact of life, and unsurprisingly there are some historians who prefer to accentuate the negative in describing eighteenth-century warfare.[20] Nevertheless it remains the view of most specialists that the eighteenth century was indeed "an era of limited war" by comparison with previous centuries, and even by comparison "with almost any other era"[21]—a remarkable era when, to borrow the language of the anthropologists, *warre* gave way to *war*.

In describing the advances made in this age of civilized "war in form," historians generally begin by pointing to a decline in the use of raiding for supplies. Seventeenth-century armies had often been indistinguishable from bands of brigands, and they often had operated through pillaging raids, ravaging everything in their paths. Like warriors of the centuries before them, they tended to rely on raiding as their fundamental form of sustenance and self-enrichment, turning their arms on the unarmed general population. Especially during the wars of religion in the earlier part of the century, fearsome gangs of troops destroyed vast tracts of central Europe in the process of seizing provisions. Indeed the entire seventeenth century was an era of chronic pillage, culminating in Louis XIV's devastation of the Palatinate in 1688–1689, much remembered and frequently denounced in the eighteenth century.

Eighteenth-century war, by contrast, was conducted by relatively disciplined professional soldiers, who did not routinely turn their arms on the general public. As Michael Howard makes the standard point, the "brigands" were "turned into soldiers, anarchic violence into the intelligent and controlled use of force. . . . European states [now had] professional armies . . . directing their activities primarily against each other and not against the civilian populations, commanded by generals who could conduct operations with restraint and skill."[22] This had particularly significant consequences for the nature of military supply:[23] pillage largely came to an end. Instead of uncontrolled pillaging and raiding, western European armies moved to the more organized and more peaceable (if still threatening) practice of demanding "contributions." This shift in the practice of supply was one of Vattel's main points of pride in his description of the high standard of civilization of his enlightened day:

> Instead of the custom of pillaging the open country and defenseless places, another mode has been substituted, which is at once more humane, and more advantageous to the belligerent sovereign—I mean that of *contributions*. Whoever carries on a just war has a right to make the enemy's country contribute to the support of his army, and towards defraying all the charges of the war. Thus, he obtains a part of what is due to him; and the enemy's subjects, by consenting to pay the sum demanded, have their property secured from pillage, and the country is preserved. But a general who wishes to enjoy an unsullied reputation, must be moderate in his demand of contributions, and proportion them to the abilities of those on whom they are imposed. An excess in this point does not escape the reproach of cruelty and inhumanity.

In this matter, Vattel congratulated himself, his age was marked by many "instances of humanity and moderation" on the part of generals.[24]

Needless to say, we should not be too credulous about the "humanity" of these "contributions": the appearance of an eighteenth-century army near a given settlement was no blessing. But it was no longer quite as much like the descent of a cloud of locusts as had been the case in the past, and would be the case again in the future. In fact Adam Smith went so far as to argue that the eighteenth-century system of supply could be economically advantageous for the peasants of the occupied country, since their landlords fled, leaving them to sell provisions to the armies and thereby "get rich."[25]

Smith's picture of eighteenth-century warfare was surely too cheery, but it is true that the practice of pillage was in some large measure tamed. The same is true of both sieges and battles. Sieges had been a particularly brutal aspect of pre-eighteenth-century warfare.[26] One of the most dramatic and welcome changes of the enlightened century was the end of the siege as Europeans had known and feared it. Sieges were still common events in warfare—more common than battles. Yet Vattel's era of "war in form" was also the era of the "siege in form," far less devastating than the monstrous sack warfare of the past.[27] An eighteenth-century siege, like an eighteenth-century demand for contributions, could be merely terribly costly for its victims rather than being ruinous or fatal. Indeed siege warfare became close in spirit to battle warfare, primarily involving a form of "open confrontation" between armed groups, and eighteenth-century war literature found it natural to class "memorable sieges and battles" together as comparable decisive events in war, both fought in comparatively orderly ways.[28]

Most important for my purposes here, pitched battle itself took on new and less unbridled forms. The eighteenth century is famous as the era of "linear warfare," characterized by pitched battles of "elegance and geometrical regularity."[29] In the linear warfare typical of the century, clashing armies lined up opposite each other, ideally on relatively open fields. Once the initial process of lining up the troops was complete—a process that could take hours—the opposing infantrymen advanced toward each other, sometimes at a trot, sometimes deliberately. These infantrymen carried flintlock muskets. Because muskets, unlike rifles, are smooth-bore weapons, they cannot be effectively aimed. Accordingly the troops approached each other very closely—proverbially until they could see the whites of the eyes of their opponent—and then fired in volleys, hailstorms of unaimed fire. Cavalry charges and artillery barrages also played an important role in the effort to put the opposing side to flight.[30]

Such was what the French called the *bataille rangée*, the orderly "lined-up" battle. It was, it can fairly be said, a relatively civilized, though hardly dainty, way to fight, especially compared with what came later. To be sure, the casualty rates in linear warfare could be staggeringly high; a cloud of musket balls can be very deadly. At the bloody Battle of Malplaquet in 1709, for example, a full quarter of the allied forces were lost to French fire. Nevertheless it is one of the critical features of eighteenth-century warfare that victorious troops did not set out to annihilate the opposing side. The evident aim of the battle was instead to force the enemy to retreat, to abandon the field. Once the losing side had retreated, the victorious side did not ordinarily hunt down the fleeing enemy in an effort to polish them off. This was even true of the most famous of eighteenth-century battle generals, Frederick the Great, who, as we shall see shortly, sometimes allowed the defeated enemy to retreat to a camp a mere few miles away without closing in to make the final kill. If linear warfare was, like all warfare, savage, it was nevertheless far less savage than it could have been.

So the eighteenth century was a period when the unbridled hunt for human prey went, almost miraculously, into decline, while sieges and pitched battle assumed relatively controlled, and in some measure temperate, forms. Yet in one critical respect it differed little from what came before. Even in this prototypical age of battles, pitched battles did not take place very often.

On the contrary, eighteenth-century commanders displayed a notorious reluctance to engage in pitched battle. On the one hand, military texts of the time idealized pitched battle, frequently describing it as the truest and above all most decisive form of warfare. As Frederick the Great put it in a famous passage, "[B]attles decide the fortune of states. It is absolutely necessary to arrive at a decisive action, whether to extract oneself from a difficult position, or to put the enemy in a difficult position of his own, or again, to put an end to a dispute that otherwise might never be settled." Many other writers said similar things. Yet if pitched battles were regarded as the prototypically decisive form of warfare, it is also the case that eighteenth-century commanders, Frederick among them, were famously hesitant to give battle and frequently tried to avoid it. As Frederick himself continued in the same passage, "The wise man does nothing without good reason, and an army general will never give battle unless it is in pursuit of some important design."[31] Another famous and frequently quoted passage, by another famous general, makes the same point. Maurice de Saxe, illegitimate son of Augustus the Strong of Saxony and a roving military hero of the early decades of the eighteenth century, wrote in his 1732 *Rêveries* that he was "not in favor of battles, especially at the beginning of a war." "I am persuaded," he added, "that a skillful general can make war all of his life without being forced into one"—though to be sure, he also insisted that a general who won a battle should be ruthless in his efforts to "profit from the victory."[32]

Military historians have laid considerable weight on such quotes. Their nearly unanimous conclusion is that eighteenth-century warfare, cursed by the reluctance of commanders to give battle, commonly degenerated into wars of maneuver, as commanders danced and prowled around each other during wars that could drag on for years with few direct engagements. That made the eighteenth century an age, as Gibbon put it in a frequently misinterpreted line, not only of "temperate" but also of "*undecisive* contests."[33] The indecisiveness of eighteenth-century warfare is indeed proverbial: almost all military historians (with the important exception of Jeremy Black, to whom I will return) have treated the eighteenth-century warfare of maneuver as a staging of "operettas" or "gavottes," incapable of achieving decisive results.[34] In short, while it is true that there were fewer raids in the eighteenth century, that does not mean that there were frequent battles, and while wars were tamer, they also tended to drag on for years on end.

Why were eighteenth-century commanders so shy about fighting battles, even though they described them as supremely important? When historians of eighteenth-century warfare try to answer this question, they do not generally refer to earlier periods in human history. Nevertheless it is important to recognize that they give a standard answer that is in essence the same as the answer given by Gat in his work on primitive and ancient warfare: battles remained rare in the eighteenth century because direct confrontation between two armed groups remained far too risky for both sides. Human "conspecifics" continued to avoid confronting each other in the open field "for fear that they might be hurt." Armed men still generally found it too dangerous to attack other armed men.

Too dangerous and, especially, too financially costly. The new armies of the eighteenth century, military historians argue, were simply too expensive to risk in battle. Assembling an army of professional soldiers costs much more than assembling a band of brigands. Soldiers must be recruited, trained, clothed, and armed. These rudimentary facts of military financial life, historians argue, affected the calculations of all sensible commanders. "Battles," as Howard explains, "were so destructive, and professional soldiers so difficult to replace" that generals like Frederick and Maurice were deeply reluctant to engage in them.[35] Fighting battles did not make good economic sense. As a contemporary report put it, the "risk of a general affair" was the risk of "losing an army."[36]

Such is the conventional account. It is important to observe that there is reason to question its force. If it is true that armies had become expensive instruments, it is also true that battle had always been rare. Indeed, as we shall see, it is easy to cite authors from the fifteenth, sixteenth, and seventeenth centuries who expressed reluctance to fight battles in exactly the same language used by Frederick the Great and Maurice de Saxe. Commanders in the age of cheap brigand armies were just as reluctant to fight battles as those in the age of pricey soldier armies. The issue cannot simply have been the cost.

That said, there is no doubt that pitched battle remained a rare event, just as it had been for millennia, and for the same reason: because it was immensely risky. The practice of raiding, the far less risky form of war involving attacks on the unarmed and defenseless, does seem to have gone into welcome decline, giving way to the less horrific if still ominous business of demanding contributions. If troops no longer casually pillaged, they still could spend years maneuvering in a given vicinity while making heavy demands on the local population. But pitched battle, direct, open confrontation between armed groups, remained what it had been in the past: a thing mostly shunned. Battle remained an activity so exceedingly risky that humans were very rarely willing to chance it.

Yet sometimes they did chance it. Sometimes, "in pursuit of some important design," as Frederick said, they did fight a battle. Sometimes, as Maurice said, they did try to "profit from a victory." Sometimes eighteenth-century commanders (like commanders of previous centuries) did accept what they called "the hazard of a general affair." Indeed amid all the maneuvering there was, in the end, no small number of important eighteenth-century pitched battles. Why? Where is the flaw in the evolutionary logic laid out by Gat, which implies so powerfully that humans would always avoid direct confrontation with their armed counterparts? Why did any rational eighteenth-century commander ever take the risk of fighting a battle rather than simply extracting contributions from the countryside, or indeed simply yielding the incentive to pillage, terrorizing unarmed victims?

There are two possible answers to this fundamental question. The first is a military answer, ordinarily founded on the analysis of Clausewitz. The second is a legal answer. The military answer is the one that dominates in our literature. But it is inadequate, which means that we must see pitched battle in general, and eighteenth-century pitched battle in particular, through the lens of the law.

Let us begin with the military answer. Our standard interpretations of the warfare of the eighteenth century betray the unmistakable influence of the most famous of battle theorists, Carl von Clausewitz. Along with Antoine-Henri Jomini, he was one of two officers writing in the wake of the Napoleonic Wars who achieved worldwide influence. Both were zealots for pitched battle, contemptuous of the reluctance to fight that had marked the eighteenth century. Napoleonic warfare, like eighteenth-century warfare, remained strongly oriented toward pitched battle. But unlike his predecessors, Napoleon was anything but reluctant to fight them. Understandably dazzled by the experience of Napoleonic warfare, both Jomini and Clausewitz defended the view that pitched battle was the natural and necessary climax of war and that the best commanders would never shy away from them.

Clausewitz developed a grand and sometimes quasi-mystical philosophy that revolved around the *Vernichtungsschlacht*, the decisive "battle of annihilation." The theory of the battle of annihilation has had a profound influence on both the practice of warfare and the interpretation of military history. It is important to review it in some detail, because it purports to offer the definitive answer to the question *Why would any rational commander ever take the risk of fighting a battle?*

Clausewitz's theory addressed a key issue in the practice of battle: Is it satisfactory to force the opposing side to retreat from the field of battle, or should the victor make the effort to destroy all of the opponent's forces? As we shall see later at greater length, when eighteenth-century commanders did give battle, they were generally content simply to force the opponent to retreat. They made relatively little effort to pursue and hunt down enemy soldiers, declaring victory once they had gained control of the field of battle. We shall also see that there was a legal reason for this:

the eighteenth-century law of war *defined* victory as forcing the other side to retreat. Once a commander gained control of the battlefield, he had won a legal victory, and that was often sufficient for his purposes.

However, with his theory of the battle of annihilation, Clausewitz firmly dismissed that attitude. As he put it in a note written late in his career, he wished to prove that "victory does not consist in merely taking control of the field of battle, but in the destruction of the physical and moral force of the enemy . . . and this is achieved principally through pursuit once the battle has been won."[37] Merely forcing the enemy to retreat was inadequate; he had to be destroyed, either through vigorous pursuit, or (as Clausewitz's later followers would often insist) through tactics of envelopment.

Pitiless destruction of the opposing army was what won wars. That, Clausewitz believed, was the lesson of Napoleonic warfare, and it meant that the fullness of victory could be achieved only if commanders consented to take the risk of fighting pitched battles. For it was only through battle that all the forces of the other side could be concentrated for annihilation. War, as Clausewitz wrote in the opening of his famous book, could be defined as a *Zweikampf*, a kind of trial by combat, in which one side forced the other to yield to its will. And, as he explained later in his text, the most secure way to win this contest was to destroy the enemy through brute force in a "great battle":

1. The annihilation of the enemy's military forces is the governing principle [of war]. . . .
2. This annihilation of the enemy's military forces transpires *principally* only in combat [*Gefecht*].
3. Only great and general combats produce great successes.
4. The results are the greatest when combats are joined together in a single great battle.

. . .

From these truths follows a double law, which can be broken down into two mutually reinforcing propositions; the annihilation of the enemy's military forces is to be sought principally in great battles, and their resulting successes; and the principal goal of great battles must be the annihilation of the enemy's military force.

To be sure, the annihilation-principle is more or less operative in
the use of other means . . . but as a general rule it remains the predominant truth that great battles are given only with the aim of annihilating the enemy's military forces, and that the latter can be achieved
only through a great battle.[38]

Successful warfare could be achieved only by those with the courage to
stage "great battles." Such was what Clausewitz called, in one of the wilder
phrases of early nineteenth-century German Idealism, the "annihilation-
principle." Armed men must openly confront armed men, and dedicate
themselves to total destruction.

It is clear that this dramatic, not to say disturbing, theory offers an answer to the question of why any rational commander would take the risk
of fighting a battle, and it is clear that that answer carries considerable
plausibility and weight. Indeed Clausewitz believed it carried the authority of Napoleon himself. It sounds right to argue that commanders must
take the risk of pitched battle, because if they do not do so, the opposing
army will survive. If the opposing army survives, it will continue to maraud and threaten. "Other means," such as raids, cannot do the necessary
work of putting the opponent out of commission.

This plausible and weighty theory has had a tremendous influence
among military historians.[39] In particular, it has dominated in interpretations of the supposed indecisiveness of the eighteenth century. The
wars of maneuver of the age of Enlightenment, those battleless wars of
the age of battles, were indeed indecisive, according to the Clausewitzian view, and inevitably so because commanders were too wary to accept the risk of mounting a truly decisive "battle of annihilation."

Even the rare battles that were fought in the eighteenth century,
Clausewitzian doctrine implies, were not *real* battles of the kind that
Napoleon would fight. They were, to quote once again the sort of language that military historians commonly use, "gavottes," "Noh theater," war that could not decide anything because it was war that did
not acknowledge the primacy of the goal of concentrating and annihilating the enemy. As Black summarizes this view in a trenchant study of
eighteenth-century warfare, "[I]t is difficult for many [military histori-
ans] to accept that warfare was 'for real' in a world in which artifice,

convention and style played such a major rôle."[40] If you embrace the views of Clausewitz, you must believe that too much artifice, too little destruction, made it impossible for eighteenth-century warfare to decide anything.

Plausible and weighty though the Clausewitzian argument may seem, however, there are some first-rate scholars who have raised doubts about it, and in fact it is far weaker than it looks. First, doubts have been raised about whether annihilation really can be decisive in the way that Clausewitz claimed. Suppose you do utterly destroy the enemy. Does that clearly mean that you have achieved a durable victory? Russell Weigley has made the incontestable observation that even Napoleonic annihilation never actually attained the lasting decisive victory it aimed for. The Clausewitzian "quest for decisive victory" proved to be a failure:

> Napoleon in particular was hailed in his time and after as the discoverer or rediscoverer of the battle so decisive in its annihilation of the enemy army in a single afternoon that the Napoleonic victories at Austerlitz and Jena-Auerstädt are regarded as the classic fulfillments of a strategy of annihilation through decisive battle.
>
> Obviously, nevertheless, Napoleon's great victorious battles were decisive only in the short run. They destroyed enemy armies effectively enough that Napoleon was able to impose upon his adversaries peace treaties favorable to himself and unfavorable to them. But the treaties did not last.[41]

Durable legal results escaped Napoleon. In fact his remaking of the European map hardly lasted more than a decade. Weigley remains Clausewitzian enough to draw from this the conclusion that decisiveness can never be achieved through war. Even total military superiority on the battlefield is not enough to create victory. The same skeptical conclusion is obviously suggested by the American experience of 2003 in Iraq, or for that matter by the long Israeli experience of warfare since 1967. In neither case has utter, annihilating superiority of force proven able to create a lasting legal settlement.

Weigley is not the only scholar to raise objections to the doctrine of decisiveness through annihilation. Black, focusing on eighteenth-century warfare, has raised an objection that is in effect the precise converse. Weigley contends that Napoleon did not achieve decisive results even though he did achieve annihilation. Black observes that eighteenth-century commanders did seem to think that battles were decisive even though they did not aim at annihilation. He notes, "[B]oth the writings and the practice of Frederick II and most of his contemporaries indicate that they held that battle could indeed be decisive—in fact too decisive for some of them some of the time."[42] Why would they believe such a thing if it were not true?[43] "[T]here was nothing inherently indecisive about seventeenth- and eighteenth-century strategy and tactics."[44]

Black is right. Eighteenth-century commanders *did* think they could achieve decisive results, and eighteenth-century wars *were* sometimes decisive. In fact I believe we must make the point even more forcefully than Black does: in the last analysis, eighteenth-century wars were significantly *more* decisive than the annihilatory wars that began in the age of Napoleon. The victories of eighteenth-century "war in form" produced legal settlements that were remarkably durable—much more so than the wars of Napoleon. Eighteenth-century wars yielded changes of immense legal importance: France's loss of Canada and India to the British; the independence of the United States; the establishment of the Bourbon monarchy of Spain; the fixing of the basic borders of the French Hexagon; and Frederick the Great's successful seizure of Silesia, which established Prussia as a leading power for the first time and inaugurated two stunning centuries in the rise of modern Germany. These were all legal events with consequences of enduring significance, sometimes down to the present day. They were all the results of decisions in war, and more particularly of decisions through the battle warfare of the eighteenth century, and all of them took place in a world of "artifice, convention and style" still innocent of the teachings of Napoleon and Clausewitz.

It is very strange to describe the eighteenth-century world as one that failed to be decisive because it failed to annihilate. It most certainly did decide. In fact, it proved more effective at making lasting decisions than the ages of either Napoleon or (to take the example of another short-lived remaker of the map of Europe through annihilation) Hitler, or, to bring matters into the present, the age of America in Iraq.

So how did eighteenth-century battle warfare manage to be decisive without obeying Clausewitz's "annihilation-principle"? Here I believe that even Black has not reckoned with the shaping power of the law. The truth is that we cannot arrive at a satisfactory understanding of eighteenth-century war and its consequences unless we understand something that military historians have proven poorly equipped to take into account: the legal framework within which eighteenth-century wars were fought.

To describe that framework, I take a famous example: one of the most celebrated, and reputedly most unlawful, military acts of the eighteenth century: Frederick the Great's seizure of Silesia in 1740–1742. The seizure of Silesia makes for an especially provocative example of the power of the law in the making of eighteenth-century war. First, it had momentous geopolitical consequences, establishing Prussia as a Great Power; second, it is universally treated as a case in which the law was unceremoniously flouted.

For international lawyers, Frederick's seizure of Silesia still counts as perhaps the classic example of an act of unlawful aggression—the classic act invoked to prove the necessity of developing a law of war with a strong *jus ad bellum* norm. When we open a standard international law text, we read that the seizure of Silesia was a case of "flagrant aggression," a lawless act "in which the realities of the situation" could not be "screened" by the specious legal pretexts that Frederick offered.[45] As Sharon Korman declares in her standard study *The Right of Conquest*, the seizure of Silesia was a paradigmatic example of the maxim *ex injuria jus oritur*, of how wholly unlawful acts could give rise to fully enforceable rights in the supposedly primitive international law of the eighteenth century.[46] Gerhard Ritter, a leading light among historians of Prussia, offered a dramatic version of the same argument in 1936: "[T]he manner in which Frederick executed his Silesian project presented him to the world as a criminal and a malevolent aggressor. . . . [H]e attacked Silesia without warning. . . . The principles of strict justice that his father and, indeed, most of his predecessors had observed in foreign affairs could not have been transgressed more sharply and suddenly. . . . There is little point in pursuing the question of whether [Frederick's] claims to Silesia were legally well-founded."[47] Ritter himself was sometimes more cautious,[48] and other historians offer less-charged accounts. Nevertheless Ritter's description captures a more or less orthodox belief among historians: Frederick had contempt for the law, or at least no interest in operating within the law.[49] Frederick's seizure of Silesia, to judge by the writings of international lawyers and historians both, was the *ur*-instance of lawless aggression in modern international law. Perhaps, authors sometimes like to suggest, it was an act of lawless aggression that established a pattern of disdain for the law that would continue in German practice down into 1914 and 1939.

Moreover since Frederick benefited from his actions, the seizure of Silesia is also frequently offered as a prime example of the profitability of lawless aggression. "Although conquest by unprovoked attack was regarded as immoral at the time," Korman writes, "as Acton observed, 'Frederick was more widely applauded for his prompt success than detested or despised for his crime.' "[50] Since the nineteenth century, historians have liked to imagine Frederick as a man who triumphed by placing himself above the law—in Carlyle's famous portrayal, a kind of proto-Nietzschean hero, capable of refashioning his world by the force of sheer genius and endowed with a healthy contempt for the moral and legal pieties of his day.[51] (*Superman: The Life of Frederick the Great* is the title of one 1931 book.)[52] Jomini portrayed Frederick in the same way.[53] So did the German General Staff of the later nineteenth century, which was particularly energetic in lionizing Frederick as a Clausewitzian before Clausewitz, a man who understood the necessity of the prompt application of decisive force without being deterred by the niceties.[54] The success of Frederick is thus taken as object proof that in the eighteenth century force was more capable of achieving decisive results than obedience to law—proof of the success of a Nietzschean willingness to take action without regard for qualms about good and evil.

But is all this correct? The truth is that the law played a far more powerful role in the seizure of Silesia than readers of either history books or international law would ever guess—in fact a dominant role. As Korman quietly acknowledges in a footnote, the seizure of Silesia "was not technically an *injuria* [an unlawful act] under the international law of the eighteenth century."[55] Indeed it was not, and the "technicalities" matter. The idea that Frederick was a "criminal and a malevolent aggressor" has firmly established itself since the early nineteenth century. More than that, his example has been taken as supreme evidence for the proposition that it is force and not law that brings success in international affairs. And the idea that Frederick's supposed "criminal aggression" was crowned with success may well have inspired authentically criminal German acts in 1939, if not in 1914. But when we wind back the clock and patiently consult the sources from the eighteenth century, we discover that the law of Frederick's own era did not by any means deem his seizure of Silesia unlawful. Seen in the light of the eighteenth-century law of war his actions are revealed to be not triumphs of ruthless force but wholly legitimate acts of war, by which he took, and won, a legal gamble in pitched battle.

Let us review the famous events. Frederick's invasion of Silesia was the opening military action of one of the major wars of the eighteenth century, the War of the Austrian Succession. Like other wars of the century, this one turned, as its name suggests, on the dominant issue in eighteenth-century international law: dynastic succession. In this case, the issue arose with the death of Charles VI, the Habsburg ruler of Austria, in 1740. Charles produced no male heir, and there were grave legal doubts about the right of his daughter, Maria Theresa, to take the throne. The law of dynastic succession lay at the foundation of eighteenth-century international law, and Charles's death set off a five-year scramble among other powers to profit from the legal vacuum in Austrian dynastic legitimacy.

In anticipation of his death, Charles had crafted a document called the Pragmatic Sanction of 1713, which guaranteed Maria Theresa's succession rights. Charles had spent years in tough negotiations inducing the states of Europe to accept the Pragmatic Sanction. Frederick's predecessor, Frederick William I, had accepted it in 1726. Nevertheless the young Frederick, newly arrived at the throne of Brandenburg-Prussia—a second-rank principality, difficult to defend and in some ways backward—refused to acknowledge the legitimacy of the Pragmatic Sanction. His house, the Hohenzollerns, was only a middle-weight player on the European stage, but it had dynastic claims to parts of Silesia that reached back almost two centuries. Proclaiming his own right of succession, he invaded in December 1740.

The war that followed escalated into a Europe-wide conflict, in which Prussia was allied with France, the traditional enemy of Habsburg power. The French monarchy made its moves with comparative deliberation, presumably expecting a multiyear conflict of the kind Europe had fought a generation earlier in the War of the Spanish Succession. To the surprise and consternation of the cautious French, however, Frederick managed to achieve rapid victory in Silesia in less than two years.[56]

The history of Frederick's sudden victory—sudden by the standards of the time—is the history of a success achieved within the familiar norms of eighteenth-century warfare. Although the Austrians had plans to station troops in Silesia, they had not yet done so when he invaded, but they quickly sent troops in. Eighteen months of maneuvering followed. Over the course of those eighteen months, the two sides met in two pitched battles: Mollwitz, in April 1741, and the decisive battle of Chotusitz (Czeslau) in May 1742. Both were victories for Frederick. Chotusitz in particular made his Europe-wide name as a military commander. After their defeat at Chotusitz, the Austrians ceded Silesia to Prussia by the Peace of Breslau, signed in July 1742, a separate peace that left the French, to their anger, unsupported in their continuing war against Austria. While the war was not over, and while the Austrians schemed to recover the lost duchy for decades thereafter, Silesia passed permanently into Prussia's possession. The result was that Prussia ascended into the ranks of the European Great Powers.

The invasion of Silesia is thus one of the epic events in the making of modern European history, and by that measure one of the great military successes of Western history. It raises two basic questions in international law: First, was Frederick justified in his initial decision to send troops into Silesia, or was his invasion a case of "criminal aggression"? Second, should international law respect the results of his victories, or should it insist that his conquest was illegitimate? To put the second question a little differently, once Frederick's troops proved victorious in pitched battle at Mollwitz and Chotusitz, should their victories count as the basis for a legitimate and durable claim of right? The first question is a jus ad bellum question; the second is a jus victoriae question. I will postpone my discussion of the first question until the next chapter. For purposes of this chapter, what matters is the jus victoriae question: the legal analysis of Frederick's battlefield victories at Mollwitz and Chotusitz.

European diplomacy—and it was European diplomacy that served to give legal effect to the consequences of war in the eighteenth century[57]— fully accepted the verdict of Frederick's battlefield victories at Mollwitz and Chotusitz, awarding legitimate possession of Silesia to him and his successors for two centuries. Why were these battles such successes?

We must begin by recognizing that the theories of Clausewitz offer no answer: neither Mollwitz nor Chotusitz was a Clausewitzian battle of annihilation. On the contrary, both battles are famous for their failure to annihilate. Mollwitz was a battle in which Frederick's forces missed what looked like an early, easy chance to destroy the Austrians in a surprise attack. Frederick's forces managed to draw up around the encampment of the unsuspecting Austrians and had the opportunity to descend on them as they were moving in casual disorder out of the town of Mollwitz, making quick work of them. They passed up the chance. Instead of mounting a surprise annihilatory raid at relatively low risk, the sort of raid that most warriors in most periods of human history would have mounted, the Prussians allowed the conflict to develop into a standard linear battle. Luckily for the Prussians, in that battle Frederick's commanders (he himself had prudently fled the scene) succeeded in forcing the Austrians to retreat from the field. Once the enemy had retreated, however, Frederick's forces engaged in only the most minimal pursuit, allowing the Austrians to escape largely intact. From the Clausewitzian point of view, Mollwitz was thus a battle in which Frederick simply let the enemy off the hook—not once but twice.[58]

The famous battle of Chotusitz, fought a little more than a year later, took a similar course. After a difficult encounter in which the Prussians suffered more casualties than the Austrians, the Austrians ultimately retreated in good order, abandoning the field of battle. Once again Frederick did not engage in a pursuit that might have destroyed the enemy, even though the defeated Austrians had fled to encampments as little as three miles away.[59] This too was a missed opportunity to annihilate, a fact that some of his contemporaries deplored.[60] Frederick's French allies in particular were agitated and angered by his decision not to hunt down and destroy the Austrian army, as their diplomatic correspondence reveals. One French commander and diplomat, the Maréchal de Belleisle, traveled to Frederick's headquarters to remonstrate with him over his failure to "draw more profit from his victory."[61] After all, Frederick's refusal to destroy the Austrians left the French alone to confront an intact army. Another French diplomat, the shrewd Marquis de Valori, railed against Frederick in similar terms: Frederick, he observed, had contented himself merely with "conquering the field of battle" while "the enemy was left unpursued, and was able to reassemble four leagues away." It was undeniably a victory for Frederick, he wrote, but it was a victory that would do little strategically to win the larger war in which the French were still engaged.[62] Yet another French commentator, the Marquis de Mauvillon, expressed dissatisfaction in similar terms: Chotusitz, he wrote, was a "victory," but he added, "I say that he won the battle because that is the usual way of thinking about things [*pour suivre les idées communes*], even though at base he won no other advantage than to remain master of the field of battle."[63]

Both Frederick and his supporters thus agreed that he could have annihilated the Austrians at Mollwitz and Chotusitz. At least some of his contemporaries thought it was a pity that he did not do so, and the French in particular grumbled. Clearly military men of the eighteenth century believed that annihilation could potentially be an advisable military tactic, just as Clausewitz did.

Nevertheless the fact remains that Frederick did not annihilate the Austrians at either Mollwitz or Chotusitz—and that he nevertheless won what all observers regarded as unambiguous victories. Indeed neither Frederick nor his contemporaries showed the slightest hesitation in calling Mollwitz and Chotusitz, these two non-battles-of-annihilation, victories. After Chotusitz, Frederick wrote a flood of letters to European monarchs claiming "complete victory."[64] Diplomatic correspondence of the time used exactly the same phrase: Chotusitz, this battle in which the Prussians left the Austrians sitting intact and unmolested a few miles away, was a "complete victory."[65] The same language was used by the French court; the draft of a letter congratulating Frederick, preserved in the diplomatic archives, described his victory as "an entirely *complete* victory," with the word *complette* underlined in the original.[66] *Complete victory* was the standard phrase used down to the end of the eighteenth century by diplomatic texts describing Frederick's triumph.[67] As the news spread through Europe, correspondents and commentators from Voltaire to Samuel Johnson agreed in calling the battle a victory for Frederick,[68] and an English diplomat quickly moved in to arrange a peace between Frederick and Maria Theresa. Within a few weeks, the Austrians agreed to the Peace of Breslau, buying peace by ceding virtually the entire province of Silesia to Prussia. Silesia would remain in the hands of the Hohenzollerns and their successors until the German defeats of 1919 and 1945.

Apparently Chotusitz was regarded as wholly decisive in the eighteenth century—decisive enough to redraw the map of central Europe for two centuries. So what made Chotusitz such a *"complete* victory"? Clausewitzian military history manifestly cannot tell us. (It is revealing that at least one leading Clausewitzian military historian feels obliged to assert, contrary to all the unambiguous evidence, that there *must* have been "vigorous pursuit" at Chotusitz, since the battle had such decisive results.)[69] Our sources for explaining Chotusitz lie not in the literature of military strategy but in the literature of law.

To begin with first principles: the law of victory of Frederick's time (and of the centuries before) made it clear that victory in pitched battle carried more legal weight than other forms of military action. Mere raiding was normally not enough to serve as the foundation for a claim of right. Full victory came to those who accepted the risk of open confrontation between armed men in pitched battle. I have already quoted Vegetius, the fourth-century military writer, who stated the basic proposition that "the plenitude of victory" came through "open martial confrontation." Vegetius's authority was relatively weak in the early modern period, but the same basic point was taken for granted by every jurist and every statesman.

A telling eighteenth-century statement of this generally accepted legal truth can be found in Vattel, who addressed a classic question in the law of war, one that was centuries old: Were deception and trickery permitted? In order to defeat an enemy, was it necessary to engage in the open

confrontation of a pitched battle? Or was it permissible to engage in
ruses? Like other jurists, Vattel held that some measure of trickery was
not only permissible, but prudent:

> Some nations (even the Romans) for a long time professed to despise
> every kind of artifice, surprise, or stratagem in war; and others went
> so far as to send notice of the time and place they had chosen for bat-
> tle. In this conduct there was more generosity than prudence. Such
> behavior would, indeed, be very laudable, if, as in the frenzy of duels,
> the only business was to display personal courage. But in war the
> object is to defend our country, and by force to prosecute our rights
> which are unjustly withheld from us: and the surest means of obtain-
> ing this are also the most commendable provided they be not unlaw-
> ful and odious in themselves.

Vattel was no more a tactical fool than Frederick or the Marquis de Valori.
He understood that the stakes in war were so high that few holds should
ever be barred. But precisely because war was not a form of dueling, "artifice, surprise [and] stratagem" were perfectly acceptable, and indeed
the prudent choice for the wise and skillful general. However, Vattel did
not stop there. Like Frederick and the diplomats who declared Chotusitz
to be a complete victory, Vattel acknowledged that there were good reasons
to opt for open pitched battle, despite the extreme risk in doing so. Victory
in pitched battle, as Samuel von Pufendorf, the greatest of authorities,
declared, empowered the victor to "dictate terms." Vattel recognized as
much:

> [Nevertheless] it must be owned that when we can defeat an army by
> open force, in a pitched battle, we may entertain a better grounded
> belief that we have subdued him and compelled him to sue for
> peace, than if we had gained the advantage over him by surprise. . . .
> [T]herefore, when plain and open courage can secure the victory,
> there are occasions when it is preferable to artifice, because it pro-
> cures to the state a greater and more permanent advantage.[70]

However advisable ruses and surprise attacks might be, victory in
open battle "procured a greater and more permanent advantage." It

permitted the victor to "impose a peace" that might be expected to endure.

Vattel was by no means the only figure to describe the significance of pitched battle in this way. He was simply stating an eighteenth-century orthodoxy. The same language was used, for example, by Valori. Frederick did not attempt to annihilate the Austrians at Chotusitz and Mollwitz, the marquis wrote, because "the design that he had to make a peace for himself led him to believe that finishing them off was not necessary."[71] As the French court put it in an internal memo, Frederick had fulfilled his hope of winning "a victory so complete that a peace would of necessity follow from it."[72] Victory in pitched battle, even without any effort at annihilation, was enough to "make a peace." Gabriel Bonnot de Mably, the author of the first systematic discussion of diplomacy, used exactly the same terms in 1757, writing that victory brought diplomatic "advantages."[73] Other diplomats agreed: Chotusitz, this battle of nonannihilation, had afforded Frederick "the advantages . . . of a peace."[74]

Victory, even the technical, non-Clausewitzian victory achieved by forcing the enemy to retreat from the field of battle, made a peace. Indeed it was a commonplace of early modern diplomacy that victory in the open confrontation of pitched battle determined the course of treaty negotiations—that, as R. R. Palmer put it, "after each battle one side or the other raised its terms."[75] Victory in open pitched battle brought victory in diplomacy. Many examples can be given. Victory at Denain at the beginning of the century shaped the Peace of Utrecht.[76] Victory at Saratoga later in the century gained a French alliance for the rebellious American colonists. In the American Civil War, Confederate leaders were still convinced in the 1860s that victory in pitched battle would earn them diplomatic recognition in Europe, just as victory had done for the Union eighty years before.

The Confederates turned out to be wrong, of course; eighteenth-century assumptions no longer held in the 1860s. But those assumptions did hold in the era of Chotusitz. As Frederick himself described it, that battle, won through "the flight and retreat" of the enemy, was "a decisive victory" that produced "advantages" in the eyes "of all Europe and the world." Through his victory at Chotusitz, he had "procured a Peace."[77] And the peace endured. It is worth quoting once more Frederick's general statement of the value of battles: "Battles decide the fortune of states.

It is absolutely necessary to arrive at a decisive action, whether to extract oneself from a difficult position, or to put the enemy in a difficult position of his own, or again, to put an end to a dispute that otherwise might never be settled."[78] Frederick and his contemporaries certainly recognized that annihilation might sometimes be wise "to put the enemy in a difficult position." They could see the sense in what Clausewitz would later say. But they also recognized that battle, in the law and diplomacy of their time, could "put an end to a dispute" and thereby "decide the fortune of state." That is exactly what Chotusitz achieved. Once Frederick had triumphed by taking the risk of an open confrontation, there was no need for him to take the further risks of engaging in a Clausewitzian pursuit. In accordance with "the usual way of thinking about things," *les idées communes*, gaining control of the battlefield had already procured him his peace.

To be sure, the achievement was open to challenge. Even after agreeing to the Peace of Breslau, Maria Theresa remained unwilling to accept the verdict of Chotusitz, and she fought for decades to undo the consequences of her defeat. Within a few years, she renewed the conflict in Silesia; fifteen years later, she joined with powerful allies in the effort to put down Prussian power in the Seven Years War.[79] The hold of the law on eighteenth-century warfare was never perfect, just as the hold of the law on international affairs remains at best imperfect today, and the armed litigation over Silesia dragged on over decades of battle warfare. The extent to which the law governed eighteenth-century warfare raises complex problems, to which I will return.

Nevertheless it should be clear that the military events at Chotusitz and the diplomatic events at Breslau make sense only if we recognize that there were rules of victory. Those rules defined complete victory in ways that had little to do with Clausewitzian analysis, and they were rules that clearly mattered.

In the eighteenth century, victory in pitched battle, even victory that consisted merely in compelling the enemy to retreat from the battlefield in good order, could bring benefits for princes who wished to "procure the greater and more permanent" advantages of a peace, in this case the Peace of Breslau. The events of the War of the Austrian Succession are unintelligible unless we recognize how seriously this proposition was taken. Frederick the Great did not succeed in acquiring Silesia because he was some kind of Nietzschean Superman who possessed enough amoral sangfroid to visit annihilation upon his enemy. He acquired Silesia because he won a technically "complete" victory whose results were treated as binding by the law and diplomacy of his pre-Napoleonic era, even though he passed up every opportunity with which fortune blessed him to annihilate the enemy. And the results of this legal victory proved much more durable than anything Napoleon and his successors ever achieved.

There is more to the legal analysis of Mollwitz and Chotusitz than that, though. We will not have fully grappled with eighteenth-century law of pitched battles until we have worked through the juristic analysis of battle as a game of chance.

According to the law of Frederick's time, an open pitched battle like Chotusitz counted as a wager enforceable under a "tacit contract of chance." So said Samuel von Pufendorf, the supremely authoritative natural law jurist of the early modern period, whose treatment, in Barbeyrac's eighteenth-century translation, was the leading text of the day. A pitched battle, Pufendorf explained, was a binding agreement by which both states consented to submit their juridical fates to "the Dice of Mars." Where the parties had forsworn peaceful settlement and taken up "the gage of battle," there was a "tacit contract that he upon whom Fortune has smiled should be able to dictate whatever terms he chose to the vanquished opponent."[80]

As Pufendorf explained, it was precisely because the parties were deemed to have tacitly agreed to this contract that the victory in battle produced results that were diplomatically binding, despite the fact that victory in battle was the product of force: "One may not reasonably challenge a peace treaty by alleging that it was agreed only under duress. Anybody who passes up the chance to come to a peaceful accommodation with his enemy, preferring to go to war, is deemed to have agreed to allow the decision about their dispute to be settled by the chance of arms; such that he has no basis for complaint, no matter how luckless his fortune."[81] Chance and force determined the outcome of a battle, but that did not make the verdict of battle any less binding. Quite the contrary: it was the very fact that the contestants had agreed to enter into a wager that made their eventual peace treaty enforceable. The loser could not plead duress. As another leading lawyer put it, "[P]rinces who engage in a war according to the rules [*dans une guerre reglée*], are regarded as having agreed that he for whom fortune decides should impose on the vanquished party such conditions as he shall judge fitting."[82] Such was the standard juristic analysis in the eighteenth-century law of victory.[83] The "fortune of arms" gave the victor full rights over the vanquished, at least once a peace treaty had been signed.[84] This analysis was absorbed by the cultured eighteenth-century public; we find it repeated, for example, in the expanded version of the great compendium of Enlightenment thought, the *Encyclopédie* of Diderot and d'Alembert, which explained, in its 1789 article "The Right of Conquest," that conquests were achieved through battles subject to "tacit conventions that have the character of a contract of a game of chance."[85]

Eighteenth-century European culture thus embraced the proposition that great geopolitical decisions could be made by a wager, a kind of game of chance in which the winner was the one upon whom "Fortune smiled." This proposition is very difficult for modern observers to digest. Our natural inclination is to dismiss phrases like "he upon whom Fortune smiles" as meaningless baroque flourishes. But we must recognize that the wager doctrine was taken entirely seriously in the eighteenth century and that it was a powerful way of conceptualizing battles and their consequences. Strange though it may seem to us, it spoke to the realities of early modern warfare; it corresponded to the way military men themselves understood battle; it had very old roots in the law; and, not least, it was well suited to the task of making legitimate decisions through contained warfare.

To begin with, the realities of battle were universally perceived as realities of chance. As military historians frequently observe, pitched battles are extraordinarily chaotic events, whose results really are the result of chance occurrences. So many combatants are engaged, so many sudden panics may intervene, so many unpredictable features of terrain and weather may factor in, that premodern observers found it impossible to pretend that the outcome of a day of battle was ever the product of pure necessity. In that respect, classic pitched battles were very different from the postclassical wars of our own day, fought over years of continuous engagement. It is possible for us to convince ourselves that the results of our long and horrible conflicts, such as World War II, are the products of necessity; in the end, our postclassical wars are probably always won by the side with deeper resources, and in that sense they can be thought of as producing the "correct" victor. For that matter, the grinding hard war of Sherman's March to the Sea or Moltke's reduction of France in 1870 can be thought of as producing the "correct" victor. But the classic single-day pitched battles of the eighteenth century were not like that. They were more like single-day sporting events, football or baseball games: the winds of chance could turn them in either direction. On any given day, either side had a chance to win. As the Latin language proverbially put it, pitched battles were *anceps*, events that "hung in the balance," events that could easily flip to the advantage of one side or the other.[86]

Everybody agreed about this in the early modern period. The sources all spoke of "chance," "hazard," of *sort* in French and *sors* in Latin. Everybody agreed that victories were the product of luck. The very word *Mars* was a synonym for the unpredictability of battle in premodern Latin. And when eighteenth-century military men in particular spoke of major battles, they used the language of chance; fighting a major battle was called "taking the risk of a decisive affair" or "hazarding a general affair."[87] That was the conventional eighteenth-century language that Frederick himself used to describe major battles. "The fortune of states often depends on a decisive affair," as he put it.[88] Other eighteenth-century texts spoke in exactly the same terms. "Combats are sometimes given by entire armies," the mid-eighteenth-century *Portable Military Dictionary* explained, "with the design of engaging a general affair." Of course, the same text continued, the results of any battle were always uncertain.[89]

This was also the language that Frederick used to describe his victory at Chotusitz. In defending the legitimacy of his victory in a manifesto of 1745, he declared, "[T]he King risked the hazard of a general affair."[90] He used the same terms in describing the whole Silesian campaign a few weeks after Chotusitz. It was a campaign, he explained in his dramatic account, in which "the chance of arms" had proven "more decisive every moment."[91] In his narrative of Mollwitz, he attributed his victory there to an "heureux hasard," a happy chance, a stroke of luck.[92]

Lawyers had their own way of talking about all this: the law described a pitched battle as a *sors*, a word for which there is no exact English equivalent. A sors is a decision-making procedure that uses chance. Casting lots and drawing straws are forms of sors; so is the *sors Vergiliana*, the practice of making a decision by jabbing one's finger at random at a passage from Virgil. It was routine in the early modern period to think of battle in this way; as the standard eighteenth-century commentary on Hugo Grotius's *De Iure Belli ac Pacis* flatly declared, "[A] pitched battle is a kind of *sors*."[93]

In line with this idea, lawyers and military men alike used another striking term as well: *eventus*, or "event." To us *event* means an occurrence of historical significance; as we shall see, in the nineteenth century battles were generally described as historical events of that kind. But in its original meaning, an event was an outcome determined by chance or fate, an outcome outside the full control of human beings. Decision through sors, as Aquinas accordingly explained, was decision on the basis of the "eventus," or, as Grotius's commentators defined it, "[A] *sors* is any type of decision procedure where the event is uncertain."[94]

The term *eventus* was routinely used to describe the outcome of pitched battle in the Latin of the Western world. Livy, for example, spoke of the *eventus belli*, the "event of war." So did Vegetius and other ancient military writers, and so did standard eighteenth-century military language: the event of a battle is always "uncertain," as they frequently declared.[95]

Battle in the time of Frederick the Great was the "hazard of a general affair," a contest that depended on the event of combat, which was always uncertain and subject to chance. To take the full measure of this eighteenth-century orthodoxy, we must reach far back in legal history.

From the Middle Ages onward, lawyers analyzed pitched battle as a form of trial by combat. And from the Middle Ages onward, trial by combat was understood in two closely related ways. On the one hand, it was understood to be a judgment of God. On the other hand, it was understood to be a form of wager, a game of chance, to which the parties agreed by a kind of contract.[96]

There was nothing strange about this. The use of wagers or games of chance to resolve legal issues is a practice documented in many premodern legal traditions, which often conceptualize trial by declaring that the parties have laid bets on the result. Such wager procedures can be found, for example, in early Roman law, in early Hindu law, in the Homeric texts, and in a variety of early Germanic traditions.[97] The use of such wager procedures has even left a terminological trace in the modern common law: we still use the word *jeopardy* to describe the stakes in a common law trial. *Jeopardy*, literally *jeu parti*, "a game of even chances," is a medieval term for the hazard of a game of risk; the term first established itself when the primitive common law spoke of the jeopardy of a trial by combat.

Using a wager to resolve legal questions sounds bizarre to us, but the evidence suggests it was not unacceptable in the past, and it is essential that we recognize that using chance can be an attractive way to serve the ends of justice in pre-state societies. This is so for more than one reason. Using chance to decide issues is attractive partly because the results can be attributed to some god: when chance decides, we may be able to convince ourselves that the goddess Fortune or some other supernatural force has, as Pufendorf put it, smiled on the victor, and this may contribute powerfully to the legitimacy of the result.

Allowing chance to decide a dispute has other advantages too. It relieves human beings of the responsibility for making the decision themselves. If chance decides the issue, no judge need put his authority on the line or accept moral responsibility.[98] Allowing chance to decide matters also means that there can be no subsequent questioning of the rational basis for the decision. If we agree to let a flip of the coin decide our dispute, we have no basis for challenging the result on appeal. A coin flip is, in that sense, an inherently contained decision-making procedure. Wagers, in their magnificent irrationality, resolve matters with perfect, unchallengeable finality. This is the notion that has survived in the modern common law ban on double jeopardy: once you have accepted and won your wager, you cannot be required to wager once again. When the bet is done, the bet is done.

Using wager procedures is also, importantly, a way of solving the basic problem of making legitimate decisions in worlds in which state power is weak or absent. In the modern world, legal decisions are accepted partly because they are backed by the power of the state. That was rarely possible in the early Middle Ages; most of the time, state power was hardly present at all. Nevertheless, even in the effective absence of a state, decision by wager can seem binding; after all, wagering taps into a kind of human gambling instinct, a deep-seated willingness to accept the results of a bet. Even where there is little by way of state authority—as was the case not only in the pre-state world of the early Middle Ages but also on the early modern international stage—the results of a wager can seem intuitively binding to the parties.

When it comes to war in particular, there is an important reason why the wager analogy seems appropriate. Using a wager appeals to a widespread, if somewhat mysterious, legal intuition: that it is through taking risks that we acquire rights. This is the intuition to which John Keegan has appealed in the interesting passage quoted earlier and worth repeating here, in which he tries to explain the supreme importance of pitched battle:

> Battle history . . . deserves a . . . primacy over all other branches of military historiography. It is in fact the oldest historical form, its subject matter is of a commanding importance, and its treatment demands the most scrupulous historical care. For it is not through what armies *are* but by what they *do* that the lives of nations and of individuals are changed. . . . [T]he engine of change is . . . the infliction of human suffering through violence. And the right to inflict suffering must always be purchased by, or at the risk of, combat—ultimately of combat *corps à corps*.[99]

At first glance, this passage may seem little better than nonsensical: Why should taking risks "purchase" rights? Why should the fact that you risked your own life have any bearing on your right to inflict suffering on anyone else?

Yet the notion that running risks purchases rights is widespread in the law; and it clearly resonates with something in the human mentality.

"He who takes the risk deserves to get the profits," reads the tagline in Roman law.[100] Risk and reward run together. Running risks gives rise to deserts. He who has accepted the "jeopardy of life and limb" cannot be denied his winnings. That is how Keegan presents the logic of battle, and it is no doubt how premodern jurists understood battle as well— though what they thought you gained through the wager risk of battle was not "the right to inflict suffering" (sovereigns had that right regardless) but a legal claim to kingdoms and territories. Risks purchase rights: that is the basic intuition behind the wager conception of battle.

In the years around 1000 CE in Europe, wager procedures were probably very widespread, not only in the understanding of battle but more broadly in legal decision making. Trial by combat in particular was used to resolve disputes, and standard legal doctrine treated trial by combat as a wager. Outside the realm of war, though, the use of wager procedures was in decline by the thirteenth century. The period from 1000 to around 1250 was a period of sustained efforts at rationalizing law and bringing it under human control, and during this period trials began to lose their character as wagers. Battles, however, did not change in the same way. (Indeed by the late thirteenth century, observers had already begun to say that battles were decided not by God but by Fortune.)[101] War is a strange and marginal border province of the law, and early medieval conceptions tended to persist much longer in the realm of war than they did elsewhere. This was true of the wager conception of battle, which survived into the eighteenth century.[102]

The eighteenth-century law of battles represented a remarkable survival of pre-state wager thinking in the complex societies of the early modern world, long after wager procedures had vanished in the rest of European law. If wager thinking survived, however, it seemed troubling to many observers. In fact much of what is most intriguing in the early modern law of war involved doubts about the implications of the idea that battle was a wager, doubts about whether it was right to let luck determine the course of human affairs. These debates engaged the minds of the most important figures in early modern political and legal thought, including Machiavelli, Bodin, Grotius, Montesquieu, and many others. They were debates that led some participants, Machiavelli and Grotius among them, to take positions that strikingly anticipated the views of Clausewitz. Most of these debates have been neglected by scholars, but they are of considerable interest.

On the one hand, many premodern authors embraced the use of chance as a fundamental tool for containing warfare. The willingness of the parties to allow the event of combat decide their dispute carried one of the greatest advantages of decision through wager: it meant that a limited battle could be sufficient. Chance was a way to contain war. On the other hand, the idea that chance could decide major questions in human affairs deeply troubled early modern observers, for reasons both theological and practical.

The classic topos for discussing the troubling role of chance in war was one institution in particular: the arranged battle, whether between two princes, two champions, or equal numbers of chosen warriors. An arranged battle is not the same thing as a battle fought in the chaotic circumstances of war. Nevertheless juristic and theological authors easily slipped from discussion of arranged battles to discussion of actual historic ones,[103] and the problem of the arranged battle offered a natural point of departure for discussions of the role of chance in war.

Classical literature included a number of examples of arranged battles. As we have seen, Herodotus, for example, reports on one conflict that was to be settled through three arranged battles: a man against a man, a horse against a horse, and a dog against a dog.[104] But by far the most frequently discussed example came from Livy. It involved a famous arranged battle, dating to early in the history of Rome, staged between the Romans and the Albans:

> It happened that there were in each of these armies triplet brothers, not ill-matched either in age or in physical prowess. . . . To these young men the kings proposed a combat in which each should fight for his own city, the dominion to belong with that side where the victory should rest. No objection was raised, and time and place were agreed on. Before proceeding with the battle, a treaty was made between the Romans and the Albans, providing that the nation whose citizens should triumph in this contest should hold undisputed sway over the other nation.[105]

As Livy explained, by means of this arranged battle, the event of war was made less awful: rather than fighting full-scale pitched battle, the Romans and Albans managed to resolve matters in such a limited way that they could subsequently fuse into a single people.[106] The battle of the two comically matched sets of Roman and Alban triplets was much invoked in the early modern period as prime evidence for the proposition that chance could be used to contain the violence of war.

At the same time, though, there were a great many doubts and a great deal of anxiety about the propriety of doing so. The first kind of doubts were theological ones, whose history reached back into antiquity. Decision by chance—drawing straws or jabbing a finger at the *Aeneid*—has the look of a superstitious practice, and the Christian tradition had some dark things to say about it. Medieval law and theology generally held that such a sors was not evil in itself, but only as long it was used to settle questions that could not possibly be resolved through the use of human reason. Trying to induce supernatural forces to make a decision simply because we lacked the nerve to do so ourselves was wrong. St. Thomas Aquinas, to take the most important example, was careful to emphasize that the use of a sors might well be sinful, especially if it was done in circumstances in which human reason was capable of resolving the matter in question. In the latter case, the use of a sors was a form of "tempting God," as medieval theology put it,[107] a way of trying to force God to make a decision that humans were capable of making through the operation of their own reason.

This theological quasi-condemnation applied to all forms of legal wagering, and so it applied to pitched battle as well. Battles involved committing a decision to chance or God when that decision could have been made through the efforts of humans themselves. As a result, medieval law insisted that battles, like other forms of trial by combat, could only be used, as Dante put it, "where human methods are not available to make the judgment, whether because matters are shrouded in the fog of ignorance or because there is no judge to preside."[108] This Christian teaching meant that battles were *only* acceptable where no "human jurisdiction" was capable of resolving the conflict.[109] To resort to a combat wager in any other circumstances was to risk committing a mortal sin.

These theological concerns survived beyond the Middle Ages, as we shall see shortly. In the early modern period they were joined by practical doubts. Much early modern political writing belonged to the Mirror of Princes genre: it concerned itself with giving princes prudent advice. Authors who wrote in the Mirror of Princes tradition routinely concluded that battle gambles were highly imprudent and thus inadvisable for any prince. A battle was, after all, a very, very big gamble. As Vegetius put it, a pitched battle was "an uncertain and fateful day for *nations*,"[110] not just for the army. Pitched battle, as Raimondo Montecuccoli, the great Austrian commander of the seventeenth century, wrote, could "give realms," but it could also "take them away."[111]

Many early modern commentators believed that the stakes in such enormous gambles were simply too high for any prudent prince to take: it was never appropriate to bet the entire fate of a kingdom on the outcome of one battle. Risking the kingdom on the outcome of a single battle was wrong, wrote Philippe de Commynes, the historian of late fifteenth-century wars.[112] Other humanist authors were also hostile to such proceedings. The gambling prince, foolishly staking the fate of a whole country on a single battle, was condemned over and over again. As Jean Bodin, one of the founding figures of modern political thought, put it in the 1570s, "[O]ne should not bet one's Kingdom on the chance of winning a victory."[113] Montaigne mocked princes who risked all on the hazard of battle.[114] This was the conventional wisdom of the sixteenth century; when authors praised great sixteenth-century commanders, such as the Duke of Alba and Henry IV of France, they did not praise them for their genius in battle. Instead they praised them for their fortitude in resisting the temptation to stake their "kingdoms and fortunes" on the "doubtful outcome" of a major battle.[115] Sixteenth-century authors were thus counseling reluctance to fight battles long before the Maréchal de Saxe and Frederick did so in the eighteenth century.

Yet there were also dissident voices. The most intriguing of them was that of the most daring of Mirror of Princes writers, Niccolò Machiavelli. Machiavelli was much more ready than others to countenance the risk of battle. One would expect no less. But that did not mean that he held conventional views. Instead of saying that princes should refuse to fight battles, he held that princes should refuse to fight *limited* battles. Indeed starting from the proposition that arranged battles were games of chance, Machiavelli arrived at strikingly Clausewitzian conclusions three centuries before Clausewitz. A man obsessed by the place of fortune in human affairs, Machiavelli simply rejected the idea that it was appropriate to allow chance to decide the event of war. Precisely because the risks of loss were so enormous, one should never fight them without committing all one's forces: "Non si debbe mettere a pericolo tutta la fortuna," he wrote, "e non tutte le forze": "One should never put all one's fortune at risk, without engaging all one's forces."[116] Certainly a prince could fight a battle, but it could not be the timid business of a limited, arranged battle. It had to be something more like what Clausewitz would demand: an unbridled effort to destroy the enemy.

Much of the early literature of international law can be read as commentary on this passage of Machiavelli, which carried the revolutionary and rather frightening implication that limited pitched battle was unacceptable. Many humanist authors were unprepared to scrap the institution of limited battle.[117] The eminent historian Francesco Guicciardini, for example, expressed discomfort in his commentary on Machiavelli. Citing the arranged battle between the Roman and Alban triplets, Guicciardini argued that limited warfare could achieve the same ends as a total commitment of force, at least where the opposing sides belonged to the same broad community.[118] It was false to imagine that total destruction was absolutely necessary. Moderate warfare through battle could be managed, in the right conditions.

The early makers of international law also wrestled with Machiavelli, slowly coming around to the view that the theological doubts of the Middle Ages could be overcome, but frequently shaken by his practical insistence on the use of "all one's forces." For example, Balthazar Ayala, a Flemish-born jurist of Spanish extraction working in the service of the Habsburgs in the late sixteenth century, found ways, drawing on the work of Spanish sixteenth-century theologians,[119] to overcome the theological objections to limited battle. But he found it impossible to escape Machiavelli's frightening conclusions. Ayala laid out the basic analysis of limited pitched battle as most early modern jurists would present it. For him, such a battle was a *duellum*, by which he did not mean what historians of international law seem to think he meant, namely an aristocratic duel. As Ayala explained clearly enough, by *duellum* he meant an arranged, limited trial by combat, meant to resolve a dispute between "the highest princes," that is, kings. Such a duellum might include either single combat of the kind fought by David and Goliath or a battle like that of the proverbial triplets: "It is not unusual for this kind of battle to be accepted by princes who stand at the highest level of power, whether through single combat or by equal numbers selected by the opposing princes, [as in the case of the Roman and Alban triplets]." This was simply a form of sors. Yet as Ayala recognized, Catholic that he was, to say that an arranged battle was a sors was to raise serious doubts about its legitimacy. Nevertheless those doubts could be put to rest: "I do not deem this species of combat to be illicit. Saint Thomas Aquinas, equating an arranged battle with a judgment by *sors*, says that it is indeed illicit, if it is done in order to provide proof or to get at the truth of something that is hidden; but not, however, if it is done in order to divide up property or to put an end to a dispute: Such was the case of the contest between David and the Philistines, which had God's approval."[120] The battle sors was not forbidden because it was not used "in order to provide proof or to get at the truth of something that is hidden" in cases where human reason could have done so for itself. Battle was not a form of proof at all. It was a means of "dividing up property or putting an end to controversies"—as Frederick the Great would say, a means of "putting an end to a dispute that otherwise might never be settled"—and as such it was perfectly licit. Yet Ayala could not escape the conclusions of Machiavelli. Even though a battle was theologically licit, it was, as Machiavelli had said (though Ayala did not, of course, cite him by name), dubious as a matter of policy, for "when the safety and liberty of us all, or the whole of our possessions, hangs in the balance, we ought to fight with all our strength."[121] Limited warfare was acceptable in the eyes of God, but it was dangerous for the princes of men despite that.

It is only against the background of debates among humanist writers like Machiavelli and Ayala that we can understand the views of Hugo Grotius, the founding father of international law. Grotius's discussion of the law of battles has attracted relatively little commentary.[122] This is a pity; his discussion is a fine example of his commitment to the Christian tradition, his cleverness, and his willingness to carry arguments to dangerous conclusions.

Grotius portrayed battle in the way other early modern authors did, as a very great gamble. This was the assumption that drove much of his discussion about the law of war.[123] The same assumption applied in his long discussion of the relationship between battles and the law of the sors and on the permissibility of arranged, limited battles. Heavily influenced by Christian theology, Grotius began his discussion of the law of battles by mulling the question of whether wars could be settled through a literal sors, a pure game of chance like the drawing of straws. The Christian tradition (unlike, let us note, some non-Western traditions[124]) firmly rejected the use of such procedures; using pure games of chance to resolve disputes amounted to tempting God. Christians were not permitted to settle their disputes simply by flipping a coin; they were obliged to use their own abilities to sort out their own affairs. This was the basic theological teaching that Christians had accepted for centuries. Within limits, Grotius too accepted it.[125]

Yet if Grotius did not deny the fundamental truth of this theology, in his characteristic pragmatic way he tried to move beyond it. Using a pure game of chance was a way of avoiding total destruction, as Guicciardini had said, and Grotius was not prepared to reject such a valuable institution out of hand. Accordingly he declared that if one of the two disputing parties was so weak that it had no hope of winning in actual combat, it was permitted to submit to a game of chance in order to avoid certain defeat. If no amount of human effort could affect the result, humans were not obliged to make any effort at all. In a hopeless case, the prospective loser could offer to draw straws.[126]

Grotius then turned to the use of arranged limited battles, like that of the Roman and Alban triplets. Those sorts of arranged battles, he observed, were certainly theoretically permissible under international law. But they were gravely questionable as a matter of theology. Christian authors had often held that battles could be distinguished from pure games of chance. This was because fighting a battle did in fact include a measure of human effort; it was not a pure exercise in tempting God. Although the outcome of an arranged battle was partly the result of chance, it also exploited human resources, human sweat and blood. Battles were mixed games of chance, not pure ones, and that might seem to give them the look of a legitimate proceeding.

Yet Grotius rejected the use of arranged battles. Their legitimacy depended on the fact that they required human effort. But if that was so, could it be theologically legitimate to use only limited human effort? In his unsettling conclusion, Grotius held that it was not. It was theologically necessary to use *all* of one's forces: unless the cause was completely hopeless, it was wrong to settle matters through the chance of battle.[127] "If the matter in question is worth fighting a war over, as would be the case when the welfare of a great number of innocents is at stake, one must deploy all of one's forces." Anything else would be "vain and impious."[128]

Grotius did not, of course, cite Machiavelli expressly, but the phrase, as his readers must have recognized, was verbatim Machiavelli's: "one must deploy all of one's forces." Yet if the phrase was Machiavelli's, the reasoning was not. Instead of growing out of a pragmatic imperative, Grotius's conclusion grew out of a very un-Machiavellian theological imperative. Theologians had always held that humans must never tempt God, must never force the Lord to decide issues that they were capable of deciding themselves. In effect, Grotius held that this Christian theological proposition required Clausewitzian methods in warfare: if Christians were obliged to use their own military efforts, then they were obliged to use *all* of their military efforts.

There was an obvious paradox in this, and an uncomfortable one. Grotius held that if a war was justified because it could save the lives of innocents, then it must be conducted with maximum force—in such a way, that is, as to kill as many as possible. It may be unsurprising that he came to this conclusion; after all, he was writing in the midst of the religious conflicts of the early seventeenth century, a time when unlimited warfare was the norm among Christians, when the battle culture of the eighteenth century had yet to emerge, when Protestants and Catholics alike threw themselves into their wars with all their forces. We shall find many Westerners drawing the same paradoxical conclusion from the mid-nineteenth century into the present.

Grotius was not the only figure to worry about the theological implications of accepting the decision of chance through battle. Other mid-seventeenth-century authors also condemned the use of contained battle as an offense against the Christian principle that humans must decide their own affairs through the use of their own efforts.[129] But as warfare moved toward its calmer eighteenth-century forms, jurists generally settled into a calmer stance. In particular, Grotius's own standard eighteenth-century commentators rejected his views. Grotius held that it was at best rarely acceptable to decide a war through a *sors*. This was unpersuasive to his commentators. "But a battle *is* a kind of *sors*," read the standard commentary on his text. The problem was not really difficult, the commentary argued; the *sors* of battle was simply a contract, an agreement by which both sides "staked their rights on a throw." It was a *transactio*, a deal, which demanded the consent of both sides.[130] It was a contractually binding gamble, and because it rested on the morality of contract, the commentators found no theological objection worth making.

By the late seventeenth century, as the horrors of the wars of religion faded, the doctrine that a battle was simply a kind of wager, a tacit contract to accept the outcome of a combat, was well established. The old theological and prudential objections faded, and the morality of contract came to dictate juristic analyses of battle. The implication of this teaching, seen against the background of the early modern tradition I have traced, was fundamental for the civilization of war in the age of Enlightenment: the wager doctrine implied that Machiavelli and Grotius were both wrong. It implied that chance could be used to settle international disputes, which meant that limited warfare was acceptable, whatever Machiavelli or Grotius might say to the contrary.

This was, in the end, not quite as strange a doctrine as it might seem at first glance. Let us understand it carefully. It was not a doctrine that endorsed the use of pure games of chance. No one (with the odd partial exception of Grotius) believed that international disputes should be settled by flipping coins. As the theologians insisted, battles were *mixed* games of chance, which were legitimate only because they included a measure of human effort. Commanders like Frederick the Great certainly could, and did, use such human effort in the hope of shaping the outcomes of their battles. They could invest, as Frederick did, in improving their cavalry, in buying better artillery, in drilling their troops more effectively. They could throw themselves into battle with the courage that taking great risks demands. The possibility of employing such efforts made the wager doctrine militarily acceptable, just as it made the same doctrine theologically acceptable. But neither military men nor theologians believed that the element of chance could be eliminated from battle, and if there had not been an element of chance, the outcomes of eighteenth-century battles would not have had the binding, decisive character that they had.

To be sure, military men did not bow completely to the law. They always recognized that visiting total destruction on the enemy might be a good idea, no matter how much the law might encourage them to be content with simply forcing the enemy to retreat. The law never completely dictated the conduct of eighteenth-century commanders. It simply gave those commanders an incentive to stop short of annihilation some of the time. It promised potential benefits to victors who met its criteria—for example, to Frederick the Great, who merely drove the Austrians from the field at Chotusitz rather than annihilating them, and so acquired Silesia. If the law succeeded at Chotusitz, it did not always succeed. But by declaring battles to be binding gambles, eighteenth-century law shifted the incentives that commanders faced and shaped the negotiations conducted by diplomats, who, after Chotusitz and other battles, fashioned durable peaces.

Such was the orthodoxy of the eighteenth-century golden age of battle warfare. To be sure, there were still voices that objected—notably that of Montesquieu, who introduced a different kind of objection from those of Aquinas or Machiavelli, an objection neither theological nor prudential. Writing in 1737, a few years before Chotusitz, Montesquieu objected to the idea that the chance of battle could decide the fate of states at all, because he rejected the proposition that chance rather than necessity ever ruled in human affairs: "Fortune does not rule the world. . . . All seeming 'accidents' are the result of deeper causes, and if the chance of a battle, that is to say of a particular cause, has been known to ruin a state, there has always been a general cause that meant that that state *had* to perish in a single battle."[131] The views of Montesquieu would eventually become the orthodoxy in the philosophy of history.

But in the eighteenth century, Montesquieu was a lone voice. (Gibbon, for example, generally saw matters more conventionally.)[132] The proposition that the fate of realms should be decided through the chance of arms was generally accepted, however much Montesquieu might grumble, and the event of the chance of arms at a battle like Chotusitz was enough to engineer one of the great developments of eighteenth-century history: the rise of Prussia to Great Power status.

I close by quoting Frederick's own account of the legitimacy of his actions, offered in 1745 as a defense against Saxon objections to his conduct. It is an account of what the law demanded in his time. Frederick insisted that he had acted to protect the Saxons themselves, and that far from pillaging, he had actually paid for the provisions he had taken: "Let us follow the conduct of the King in his expedition. . . . [T]he troops almost never stayed in any one locality [where they might have consumed all the resources], they paid for everything that was provided for their subsistence. . . . And is it possible that this ungrateful nation [i.e., the Saxons] has already forgotten the memory of Chotusitz, where the King risked all of the hazards of a general affair in order to guarantee their frontiers against the incursions of the Austrians?"[133] This was, of course, specious special pleading. But like all special pleading, Frederick's declaration was tailored to the demands of the law and morality of his time. What law and morality demanded was that armies not pillage and that commanders accept gracefully the "hazard of a general affair"— with the understanding that they had every right to collect the profits if they won.

Let me emphasize the contrast between the picture painted here and the pictures painted by our standard histories. Battles in the eighteenth century were not aristocratic duels; they were more like trials by combat. Victors in these trials by combat could achieve results of remarkable legal durability. This had nothing to do with dueling culture and nothing to do with Clausewitzian conceptions of battle. It had to with the well-understood and generally accepted legal truth that battles were gambles whose outcomes were enforceable in law, and that complete victory could be achieved by putting the enemy to flight after an open confrontation.

If we understand how well-accepted that legal truth was, we can find an answer to our earlier question: *Why would any rational commander ever take the risk of giving battle?* Maybe some commanders did so in order to display their courage. But the law gave commanders a different, and arguably better, incentive than that: by accepting the gamble of battle, princes like Frederick could potentially "gain a kingdom," in the words of Bodin. The evolutionary logic of Gat could never give us that answer, of course, and neither could the social scientific definition of war as "a series of acts of violence." "To gain a kingdom" is not a concept that has any place in the world of evolutionary survival pressures, and the description of a human act as violent, correct though it may be, cannot fully capture the social meaning of that act. Kingdoms are gained and lost in the realm of law and legitimacy. It is only if we remember this truth that we can fully grasp why pitched battles were fought by Frederick and others like him, despite the extraordinary risk of death that they carried. Though there was a great deal to be lost in these "acts of violence" against "armed conspecifics," there was also potentially a great deal to be gained, as Frederick knew when he met the Austrians at Chotusitz.

CHAPTER 3

Laying Just Claim to the Profits of War

Comrades in arms join together to seek the profits of war, their aim
being either booty or victory over the enemy or the capture of a city.
—Aristotle, *Nicomachean Ethics*

AT 5:00 ON THE MORNING of April 10, 1741, with two feet of snow
covering the uplands of Silesia, Frederick the Great began arraying
his forces around the encampment of the Austrians in the village of Mollwitz in preparation for battle. The Austrians were unaware that the
Prussians were drawing up around them; as Frederick later wrote in his
dramatic narrative of the battle, the experienced Austrian general, Wilhelm Reinhard, Count of Neipperg, had allowed himself, stunningly, to
be taken by surprise.[1] As Frederick's advance guard took up its position,
they detected the unsuspecting Austrians moving into the open in casual disorder, exposed to an easy attack.

In earlier periods of human history, the Prussians would presumably
have done what humans have generally done in war: with surprise on
their side, they would have seized the opportunity to charge in and slaughter their unprepared enemy. As Lawrence Keeley writes, there have been
few more common forms of land warfare than the massacre, "surrounding
or infiltrating an enemy village and, when the signal is given, attempting
to kill everyone within reach."[2] "[T]he most lethal and common form of
warfare," Azar Gat observes, has always been "the raid, using surprise
and taking place mostly at night."[3] Even for the classical Greeks, "ambushes and surprise attacks" were the norm.[4] No other form of warfare

seems entirely rational: Why allow a dangerous armed enemy to prepare for battle when you can kill him first in a sudden surprise attack in the cold, early morning hours?

But this was the eighteenth century, and there was no early morning surprise massacre. Instead the Prussians, following Frederick's orders, allowed the Austrians to form into their own battle order—though to be sure, the Prussians bombarded them while they did so—and Mollwitz emerged as the first of Frederick the Great's pitched battles.

Why was eighteenth-century war fought in this way? What held eighteenth-century commanders back? Why did Frederick give the Austrians a chance? Why did eighteenth-century armies take the risk of forming into lines for battle rather than mounting surprise massacres?

Eighteenth-century lawyers had an answer: they gave the credit for the civilized character of warfare in their age to what they called the "manner" of war—in German, the *Kriegsmanier*. Georg Friedrich Martens, the German diplomat and leading European scholar of international law, explained the Kriegsmanier in 1789, just as the old civilization of the eighteenth century was about to shatter. Under the letter of law, annihilation of the enemy was perfectly permissible: "*Ius belli infinitum*: the law of war gives us unlimited rights against the enemy. Under international law all means necessary to achieve the goals of war are permitted, so that as a general matter no means of harming the enemy is considered unacceptable." Nothing in the letter of the law forbade a massacre. "Nevertheless," Martens continued, "the civilized Powers of Europe, animated by a desire to diminish the horrors of war, and convinced that there are means that are equally destructive for both Powers and therefore senseless as a matter of policy, recognize, in virtue of customs and treaties, certain means as illicit even though they are not entirely forbidden according to the rigors of the law. It is from this that were born those customs that are today designated by the name 'the laws of war' (*Kriegsmanier*, ['manner of war']), laws that have been observed above all since the introduction of regular troops."[5] Though annihilation was permitted "according to the rigors of the law," eighteenth-century law had established a "manner of war" that set limits.

Other eighteenth-century authors had similar things to say about the "manners" of warfare in their age. The Scottish philosopher Adam Ferguson put it particularly handsomely: "The foundation of the law of war was laid in the manners of Europe. . . . [W]e have improved on the laws of war, and on the lenitives which have been devised to soften its rigours; we have mingled politeness with the use of the sword."[6] As Martens would say in later years, the eighteenth century lived by the rule that "the legitimate goal of war is never to exterminate the enemy. Instead it is to oblige him to accept a peace that satisfies our demands."[7] We have already seen that this was the attitude Frederick brought not only to Mollwitz but also to Chotusitz, where "the design that he had to make a peace for himself led him to believe that finishing [the enemy] off was not necessary."[8]

How did this manner of war emerge, and how did it succeed in inducing eighteenth-century commanders to accept the un-Clausewitzian principle that "finishing the enemy off is not necessary"? Legal historians and international lawyers have a standard answer to this question, an answer framed in the terms of the modern humanitarian law of war. According to this standard answer, the eighteenth-century manner of war was the product of two great legal developments: the decline of a Christian jus ad bellum that was preoccupied with the problem of good and evil, and the rise of the cultural domination of the dueling aristocracy, which encouraged a kind of chivalric jus in bello.

The standard narrative begins with the just war theories of the medieval Church. Before the eighteenth century, scholars explain, medieval just war theories of the jus ad bellum held sway. These just war theories were the products of an age of deep and dangerous religiosity, which treated war as a way of punishing crimes. In the words of Stephen Neff, medieval theories declared the aim of war to be "the subduing of evil and the promotion of good."[9] This moralistic attitude toward war may at first sound admirable, but dangerous indeed it was. Carl Schmitt offered the best-known statement of this danger; the treatment of "the enemy as a criminal" and the associated invocation of the principle of a "just cause," he argued, "runs parallel with the increased use of weapons of annihilation and the displacement of war beyond the field of battle."[10] If you label your opponent evil, you find it all too easy to aim at exterminating him. Schmitt is by no means alone in this belief. "Most international lawyers," write Benedict Kingsbury and Alexis Blane, agree that the idea of war as a form of punishment is "awful," countenancing "annihilation . . . genocide . . . arbitrary violence," and more.[11]

Happily, the standard account continues, the eighteenth-century law of war took a less morally charged attitude. The wars of religion had deeply discredited older approaches, and the eighteenth-century law of war, in a way typical of the Enlightenment, put distance between itself and Church tradition.[12] To be sure, eighteenth-century jurists continued to speak of just war occasionally, but these invocations of just war theory, Schmitt insisted, were merely "empty commonplaces."[13] Moreover even when they did speak of just war, they held that wars could be "just on both sides," thereby eviscerating the traditional Christian teachings.[14] Vattel was the embodiment of these eighteenth-century attitudes. He maintained that wars should be viewed as "just on both sides," and he declared that even unjust wars could yield legally enforceable rights, as long as they were "wars in form," wars observing "all the rules of formal warfare."[15]

Just war theory was dead. In its place, scholars tell us, the eighteenth-century law of war embraced the *guerre-duel*,[16] the duel-war, dominated by the courteous and inherently restrained chivalric values of the dueling class of aristocratic officers. The manner of war that Martens celebrated was an *aristocratic* manner of war, and in particular a duelists' manner of war. The French historian David Bell has recently given a concise summary of this standard interpretation: "Unlike medieval commentators . . . jurists like Vattel devoted relatively little attention to the questions of justice. . . . [T]hey focused less on which, if any side, had the morally superior cause. . . . [Instead] they treated war as something like the formal duel. . . . If the forms were honorably observed, it did not matter which side was in the right. Nothing could be closer to the aristocratic code."[17] As Schmitt famously put the same claim, "[T]he contained war of classical European international law, proceeding by recognized rules, [became] little more than a duel between men of honor seeking satisfaction."[18]

Frederick did not take the easy route of a surprise massacre at Mollwitz, the standard account thus suggests, because there was no great conflict over religious truth at stake. He was willing to accept the heightened risk of a pitched battle because he understood himself to be a man of honor, challenging the Count of Neipperg to a grand duel.

This interpretation is repeated, in some form, by almost every scholar writing about the eighteenth-century law of war, and it may seem improbable that it is fundamentally flawed. Nevertheless, it is my purpose to show exactly that is this case. The standard account is wrong about the just war tradition of the Middle Ages and wrong in supposing that the eighteenth century abandoned earlier Christian theory. In the next chapter I show that it is wrong in its claims about how aristocratic values dominated in eighteenth-century war as well.

I begin here with the standard account of just war theory. It may indeed sound plausible to claim that Christian just war theory was about "the subduing of evil and the promotion of good" and that the eighteenth century prospered by rejecting older Christian legal traditions. What else would Christian law be about? But in fact it is not so. In large measure, just war theory was about something quite different: the rights of the victor, and especially the claims of the victor on property, on lands and booty. Improbable though it may sound, medieval just war theorists thought of war as a means of establishing property rights.[19] For them, ordinary wars were not criminal prosecutions, but civil litigation over property disputes. Their just law of war was largely law of victory: it was law about the justice of the property claims made by victors, law about *what you win by winning*, and it was deeply concerned with the division of the spoils. As a result, classic just war writings often sound barbaric to modern humanitarians.

Such was the attitude of medieval just war theory, and lawyers of the civilized eighteenth century did not by any means reject it. Just war theory was *not* dead. It is true that the eighteenth century rejected the fury of the religious wars of the sixteenth and seventeenth centuries—though it is also true that there was an undoubted religious element in the War of the Austrian Succession.[20] It is also certainly true that there were significant innovations in the law. But there was no radical break with the Christian traditions of just war theory. The proposition that a war could be just on both sides had been advocated for centuries. Most important, war was still, at bottom, a means of settling disputes over property. Correspondingly there was no need for eighteenth-century jurists to reject the traditions of just war theory, and they did not do so. They regarded themselves as applying traditional just war principles right down until the end of the century, and they were perfectly right. The idea that the eighteenth-century law of war was the product of a great Enlightenment rupture with the good-versus-evil moralizing of an older Christian tradition is simply false.

That matters for understanding the history of war. In particular, it matters for understanding the events of the invasion of Silesia, of which Mollwitz was the opening engagement. Under traditional just war principles, strange though it may sound, the case for the justice of acts like the seizure of Silesia was quite strong; and such innovations as there were in eighteenth-century law only made the case for Frederick stronger. It may seem self-evident to modern humanitarians that Frederick's epoch-making land grab was a criminal act of aggression—the original sin of modern warfare, the first outburst of a style of Prussian aggression that would set the tone for two centuries of criminal violence in defiance of the humanitarian jus ad bellum. But in fact Frederick was acting in perfect obedience to the law of his time. The eighteenth-century law of war, like the just war theory of centuries before it, was largely the law of victory, and it saw nothing inherently wrong in Frederick's acts.

People who know nothing else about the premodern law of war know that there was a medieval Catholic tradition of just war theory. College courses on the law of war often start with one book in particular, Michael Walzer's *Just and Unjust Wars*, which asserts that "medieval writers" distinguished the "*jus ad bellum*, [which] requires us to make judgments about aggression and self-defense," from the "*jus in bello*, about the observance or violation of the . . . rules of engagement."[21] There are numerous other texts as well, all intended to facilitate classroom discussion of just war analysis. These books all cite Thomas Aquinas. They explain that just war theory is founded on the idea that war is appropriate only as a response to "injustice,"[22] and they give the strong impression that Christian just war theory involved, as a typical college instructor will say, "the recourse to war as punishment," the recourse to just war as a Christian response to the problem of evil.[23] They further explain that just war established certain basic criteria for the moral evaluation of war:

Aquinas . . . laid down three conditions: (1) legitimate, that is consti-
tutional, authority should make the war decision; (2) war should be
waged for a just cause; (3) statesmen should resort to war with right
intention. The sixteenth-century theologian-philosophers Francisco
de Vitoria and Francisco Suárez added three further conditions: (4)
the evils of war, especially the loss of human life, should be propor-
tionate to the injustice to be prevented or remedied by war; (5) peaceful means to prevent or remedy injustice should be exhausted; (6) an
otherwise just war should have a reasonable hope of success.[24]

Texts like these are the bread and butter of education in the law of war,
familiar to everyone with a good liberal education and fundamental to
the humanitarian commitments that guide our modern law of war.

The idea that just war theory was about "the recourse to war as punishment" has driven deep roots into our common culture—so deep that it
may be hard to imagine that it is mistaken. Nevertheless it is so. Classic
just war theory was not what Walzer supposed it was, an early variety of
the modern humanitarian law of war, revolving around the punishment
of evil. While it certainly included reflection on the jus ad bellum, and
sometimes reflection of a humanitarian kind, it also included a great deal
of law of victory, and in the last analysis it had a thoroughly nonhumani-
tarian cast. As a few fine scholars, especially Peter Haggenmacher,[25] have
recognized, classic just war theory was in fact largely about the just property claims of the victor, and it assumed and tolerated rapacious and even
savage forms of war.

To understand how the standard account of just war theory went astray,
it is useful to go back to its origins. Our literature can largely be traced to
late nineteenth- and twentieth-century pacifists committed to the creation
of a humanitarian law of war. In particular, it can be traced to the energetic
work of Alfred Vanderpol, a French engineer who passionately promoted
the cause of pacifism in the decades before World War I. When Vanderpol began his pacifist activities, the technical law of war was still largely
law of victory: it still assumed that war was a perfectly legitimate procedure for claiming rights. Like his fellow pacifists, Vanderpol vigorously
rejected that traditional juristic view. He was one of the pioneers of the

proposition that war, instead of being treated as a legitimate legal procedure, should be criminalized—a view that would become widespread
only in the 1920s, after his death.

Vanderpol was also, like a number of important late nineteenth-century
French intellectuals, a committed Catholic. Many of these French Catholic revivalists thought that a more just modern society could be built on the
foundation of the legal tradition of the medieval Church,[26] and they trolled
through the medieval texts in search of authority for their programs. That
was what Vanderpol did, devoting his after-work hours, and his high
school Latin, to the industrious research that was published posthumously
in his influential 1919 book *The Scholastic Doctrine of the Law of War.* The
material he presented there became the basis of the modern historiography of just war theory.

Understandably Vanderpol was particularly eager to find support for
his belief that war should be treated as a crime. And it is certainly the case
that there are medieval Christian texts that could be cited in support of a
humanitarian view of the just war tradition, and even in support of the
idea that the law of war should be close in spirit to criminal law. In particular Vanderpol could cite texts of that kind from the Thomist theological
tradition; he observed, with perfect justice, that Aquinas's theology demanded "that those against whom we make war must deserve to be fought
against because of some evil act [*propter aliquam culpam*]."[27]

This was not false. Aquinas did indeed develop a theory of the jus ad
bellum according to which wars should be fought because of some *culpa*,
and he was not entirely alone in his views. The language of punishment
was also to be found in some other medieval authors and among sixteenth-
century theologians working in the Thomist tradition.[28] The same language of punishment sometimes also made its way into the writings of
early theorists of the law of war such as Alberico Gentili and Hugo Grotius. Thus Gentili wrote, around the end of the sixteenth century, that
war was just "to avenge wrongs [*injurias*], to punish those who do harm,
and to claim one's rights [*ius suum vindicare*]. . . . For we should not
properly speak of 'war' unless there is an element of justice, which seeks
to punish crimes."[29] As for Grotius, he certainly included punishment
among the generally accepted purposes of just war: "It is a commonplace
to declare that war has three just causes, defense, the recovery of prop-

erty, and punishment."[30] There is no doubt that some theologians spoke, some of the time, about punishment, and no doubt that some jurists, some of the time, echoed them.

Nevertheless the image of just war theory that Vanderpol extracted from his readings was a pacifist distortion—a noble distortion perhaps, but a deep one. It rested on a caricature of the medieval Church, and it misrepresented a medieval juristic tradition that in fact was largely about specifying and enforcing property claims.

Caricatures of the Middle Ages often take the form of exaggerating the dominance and intrusiveness of Church moralizing, imagining that the Church, with its Dominican inquisitors peering darkly out from their cowls, exercised an invasive control over every corner of daily life. The image of just war theory that established itself in the wake of Vanderpol's work has the air of just this kind of caricature. It is too quick to think of the Church as obsessed with the inquisitorial task of ferreting out and punishing evil and too quick to assume that the Church was in a position to dictate the form of war to be fought in the Christian world.

Medievalists know that the medieval Church was a more flexible institution, with much more willingness to compromise with the society around it. The Church had to govern, not just preach, and like any governing institution it frequently accommodated itself to the needs, interests, and customs of the governed. This is especially true of Church lawyers, who were almost always more flexible and open in their approaches than theologians like Aquinas.

It is especially important to remember that the just war theory of the Church belonged to the law of *conscience.* That is to say, its aim was to instruct Christians on how to protect their souls against the threat of damnation. The Church had little hope of remedying all the evils of this world but at least some hope of shepherding souls safely into the next. Correspondingly when medieval theologians and canon lawyers spoke of a war as unjust, what they meant was that it was dangerous for the salvation of Christians to participate in it. Medieval just war theory was thus not law in the modern sense at all, but counsel of conscience of the kind a confessor would give to an individual Christian.[31] It was precisely because just war theory was counsel of conscience that it focused heavily on the state of mind of the Christian engaging in war, who, as Isidore of

Seville explained around the turn of the sixth and seventh centuries, was to act "with legitimate reason" and without "fury."[32] Only by keeping one's mind free of anger and frenzy could one avoid the risks of the damnation of one's soul.

The fact that just war theory was directed to the individual conscience and focused on the individual state of mind is of fundamental importance for understanding its history. For example, the fact that just war theory was counsel of conscience helps explain why lawyers and theologians, centuries before Vattel, were already arguing that a war could be just on both sides. As early as the fifteenth century, lawyers embraced this seeming paradox. They could do so because they held that both sides could experience unconquerable uncertainty about the justice of the war. If there was no way to be sure who was in the right, neither party risked damnation by fighting.[33]

It is especially important to remember that, in offering their counsel of conscience, medieval theologians and lawyers took it for granted that unjust wars would be fought in practice. They could hardly do otherwise: the medieval Church had nothing like sufficient power to prevent unjust wars, and it belongs to the caricature of the Middle Ages to suppose that the Church was moved by such unrealistic aspirations. In fact medieval just war theorists never set out to regulate the practice of war in the way modern lawyers do. Their purpose was to advise pious Christians to steer clear of unjust wars if possible, not to establish a detailed code for the conduct of war. Churchmen generally had to take the practice of war in the world around them as they found it.

That matters a great deal, because the practice of war in the world in which premodern theologians and lawyers lived generally had little to do with the punishment of evil. It had to do mostly with the acquisition of property. Just war theory emerged in antiquity, in a world in which war generally took the forms described by Aristotle and Cicero. Aristotle described war this way: "Comrades in arms join together to seek the profits of war, their aim being either booty or victory over the enemy or the capture of a city."[34] A war was a partnership for profit. For Cicero too war was naturally a matter of seizing booty.[35] From the Homeric tradition onward ancient literature assumed that it was natural and normal to seize booty. The *Iliad*, after all, is about nothing other than a squabble over a piece of war booty, the slave girl Briseis. Other epic poems dwelt on the Sack of Troy and subsequent division of spoils.[36] The Qur'an too, for that matter, addressed the standard problem of the division of booty.[37] Max Weber made the point forcefully in his account of the ancient world: ancient democracies, he wrote, were a kind of citizen guild dedicated to collecting and distributing "booty in slaves, land, and tribute."[38] Profit seeking in the ancient world, he argued, did not involve capitalist production.[39] Profit seeking paradigmatically involved war: men grew rich by seizing the goods and bodies of others.

In fact among the Greeks and Romans, whose teachings formed the juristic basis of just war theory, it was a commonplace not only that war was a way of acquiring property but that war was the *best* way of acquiring property. War, the ancients held, gave the clearest title. While acquisition through inheritance or purchase might be challenged, there was, as the Roman jurist Gaius declared, no more clear root of title than "seizing something from the enemy."[40] In the Greek tradition too "[a]cquisition in war was seen as establishing the strongest, the clearest, and the most just title of property."[41] It is a striking fact that in both Greek and Roman traditions, claims on property were symbolized by the spear, the implement of war. "Spear-won" property, as the Greeks called it, was the most natural form of asset.[42]

War was a means of acquiring property. So indeed did matters generally stand, not only in antiquity, but right down into the eighteenth century. As late as 1804, when the French Civil Code was promulgated, it was understood to include seizing booty as one of its "natural modes of acquiring property," and throughout the Middle Ages and the early modern period the same attitude prevailed. War was at base a form of the pursuit of profit, a way of sorting out conflicting property claims.[43]

Such was the premodern world in which just war theory formed, and just war theorists were in no position to transform it completely.[44] They had a different aim: to induce victors to submit to some measure of the rule of law. Rather than rejecting the proposition that war was an acquisitive enterprise, they insisted that Christians should make war only in order to vindicate plausible property claims. Rather than regarding war as akin to criminal prosecution, most of the time they treated it as a kind of civil action. As an ordinary matter, a war was a kind of trial over a property dispute. Correspondingly, the law of war developed by the Church was largely law of property—law about the just seizure of booty, lands, and thrones. The efforts of just war theorists to make war just were *not* all early humanitarian efforts to criminalize aggression. They were largely about subjecting the profit-seeking enterprise that was war to norms of property law justice, and the rules they established were still entirely alive when Frederick the Great invaded Silesia in 1740.

The unhumanitarian tenor of classic just war theory emerges clearly enough if we read its principal texts closely, maintaining a resolutely open mind. In the West, the great line of authority on just war begins with the late antique writings of Saint Augustine and Isidore of Seville. Both men were working within traditions, biblical and Roman, that treated war fundamentally as a permissibly violent means of acquiring property, and their understanding of the problems of just war reflected that fact.

Let us begin with Augustine. Like later Thomists, Augustine did sometimes speak the language of punishment. But his concerns belonged to the theology of conscience, and when he spoke of punishment, he did so in an Augustinian way that was quite different from the modern humanitarian law of war.[45] Moreover, and more important, he did not by any means always speak the language of punishment. His aim instead was to create a just war theory that tolerated the notion that war was a kind of profit-seeking enterprise.

The key text is Augustine's highly influential commentary on the Book of Joshua. The Book of Joshua is one of the most challenging texts for Jewish and Christian interpreters both, because of its frighteningly brutal account of the conquest of the Holy Land.[46] The passage that Augustine commented on was typical: Joshua 8:1–2, in which God directs Joshua to slaughter the people of Ai and seize and distribute their goods: "Then the Lord said to Joshua, 'Do not be afraid; do not be discouraged. Take the whole army with you, and go up and attack Ai. For I have delivered into your hands the king of Ai, his people, his city and his land. You shall do to Ai and its king as you did to Jericho and its king [i.e., slaughter them], except that you may carry off their plunder and livestock for yourselves. Set an ambush behind the city.'" A modern humanitarian reading this passage, and so many other passages from the Book of Joshua, can only be appalled by the horrific and, by our standards, manifestly criminal practices it describes. Augustine did not react that way. He could have. He could presumably have treated Joshua the way he treated some other aspects of the Old Testament; he could have held that it embodied a special rule or "dispensation" that applied only to the ancient Israelites, not to Christians. That is what earlier Church Fathers did.[47] He could have searched for a way around this awful passage in the effort to build a just war theory that bore some resemblance to modern International Humanitarian Law.

But Augustine was not in the business of creating a modern humanitarian law, and that is not what he did. Instead, as so often, he made an effort to reconcile Christian ideals with the practical needs of government in this world. Augustine was a man who had to govern, and that meant that he had to compromise. Rather than condemning the practices described in Joshua, he set out to tame them. His commentary on this passage would eventually make its way into the standard canon law compilation of the Middle Ages: "Just wars are customarily defined as those that avenge wrongs, where we seek out a people or a polity that has failed to vindicate [*vindicare*] something that has been dishonestly [*improbe*] done by its members, or that has failed to return something that has been wrongfully [*per injurias*] carried off."[48] The key term in this passage is *injurias*. *Injuria*, as Haggenmacher has pointed out, is different from *culpa*, the term used by Aquinas.[49] In the Latin of Augustine and his successors, *injuria* is a term, not from criminal law, but from what we would call tort and property. It is a wrongful injury to private rights. Augustine's reading of his text from Joshua characterized the war as undertaken to force the return of things unjustifiably taken away: "reddere quod per iniurias ablatum est." It assimilated the wars of Joshua to mounting claims on property unrightfully denied, and where it did not speak the language of property, it spoke the language not of punishment but of vengeance.

In short, Augustine treated the Israelites as the injured parties in a property dispute, people whose property had been unjustifiably carried off or whose debts had gone unjustifiably unpaid. Now, this was hardly convincing as a reading of Joshua 8. The Book of Joshua is an unrelievedly horrifying narrative of mass killing and pillage—about as depressing a read about war as you can find in the literature of the ancient world. More of the same is found, moreover, in other Old Testament passages, notably Deuteronomy 20:10–14:

> When you draw near to a city to fight against it, offer terms of peace to it.
>
> And if it responds to you peaceably and it opens to you, then all the people who are found in it shall be your slaves and pay you tribute.[50]
>
> But if it makes no peace with you, but makes war against you, then you shall besiege it.
>
> And when the Lord your God gives it into your hand, you shall put all its males to the sword,
>
> But the women and the little ones, the livestock, and everything else in the city, all its spoil, you shall take as plunder for yourselves. And you shall enjoy the spoil of your enemies, which the Lord your God has given you.

This is chilling stuff, from the modern humanitarian point of view, and it seems wholly forced to pretend that the marauding Israelites of these passages were simply the wronged plaintiffs in a property suit. Nevertheless Augustine was only the first in the Western Christian tradition to make just such a forced argument. He was only the first to propose that a just war was a war that could be characterized, no matter what its brutality, as an effort to recover property that had been unrightfully denied. We shall find lawyers taking exactly the same tack right down into the time of the seizure of Silesia and after.

That Augustine took this attitude is a truth that Vanderpol and his followers were not prepared to accept, and modern humanitarians are still likely to rebel against it. Yet the fact that he took this attitude does not imply that Augustine condoned or connived in the brutality of war. The issues are more complex than that, and they go to the heart of the value of a law of victory of the kind that Vanderpol rejected.

Yes, it is true that Augustine did not take a modern humanitarian view of war. He did not simply condemn the horrific practices described in the Book of Joshua as evil or aim to make out war to be a species of crime. But that does not mean that he was a quietist or a fellow traveler. He, and his followers, were trying to subject the practice of war to the rule of law. They were trying to coax combatants to keep their war making within the limits of just claims to property. In insisting, however improbably, that the Israelites of Joshua were simply claiming property that had been taken from them, Augustine was addressing a plea to the war makers of his time: they too should confine themselves to making wars to execute plausible legal claims. In making this plea, Augustine and his followers implied, in a way repugnant to modern lawyers, that war was an appropriate way of claiming property through slaughter. But their aim was not by any means to permit combatants to engage in an unbridled practice of horror. Their aim was to govern the human society that they found around them. Their aim was to induce the combatants of the violent world of late antiquity to act with some of the controlled sobriety of litigants in their pursuit of victory; and that represents a real advance in the project of civilizing war.

Henry Maine, the pioneer of modern legal history, understood that aim. Maine left us a brilliant description of the value of the kind of approach Augustine pursued. "The rules," he wrote in 1861, "have sometimes been stigmatised as needlessly indulgent to the ferocity and cupidity of combatants, but the charge has been made, I think, by persons who are unacquainted with the history of wars, and who are consequently ignorant how great an exploit it is to command obedience for a rule of any kind."[51] Commanding obedience for a rule of any kind was indeed the exploit at which just war theory aimed for centuries. The true aim of Augustine and his followers was precisely the aim that Kant would reject fourteen centuries later: It was the aim of guaranteeing that a war would be regarded as a legal procedure, precisely in order to keep it within civilized bounds.

We find the same aim in Isidore of Seville, the other late antique font of medieval just war theory, who also treated just war largely as a matter of claiming rights in property. Where Augustine commented on the Old Testament, though, Isidore drew principally from the Roman tradition. His formulations were principally taken from Cicero, who declared that no war was just unless it was fought "to claim things back that are ours [*de rebus repetitis*], or after a warning and a declaration."[52] Claiming things back, *rerum repetitio*, had a long Roman history. The Romans, who were among the most savage war makers of Antiquity, always justified their wars, at least as far back as we can read the historical record, as efforts to vindicate a lawful claim to property that had been wrongfully denied to the Roman people, and ancient records of the Roman rituals for the declaration of war required that a Roman priest repeat three times the rerum repetitio, the demand that things be given back.[53] In particular, the rituals involved casting a spear, also used as the symbol for making property claims in ordinary trials: "It was customary for [the priest charged with declaring war] to carry a . . . spear . . . to the borders of the people in question and to pronounce in the presence of not less than three men of military age [a traditional formula]. When he had said these words, he cast the spear across their borders. This was the traditional means by which the Latins claimed their property back and declared war."[54] The difficulty of conducting this ritual as Rome expanded led to one of the most famous of Roman legal fictions: "When in the time of Pyrrhus the Romans were about to wage war against an enemy across the sea, and could not find a place where they might perform . . . this ritual for declaring war, they compelled one of Pyrrhus' soldiers whom they had captured to buy a plot of land [in Rome], so that they might fulfill the law of declaring war [by casting a spear into it.]"[55] In all of this, the forms of war closely paralleled the forms of property litigation.[56] And as we have seen, Roman legal texts too simply assumed that war was a mode of acquiring property rights.[57]

These classical traditions guided Isidore, who declared that a war was just if it was waged "to claim back things that are ours, or to repulse an invasion."[58] Isidore's approach joined Augustine's in establishing the basic foundation of medieval just war reasoning that focused heavily on property rights. Of course, as Isidore's language suggests, self-defense too had its place among the just causes for war that emerged in subsequent centuries. Nevertheless he listed it second, and as Haggenmacher observes, self-defense would tend to fade into the background in later centuries, as just war theory developed under the influence of Augustine and Isidore. Thus the standard twelfth-century Canon text of Gratian tended to eliminate everything other than material considerations in the causes of war, and the same remained true of subsequent developments in medieval law.[59]

When we turn to the Middle Ages, we find that the ties between the law of war and rerum repetitio, the making of property claims, remained tight—so tight that most medieval legal analyses of war were conducted as exercises in property law. Thus for Baldus, the most ingenious jurist of the later Middle Ages, it came naturally to found his discussion of the law of war on the Roman law of possession.[60] Raphael Fulgosius, who pioneered the idea that wars could be just on both sides around the year 1400, took it for granted that wars were a form of litigation over property between sovereigns.[61] Similarly in standard canon law basic questions about the law of war were understood as property questions.[62]

All of these authors, from Augustine on, simply assumed that war was generally fought over material claims and consequently that the justice of a given war was primarily about the justice of claiming property rights, requiring careful property law analysis, and imposing on combatants the obligation to pursue only colorable claims. Correspondingly, most of the time, the Latin technical term used by just war theorists was not *culpa*, criminal guilt, the term used by Aquinas, but *injuria*, unjustified invasion of rights. Most of the time, the fundamental orientation of just war theorists was much closer to civil litigation than to criminal litigation.[63] Even Thomist theologians like Vitoria, though they did sometimes speak of punishment, always also spoke of recovering property—of war as having a kind of property as its object of litigation.[64] As Gentili said, it was just to make war "to claim your rights." In fact the bulk of just war theory was precisely about claiming rights. It was about the first two of Grotius's "just causes": self-defense and most especially "the recovery of property." As we shall see shortly, by the eighteenth century even self-defense was regarded as an exercise of property rights.

It is important to underline how comfortably the emphasis on property claims fit with the practice of war in the world in which medieval authors lived, and how well it would still fit with the practice of war in the age of the military gambler Frederick the Great. First of all, the proposition that war was about "demanding property that has unrightfully been denied to us" made eminent sense in a world in which wars were fought over title to lands and castles and especially over claims of royal succession. As a matter of law, a claimant to a throne was precisely a person whose property was being unrightfully denied to him. Such was the legal basis of the major conflicts of the Middle Ages, as it still would be in the eighteenth century. The Norman Conquest of England, justified by William the Conqueror's assertion that he had been denied his rightful claim to succeed to the throne, is a familiar example. Another is the Hundred Years War, a contest technically fought over the interpretation and application of the Salic law of succession in France. Many other examples can be cited as well. The claims in such wars of succession were easy to frame in just war terms, precisely because just war theory revolved so much around the rerum repetitio: *The throne is mine by right of succession, but it is being unjustly withheld from me! I am the rightful heir of that duchy, that castle, but you are denying it to me!*

Second, the emphasis of just war theory made sense in a world in which many of the legal disputes arising out of war had to do with the seizure of booty. Soldiers had well-established and extensive rights to claim booty in premodern warfare, and any useful theory of the law of war had to concern itself with the contours of those rights. When did soldiers acquire title? How was booty to be distributed? These were important and complex practical questions in property law, and just war theorists put considerable effort into resolving them. The passage from Joshua that Augustine commented on was of course about the distribution of booty: "[Y]ou may carry off their plunder and livestock for yourselves," declared the Yahweh of this text, meaning that He did not insist on taking it for Himself. Isidore's just war theory too concerned itself with booty: military law was inevitably partly about "the booty decision: that is to say the just division of booty, which depends on the relative social rank of individuals and on their relative contributions to the war effort, as well the portion due to the prince."[65]

Justa divisio, just divvying up, was Isidore's just war concern here. This passage too was incorporated into standard Canon Law, as booty law retained a central place in just war analysis.[66] Leading canon lawyers like Raymond of Peñafort declared that as long as the war was just, "anything you take from the enemy is yours."[67] Medieval canon literature went out of its way to insist that booty could be taken not only from heretics but from any enemy in a just war.[68] The great Bartolus declared the basic rule: real property went to the victorious prince, while mobile goods were to be distributed to the soldiery.[69] Sixteenth-century just war theorists too, even Thomist ones, continued to work out lengthy legal treatments of the problems of rights in booty.[70] The same was true of pioneers of the early modern law of war like Balthazar Ayala, to say nothing of Grotius, whose early work involved nothing other than *The Law of Booty*.[71] All of this sounds sinister to us today, but it lay at the foundation of the just war theory of the past.

What I have offered here is a rapid overview of medieval and early modern material, but it is enough to make the critical point. The medieval just war tradition was *not* all about punishing evil. It is thoroughly anachronistic to think of it simply as a primitive version of the modern humanitarian jus ad bellum, dedicated to the proposition that the law of war was a close cousin to the law of criminal prosecution. Like the rest of premodern law, medieval just war theory was largely jus victoriae, and its tone was very remote from the tone of modern humanitarianism. It took for granted the legitimacy of acquisition through war, and its concern with justice was largely a concern for property rights. People went to war to seize goods and lands, and the law of war was concerned with giving sanction to the just claims of victors.

The same remained true in the eighteenth century, which means that there was no need for eighteenth-century jurists to break radically with medieval just war traditions. One tends to think of the eighteenth century as deeply different from previous ages—a time when the "crisis of European consciousness," famously described by Paul Hazard in 1935, ushered in a new intellectual and social era.[72] This is part of the reason why the conventional account, with its insistence that the eighteenth century rejected medieval traditions in the law of war, sounds so plausible. But there have always been historians who doubted that the eighteenth century really broke so thoroughly with the Christian past,[73] and doubt is wholly in order when it comes to the law of war. There were certainly some aspects of eighteenth-century law that departed from the older traditions, but the spirit of the law of war remained unchanged. Wars were still being fought over territory, booty, and the right to succeed to thrones. Correspondingly there was no need for eighteenth-century jurists to discard the just war tradition.

In fact it is flat-out false to say, as Bell does, that "jurists like Vattel devoted relatively little attention to the questions of justice," and flat-out false to say, as Schmitt does, that eighteenth-century invocations of just war theory were simply "empty commonplaces."[74] As Jean-Mathieu Mattéi has demonstrated in his meticulous study of the eighteenth-century law of war, the jurists of the Enlightenment, who were "infinitely indebted" to the medieval scholastic analyses, generally considered their own work to belong to the just war tradition right down until the end of the century, and they generally continued to speak in the same terms as their medieval predecessors had done, Vattel included.[75] We must understand this if we are to understand the idea of justice in the eighteenth-century law of war, which remained a species of the law of victory and therefore a species of law thoroughly foreign to our modern humanitarian way of thinking. We must understand it, in particular, if we are to understand the eighteenth-century justice of Frederick's seizure of Silesia.

There were certainly some aspects of medieval theory that eighteenth-century jurists rejected outright. Occasionally—though only occasionally—medieval authors held that it was just to fight wars in the name of religious orthodoxy. That view was roundly rejected in the eighteenth century.[76] In that sense at least it is true that the eighteenth century represented a rupture with an older religious approach to war. There were also distinctive innovations in eighteenth-century just war theory. One reflected the greatest innovation of eighteenth-century diplomacy: jurists sometimes, but only sometimes, were ready to hold that it was a just cause to go to war in order to maintain the balance of power.[77] This was of some relevance to the invasion of Silesia: contemporaries did worry that Frederick, bold gambler that he was, was a "disturber of the balance of power."[78]

For the most part, however, jurists of the Enlightenment era regarded war as a means of acquiring territory and booty, as just war theorists had always done, and the tenor of their texts was accordingly perfectly consonant with what had been said in previous centuries. That means that, like their predecessors, they occasionally used the language of punishment,[79] while much of their law was about the unhumanitarian business of specifying and analyzing the just property rights that arose out of war. In particular they were preoccupied with analyzing the just property claims of sovereigns.

Like their predecessors, eighteenth-century jurists had no doubt that war was a "legitimate mode of acquisition." As Robert Pothier, the leading French treatise writer of the century, explained, "The right of conquest is the right of a sovereign . . . to acquire . . . the ownership of the cities, castles and lands of the enemy by seizing them. . . . The term 'booty' refers to all mobile goods seized by the victors from the vanquished. . . . [When booty is seized in battle] it is customary to give part of it to the troops, in order to encourage them."[80] Some of the spirit of the Book of Joshua still clung to Pothier's property doctrine. Writers on the law of war took the same point of view. Vattel, for example, declared that "a just war is a legitimate means of acquiring property according to natural law."[81] Long passages in Vattel's writings, and the writings of others, made the point that had been made for centuries in just war theory: rerum repetitio was, as it had always been, a just cause,[82] and a just war conferred property rights on the victor. War remained a rapacious activity, and just war theory continued to reconcile itself to that fact. Property claims lay at the foundation of the law of war for well-known jurists like Christian Wolff:

> Nations have the right to acquire rights, and to demand that other nations fulfill the obligations that grow out of the rights they have acquired.
>
> From this is born the right to go to war, in virtue of which a nation defends its natural liberty, and engages in the legitimate pursuit of its rights.[83]

Acquiring rights, in the technical language of Roman law used in this passage, means acquiring *property* rights.[84] Similar language can be found in all the standard eighteenth-century jurists.[85] Perhaps even more revealingly, similar language is found in forgotten figures like the Abbé de Fleury, the aged theologian who was made the confessor of the young Louis XV in 1715:

> War is the right of sovereigns to claim justice by force. . . .
>
> The causes of war are the same as those for which private persons file lawsuits. Defense, to prevent a harm threatened against persons or property. . . . [T]here is no need to wait for the damage to occur,

nor to be too slow to prevent it. . . . Claiming back things that have been usurped . . . claiming things owed to us for reparation of damages . . . including for the execution of treaties [among them a promise to make a marriage] . . . also property that is owed to us because it has been given, bequeathed, or because we have succeeded to it by testamentary or intestate successions following the laws of the relevant country. [War is] private law applied to the interest of sovereigns . . . though the rules of prescription [statutes of limitation] do not apply. From all this arise the pretentions of so many sovereigns against other sovereigns.[86]

No text could have presented a more perfect picture of accepted orthodoxy than the book of instructions prepared by his confessor to guide the conscience of the King of France. The doctrine in these passages was close to indistinguishable from the doctrines of the Middle Ages. Like their medieval and early modern predecessors, eighteenth-century jurists also engaged in refined debates about rights in booty, to which we will return later, along with a variety of other questions surrounding property rights acquired through war.[87]

In particular, as the passage from Abbé de Fleury suggests, they delved into two critical areas of law in the creation of monarchical rights: the law of marriage and especially the law of succession.[88] As the abbé declared, it was just for a sovereign to go to war, under the rubric rerum repetitio, to claim "rights of testamentary or intestate succession . . . following the laws of the country in question." This was how "private law applied to sovereigns."[89] In this respect too nothing had changed since the time of Hastings and the Hundred Years War.

Indeed because war was "the right of sovereigns to claim justice by force" and because the claims of sovereigns were preeminently claims to property under the law of dynastic succession, the law of war texts of the eighteenth century frequently discussed the private law problems of succession and royal marriage. These passages have puzzled modern scholars, wedded as they are to the idea that the law of war must have been either about the problem of punishment or about dueling rather than about the law of royal succession. For example, Arthur Nussbaum, in his *Concise History of the Law of Nations*, found it inexplicable that

Richard Zouche, the seventeenth-century English jurist, should have written about problems in the law of succession: "The alleged connection with the *ius inter gentes*," wrote Nussbaum in puzzlement, "is limited to the observation that contests over succession to a throne sometimes lead to war." No less mysterious to Nussbaum was J. J. Moser's discussion of the law of royal marriage in his own mid-eighteenth-century treatise. "Royal marriages," opined Nussbaum, have after all "very remote bearing upon international law."[90] Other historians have treated eighteenth-century discussions of the law of succession in international affairs as simply irrelevant or specious. This is notably true of Sharon Korman's account of the legal conflicts behind the War of the Austrian Succession; disputes over dynastic rights to succession, she writes, in reality "played no part."[91] The truth is that it was all about Frederician power politics. Other historians, even very careful ones, regard the law of succession as so irrelevant to international law that they spill no ink on it at all.[92]

Yet eighteenth-century writers on international law put considerable energy into the law of royal marriage and royal succession—naturally enough, since they all regarded war as a normal means for dynastic sovereigns to lay claim to their succession rights. Moser, for example, explained in the opening pages of his 1752 treatise that "[s]uccession to the throne in hereditary monarchies has often created the occasion to take up arms, by which the claimants hope to establish their rights." Accordingly he passed in his next paragraphs to the consequences in international law of the extinction of a royal male line.[93] One assumes that he reached the topic of the law of royal succession on the second or third day of his lectures. Vattel, displaying his humanity and originality, deplored the conventional approach to the connection between war and the law of succession. He rejected the hallowed view that such disputes could not be resolved in a human court and therefore must be settled by force: "Some scholars have argued, on the basis of the proposition that sovereigns recognize no judge but God, that the pretenders to the crown, if their claim is uncertain, should either negotiate or contract among themselves, or choose arbiters, or even use a game of chance [*sors*], or finally settle their differences through armed force, while the subjects of the realm in question are by no means entitled to decide for themselves."[94] Vattel admirably insisted that the question ought instead to be decided .

by domestic legal procedures, effectively forcing sovereigns to submit to the judgment of a human court.[95] This was quite a radical view, but let us note that Vattel did not for a moment suggest that disputes over succession should not be taken seriously. To him, problems in monarchical succession were real problems in international law, not irrelevancies. Martens, writing toward the end of the century, took a somewhat harder realist line. In the end, he said, disputes over succession were always decided by the larger constellation of military powers involved.[96] But he too did not suggest that succession disputes were not completely serious and important causes of war, indeed the prime causes of war among the civilized European powers.

The law of succession mattered to these authors; war was how the private law of succession "applied to the interest of Sovereigns." Sovereigns were, by definition, not subject to any court, which meant that they had the license to resolve their succession disputes through the legal procedure that was war. That indeed is why the continental wars of the century were ordinarily captioned "the War of the Spanish Succession," "the War of the Austrian Succession," and the like. From a technical standpoint, these wars were legal procedures, undertaken by sovereigns to enforce private law claims in the law of succession—as we would call them, *In re* Spanish Succession, *In re* Austrian Succession, and so on. As this suggests, it is a basic mistake not to take what eighteenth-century authors wrote about the law of succession at face value. The fashionable realism of the nineteenth century, with its hard Clausewitzian view of war and its lionization of Frederick the Great as an avatar of ruthlessness, naturally preferred to dismiss the legal debates of the eighteenth century. But the eighteenth century itself was a century of law, and the law of royal succession in particular was taken with utter seriousness. People cared.

Nor should it surprise us that they cared. There were great questions of legitimacy at stake. Monarchical rule mattered in the eighteenth century. Princely courts were at the center of life for people who came into any contact with them; the sense of what was legitimate and right was deeply tied up with monarchical government for most people; and the legitimacy of a royal family rested on its rights under the law of succession. To anyone fascinated by royalty—and after all, most people are fascinated by royalty—the question *Who has the right to the throne?* was inevitably riveting, indeed fundamental to their respect, or lack of respect, for the state. Moreover the very right to go to war announced to the world that a prince was sovereign. Disputed successions were no more irrelevant on the eighteenth-century international stage than disputed elections are irrelevant on the international stage today: they went to the heart of state legitimacy in an order founded on dynastic monarchy.

As for the proposition that a war could be just on both sides: It is true that eighteenth-century jurists endorsed it. Most especially Vattel endorsed it, and he may well have viewed it as a healthy antidote to the dangers that grew out of deeming one's enemy to be evil. But it was a proposition that had been endorsed by just war theorists for more than three hundred years, and properly understood it fit perfectly comfortably within just war traditions.[97]

If just war theory had regarded war as a form of punishment, then it would indeed have been strange to say that a war could be just on both sides. After all, in a criminal prosecution only one side, the state or the defendant, can be in the right. But the same is not true in civil litigation. Both parties in a civil matter typically have plausible legal claims, which they typically bring in good conscience; the task of the court is not to punish evil but to sort out the inevitably conflicting interpretations of the two sides. War, from the point of view of much just war theory, was nothing other than a form of civil litigation over property claims; it was how private law applied to sovereigns. As long as the sovereigns on both sides had colorable legal claims, it made perfect sense to deem their war just on both sides.

With that in mind, let us turn once again to the invasion of Silesia in 1740. As we have seen, scholars treat the invasion of Silesia as a lawless act, indeed the classic act of criminal aggression on the international stage. "[T]he manner in which Frederick executed his Silesian project presented him to the world as a criminal and a malevolent aggressor. . . . [H]e attacked Silesia without warning. . . . The principles of strict justice that his father and, indeed, most of his predecessors had observed in foreign affairs could not have been transgressed more sharply and suddenly."[98] Frederick's claims of succession rights are dismissed as hypocritical window-dressing, and the abrupt march of his troops into Silesia is regarded as a piece of brigandage, perhaps even as the model for the German aggressions of the twentieth century. How well does this view comport with the views of the eighteenth century?

Unsurprisingly, not well at all. Frederick was a sovereign, subject to the jurisdiction of no human court. He had colorable legal claims, and the law of his time permitted him to litigate those claims through war. Moreover the law imposed no obligation on him to issue a formal declaration or warning before invading. It did not even impose any obligation that he offer the legal justifications for invading in good faith.

Let us begin with Frederick's claims in the law of succession. If those claims had been regarded as dishonest nonsense, we would expect contemporaries to treat them dismissively. Nothing of the kind is the case. The literature of the 1740s treated his claims, not only as plausible, but as fascinating. Debating Frederick's rights of succession seems to have been a major parlor activity, generating hundreds of pages of disconcertingly arcane juristic discussion in newssheets and pamphlets in all European languages. For example, Richard Rolt, who reviewed the events of the war in his four-volume 1749 *Impartial Representation of the Conduct of the Several Powers of Europe Engaged in the Late General War*, described the legal dispute at length—enormous length—after acknowledging that Frederick had both "powerful incentives" *and* "plausible pretences":

> [H]e was neither in want of powerful incentives, or plausible pretences. He insisted on an incontestable right, in the royal and electoral family, of Brandenburgh, to the principalities and lordships of Jagerndorff, Lignitz, Brieg, Wohlau, Beuten, Oderberg, and other territories in the duchy of Silesia; partly founded upon antient pacts of succession and cofraternity, between his predecessors in the electoral dignity, and the dukes of Silesia, Lignitz, Brieg, and Wohlau; as well as upon other controvertible titles. For George Frederick, Duke of Jagerndorff, having no children, by his last will, bequeathed that duchy, which he had a right to dispose of under the permission granted by Lewis King of Bohemia, to the Margrave George, who had purchased the duchy from the lords of Schellenberg in 1524 . . .

[several pages of dense discussion of the law of succession omitted] [and so] his Prussian majesty insisted, that those duchies are heredi- tary estates only in the male line, and were never transmitted to the females; besides those states had surrendered a formal homage to the house of Brandenburg: and as the electors had never been able to obtain redress on account of the great power to which the house of Austria had arrived by sitting on the Imperial throne; on the declen- sion of their grandeur, his Prussian majesty embraced the opportu- nity of asserting his rights.[99]

It is no easy task for modern readers to wade through this stuff. But Rolt and his publisher evidently believed that eighteenth-century readers were ready to pay money for a book that included lengthy legal disquisi- tions of this kind, and one guesses that the attendees at the salons and dinners of 1741 and 1742 spent their time discussing exactly the same questions in the same terms.

Many other authors wrote in the same vein, often producing detailed accounts of the disputed law of succession. *Scots Magazine*, for example, published a long account of the "disputable point" in "The King of Prus- sia's Rights to Silesia" in March 1741. It reviewed Frederick's claims en- tirely seriously.[100] Similarly a sheet called the *Europäische Fama*, which reported on the politics of various courts for its German readership, pre- sented Frederick's legal claims under the law of succession of the relevant duchies without irony or derision.[101] None of these commentators thought that the law of succession had "very remote bearing upon international law."[102] In fact, for them, the law of war *was*, for most purposes, an aspect of the law of dynastic succession. Modern humanitarians may find it dif- ficult to grasp that eighteenth-century readers could have accepted ar- cane and "disputable" claims in the law of succession as justification for the bloodshed of war, but it is plain that they did.

The law of succession was particularly important with regard to one of the crucial details in the Silesian dispute. Frederick's predecessor Frederick William had executed the Pragmatic Sanction in 1726, guar- anteeing the succession rights of Maria Theresa. Did that not mean that Frederick had no claim? Modern commentators often say so, but the eighteenth century did not find the issue so clear-cut.[103] In fact the law raised serious questions about the enforceability of the Pragmatic Sanction. It was Frederick's claim that, under the law of succession, Frederick William simply did not have the legal power to sign away the rights of his heirs. Modern historians may sneer at this supposedly cynical argument, but under eighteenth-century law it is by no means obviously flawed.[104] The law was very solicitous of the rights of heirs, and it frequently frowned on cases in which the older generation signed away the succession rights of the younger.[105] It may indeed be the case that Frederick William had no legal power to execute the Pragmatic Sanction.

To be sure, the Austrians contested Frederick's arguments. As *Scots Magazine* reported, Frederick's rights were "a disputable point." So they were. Premodern law was disorderly and uncertain. That is why the dispute in question stirred up so many hundreds of pages of elaborate discussion of the law of succession in contemporary literature. In fact the issues were so disputable that they could ultimately have been settled only through long battles in a court with jurisdiction to hear the case.

But there was no court with jurisdiction to hear the case. The orthodoxy of the Middle Ages remained the orthodoxy of the eighteenth century: war was a necessary procedure for claiming rights in a setting in which no human court had jurisdiction, and to be sovereign was to be subject to no human jurisdiction. That meant that sovereigns had as much right to go to war as their subjects had to file suit. Most especially, as the Abbé de Fleury explained, sovereigns had the right to go to war to claim "rights of testamentary or intestate succession . . . following the laws of the country in question."[106]

To be sure, the Austrians made a game effort to deny that Frederick counted as a sovereign. Their cleverest argument was that he had violated his duties as head of a subordinate house of the Holy Roman Empire— that is to say, that he did not in fact enjoy fully sovereign rights.[107] In the end, though, that argument was hardly a winner: nobody doubted that Frederick of Prussia was a king.

Nevertheless modern readers may not yet be satisfied. However plausible his rights may have been, wasn't Frederick's invasion an unprovoked act of aggression? Wasn't it self-evidently wrong simply to march troops into Silesia? And in any case weren't his legal arguments mere pretexts, offered in bad faith? The question, after all, is not just whether Frederick had colorable legal claims; it is whether he acted unlawfully in pursuing those claims.

To modern readers it may seem obvious that Frederick acted unlawfully, but once again eighteenth-century law gave answers very different from the answers the law would give today. To understand those eighteenth-century answers, we must examine two bodies of legal doctrine that are both quite strange from the modern point of view: the law of the initiation of war for what Vattel called the "maintenance of one's rights" and the law of pretexts.[108]

First, the law of maintaining one's rights. Under modern law, wars are generally supposed to be conducted only in self-defense, but in the eighteenth century the license to make war was broader. Indeed it had always been broader. As Isidore explained, just wars were fought "*to claim back things that are ours*, or to repulse an invasion."[109] The eighteenth century continued to view matters in the same way. In Vattel's formulation, "the right to use force, or make war, belongs to nations only for defense *or for the maintenance of their rights*."[110] The second category mattered. Sovereigns could go to war to maintain their rights, and in doing so they did not have to wait until there was the kind of threat that ordinarily justified acting in self-defense. "There is no need to wait for the damage to occur, nor to be too slow to prevent it!" the Abbé de Fleury instructed young King Louis XV of France.[111] Martens gave a particularly sharp statement of the doctrine: war was permitted "to maintain oneself in possession of a right *outside one's territory* to which one is entitled and which has been improperly impaired." Such a war would be technically "defensive" if it involved "forestalling a threatened attack," and it was not necessary to give a warning.[112] Vattel deemed a war to be just when it was undertaken "to avenge *or prevent* a wrong."[113] Wolff declared similarly that "an offensive war is licit, when your right is certain, and you face an adversary who refuses to accede to it, or to repair a manifest civil wrong."[114] By the end of the century, it was common to declare that wars "to maintain one's rights" were by their very nature wholly defensive.[115]

Maintaining one's rights was such a preponderant concern in the princely law of the eighteenth century that the literature was prepared to treat preemptive wars based on claims of sovereign right as just. This is law that we must remember if we hope to appreciate the eighteenth-century significance of Frederick's supposedly illegal invasion of Silesia. Even before he acceded to the throne of Prussia, Frederick addressed the question of preemptive wars for the maintenance of rights in his *Anti-Machiavel*. The *Anti-Machiavel*, famously sponsored and promoted by Voltaire, was Prince Frederick's description of the high moral standards of the enlightened monarch. It is often derided as a text whose teachings Frederick would rudely jettison when he embarked on his "lawless," and wholly Machiavellian, invasion of Silesia, but in fact it already defended the sort of war that he initiated, and on orthodox legal grounds. Even wars that were offensive as a matter of military strategy, the young Prince Frederick wrote, might nevertheless count as just under the law of war:

> Wars made by sovereigns to maintain certain rights or certain pretentions that others dispute are no less just than [wars of self-defense]. . . . Since kings are subject to no superior tribunal . . . it is for combat to decide their rights and to judge the validity of their reasons. . . .
>
> There are wars of precaution, which princes are wise to undertake. They are in truth offensive, but they are no less just for that. . . . It is a well-established maxim that it is better to forestall than to be forestalled; great men have always put themselves in the best position by using force before their enemies have arranged matters so as to tie their hands and destroy their power.[116]

This sounds ruthless enough to the modern ear, but it was a wholly conventional reading of eighteenth-century doctrine. It was hornbook law to say that you had the just license to move first against an adversary who was disputing your pretentions.

In light of these doctrines, it should come as no surprise that contemporaries were not notably troubled by the fact that Frederick attacked "without warning." One might have imagined that the "code of conduct" approach of the supposedly chivalric eighteenth century would have required a proper declaration of war. Vattel, the humane reformer, certainly thought so.[117] However, in practice the law of what Frederick called "wars of precaution" left little room for such niceties, and contemporaries do not seem to have worried much about them. The law clearly required only one measure: sovereigns were expected to issue a manifesto for the benefit of the general public describing the rights that they aimed to maintain.

Martens surveyed the law at the end of the century and summarized it this way: "[t]he strict law of nations" had not required a formal declaration to the enemy since the mid-seventeenth century. "Instead," he explained, "one announces the war to one's own subjects through manifestoes, and elaborates the causes of the war in pamphlets that it is customary to communicate to the various [princely] courts."[118] The law required sovereigns to declare their cause to the world, not to their enemy. Similarly Moser, writing at midcentury, declared that it was neither "necessary" nor "customary" to make a formal declaration of war. It was "often" the case that sovereigns initiated military action without any even informal declaration, simply publishing a manifesto laying out the "cause" that had led them to attack.[119] Other jurists too spoke only of the obligation to publish a general manifesto laying out one's claims.[120] That is exactly what Frederick did.[121]

To be sure, as in so much of the law, the point was disputable. Moser noted that "there is debate" over the question of whether "an informal declaration of war should precede the initiation of hostile operations by a sovereign."[122] The Austrians *did* find arguments to mount in favor of the proposition that Frederick should have made a prior declaration before invading.[123] But the Prussians had their legal arguments too, and journalistic reports at the time of the invasion presented the arguments of the two sides in an agnostic way.[124] Once again the question was one that would have called for litigation in court, had litigation in court been possible. On balance, though, it must be said that eighteenth-century law quite clearly favored Frederick.

Yet even if the law favored Frederick in some ways, even if his claims had some plausibility, isn't it the case that he offered his legal arguments in bad faith? Weren't his claims mere pretexts, mere sham arguments, intended to cloak an exercise in pure power politics? Shouldn't such pretexts be condemned by the law of war? This is perhaps the most frequently and fiercely repeated charge against Frederick. To answer it, we must examine one last striking body of doctrine: the eighteenth-century law of pretexts.

It is commonplace to condemn Frederick as an opportunistic manipulator of pretextual legal arguments, a man who, in the words of Jomini, "evoke[d] old parchments [and] enter[ed] Silesia by main force."[125] "Frederick," writes Korman, "took great pains to produce a pretext for his invasion . . . [but] nobody believed it, least of all himself."[126] His true motives had in fact nothing to do with "questions of the law of succession" and everything to do with Machiavellian *raison d'état*. So Korman insists, and so do other historians insist as well.[127]

Korman cites in particular the great German historian Gerhard Ritter, who painted just such a picture of Frederick in 1936, at a time when the then-ruler in Berlin, Adolf Hitler, was setting new standards of contempt for the law. Ritter intended his book as a sly critique of Hitler,[128] and the picture he painted of Frederick could hardly have failed to resonate in the fourth year of Hitler's rule. Frederick, wrote Ritter, was an "arrogant and cynical" manipulator of legal arguments that he never expected anyone to take seriously: "At bottom the appeal to venerable dynastic treaties of inheritance had no place in his diplomatic style. He left this sort of thing to his jurists and ministers—let them see how far they could convince the world."[129]

Such is the prevailing image of Frederick. It is indeed the image of a proto-Hitler, an "arrogant and cynical" abuser of specious legal claims, the first of the modern villains of wars of aggression, whose crimes the modern law of war has been invented to combat. It is the image of a criminal warmonger who justified his aggression through specious legal pretexts.

Yet it is a false image—not only because it rests on a questionable use of the historical record,[130] but also, and more importantly, because it rests on a deep misreading of eighteenth-century law. Of course Frederick's claims were pretexts. No one could doubt it. But the fact is that eighteenth-century law did not necessarily condemn the use of bad faith pretexts. On the contrary, bizarre though it may sound, eighteenth-century jurists regarded the use of pretexts as something of a *good* thing. If we can understand why, we can gain some critical insight into how the eighteenth century managed to maintain a culture of civilized, limited war.

The eighteenth-century doctrine of pretexts is one of the most striking products of the premodern law of victory tradition. As we have seen, the drive of the law of victory in the just war tradition was not to condemn war outright but to coax combatants into stating legal claims. In Maine's words, just war theory aimed at the "exploit" of "command[ing] obedience for any rule at all," while remaining "indulgent to the ferocity and cupidity of combatants."

The doctrine of pretexts was the ultimate expression of that drive. Eighteenth-century jurists certainly did not think that pretextual wars were just wars. They uniformly held that just wars should be fought on the basis of good faith claims. But they did not stop there. Like Saint Augustine, they understood that they had to govern and not just preach, and while they expressed the pious hope that wars would be fought in good faith, they also accepted the proposition that enforceable rights could arise from a war fought on the basis of mere pretexts. In fact they thought it was a mark of civilization that sovereigns should feel obliged to offer pretexts. What mattered most, they argued, was that civilized wars be fought on the basis of *some* legal claim, even a bad faith one. The alternative was nothing less than barbarism.

Christian Wolff gave a fine statement of the eighteenth-century view. Although only some wars were just, he wrote, some unjust wars were worse than others. The worse wars were wars for which no pretext whatsoever was given. Wars without pretexts belonged to the category *bellum ferinum*, "wild beast wars," "unworthy of humanity."[131] Civilized warfare, as Wolff saw it, warfare preceded by the giving of reasons, was warfare that rejected the mere animal rapacity of an Attila or a Genghis. Others spoke in similar terms. The Abbé de Fleury, for example, declared that wars without a pretext were "brutish," whereas wars on a false pretext were merely unjust.[132] As another eighteenth-century author put it, those who made war "without reasons or pretexts" were simply "monsters, unworthy of the name 'human.'"[133] These jurists were not interested only in drawing a line between just wars and unjust wars. They also wanted to draw a more basic line between humans, beings oriented toward law, and mere beasts.

Vattel offered the most elegant statement of this eighteenth-century teaching. "Pretexts," he wrote, "are at least a sort of reparations that the unjust pay to the just. He who covers himself with a pretext at least shows some shame. He does not openly declare war on all that is sacred in human society. He tacitly admits that injustice deserves the indignation of all men." The belligerent who offered pretexts was at least a civilized European. This had a highly significant implication for the law of war, as Vattel understood it, and in turn for the legal consequences of the invasion of Silesia. While it was of course true that the best wars were just wars, fought in good faith, Vattel declared, a realistic view of human society made it clear that customary international law recognized property rights growing even out of an unjust war—as long as it was a war in form and as long as it was conducted by a belligerent who offered *some* pretext: "War is a means of acquiring property. . . . Every acquisition made in a war in form is valid under voluntary international law, irrespective of the justice of the cause. . . . Thus conquest has always been regarded as conferring legitimate title as between nations; and no such title has been contested, unless it is the result of a war, not only unjust, but devoid even of any pretexts."[134] On a stern humanitarian view of the law of war, this quote seems highly dubious, a kind of surrender to the amoral raison d'état attitudes we associate with Machiavelli. How could any jurist concede that the results of an unjust war, initiated on the basis of a mere pretext, could give rise to legally enforceable rights? If Vattel said such a thing, is that not proof that just war theory was dead?

Nevertheless Vattel's treatment of pretexts was in fact not a piece of pure raison d'état cynicism. It was a sample of fine civilized reasoning within the law of victory tradition, of a kind that deserves a place in international law to this day. On an international stage on which the grip of the law is never perfectly secure, it *is* a mark of civilization when actors feel obliged to justify themselves by law, however disingenuously. The alternative really is bellum ferinum, "wild beast war," and in the effort to subject human barbarism to the rule of law, the requirement that belligerents state legal reasons, even specious ones, marked a major step forward in the civilization of warfare.

It is certainly true that the eighteenth-century treatment of pretexts departed from the older just war tradition. This may be the aspect of the law in which eighteenth-century jurists were most innovative. Yet for all that, we must recognize how comfortably this innovative doctrine fit within the Augustinian spirit of the just war tradition. Just war theorists had always aimed to coax warriors into acting like litigants. The doctrine of pretexts aimed to achieve exactly that effect.

The lawfulness of Frederick's acts has been forgotten since the early nineteenth century, and it remains immensely difficult for us to appreciate it today, because our attitudes have grown so distant from the attitudes of his time. Eighteenth-century jurists did not set out to do what modern advocates of a humanitarian law of war set out to do. It was not their ambition to construct a world of perfect justice or to impose standards of unimpeachably high conduct. It was not their aim to limit war to the task of punishing or preventing evil. They were the true heirs of Saint Augustine; they knew that they had to govern; and they understood that in trying to govern war they were riding a whirlwind. Correspondingly their ultimate ambition was more modest than the aim of modern lawyers. They hoped to create a world in which sovereigns like Frederick the Great would at least refuse to behave like wild beasts, like Attila or Genghis.

That aim may seem depressingly modest to modern lawyers, depressingly "indulgent to ferocity and cupidity." It certainly seemed depressingly modest to Kant; he denounced Pufendorf and Vattel as "peddlers of false comfort."[135] But we should think long and hard before we condemn the law of the eighteenth century. The hand of the law rested lightly on eighteenth-century war. Its purpose was more to steer the conduct of war than to condemn it. Rulers like Frederick, who would be denounced as dangerous aggressors today, were tolerated. In the words of the modern American international lawyers Derek Jinks and Ryan Goodman, eighteenth-century jurists worked more through "socialization" and "acculturation" than through imposing obligatory humanitarian norms.[136]

Yet the fact is that eighteenth-century jurists succeeded. At the end of the day, eighteenth-century warfare *was* remarkably civilized. At the end of day, the eighteenth century *did* manage to inculcate an attitude of restraint in princely war, creating a culture of war that abjured the practices of an Attila or a Genghis. Frederick gambled boldly in invading Silesia, and that made him something of a fearsome figure.[137] But he acted lawfully, and when direct engagement finally arrived, he did not descend to slaughter the unprepared Austrians at Mollwitz. He fought a civilized war.

The state of eighteenth-century law was faithfully reflected in the reasons that Frederick gave in justification of his invasion of Silesia. Those reasons appeared, as the law required, in a manifesto, addressed by "His Royal Majesty in Prussia" to the inhabitants of "the Duchy of Silesia and all of the Principalities and Territories incorporated within it" in late 1740. They were reasons founded not only in the law of succession but also in the right of self-defense, though a right of self-defense that extended much further than it would extend today.

The death of Charles VI, Frederick announced to the world, "with the extinction of the male line of succession," had created the risk of "many dangerous eventualities, some of which have already presented themselves, some of which are on course to burst out in a full-scale conflagration." The dangers threatened Silesia in particular, where the "pretensions of the Austrian house" were all too likely to result in a "violent seizure of possession." For that reason, he continued,

> in order to prevent a worrisome sequence of events, and for the necessary defense of the lands and peoples that the Almighty has entrusted to us, as there is a clear and present great danger of a general war, and according to permitted principles of necessary defense acknowledged by the law of all peoples, with the aim of forestalling intended hostile actions, some of them as yet secret but some already openly declared to a satisfactory degree, as well as for other relevant and weighty reasons which we will present in due course, we have found ourselves obliged to send our troops into the Duchy of Silesia.[138]

To the modern ear this sounds like dishonest, indeed criminal, blather. We have grown accustomed to the idea that force should be used as a kind of desperate last resort. Under modern international law, there is little doubt that Frederick's claims, even if legitimate, should have been adjudicated peacefully, and it is no surprise that modern lawyers declare Frederick to have been a "criminal aggressor." Under modern law disingenuous legal claims are no good basis for an act of war.

But such was not the law of Frederick's time. Far from it. The "permitted principles of necessary defense acknowledged by the law of all peoples" were different from what they are today. Sovereigns were permitted to go to war. Wars to counter threats against claims in the law of succession were perfectly lawful. Princes were expected to publish a manifesto that listed plausible reasons for going to war. Frederick did so. He was a daring man, but he did not defy the law.

The eighteenth century knew that perfectly well. Fifty years after the invasion, the philosopher Mirabeau summarized Frederick's actions with Voltairean irony: "This war, and this conquest, were just—insofar as wars and conquests are ever just."[139] There was certainly an element of condemnation in Mirabeau's condescending verdict. But what he was condemning was not Frederick's invasion of Silesia but the state of eighteenth-century law. It was perfectly permissible under the eighteenth-century *jus ad bellum* for Frederick to make war; and once he achieved a complete victory at Chotusitz, it was perfectly permissible under the law of victory for Maria Theresa to bargain her way out of trouble by ceding to him the Duchy of Silesia. Conquest, as the lawyers explained, was a natural means of acquisition.[140]

The doctrine of pretexts was something new in the eighteenth century, but it breathed the venerable spirit of the law of victory, and much of the rest of eighteenth-century law simply restated centuries-old just war doctrine. It is very far from the truth to describe the eighteenth-century law of war as the product of an Enlightenment breach with earlier just war traditions. It was overwhelmingly a continuation of those traditions. The jurists thought they were still speaking the ancient language of just war, and that is what they were doing.

In the last analysis, their position, despite their innovations, was little different from that of Augustine, the commentator on the Book of Joshua, or that of Isidore, the student of Roman law. Just war theorists had al-ways lived in a world in which wars were made in a spirit of "cupidity and ferocity" to take territory and goods, and they had always accom-modated themselves to that reality. Importing justice into war, for them, usually meant, not criminalizing it, but insisting that legal reasons be given. It meant subjecting war to such teachings as Isidore's justa divisio, the rules for the just divvying-up of booty. It meant insisting, as Bartolus did, that real property justly went to the conquering prince, while mobile property justly went to the soldiery "in order to encourage them." In the eighteenth century nothing had fundamentally changed. The big differ-ence between the Middle Ages and the eighteenth century lay elsewhere: unlike their medieval predecessors, eighteenth-century authors could feel confident that only sovereigns retained the practical power to go to war rather than going to court.

CHAPTER 4

The Monarchical Monopolization
of Military Violence

In the frenzy of duels, the only business is to display personal
courage. But in war the object is to defend our country, and by
force to prosecute our rights which are unjustly withheld from us.
—Emer de Vattel, *The Law of Nations*

A GENEALOGIST"—so began Voltaire's satirical definition of *war* in
his *Philosophical Dictionary* of 1764—"proves to a prince that he
descends in a direct line from a count whose relatives had made a family
pact three or four hundred years before with a house of which no memory
subsists."

This house had distant pretensions to a province whose last pos-
sessor has died of apoplexy: the prince and his council find his
rights perfectly obvious. This province, which is several hundred
leagues away, may protest that it does not know him, that it has no
wish to be governed by him; that to give laws to nations one must at
a minimum have their consent; these declarations do not even reach
the ears of the prince, to whom his rights are incontestable. He finds
forthwith a large number of men who have nothing to lose; dresses
them up in an imposing blue outfit at a hundred sous per ell, runs a
fat white thread around their hats, has them do a few turns to the
right and the left, and marches off to glory.

The other princes who hear about this undertaking join in, each according to his abilities, and cover a little stretch of country with more murderous mercenaries than Genghis Khan, Tamerlane, or Bajazid ever had trailing after them.

People from far away hear that there is going to be a fight, and that they could earn five or six sous a day if they get in on it; they immediately form themselves into bands like migrant fruit-pickers, and sell their services to whoever wants to hire them.

These multitudes fight violently against each other, not only without having the slightest stake in the dispute to be resolved by this trial by battle [*sans avoir aucun intérêt au procès*], but without even knowing what it's about. . . . The marvelous thing about this infernal enterprise is that each of the leaders of these murderers has his flags blessed and solemnly invokes God before going to kill his neighbor. If a leader does not have the good fortune to slit the throats of two or three thousand men, he doesn't give any thanks to God; but when ten thousand or so are exterminated by fire and steel; when—O height of good fortune!—a city is destroyed from top to bottom; then one sings a rather long song in four-part harmony, composed in a language unknown to all those who have fought, and what's more thoroughly stuffed with barbarisms. The same song is used for marriages and births as well as for murders; which is unforgiveable, especially in a country famous for inventing new songs.[1]

No one could fail to appreciate Voltaire's humane and enlightened sensibility, just as no one could fail to appreciate his gift for irony. But one should not fail to notice the larger irony clinging to this pretty little sally of Voltairean satire: the eighteenth-century style of warfare that Voltaire was satirizing was in fact remote from the "wild beast war" of "Genghis Khan and Tamerlane," as remote as the warfare of the past few centuries has ever managed to get. The style of warfare that Voltaire chose to condemn, with its seemingly absurd claims in the law of dynastic succession, its arrogant and dim-witted princely court culture, its indifference to the consent of the people, its pompous colored uniforms, and its elaborate victory ceremonies, was in fact far tamer than what was seen before or has been seen since.

That said, the legal basics of Voltaire's entry on *war* were perfectly accurate. Indeed they were quite a bit more accurate than the accounts given in our standard literature on the history of the law of war. Eighteenth-century war, as Voltaire presented it, was fought by princes, under the color of genealogical claims in the law of succession. It was fought by soldiers who were equipped by princes, dressed in uniforms, and paid for their services; Voltaire said nothing about aristocrats or chivalry. Many powers might be drawn into the sort of conflict he satirized, but the war itself was still a *procès*, a kind of procedure or trial intended to resolve a dispute. And victory was to be followed by a "a rather long song in four-part harmony, composed in a language unknown to all those who have fought"—that is to say, a Latin "Te Deum," a high ceremony of victory about which we shall hear more later.

This picture of war corresponded perfectly to the law of the eighteenth century. For jurists of the period too war was a princely activity, a kind of *procès* in the law of dynastic succession. By contrast, the accounts of eighteenth-century war by modern historians of the law of war bear little resemblance to what either Voltaire or eighteenth-century jurists described.

The proposition, so widespread in the modern literature, that eighteenth-century warfare was an expression of aristocratic dueling culture is deeply alien to the views of eighteenth-century jurists; they would have deemed the idea that a war was a kind of aristocratic duel to be a clumsy error in legal analysis. Still more alien is another familiar proposition in modern literature: that the eighteenth century saw a revival of medieval chivalry. Historians often assert that the civilized practices of the age of Voltaire can be traced back to the law of arms, the ritualized law governing medieval knights. Geoffrey Best, the prominent historian of the modern law of war, gives a statement of this modern commonplace: "Chivalry, honour, discipline, and self-restraint had been common enough concepts among the military-minded time out of mind. . . . But it was only during the maturity of the Enlightenment that . . . it entered into the common discourse of the ruling élites of the whole European states-system."[2] Many other modern authors, such as Michael Howard, speak similarly: "[T]he chivalric constraints developed during the later Middle Ages became generalized."[3] The aristocratic eighteenth century, according to this line of thought, was an age when one medieval tradition, the moralistic tradition of just war theory, gave way to another, the tradition of noble warrior self-restraint.

Yet eighteenth-century jurists themselves saw the warfare of their time very differently. They made a sharp distinction between war and dueling. As Vattel wrote, "[I]n the frenzy of duels, the only business is to display personal courage. But in war the object is to defend our country, and by force to prosecute our rights which are unjustly withheld from us."[4] Duels were dubious, "frenzied" affairs, fought in defiance of the law; wars, by contrast, were "the right of sovereigns to claim justice by force." Duels were fought over insults; wars were premised upon carefully framed legal claims about territories and dynastic succession, published in manifestos. Duels were the acts of hotheads; wars were carefully considered acts of state, weighed after taking legal advice by "the prince and his council." It is a jarring anachronism to call eighteenth-century wars aristocratic duels.

It is no less jarring to call them the product of a flowering of the noble chivalry of the Middle Ages. Eighteenth-century authors sometimes found kind words for medieval chivalry. But there was no cult of chivalry in the law. In fact Vattel was at pains to deny that "the laws of chivalry" and the practices of dueling applied to nations.[5] Far from thinking that they lived in an age of revived medieval practices, the jurists of the eighteenth century typically thought of the warfare of the Middle Ages as something their own enlightened age had left behind. What the jurists noticed about the armies of their time was not the presence of chivalric officers but the presence of a paid and disciplined soldiery in royal livery. Unlike Romantic-era idealizers of medieval knighthood, eighteenth-century authors believed that there was a gulf between their own enlightened world and the baronial world of the Middle Ages, an age they generally regarded as dark and violent.

None of this is to deny the truth that the nobility played a highly visible role in military life. Many nobles were drawn into service in royal armies in the eighteenth century, and of course they maintained a firm control over the European officer corps. Their social standing too often depended on their claims to be the "estate of those who fight" rather than the estate of those who prayed or those who tilled the land, and they celebrated military glory when they could acquire it. Moreover their tax exemptions, when they enjoyed them, were defended on the grounds that they rendered military service. There is no doubt that eighteenth-century nobles were, in large measure, a military class. As Montesquieu wrote, "[T]here is nothing that honor prescribes more for the nobility than to serve the prince in war."[6]

Nevertheless, from the point of view of the law, it matters immensely that eighteenth-century nobles had become the *servants* of their prince. Jonathan Dewald has rightly summarized their place in the military world of their age: "Here ultimately was the bargain struck between nobles and governments. Nobles relinquished their habits of violence, both public and private. They accepted the idea of kings' authority over their lives, and gave up belief in their right to an autonomous political stance. They ceased to support the dozens of followers who had been the foundation for political power in the fifteenth century. In exchange, they received the vague benefits of civic peace and the more concrete advantages of government service."[7] This is a wise summary from a learned historian. The organization of military life, understood properly, symbolized not the triumph of the nobility but its subordination. Nobles who had once boasted "dozens of followers" and indulged manifold "habits of violence" had now been compelled to submit to the military authority of the king. Eighteenth-century jurists understood that perfectly well.

That said, the proposition that eighteenth-century warfare was related to the law of the medieval nobility is certainly not entirely false. We shall see in this chapter that there *were* connections between medieval forms of noble combat and the practice of eighteenth-century battle war. As a matter of legal history, it is impossible to understand eighteenth-century battles unless we are familiar with legal traditions of noble combat that stretched back into the High Middle Ages, and more broadly with noble rights to engage in legitimate violence. The right to go to war belonged to a much larger class of rights to do violence, and princes had historically shared all of those rights with nobles.

Nevertheless it is a real mistake to think of eighteenth-century warfare itself as aristocratic or chivalric. To do so is to obscure hopelessly what mattered most about the civilized law of war in the age of Voltaire. What mattered most, in the eyes of eighteenth-century jurists, was that only sovereigns were permitted to engage in war, and more broadly in legally sanctioned violence, whereas nobles in particular had lost all such rights. What mattered was not the supposed rule of a chivalric jus in bello but the triumph of a jus victoriae that accorded sovereigns the exclusive power to pursue their rights through lawful war. What mattered most was that monarchs had finally achieved, after a history of conflict that extended from the Middle Ages deep into the seventeenth century, a monopoly on legitimate military violence.

War, according to the eighteenth-century legal definition, was how "private law applied to *sovereigns*."[8] Nobody else, nobles included, retained the power to enforce their rights through violence. By the eighteenth century, this was the undoubted rule, the basis of the civilization of war, but everybody understood that this state of affairs was a recent achievement. It was the product of a long process of princely struggle—a process that was still much in doubt as late as the Fronde, the mass French noble uprising of the mid-seventeenth century.

The story of the rise of the Enlightenment law of war really starts around 1660, roughly at the time of Louis XIV's assumption of personal rule in France and shortly after the great French noble revolts ended in the 1650s. It was in the subsequent decades that the basic teachings of the eighteenth-century law of war began to emerge.

They emerged, notably, in the writings of Samuel von Pufendorf, who died in 1694 but whose work remained highly authoritative in the generations that followed. Writing after the havoc of the first sixty years of the seventeenth century had died down, Pufendorf adopted a tone of understandable satisfaction over the standard of civilization that had been attained in the later seventeenth century. It was Pufendorf, as we saw earlier, who gave his sanction to the "tacit contract of chance" theory of battle; and it was he who gave the most elegant account of the political foundations of the civilization of war.

In particular he described the contrast between his own age of princely pacification and the disorderly past using the language of classic political philosophy. Once upon time, he wrote, in the usual fabulous vein of early modern political theory, there had been a state of nature, in which all individuals had the right to make war in order to protect their rights. In modern times, however, individuals had lost that right. Every individual, with the sole exception of the sovereign, was now required to go to a judge rather than "avenging injuries by his own power or claiming rights due to him by the use of violence."[9] In the post-state-of-nature world of the late seventeenth century, only sovereigns retained the primitive right to "claim rights due to them" through violence.

Such was the basic proposition of the Enlightenment law of war. It was not an entirely simple proposition, since the concept of *sovereign* had undergone some important development over the course of the previous centuries. By the end of the Middle Ages, it went without saying that for most jurists, the war-making power belonged, at least in theory, exclusively to monarchs—and in particular to the highest prince, "recognizing no superior."[10] At least that was the rule on paper. But if that much was clear, it was not entirely easy to say which princes counted. A late medieval author such as Juan López, for example, had doubts about whether any person other than the pope or the emperor could make war or whether perhaps the kings of France and Spain could also do so.[11] Gentili was still wrestling with the same problems at the end of the sixteenth century. Wars could be mounted only by princes; anybody else who made war was a "bandit." Yet even this seemingly simple rule raised tough legal questions about whether such powerful personages as the dukes of Parma or Mantua or Braunschweig counted as princes or bandits.[12] Where was one to draw the line between the sovereign prince and the mere subject nobility?

Nor were those the only complications. The existence of republics muddied the juristic waters as well. There had been European republics of various sorts since the Middle Ages, and there were three leading republics, or at least quasi-republics, on the eighteenth-century scene as well, in the form of Venice, the Swiss Confederation, and the Netherlands. Both Grotius and Zouche, for example, wrote in seventeenth-century republics. Those republics made war. On what authority could they do so? Grotius dealt with this difficulty by insisting that "private" wars were permissible.[13] Even if the Netherlands were not monarchical, they nevertheless had the right to make war. Zouche, writing in the English

Protectorate, took a different tack: he avoided the problem by defining war, in language lifted from Vegetius, as "a lawful contention between princes *or peoples*."[14] Later in the seventeenth century, Johann Wolfgang Textor tried to resolve the issue by according the power to make war to "royal or quasi-royal powers," thus apparently classing republics, strangely enough, as "quasi-royal."[15] It is not until Vattel that we find a clear statement of what may seem the obvious solution to the problem: Vattel, fine lawyer that he was, simply held that the sovereign of any given polity should be identified by the internal law of that polity.[16] Republics could be sovereign too, which meant that they too could engage in public wars.

The very fact that this was a novel solution, though, suggests how deep the association between monarchy and the power to make war ran. Sovereigns were normally monarchs; war was the prototypical activity of sovereigns; and the best way to understand the genesis of the eighteenth-century law of war is to see it against the backdrop of centuries of conflict between sovereign dynastic monarchs on the one side and their nobilities on the other over the right to engage in violence—to see the eighteenth century in the way Pufendorf did, as an age when sovereign monarchical power had succeeded in putting an end to the violence of a quondam state of nature.

Pufendorf's political fable in a real sense painted an accurate picture of European legal history. There had indeed been an age when private persons—or at least noble private persons—had enjoyed the right to make war "to avenge injury by their own power or claim rights due to them by the use of violence." In fact nobles were still claiming that right in the mid-seventeenth century, in Pufendorf's own youth. As a matter of law, though, their claims rested on traditions that were much older. To understand the legal history of eighteenth-century battle warfare, we must begin in the High Middle Ages, a period that, for purposes of legal history, we can date principally to around 1100, and a period that saw the flourishing of what the Dutch medievalist Johan Huizinga called the "system of noble combat."[17]

What was the "system of noble combat?" It rested on a basic legal idea very alien to the modern mind: the idea that there was an intimate connection between high social status and the right to do violence. As Dewald writes, the pre-eighteenth-century nobility had "habits of violence, public and private." More than that, they had as a matter of law *privileges* of violence. Nobles were marked off from their social inferiors not just by their titles, not just by their dress, not just by their wealth, but also by their privileges, symbolic or real, of inflicting violence on others. Historically these privileges of public and private violence included "high justice" (the privilege of sentencing dependents to death), the privilege of hunting, the privilege of thrashing inferiors, and the complex privilege that goes by the name of "the right to bear arms." The character of these privileges varied over the centuries, but from the central Middle Ages onward the symbolism of the law of noble status was consistently a symbolism of the "right of the stronger," as the medievalist Wolfgang Schild has put it.[18] Noble status was largely defined and displayed by the right, whether or not exercised, to commit violent acts.

Huizinga's "noble combat" was prominent among these symbolically charged privileges. High status was partly defined by the privilege of doing violence not only to inferiors but also between equals, and aristocracy, as one medievalist has said, with a shade of exaggeration, was based "first and foremost on the capacity to assert oneself in and through combat."[19] In that sense, engaging in combat was closely akin to such acts as sentencing one's dependents to death: it was a resonant marker of high status rich in the symbolism of "the right of the stronger."

This symbolically charged law of noble combat deeply colored the law of war. War too, at least in its more ritual aspects, was an exercise of a primitive right of violence "to avenge injury or claim rights," and so war was understood in the law as a form of noble combat. Scholars like Howard and Best are thus perfectly correct in declaring that the law of the war in the eighteenth century was related to the law of the high medieval nobility. But it must be emphasized how wrong it is to imagine that the system of noble combat of the medieval state of nature represented the same changeless form of chivalry that would emerge centuries later in the age of Pufendorf and his successors. The proposition that medieval warfare was a world of "chivalry, honour, discipline, and self-restraint" that would blossom once again "during the maturity of the Enlightenment" rests on a wild-eyed Romantic-era idealization of high medieval chivalry.

To get a proper fix on the relationship between military violence in the eighteenth century and military violence in the Middle Ages, we must begin with a fact that is familiar to every scholar of the history of war: the bulk of medieval noble warfare was anything but chivalric and restrained. "The rules and practices of knighthood and chivalry," as Stephen Neff remarks, "did little in practice to mitigate the horrors of war. . . . For the most part, medieval warfare presented a shocking picture of horror and brutality."[20] In particular we must remember how much of medieval warfare involved horrific raids mounted by nobles against their social inferiors. The late medieval archives are full of accounts of raids that "invariably involved surprise, the violence of armed men (usually nobles) against unarmed people (usually non-nobles), and the destruction or appropriation of productive resources. Again and again the sources tell of sudden, unadvertised attacks, of peasants murdered or mutilated in their fields, of women raped, of vines and trees cut down, of tools destroyed or taken, and of livestock stolen."[21] A typical medieval document reproduced by Maurice Keen gives the flavor of the "hideous brutalities" visited on the lower orders: "femme violée; gens crucifiez, rotiz et penduz; homme roty," "a woman raped; some people crucified, roasted and hung; a man roasted."[22] To quote John Lynn, "[C]hivalry may have tried to moderate violence among the elite, but peasants and townspeople were subject to horrendous abuses, which included murder, rape, and torture."[23]

Social superiority meant doing violence to others, and the forms of medieval warfare reflected that fact. Just as nobles wished to exercise the right to execute their dependents, they wished to exercise the right to prey on inferiors. Norbert Elias, the great sociologist of violence and noble status, put the point memorably: "[R]apine, battle, hunting of people and animals—all these were vital necessities which, in accordance with the structure of society, were visible to all. And thus, for the mighty and strong, they formed part of the pleasures of life. . . . War, one of the *chansons de geste* declared, was to descend as the stronger on the enemy . . . lay waste his land . . . and kill his people."[24] A famous passage from Nietzsche comes to mind as well: "It is impossible not to recognize, lurking under the surface of all nobilities, the beast of prey, the glorious and joyful blond beast roving after booty and victory; from time to time the hidden urge must be discharged, the beast must emerge, it must head back into the wild:—Roman, Arab, German, Japanese nobles, homeric heroes, Scandinavian Vikings: When it comes to this urge, they are all alike."[25] This is a piece of hopelessly overheated writing by a sometimes hopelessly overheated philosopher, of course, but it does capture something about the behavior of medieval nobles.

The inveterate brutality and violence of European noble behavior did not end with the Middle Ages. On the contrary, it was still alive in the mid-seventeenth century. Here the case of France, whose culture dominated so much in the eighteenth century, is particularly pertinent. We possess a rich literature on the seventeenth-century French nobility, a literature that shows how tenacious the traditions of violence and private war-making remained right up until the moment in the 1660s when Louis XIV finally succeeded in concentrating in his own hands the authority to make war. Arlette Jouanna has sketched a vivid picture of noble values and behavior during the century of noble revolts that ended in the 1650s, a period when nobles insisted on marking themselves off, not only by their garments, but also by their gallows, and maintained familiar rituals for summoning their followers into war.[26] William Beik describes the near impossibility the authorities in the South faced when aiming to control the behavior of the powerful, and Brian Sandberg shows, in a richly documented study, how little had changed in the Midi since the Middle Ages: "The destruction or seizing of livestock was often a main rationale for raids. . . . A group of Catholic nobles planned to launch a raid in the Alès region in 1621 with at least two hundred infantry and a hundred cavalry drawn from their châteaux and governments in the area, targeting livestock especially. Assembling at dawn near Alès on the chosen day, this force followed the Gard river, 'ravaging the entire plain' and stealing 'a great many animals.' "[27]

This book is not the place to review all of this literature on the seventeenth century, and certainly not the place to add to it. What matters is to remind specialists in the law of war of something early modern historians like Dewald well know: how pressing the problem of controlling the nobility could seem from the point of emerging absolutist monarchies.

Authors of the Romantic era would find it easy to forget these truths, but authors of the eighteenth century did not. When Pufendorf and his contemporaries and successors lived, the defiance and brutality of traditional noble conduct were not far in the past at all. Correspondingly when they wrote about traditions of noble warfare, they generally shuddered. As the pioneering medievalist Charles du Fresne du Cange put it in a fundamental article on "private wars and the customary law of war" published in 1678, at the moment when Louis XIV was finally succeeding in eliminating private noble warfare, the wars of medieval barons were "entreprises funestes" (baleful enterprises).[28]

Even those eighteenth-century authors who spoke most admiringly of chivalry felt obliged to admit that the medieval nobility had tended toward a frightening barbarism that only princely power was in a position to curb. It is striking, for example, to read the most eminent eighteenth-century student of knightly values, Jean-Baptiste de la Curne de Sainte-Palaye, whose 1753 *Memoirs on the Chivalry of the Past* made a literary sensation. La Curne de Sainte-Palaye devoted many pages to the chivalric training of squires and courtly etiquette, but he also felt compelled to add a dissertation on the horrors of medieval knightly warfare:

> [Medieval] authors declaim against . . . the pillage, theft, brigandage and all the other excesses of a militia that accepted no limits. . . . Even those knights who had dedicated themselves to a more regular life, who had embraced the religious orders of chivalry, were no more shielded from the reproach of the literature of their age. . . . Arrogance, vanity, and pride were, above all, the vices of knights, despite all of the lessons of humanity, *politesse* and modesty that were so frequently repeated: this was the dominant character of their station, the motive of all of their activities, the principle of all of their actions. . . . One frequently sees the finest leaders of chivalry soil themselves with all of the crimes to which barbarism can give birth.

Everybody, La Curne de Sainte-Palaye concluded, knew about the evils of these private wars.[29]

Everybody did indeed know. As a result, eighteenth-century authors who praised chivalry praised it circumspectly, as a lesser substitute for royal control of medieval noble barbarism. For example, the most influential advocate of noble values of the early part of the century, Henri de Boulainvilliers, whose *Essay on the Nobility of France* was published in 1732, declared that "the laws of chivalry" had brought a necessary improvement to the mores of the medieval nobility—but one that was necessary because royal power was as yet too weak to control the "depravity" and "barbarism" of the nobility. Because "the authority of the Kings" was as yet "feeble, or rather still too little known," the Church had stepped in to inculcate more civilized values.[30] Boulainvilliers may have been "the staunchest and most persistent proponent" of the importance of noble power against royal power,[31] but even he declined to make extravagant claims about chivalry in medieval war.

To be sure, not all medieval noble warfare involved unbridled barbarity. Noble warfare against inferiors was savage, but when nobles fought each other they did adopt more or less chivalric practices, as early modern authors knew.[32] There was indeed a chivalric law of arms, and it did involve a species of temperate warfare. When medieval nobles fought each other their ordinary aim was not to kill each other but to capture and hold each for ransom.[33] By its nature, warfare that aims at collecting ransom is warfare that obeys a kind of humane jus in bello; there is no point in killing your opponent if you hope to profit from taking him prisoner. Correspondingly chivalric practices sometimes encouraged more moderate forms of warfare.[34] In that sense, chivalry and moderation went hand in hand.

Moreover when princes and nobles fought each other, all of the ritualized forms of trial by combat—naming a time and place for battle, for example—could be found in the Middle Ages, just as in other eras. As Keen, Kurt-Georg Cram, Robert Stacey, and other scholars have shown, there were well-understood norms for governing behavior in ritualized combat, which did have the same chivalric feel as the ritualized combat that was periodically fought in other times and places. Medieval knights were also subject to various courts for the enforcement of the laws of war that governed their order.[35] All this is true, and all of it was known to eighteenth-century authors.

Nevertheless to describe the civilization of eighteenth-century warfare as a revival even of such medieval chivalry as there was is to distort it profoundly. Eighteenth-century authors knew that medieval chivalry had existed, but they did not describe it as a model for their own time. Moreover they were amply aware of a fact that was emphasized until the 1830s: medieval knights were out to claim the profits of war. Like every other participant in war, their wars were wars of cupidity and rapacity. Yes, they spared their opponents, but they did so in order to claim ransom. Yes, there were courts to enforce their duties, but the dockets of those courts did not all involve holding knights to some general high standard of "honour, discipline, and self-restraint"; they heavily involved the enforcement of ransom claims.[36]

This truth was frequently repeated in the eighteenth century. When it came to the practice of war, eighteenth-century authors (like late medieval ones) understood that chivalry meant "having no fear of dangers" while "claiming ransom from prisoners."[37] Here we may quote once again La Curne de Sainte-Palaye, who presented medieval chivalric warfare this way: "In all ages merit denuded of riches has encountered great obstacles; Chivalry, or the military of government, furnished several means for overcoming those obstacles. War, with its booty and its ransoms, enriched the man who conducted himself with the greatest valor, vigilance, and energy."[38] *That* was how the eighteenth century understood chivalry. La Curne de Sainte-Palaye never entertained any doubt about the aims of the medieval nobility at war: they wanted to enrich themselves. Of course it is true that war for ransom is war that in some sense obeys jus in bello norms of moderation. But we should not exaggerate the nobility of ransom taking. Medieval knights were rapacious; in the "baleful enterprises" that were their endemic private wars, they preyed on social inferiors without mercy, and eighteenth-century jurists knew it.

In the latter part of the century, attitudes changed somewhat. Some historians, like William Robertson and Edward Gibbon, spoke of chivalry with more unreserved warmth. Robertson in particular set the tone for the idealization of chivalry that would emerge in the legal literature of the Romantic era: "War was carried on with less ferocity, when humanity came to be deemed the ornament of knighthood no less than courage. More gentle and polished manners were introduced, when courtesy was recommended as the most amiable of knightly virtues. Violence and oppression decreased, when it was reckoned meritorious to check and to punish them."[39] Even these historians, however, did not exaggerate the importance of the chivalric jus in bello. They still believed that monarchical government was the agent that had civilized warfare. If Gibbon praised chivalry, for example, he did not give it the credit for civilizing the warfare of his time; for him, as for Voltaire, what mattered was that "the calamities of war . . . are now moderated by the prudence or humanity of the *princes* of Europe."[40] In any case, the legal literature did not begin claiming that aristocratic chivalry was the force that civilized warfare until after the French Revolution: it was the Romantic era that invented timeless chivalry in the law of war.

One especially important point remains to be made. Even such chivalry as medieval knights practiced in combat was, as a matter of law, critically different from the forms of eighteenth-century aristocratic duelists. For what matters most about medieval noble combat, even in its moments of chivalric restraint, is what Pufendorf said about it: unlike their eighteenth-century successors, high medieval nobles claimed the *right* to engage in violence, the right of "avenging injuries by their own power or claiming rights due to them by the use of violence."[41] Indeed their social status was partly defined by their proud and often terrifying right to engage in legitimate violence, and in particular to pursue their interests through private wars.

By contrast, the key truth about the legal history of the eighteenth century is that that right had been quashed. After centuries of struggle, the nobles of Pufendorf's time had been subjugated as a matter of law, surrendering their state-of-nature right to engage in legitimate violence. To speak of their chivalry without many words of qualification is to obscure the most fundamentally important legal dimension of their place in the eighteenth-century world.

With those facts in mind, we may turn to the connections between the eighteenth-century law of battles and the medieval law of noble combat. Those connections certainly did exist. There are even good reasons to speak of eighteenth-century princely battle warfare as a form of *duellum*, or duel—what Clausewitz called, using the German equivalent of duellum, *Zweikampf*. But it is a real error to think of duellum or Zweikampf simply as a kind of eighteenth-century aristocratic duel. The juristic tradition was much more complex and much more interesting than that.

In the centuries of noble violence, the European juristic tradition recognized four different kinds of noble combat: trial by combat, jousting, dueling over a point of honor, and battle warfare, especially as fought through either a challenge between princes or a limited pitched battle. All four of these forms of high-status combat were sometimes called by the same Latin name *duellum* and sometimes by the modern European term *duel*, but we must understand that they took different forms and served different ends. In particular, trial by combat, sometimes called "the judicial duel," differed from dueling over a point of honor. Trial by combat was a legal procedure used, to borrow language employed by Cardinal Cajetan in the sixteenth century, for the "manifestation of truth" and the "termination of a criminal or civil dispute," whereas dueling was an outlawed activity, used for "the avoidance of ignominy, since any man who does not accept a duel is deemed to be vile and of degenerate soul."[42] The difference between the two ran deep, and if we do not understand the difference we will misread the legal nature of war in the eighteenth century.

Let us begin with trial by combat. This was one of three forms of what medieval law called *iudicium dei*, the "judgment of God," the other two being ordeals and pitched battles. It is often misdescribed, and it is important to review it carefully. The privilege of proof through trial by combat was one of the basic rights of high status in the Middle Ages. "A free man defends himself by battle," as the often-repeated rule read, "whereas a servile man must go to court."[43] From this it followed for medieval jurists that trial by battle was in the ordinary case a practice for the nobility[44]—just as by the eighteenth century it would be held that sovereigns, and sovereigns exclusively, "recognize no arbiter of their quarrels but the chance of arms." Trial by combat was thus an institution of large symbolic importance in a world in which monarchs had not yet successfully monopolized violence. It was the privilege of not undergoing the humiliation of being subject to someone else's court, the privilege of not submitting to the authority of a superior, the privilege of instead exercising violence to prove one's claims.

But how exactly did this privilege work? As Cajetan said, trial by combat was combat for "the manifestation of truth." How can combat be thought of as manifesting the truth? To understand the answer given by premodern law, we must understand something of the medieval law of proof, and in particular another symbolically charged aspect of the law of noble status: oathworthiness.

The law of proof in the premodern world—not only in Europe but elsewhere as well—commonly rested on the proposition that the oaths of honorable, high-status persons should be respected. Oaths mattered for a reason. Law in the premodern West, like premodern law elsewhere, relied heavily on the testimony of witnesses—inevitably so in societies with few or no means of forensic investigation. In societies with no police forces, no detectives, and often few reliable written documents, the only way to resolve cases was to collect trustworthy testimony.

The law in the medieval West, as elsewhere in the premodern world, took the strong view that trustworthiness and high social status went hand in hand. A person of high social status was a person whose word had to be taken as good. Here another famous passage from Nietzsche comes to mind: noble status is partly characterized by the assertion "We, the nobles, are the truthful ones; you of low status are liars."[45] High status was defined not only by the privilege of doing violence but also by the privilege of being treated as one of "the truthful ones," as a man of one's word, whose declarations should not be challenged—what was called an "oathworthy" person. The testimony of others was systematically distrusted; indeed much of premodern law involved careful social distinctions in degrees of trustworthiness. The testimony of a male might outweigh the testimony of a female; the testimony of a Christian might outweigh the testimony of a Jew; the testimony of slaves might be accepted only if they had been tortured.

The medieval law of proof thus rested on the same assumptions about social hierarchy as the medieval law of violence, and it held that disputes should ideally be resolved by an oath sworn by such an oathworthy person, ordinarily to be taken on the relics of a saint. That oath, once sworn, would definitively establish the truthfulness of the man taking it, and the dispute would be at an end. Nonoathworthy persons did not enjoy the option of swearing such a decisory oath. Instead they were obliged to undergo an ordeal, such as the ordeal of the hot iron, before their word would be accepted.[46]

So where did trial by combat come in? It was an alternative to giving sworn testimony. High-status, oathworthy disputants often refused to swear oaths. Our medieval sources tell us that this was because of fears about the danger of perjury: medieval authors worried that conscious self-interest, or even a careless self-interested slip, might lead even honorable men to swear falsely and so endanger their salvation.[47] Perhaps fear of careless perjury was the reason; perhaps high-status persons did not want to accept the proposition that their disputes should be resolved by a court at all. In any case they often took an alternative honorable route, the route of trial by combat. When their word was questioned, rather than swearing an oath to affirm it, they insisted on their privilege of violence and took up arms.[48] Trial by combat was thus a proof procedure, fought by "truthful ones" whose sworn word was legally sufficient to prove their case but who preferred to resort to the force of arms.[49]

From the later Middle Ages onward, this privilege of trial by combat came under growing assault, partly mounted by the Church. Trial by combat was understood to be a judgment of God; yet as we saw earlier, theologians objected to any procedure that tempted God—that demanded that God decide questions that human beings could resolve through their own efforts. As a result of these theological objections, procedures like the ordeals of the hot iron or the cold water went into decisive (if sometimes slow) decline after the early thirteenth century.[50] So, even more slowly, did trial by combat, though it survived at least into the sixteenth century.

The Church was not the only agency at work, though. Monarchies too, in their determination to limit private violence, assailed trial by combat. Beginning in the mid-twelfth century, emperors and kings made growing efforts to clamp down, insisting that to the extent possible matters be resolved through sworn testimony instead.[51] That is to say, they tried, with increasing success by the end of the Middle Ages, to compel nobles to take the "servile" route of going to court. By the eighteenth century, they had long since succeeded.

Trial by combat was thus a legal privilege, the privilege of oathworthy persons to refuse to submit to the ordinary process in a court. The duel over the point of honor was fundamentally different; it has a long medieval history, but classic dueling culture emerged into particular prominence around the same time that trial by combat was going into decisive decline,[52] principally in later medieval Italy and perhaps Burgundy, and it spread throughout Europe in the sixteenth century. It survived long after noble trial by combat had disappeared, flourishing throughout continental Europe until World War I.

The two forms of noble combat certainly did bear some resemblances. As we have seen, trial by combat rested on two assumptions about high status: high-status persons were persons whose word had to be accepted as true, and they had the privilege of settling their disputes through violence. Dueling rested on the same two assumptions, at least to some extent. The starting point for a duel might well be some form of the insult "You lie." Just as the honorable truthfulness of an oathworthy person was theoretically proved by victory in trial by combat, the honorable truthfulness of the challenger could be proved by a duel. In that sense the purpose of dueling, in its early history, was close to the purpose of trial by combat.

Yet at their core the two institutions were deeply different. Dueling, unlike trial by combat, was not a proof procedure, and it did not symbolize the lawful nonservile privilege of settling one's disputes without going to court.[53] Trial by combat was an alternative to ordinary trial, used by privileged oathworthy persons to resolve a legal question—as Cajetan put it, to "manifest the truth" or "terminate a civil or criminal dispute." Dueling, by contrast, was purely a contest over the honorability of the duelists, used to dramatize the fact that the challenger was not "vile and of degenerate soul," and apart from the possible criminal liability of the participants, it had no legal consequences whatsoever.

Thus it should come as no surprise that historians generally hold that the rise of early modern dueling culture reflected, not the triumph of the privileged medieval warrior nobility, but its decline. That decline had to do partly with the loss of the privilege of trial by combat. As nobles were forced to give up this resonant privilege, they took to dueling, an ostentatious substitute for trial by combat that proclaimed their insistence on their continuing right to do violence.[54] There were also changes of fundamental importance in the practice of warfare. Before the fifteenth century, knights could claim the leading role in battle warfare. By the fifteenth century, however, infantry had unmistakably begun to assume the dominant role, and battle warfare had become more lethal, for knights as well as for everybody else.[55] The place of traditional knightly combat in war only declined thereafter.[56] That dueling began its cultural ascent at the same time that knightly warfare disappeared is not an accident. Dueling over a point of honor emerged as a kind of substitute form of combat, which permitted nobles who could no longer easily display their manly virtues on the battlefield to do so on the dueling pitch instead.

Nor was the rise of infantry warfare the only change at work. Like Pufendorf, du Cange, La Curne de Sainte-Palaye, and so many eighteenth-century authors, historians of dueling observe that the private wars of the nobility were under steady, grinding pressure from monarchical governments. Throughout the Middle Ages, nobles in many parts of Europe maintained private armies and fought their territorial disputes in small-scale wars. These private wars constituted a major challenge to royal control over the realms of the continent in the Middle Ages. Recent scholarship has demonstrated, moreover, that princely efforts to suppress private war were enjoying only modest success at the end of the Middle Ages.[57] Monarchies met the challenge of private warfare only slowly, in a process that extended from the late Middle Ages deep into the seventeenth century, a long "effort to bend nobles to the will of the monarchy."[58] Still, slow though the process was, they did eventually succeed in stamping out private armies and private warfare, just as they eventually succeeded in curbing the practice (though not the symbolism) of high justice.

This gradual suppression of private war inevitably brought a deep-seated change to noble military identity. As François Billacois put it, in the midst of a great royal crackdown, which hurled them down from the "summit" of society, nobles took refuge in a "state of nature," the "Eden of conflict" that was dueling culture.[59] What had been an autonomous baronial military class, accustomed to leading crowds of followers into battle to claim rights, gradually became a dueling class, deprived of their private armies but resistant to all efforts to outlaw their right to prove their individual honor through arms.

For dueling, it must be emphasized, was indeed outlawed. Trial by combat was a lawful privilege, a privilege that proclaimed to the world that medieval nobles were not servile. Dueling, at least by the sixteenth century, was anything but lawful. Early juristic writing on dueling over a point of honor did not condemn it. From the mid-sixteenth century onward, though, prohibitions both ecclesiastical and secular multiplied. The Council of Trent, which established the basic law of the Counter-Reformation Catholic Church, strongly condemned dueling. Secular governments too prohibited dueling in a legislative tradition that extended into the nineteenth century.[60]

None of these prohibitions put an end to the practice, of course. On the contrary, dueling remained widespread and took on the character of a kind of demonstrative aristocratic defiance of the law—a way of displaying that aristocrats still claimed the privilege of violence despite generations of declining status. This lawless defiance was largely tolerated de facto; with a few spectacular exceptions, duelists did not ordinarily risk severe punishment. Nevertheless the very fact of its lawlessness set dueling crucially apart from trial by combat—and from war. War symbolized the legal supremacy of the prince; dueling, properly understood, symbolized the legal impotence of the nobility.

If we use the term with care, there is nothing wrong in calling the princely wars of the eighteenth century *duel-wars*. They were indeed a form of duellum. They were, however, not aristocratic duels but the last surviving form of trial by combat. They belonged to a world in which the nobility had been stripped of most of its medieval privileges, and only sovereigns retained the symbolically powerful privilege of proving their private law claims through the chance of arms, just as only sovereigns retained the symbolically powerful privilege of executing malefactors. This is the straightforward lesson of legal history, as Huizinga and a few other scholars of the 1930s, notably the learned French international lawyer Georges Scelle,[61] recognized. And it is how we should ultimately understand eighteenth-century princely war. Eighteenth-century battle warfare was, at base, a form of princely trial by combat.

To be sure, the point must be made with care. Dueling culture *was* influential, and there were occasional moments when jurists, like Johann Wolfgang Textor in the seventeenth century, spoke of the possibility that wars, like duels, might be fought over a point of honor[62]—though Textor immediately added that "the farthest-reaching cause of war is that on account of injury to property." Vattel believed that at least one seventeenth-century monarch, Louis XIV, had alleged the point of honor in justification of at least one war and that the czar had done the same in 1701.[63] To the extent that the norms of "war in form" applied in the eighteenth century, there was certainly a kinship between the dueling challenge and the declaration of war.

It is furthermore certainly the case that dueling practices colored the culture of military violence. Duels bore an obvious resemblance to the trials by combat that were legitimate war. They were a kind of aristocratic apery of the legitimate forms of war, and apery can certainly sometimes influence its original. The technical language of the law of war was sometimes close to the language of dueling: not only were both sometimes called duellum, but both also sometimes spoke of "injuries" and "satisfaction."[64] We can find aristocratic authors who struggled to recast military norms in ways that would bring them closer to the norms of dueling.[65] There are reasons why historians have confused the two.

It is also no doubt the case that there were sometimes resemblances between the culture of war and aristocratic patterns of dueling behavior. When Bell asserts that monarchs simply *were* aristocrats, what he says is not entirely false: "On the battlefield, European monarchs and generals did not practice the new style of warfare because of conscious calculations about the balance of power or conscious reflections about the waning of religious passions. They did so because it came naturally to them as aristocrats: to fight, to fight bravely and gloriously, but also with restraint, with self-control, with honor. . . . What governed the experience of warfare for Europe's ruling classes and kept it functioning as a system was aristocratic culture."[66] There is certainly a grain of descriptive truth in this. Kings lived among aristocrats, often spoke with them, and sometimes thought like them. There was a culture of aristocratic violence, and monarchs no doubt participated in it some of the time. The social history of the eighteenth century is necessarily in part a social history of aristocracy.

But (to say it once again) there is more to war than a "series of acts of violence," and the social history of war can never do justice to its larger legal significance. War is not just violence; it is a legal act with legal meaning, and that legal meaning is of great symbolic importance for the organization of society.

Once we understand the legal meaning of eighteenth-century war, we must necessarily see it, not the way Schmitt and Bell see it, but the way Pufendorf, du Cange, and Voltaire saw it: as an enterprise whose very structure proclaimed the downfall of the independent nobility. In the last analysis, aristocratic dueling was a kind of sham, a pretense evolved by European societies to allow nobles to act as though they still had the sovereign right to do violence. Maybe some of those nobles were fooled by that sham, but there is no reason it should be allowed to fool modern scholars. Yes, in a sense it was true that monarchs were aristocrats. Yes, the language of war sometimes echoed the language of dueling. But the symbolic message of the law of war and of the law of dueling—and, for that matter, of court ceremonial—was that an immense legal chasm separated an eighteenth-century prince from eighteenth-century nobles. Eighteenth-century wars were *public* wars, and that is the critical truth about them.

Thus it is no surprise that eighteenth-century continental wars, unlike eighteenth-century duels, were not normally fought over points of honor. As Voltaire's satire suggests, and as the manifestos described earlier make clear, continental wars were fought over carefully specified legal claims, almost always in the law of succession. War was indeed a kind of *Zweikampf*, as Clausewitz wrote, a kind of duellum. But it is thoroughly misleading to translate Clausewitz's *Zweikampf* as *duel* without making some energetic juristic distinctions. As a matter of law, the form of duellum to which eighteenth-century war was by far the most closely related was trial by combat, the form of combat that produced a verdict, the form of combat based on legal claims, the form of combat that consisted in the legitimate privilege of "avenging injuries by one's own power or claiming rights due to one by the use of violence."[67] As Frederick declared in the *Anti-Machiavel*, "[S]ince kings are subject to no superior tribunal . . . it is for combat to decide their rights and to judge the validity of their reasons."[68]

That is exactly how Frederick's contemporaries understood matters. We can see the kinship between eighteenth-century battle warfare and trial by combat both in the literature of eighteenth-century law and in the imagery of eighteenth-century popular culture. Premodern juristic discussions of the law of war typically began with the problem of single combat between princes or princes-to-be—the *singularis pugna*, the single battle, or the *monomachia*, the contest between two heroes. In particular, premodern legal analyses typically revolved around a few famous exemplary monomachies, including the combats of David and Goliath, Menelaus and Paris, Alexander and Porus, Aeneas and Turnus, and Heraclius and Chosroes II.[69] As Huizinga rightly observed, lawyers slipped easily from discussion of such heroic monomachies to the discussion of pitched battles.[70] Indeed the classic terminology made little distinction between trial by combat and battle in war, whether in the Middle Ages or in the early modern period;[71] jurists found it natural to lump heroic monomachies together with both arranged battles and the improvisatory battles of actual warfare. In effect premodern law treated contained pitched battles as a large-scale form of princely single combat.[72]

The notion that battles were a form of princely trial by combat was not just a matter of legal theory. The actual practice of European princely war always had the air of single combat between rivals. By tradition, princes directly challenged each other to personal combat as a ritual prelude to war.[73] The literature of the Middle Ages through the sixteenth century preserves dozens of examples, notably in the iconic conflicts between François I and Charles V.[74] These challenges occurred in a particularly revealing legal context: they were issued over rights of succession. As Werner Goez demonstrated, medieval princely challenges were issued only where there were questions concerning hereditary monarchies. Elective thrones were filled by elections, not by combat, while down into the sixteenth century in "hereditary monarchies there is never any shortage of examples of rulers declaring themselves ready to resolve disputes through a trial by combat between princes."[75] In that sense, the princely practice of issuing a challenge to trial by combat formed part of the historic mingling of the law of war with the law of royal succession.

Of course, these formal princely challenges never resulted in literal one-on-one combat. (Jurists insisted that princes should do nothing of the kind, since their death might threaten general disaster.)[76] In practice princely challenges were, as Huizinga put it, a mere "empty ceremonial between royal houses."[77] The notion that a battle might devolve into a direct conflict between two princely contenders was "a motif of fine literature from the earliest times," and the Middle Ages produced some accounts of princely encounters on the battlefield. But those accounts, Goez concluded, were clearly fabulous.[78] All this led Goez to declare the monomachies of princes to be nothing but a fiction, unworthy of the serious attention of historians.

Yet we should not minimize the importance for popular culture of the tradition of princely challenges or the larger resemblance between the princely battle warfare and trial by combat. The law is full of "mere" rituals.[79] Yes, larger-scale battles were always substituted for direct trial by combat between individual monarchs. But the very fact that battles could serve as substitutes reflects the legal truth that battle and trial by combat were closely associated.

Most of all, we must not forget that once the pro forma challenge had been issued, major disputes and claims of royal legitimacy *were* in fact frequently decided by pitched battle. This is especially true of cases in which battles tested the dynastic claims of two rival houses to a throne. It was very common in the Middle Ages for royal houses to establish their legitimacy through pitched battle. The epochal Battle of Fontenoy-en-Puisaye in 841, the arranged battle that established the basic lines of succession to Charlemagne, is a leading example.[80] There are many others, including the Battle of Hastings, which established the claims of William the Bastard to the English throne; the Battle of Bosworth Field, the foundation of Tudor legitimacy, in 1485; the Battle of Mühldorf in 1322, which put Ludwig of Bavaria on the imperial throne. Formal battles *were* used to resolve contests over succession between two claimants, and contemporary reports clearly show that those battles were regarded as trials by combat.[81] There were even attempts at formal arranged battles to settle a dispute over a throne.[82]

Moreover princely battles sometimes did take the life of one of the claimants to the throne, as a trial by combat might have done, and sometimes with immense historic consequences.[83] The death (or reported death) of a monarch in battle could have a powerful ritual effect in establishing the legitimacy of a new pretender. A famous English example makes the point. Here is Francis Bacon's account of the Battle of Bosworth Field: "After Richard III, de facto King of England but a tyrant . . . was overthrown and slain on Bosworth Field . . . Sir William Stanley, after some acclamations of the soldiers in the field . . . put an ornamental crown, which Richard wore in battle and was found amongst the spoils, upon King Henry's head."[84] Yes, there was no direct one-on-one monomachy between Henry and Richard, but all of us can appreciate the symbolic power in the reported gesture of Stanley, taking the crown that had fallen from the head of the dead Richard and placing it on the head of the surviving claimant, like a referee raising the hand of one princely prizefighter.

Battles over thrones were never literal trials by combat, but the human imagination naturally perceived them as a kind of grand monomachy between princes. This was true in the Middle Ages, true in the early modern period,[85] and it remained true in the age of Pufendorf and Voltaire.

Thus even Pufendorf was still discussing the traditional problems of monomachy and war in the traditional terms.[86] So were his eighteenth-century readers. Consider the Austrian canon lawyer Franz Schmier, who summarized the key debates in 1742, exactly at the time of the Battle of Chotusitz. Single battles like those between Aeneas and Turnus, Menelaus and Paris, or David and Goliath were licit, Schmier wrote. By the same token so were battles of several or "war of several thousands"—at least as long as they were undertaken "by public authority."[87] Wars had to be public, but otherwise they were not categorically different from the combat of David and Goliath. In that respect, Schmier still saw matters in just the way his medieval predecessors had.

Other authors also kept alive the connection between single combat and war, at least when it came to public wars. In 1738, for example, two years before the invasion of Silesia, Jean Barbeyrac, the translator of Pufendorf and a shaper of eighteenth-century international law, published a translation of the sermons of John Tillotson, the late seventeenth-century archbishop of Canterbury. He included a sermon on the military subject of glory, which used the example of the single combat between David and Goliath to address the classic question of the law of war that we explored at length in Chapter 2: "the uncertainty of the events of war."[88] Whole books could still be devoted to monomachies around midcentury, such as Giacinto Sigismondo Gerdil's 1759 *Treatise on Single Combats*, a "solid work" taken sufficiently seriously that it was excerpted at length in the *Journal des Sçavans* in 1761.[89] Whatever "crisis of European consciousness" may have intervened, the eighteenth century remained entirely capable of succumbing to the fascination of trial by combat in general, and of the notional monarchical trial by combat in particular. Wars were still combat wagers between princes.

Here again there is meat for the discussion of Frederick's conquest of Silesia, particularly in the popular literature describing his victory at Chotusitz. Chotusitz, readers will recall, was Frederick's second Silesian victory and the one that sealed his conquest. It differed from the previous battle at Mollwitz in a notable way. Frederick himself had not been present at Mollwitz—he rode off to safety when the battle began— and the opposing Austrian forces had been generaled by the Count of Neipperg, an honorable member of the military aristocracy but not himself a Habsburg. In that sense Mollwitz did not have the look of a monomachy between the two rival princely houses. By contrast, the Prussian forces at Chotusitz were commanded by Frederick in person, and on the other side of the field, the Austrians were led by Charles of Lorraine, the brother-in-law of Maria Theresa and the senior Habsburg capable of battlefield service.

Chotusitz thus looked something very much like a classic battle or monomachy between royal houses, and the popular literature of the day presented it in exactly that way. For example, the *Lettres Politiques, Historiques et Galantes*, a compendium of current news and culture published for cultivated society in Amsterdam, described the events for its readers this way: "The Prince *Charles of Lorraine*, a young hero who began to march in the footsteps of his ancestor Duke Charles IV, had taken command of the army of Silesia. . . . This Prince followed the armies that had moved out of Moravia [and] having reached the army commanded by the King in person, these two heroes did not miss the occasion to measure themselves against each other on the plain of Chotusitz."[90] Johann Joachim Schwabe, a fertile German Enlightenment publicist, published the following brief heroic verse:

> Du kämpfest, tapfrer Karl, wie deine Anherrn fochten,
> Die noch zu keiner Zeit ihr Heldenblut gespart:

Doch Preußens Friedrich thut nach seiner Ahnen Art,
Die sich in jeder Schlacht den Siegeskranz geflochten.[91]

You fight, brave Charles, as your ancestors did,
Who never spared their heroes' blood, and never hid;
But Prussia's Frederick fights like *his* forebears:
In battle, victory was always theirs.

No doubt no eighteenth-century observer was entirely serious in offering these heroic descriptions of the battle between Frederick and Charles. Everybody knew that battles were not in fact heroic trials by combat, even on the rare occasions when they opposed a Hohenzollern directly against a Habsburg. Yet at the same time, the human imagination found it very easy to conceive of them as exactly that.

To call eighteenth-century wars aristocratic duels is to commit a basic error in interpreting their legal and social meaning. It is to deprive ourselves of our best chance for understanding how eighteenth-century warfare became the civilized affair that it was. It was not the revival of noble chivalry that held warfare in check, but the success of monarchs in establishing a monopoly of military violence—in establishing the principle that they alone were "subject to no superior tribunal" and so eligible to prove their claims through combat.[92] It was not the jus in bello that lay at the foundation of the old civilization of the eighteenth century, but the jus victoriae.

In one respect, though, I think our literature is on target: in a striking effort, made by Bell, to bring to the table Norbert Elias's sociology of the "civilizing process." Elias's illuminating sociology is an attempt to explain how the violence and coarseness of everyday European life in the sixteenth century gave way to the norms of self-control and elaborate courtesy that dominated by the nineteenth and twentieth centuries. The answer, Elias believed, was to be found in transformations of daily life that began in aristocratic court society, especially in the seventeenth century: patterns of self-restraint that first took hold in the courtly society of Versailles and other courts subsequently spread to European societies more broadly, as aristocrats came to set the tone for all social strata. Bell makes the case that eighteenth-century warfare, with the civilization that its jurists boasted about, was an instance of Elias's aristocratic civilizing process. After all, the aristocratic culture of both etiquette and war, Bell writes, citing Elias, imposed "astonishingly difficult standards of self-control."[93]

Here Bell seems to me to have it quite right. The restrained warfare of the eighteenth century is indeed well-described as a case of Elias's civilizing process. If we are to invoke Elias, however, we must bear in mind the full scope of his argument. His argument was not a claim about the dominance of aristocratic culture, but about the monarchical monopolization of violence.

Elias, who wrote in the terrible years leading up to World War II, regarded himself as a student of Weber, and he described his project precisely as an attempt to explain the "psychogenetic" process that ran parallel to the "sociogenetic" process of the monopolization of violence by the state. The monopolization of violence was not just a matter of the confiscation of weapons by the state or the state promulgation of criminal prohibitions on violence. It was also a matter of "affect control"—of changing the patterns of behavior that led human beings to engage in routine acts of violence and brutality.

It was for this reason that Elias laid so much emphasis on the transformation of aristocratic behavior. The taming of violent affect was something that happened first and foremost to the nobility over the centuries of European development, and Elias set himself the task of explaining how the brutish nobility of the Middle Ages had become the polite aristocracy of the eighteenth century. I have already quoted his description of medieval life: "Rapine, battle, hunting of people and animals—all these were vital necessities which, in accordance with the structure of society, were visible to all. And thus, for the mighty and strong, they formed part of the pleasures of life." As Elias argued, these forms of "mighty and strong" barbarism were under attack from the moment that court society began to establish itself in the Middle Ages, and they came to be thoroughly controlled in the age of Absolutism: "Within the restricted court circle . . . more peaceful forms of conduct became obligatory. Certainly [in the Middle Ages] pacification was not nearly so far advanced as when the absolute monarch would even prohibit dueling. . . . But the moderation of passions, sublimation, is unmistakable and inevitable."[94] Elias did not make use of legal sources or talk much about war, but he was a connoisseur of continental culture if there ever was one, and his topic was the same topic we have been exploring here: how a thuggish continental nobility had become domesticated, as Elias saw it, through the pressures of life in court society, becoming a "courtly" aristocracy.

Of course, the agency that was domesticating the aristocracy, in Elias's view, was the absolute monarch, most notably the monarchical government of Louis XIV. This domestication was achieved through the inculcation of the elaborate ritual ceremonial of court etiquette, the mastery of which required court nobles to develop precisely the "affect control" that mattered most for the civilizing process. Elias argues that this ceremonial court etiquette spread from absolutist France throughout Western Europe as a basic feature of princely government: "In taking over French etiquette and Parisian ceremony, the various rulers obtained the desired instruments to express their dignity, to make visible the hierarchy of society, and to make all others, first and foremost the courtly nobility themselves, aware of their dependence." In all of this, Elias was emphatically not offering an account of how aristocratic culture had shaped society. He was offering an account of how princely power had shaped aristocratic culture—of how nobles were domesticated and made "dependent" on princes, in a process that pushed Europeans on the path to overcoming what he called their "brutish animal" instincts.[95]

It should be evident how comfortably Elias's sociology fits into the account of legal history I have given, and it is with Elias in hand that I would like to return to Martens's description of how the "civilized Powers of Europe" had overcome the "horrors of war" through their obedience to "'the laws of war' (*Kriegsmanier*),"[96] and more broadly to the idea of civilization that we find among eighteenth-century jurists.

Eighteenth-century jurists were proud of the fact that their law was law for "civilized Powers." But what did they mean by *civilization*? In part, of course, as historians often like to emphasize today, they meant that the norms that they celebrated applied only to western European societies and not to indigenous peoples in the colonial world or to Asiatic potentates. But civilization was more than just that for the jurists.

Civilization was also the *Kriegsmanier*, the style, manner, or etiquette of war that Martens credited with "diminishing the horrors" of warfare in his time. Civilization was the set of practices that allowed Europeans to overcome what Wolff called the bellum ferinum, the "wild beast war" of the uncivilized past. It was civilization that demanded that sovereigns making war offer at least polite pretexts. And it is when we study the concepts of Kriegsmanier and bellum ferinum that Elias becomes our surest guide to the eighteenth-century mentality.

Let us begin with the Kriegsmanier, the "proper manner of war." Martens wrote in 1789 that war had been tamed by "those customs that are today designated by the name 'the laws of war' (*Kriegsmanier*), laws that have been observed above all since the introduction of regular troops." Like other eighteenth-century jurists, he thus agreed with modern military historians: the key shift came with the introduction of regular troops, with the transformation of "brigands . . . into soldiers [who formed part of] professional armies."[97] Like Voltaire, he noticed not the presence of aristocratic officers but the presence of a paid and disciplined soldiery wearing royal livery. But what was the Kriegsmanier that Martens associated with this transformation?

Kriegsmanier is ordinarily translated as "customs of war"; in particular it is understood to be a term for the jus in bello.[98] But to translate it so baldly into the terminology of modern International Humanitarian Law is to miss much of its eighteenth-century resonance. *Manier*, like the plural *Manieren*, was a term rich with meaning in the early modern period. It meant both "manners," as we still use the term to refer to etiquette, and "manner" or style—as, for example, the *maniera*, the recognizable masterly style of mannerist painters. A manner was the pattern of comportment and accomplishment of a master in a realm of human activity; that is why accomplished painters had a manner and accomplished courtiers had manners. It is in that same sense that eighteenth-century authors spoke of the Kriegsmanier; it was both the art of regulating the etiquette of military life, in such a way as to foster good manners and discipline, and the art of putting disciplined, regular troops to effective use on the battlefield. As such, it was closely associated with the forms of ritual etiquette that governed other aspects of eighteenth-century life.

Thus the Kriegsmanier was discussed in a general text on social ceremonial, the Saxon jurist Johann Christian Lünig's fascinating *Historical-Political Theater of Ceremonies*, published in 1719–1720. Lünig's book is principally remembered today by historians of court etiquette, since it is a rich source of information on ceremonial in the court sphere.[99] His book, however, extended well beyond princely courts to cover such topics as the ceremonies upon executing a will, the ceremonies upon agreeing to an engagement or a marriage, the ceremonies of diplomatic precedence (covered at great length)–and the ceremonies of the Kriegsmanier. Lünig's account, which proved influential on other eighteenth-century jurists, is vivid testimony to the social setting in which eighteenth-century war was fought.

Lünig began his book by explaining that ceremony was necessary only because of original sin: when humans lost their innocence, they fell prey to the desire to lord it over each other. The purpose of etiquette was to gratify that desire of some humans to feel superior to others. Obnoxious though such hierarchical conduct might seem, Lünig explained, it was necessary in a fallen world: "certain Rites and Ceremonies" were necessary "for the maintenance of a certain order, without which human society cannot exist."[100] The Kriegsmanier was an example of exactly that; it was a means of introducing a courtly, hierarchical form of disciplined subordination, which permitted the maintenance of "a certain order" in war. Lünig's description of how this courtly order of war worked bears reproduction at some length:

> The *Kriegsmanier*, which is little discussed in the literature, has a great influence in many questions of law and policy [*in vielen Casi-bus*] in the contemporary practice of warfare, and it deserves to be carefully studied by all specialists in international law, along with all related topics. Despite the neglect of the topic, one must be aware of the importance of war ceremonial when one considers recruitment, mustering, presentation of officers, flag ceremonies, staffing, watches, marching, quartering, honors given to ruling lords, commanding generals, foreign troops, the officers of one's own army . . . declarations of war, attacks and sieges of fortresses, demands, capitulations, surrenders, military exercises and all manner of other actions, in

which civilized nations submit to appropriate forms of military reason [*die billige Kriegs-Raison*]. . . .

When a great lord declares war on another, this customarily takes
place by means of a Manifesto, which contains the causes that have
brought him to this action. . . .

The commanding General of the Army salutes the King with his
weapon in his hand, all other higher officers, however, merely by
removing their hats.[101]

Many other topics were covered as well. How to demand and accept surrender at a siege; how to conduct courts-martial and administer punishment to troops; and much more, including lengthy discussion of the various victory ceremonies, war monuments, and celebratory poems—all of
this counted as "the proper manner of war" for Lünig. Managing war
meant subjecting it to the same elaborate rites and ceremonies that governed life in a princely court. Lünig was thus a theorist of the same strange
forms of courtesy that Elias found so riveting, and he thought that all jurists with knowledge of international law needed to be theorists of those
forms of courtesy too.

And such matters did indeed interest jurists. Martens, for example,
cited a text that was indebted to Lünig: the 1745 *Brief but Thorough Account of the Ceremonial of War and the So-called Kriegsmanier*. After a
survey of military discipline and practice in the various countries of Europe, this book devoted itself primarily to matters of military protocol
and etiquette, beginning with the proper manner of saluting "princes of
the blood" and going on down through the ranks.[102] Pufendorf too concerned himself with the problems of the Kriegsmanier in his general
survey of the *Leading Empires and States of Europe*, published in 1705.
The Kriegsmanier was of particular interest to Pufendorf in describing
Russia, an uncivilized nation in his eyes, in which there was "no such
culture as is found elsewhere in Europe." This absence of culture showed
up particularly in the behavior of Russian troops, who had to be beaten
before they would obey. Because they were not susceptible to the more
civilized and ceremonious forms of discipline known in Western countries, they made poor soldiers in pitched battle: "In battles in the open
field and in besieging cities they are not worth much."[103] In recent times,

however, Pufendorf noted, German and Scottish officers had been brought in to subject the loutish Russian troops to the civilized Kriegsmanier, and they had greatly improved. This showed that the discipline of the civilized Kriegsmanier, with its elaborate hierarchical protocol, was more effective than the knout. In fact, as Pufendorf's account implied, it was only the civilized Kriegsmanier that made the battle warfare of the eighteenth century possible: hierarchical protocol instilled in soldiers the courage without which they could not stand and fight, as the knout could never have done.

The French-language authors also discussed these issues, though of course they did not make use of the German term *Kriegsmanier*. We may quote Vattel: "Good order and subordination, which are useful everywhere, are nowhere more necessary than in the management of troops. The Sovereign must determine exactly the functions, the duties, and the rights of military men, soldiers, officers, *chefs de corps*, generals; he must regulate and fix the authority of commanders in all grades, the punishments attached to offenses, the form of judgments, etc. The laws and ordinances that concern these different points form the Military Code."[104] Many such passages could be cited.[105]

What we see in all this is an unmistakable example of the formation of civilized European society through the imposition of hierarchical forms of etiquette—precisely the civilizing process that Elias famously described. None of the passages I have quoted may seem startling to military historians, who are well aware of the importance of hierarchical military discipline in the making of early modern warfare. A representative quote from the finest of specialists, John Lynn, is enough to make the point:

> The character of discipline within the army of the *grand siècle* rested on assumptions basic to the culture of command with the army. That culture posited a rigid social class structure and ascribed honor only to the aristocratic upper strata. By this logic, because common soldiers were men of low class and, therefore, devoid of true honor, they could hardly be trusted to comply voluntarily with high military standards. Such assumptions, though based upon class prejudice, also reflected the reality that a great many soldiers within the army had been forced into the ranks against their will. Harsh discipline

and brutal punishment were essential to enforce compliance upon individuals held in such low esteem.[106]

Lynn's picture of army discipline is much the same as Lünig's, with its focus on hierarchical honor and punishment by courts-martial in the "fallen world" of human ceremony. Nevertheless Lünig makes a critical observation that Lynn and other military historians do not: the *Kriegsmanier* and the ceremonial of war were simply one corner of a grander "theater of ceremonies" whose main stage was the princely court. As Vattel put it, "order and subordination" were useful *everywhere*, not just in the army.

Moreover the pyramid of rank rose, as eighteenth-century texts recognized, not just to the "aristocratic upper strata" but to the "princes of the blood," to Vattel's "sovereign," to Lünig's "ruling lords." The deep truth about this theater of ceremonies, as contemporaries perceived it, is the one that Elias gave us: this was a world in which everybody, the aristocratic strata included, had been forced into a pyramidal system of princely hierarchical subjection. As Louis XIV himself wrote, in a passage quoted by Lynn, "I was resolved to spare nothing to reestablish, at every point, discipline in the troops that served under *my* authority."[107]

The wars of the eighteenth century were not wars of aristocrats. They were wars of dynasts who had succeeded in claiming sole supremacy. That is what gave them their distinctive legal character, their ultimate meaning, and their culture of controlled restraint. By the eighteenth century, continental monarchies had finally established the principle that war was to be fought, not to further the aspirations of local magnates, nor for that matter to impose one form of Christian belief. War was public war, to be fought strictly for dynastic interest. That is what matters most about the eighteenth-century law of war.

There should be nothing surprising in this conclusion. All historians know that eighteenth-century wars were dynastic wars. As Roger Chickering has recently summarized the wisdom of scholars, "[W]ars were fought in the Age of Reason for the sake of calculated dynastic ambition by small professional armies according to generally accepted rules of engagement and conventions that reflected the mores of the aristocratic officer class."[108]

That is precisely right—except for its deeply misleading last clause. Yet all too often it is the matter in the last clause, "the mores of the aristocratic officer class," that has gripped the attention of even the finest historians, while the dynasts have too often receded into the shadows.

That is not to say that aristocrats deserve no attention at all. It is true that if we ask social historians' questions—if we ask what military life was really like in its day-to-day forms, what it was really like to stand there on an eighteenth-century battlefield, what it was really like to live in an eighteenth-century camp—we find many signs of "the mores of the aristocratic officer class." There can be no doubt that aristocrats set the tone in eighteenth-century military camps, in which they stood out like so many cocks in a hen yard. If is true that if we ask how men mustered the courage to face possible death in battle, we no doubt find that norms of aristocratic honor motivated at least some of them, some of the time. It is true that if we wish to understand, as it were, the microcultures of violence, we naturally find ourselves focusing on aristocratic duels; after all, anyone seeking a social model for restrained and courteous violence— anyone seeking, in the words of Best, a restrained "code of conflict behavior"—is likely to light on the duel as the best possible example.

Nevertheless to put the focus on the role of aristocrats in eighteenth-century warfare is to miss its ultimate meaning. War was emphatically a business for princes. Duels were a dim, illegitimate echo of the real thing. Aristocrats benefited from their association with war, and the culture of aristocratic honor depended in many ways on their association with war. But to benefit from a business is not to control it, and if the eighteenth century succeeded in restraining warfare, it is first and foremost because it marked the acme of the exclusive monarchical possession of the instruments and symbols of legitimacy.

It is no coincidence that this moment of dynastic triumph in monopolizing legitimate military violence was also a moment of comparative restraint in warfare. This is partly for the reasons given by Elias: the monarchical culture that grew up after the sixteenth century was founded on a systematic commitment to the restraint of violence, expressed through forms of etiquette that emanated from princely courts throughout society, military society included. This is in large measure how we should understand the Kriegsmanier, the "proper manner of war" of the eighteenth century. It is surely also how we should understand the self-control that characterized eighteenth-century aristocrats, as Bell writes.

But there were other factors at work as well. It is fundamentally important that the aims of eighteenth-century warfare had been sharply limited. Eighteenth-century continental wars, as we saw, were fought essentially over dynastic claims in the law of succession. Indeed legal writers sometimes treated the law of war as though it were simply an aspect of the law of dynastic succession. It matters that other considerations had mostly vanished—in particular religious considerations, still perhaps present in conflicts like the Nine Years War (1688–1697) but largely (though not entirely) absent in the eighteenth century. Wars with limited aims tend by their nature to be limited wars, and the aims of eighteenth-century wars were particularly limited because they fell so clearly within the defined parameters of a body of quasi-private law, the law of dynastic succession.

It is also essential to acknowledge the extent to which eighteenth-century wars could be limited because they were not troubled by basic questions about the nature of political legitimacy. To understand why, we must reflect for a moment on the complexity of the relationship between the two elements of Weber's famous formula: legitimacy and violence. When we hear the phrase "monopoly of legitimate violence," we naturally interpret it as though legitimacy were the premise of the right to do violence—as though we could begin by establishing as a fact that regime X has legitimacy and then conclude from that fact that regime X has the right to do violence. But historically the relationship between violence and legitimacy has been more complex than that. Historically violence has been used to *create* legitimacy. By very virtue of the fact that I visit violence upon you, I claim to be your legitimate lord. That is why public execution was so important for establishing the legitimacy of regimes in the past: sovereignty was by definition the authority to kill without committing a crime. Accordingly making wars and executing criminals were kindred activities of lawful rulers. As Saint Augustine explained: "If murder means killing a man, nevertheless sometimes this may happen without sin: after all, a soldier can kill an enemy; and a judge, or the judge's minister, can kill a malefactor."[109] Such was the mark of a legitimate sovereign: a sovereign had the license to do what would be murder if done by any other agent.

The right to use lethal violence expressed legitimacy, and therefore the use of violence could help create legitimacy. We can see the use of violence to create legitimacy in the barbarous practices of medieval warfare. David Whetham describes the *chevauchées*, the raids of devastation, conducted by Edward III during the Hundred Years War, as part of a contest over legitimacy. These acts of unrestrained violence were mounted in territories that Edward claimed as his own, and they were intended to dramatize his superior rights: "In a period that had a very positivist conception of rights if one was unable to defend something, one did not have a right to it. Therefore a *chevauchée* could be used to, very publicly, call in question the legitimacy of the position of the impotent lord and demonstrate the justice of one's own cause at the same time."[110] Something similar could be said about the most infamous campaign of devastation in the years preceding the eighteenth century, Louis XIV's ravaging of the Palatinate. Here, for example, is a contemporary report of the burning of Heidelberg:

> They completely burned the city of Heidelberg, and what remains is so little that it serves only to display all the more their cruelty to the world [*faire eclatter d'avantage leur cruauté*]. . . . They desired, out of a completely extraordinary harshness, that the inhabitants should be the witnesses of their own misery, and so they refused to permit anyone to leave the city; instead they were all shut up in a church that was exempt from the furor. . . . Many places in the surrounding area suffered the same fate, and that perhaps because a few days earlier they had witnessed the defeat of the French troops.[111]

The violence served to make everybody "witnesses" of French power. What was true of kings like Edward III and Louis XIV was also true of medieval nobles. The fact that medieval nobles used violence did not just follow from their social supremacy; it helped create their social supremacy. To engage in acts of violence was in effect to declare oneself sovereign over one's victims.

We can see the same pattern in fascist movements, which claimed a right to do violence precisely in order to proclaim their legitimacy. By the same token, early modern republics *had* to claim the right to make war in order to establish their legitimacy. The right to use violence and the acquisition of legitimacy went hand in hand. This is why Grotius, the former advocate of the Dutch Republic, felt obliged to insist that private wars were permissible.

The point is simple enough, and even obvious. Contests over legitimacy are always likely to breed violence. Those whose legitimacy is unsure will always be tempted to use violence to prove it. In that sense, Schmitt was wrong when he famously declared that the sovereign is "he who decides the exception." The better definition came from Schmitt's teacher Weber: the sovereign is one who can succeed in claiming the right to exercise unrestrained violence, especially the license to kill. For most of the eighteenth century, though, legitimacy was blessedly uncontested. Few doubted the right of dynastic monarchy to rule, and princes had many ceremonial means of maintaining their legitimacy. Unbridled violence was correspondingly less necessary for them than it would be for the new forms of government that would succeed them.

Eighteenth-century wars were fought under the star of clearly legitimate rulers, for clear and legally defined material ends, in a legal culture oriented toward the restriction of violence. It is not surprising that they were relatively contained wars. But wars would not be fought over legally defined material claims forever, and questions of legitimacy that were closed in the eighteenth century would not stay closed in the nineteenth.

CHAPTER 5

Were There Really Rules?

It is worth asking why Frederick's great victories were not more decisive than they actually were: why he restricted himself to gaining control of the battlefield.

—Jeremy Black, "Eighteenth-Century Warfare Reconsidered"

T HE EIGHTEENTH CENTURY was an age of exceptional military restraint, but that does not mean that it did not witness terrible battles. Among the most terrible was Malplaquet, "the battle that averted the collapse of France."[1] Malplaquet was a nightmarishly bloody exchange fought in early September 1709 between France and its opponents in the War of the Spanish Succession. It is using the example of the bloody battle at Malplaquet that I now turn to a crucial, and much debated, question about the civilization of warfare in the eighteenth century: whether there were really rules.

The Battle of Malplaquet is a classic example of a battle that brought a sudden reversal in the fortunes of war. In the summer of 1709, eight years into the long War of the Spanish Succession, France seemed close to defeat. The war had begun in 1701, after Louis XIV, profiting from some clever maneuvering by his diplomats forty years earlier, made his grandson, Philip V, king of Spain under the Spanish law of succession.[2] This was a risky and provocative decision, and it triggered one of the most momentous and exhausting wars of European history, as a coalition formed to oppose Louis that included Britain, Austria, and the Netherlands.

There was inconclusive fighting in the early years of the war, but in 1704 the Allies enjoyed some significant successes against France, among them the famous Battle of Blenheim, at which the Duke of Marlborough and Prince Eugene of Savoy, the allied generals, defeated a large French force, thus thwarting a planned attack on Vienna. By the spring of 1709, things were going badly for France—so badly that the Allies were demanding not only that the French make territorial concessions but also that Louis commit his own troops to the task of driving Philip from the French throne.[3] Louis resisted, mounting an unprecedented propaganda effort to rally public support, but his prospects looked grim. In late summer, Marlborough and Eugene undertook what they hoped would be a definitive invasion of France, to be mounted by way of Flanders, so often the theater of western European conflict.

The Allies began by taking Ypres and Tournai by siege, then moved to attack the fortress of Mons. Before they reached Mons, however, they were met by the French at Malplaquet, where a monumental battle ensued on September 11. The casualties on both sides were terrible, but the Allies suffered far worse than the French, losing about 21,000, a full quarter of their men, whereas the French lost only 11,000.[4] No comparably bloody battle would be fought for more than a generation.

The immense bloodshed made Malplaquet an eighteenth-century byword for battlefield carnage. It even gave rise to a cruel children's song that is still sung in France today, three centuries later. This was "Marlbrough s'en va en guerre," sung to the tune of "For He's a Jolly Good Fellow" and celebrating the rumor that the Duke of Marlborough had been killed on the field of Malplaquet. Marlborough was not in fact dead. Nevertheless by holding off the allied invasion, Villars, the French commander, saved France from almost certain defeat in the war. The allied campaign had effectively failed. Three years later the French would manage a victory at nearby Denain that allowed them to procure a compromise peace leaving Louis's grandson on the Spanish throne, thus salvaging what had seemed an almost hopeless cause three years earlier.

Malplaquet was the battle that saved early eighteenth-century France. It may seem bizarre, then, that contemporaries universally declared it to be a victory for the *Allies*—indeed a "complete victory." "The good lord has given us a complete victory," exulted Marlborough in a letter to the Holy Roman emperor on the evening after the battle. This despite the fact that the battle had taken such a toll that the allied war effort was crippled.[5] The Dutch commander Frans Nicolaas Fagel used the same phrase the next day: the battle had been a "complete victory," though Fagel added that "the corpses lay on the ground in their ranks and files." "Our troops could not have acquired more glory," boasted another allied commander, the Count of Albemarle, that day, "but I admit that it has cost us dearly: Our poor Dutch infantry has been cut to pieces."[6] In fact the Dutch suffered such calamitous losses that they would find it difficult to muster new forces for the remainder of the war. Yet the battle was a complete victory for their side, the Allies rejoiced, and the French sources would continue to describe Malplaquet as a "complete victory" for the enemy down into the nineteenth century.[7]

Why was Malplaquet, a battle that took the lives of a quarter of the allied troops, a battle that by any strategic measure should have counted as perhaps the most critical French victory of a momentous war, the battle that saved France, understood to be a French defeat? If eighteenth-century observers were not judging it by the modern standard of military strategy, what standard *were* they applying?

The answer belongs to the standard premodern law of victory, and it is an answer that suggests powerfully that there were rules in eighteenth-century warfare and that those rules mattered. Under the premodern law of victory, the French counted as the losers at Malplaquet because they were the ones who retreated. The rule that made Malplaquet a complete victory for the Allies was thus the same rule that would make Chotusitz a complete victory for Frederick the Great thirty-three years later: it was what I shall call *the retreat rule*. Malplaquet was a complete victory for the Allies because they managed to gain control of the field of battle, despite the fact that they did so only at the cost of devastating and hugely disproportionate losses. As an eighteenth-century report explained, "The massacre was great. . . . [O]ne saw the battalions of the Allies . . . lying dead in ranks. . . . But [the French] yielded the field of battle."[8] To be sure, the French, like the Austrians at Chotusitz, retreated "in good order," "with flags waving, drums beating, and drawing off sixty-five of their cannon with them."[9] A retreat could be as ceremonious and colorful an event as any other in the age of eighteenth-century Kriegsmanier. But a retreat was a retreat: the side that yielded the field of the battle, no matter how great its strategic gains, no matter how awful the cost it imposed on the enemy, was the loser.

But did it really matter to be the technical loser? What difference could it possibly have made, as long as you were (as Louis XIV clearly was) the strategic winner? Could anybody really have cared? Modern military historians certainly do not seem to think that being the technical loser mattered. When modern historians discuss Malplaquet, they do not pause to dwell on the fact that the eighteenth-century sources declared the battle to be a complete victory for the Allies. What interests them is analyzing the strategic consequences of the battle that very likely "saved France."[10]

Yet it is clear that people in the eighteenth century took the question of who counted as the loser very seriously. In part this had to do with diplomacy. As we have already seen in the case of the Chotusitz, a technical battlefield victory, however limited by modern tactical standards, could result in a diplomatic triumph in the eighteenth century. Chotusitz, like Malplaquet, was a battle in which the Prussians took heavier losses but gained control of the field, while the defeated Austrians retreated in good order to encampments a few miles away. This was certainly not the kind of crushing Clausewitzian defeat that modern military commanders seek. Nevertheless Chotusitz was universally declared to be a complete victory for Frederick, and as a result of that complete victory, English diplomacy stepped in, and Frederick "procured a Peace" which gave him possession of Silesia.[11]

The same language was used to describe the allied complete victory at Malplaquet, though it certainly did not have the kind of decisive diplomatic impact that Chotusitz had. According to contemporary reports, after they had driven the French from the field "Marlborough and his other principal officers . . . hoped that this action would procure a rapid Peace."[12] They saw reason to believe, despite their fearsome losses, that their success in gaining control of the field might be enough to put an end to the war. And indeed, as a report from the year 1710 reveals, the high powers then negotiating the Treaty of Utrecht were prepared to

acknowledge that the allied campaign, including "the victory of Malplaquet," added "rather strong reasons" why Louis should be compelled to
yield.[13] The fact that the Allies had been "cut to pieces" was not, apparently, of critical importance in the eyes of the diplomats. They thought
the diplomatic consequences of Malplaquet were adverse to the French,
not the Allies.

Nor were the potential diplomatic benefits the only ones, or even necessarily the most important ones. Gaining control of the battlefield also
carried political and propaganda benefits, both on campaign and on the
home front—benefits that eighteenth-century observers clearly valued
highly. First and foremost, the technical victor had the privilege of
mounting a victory ceremony. Elaborate and ostentatious victory celebrations had been a part of royal propaganda since antiquity,[14] and that
remained the case in the eighteenth century. The forms for the celebration of victory played a central role in eighteenth-century accounts of
war. Recall that Voltaire's satirical article on war culminated with the
victory ceremony. "[O]ne sings," he noted nastily, "a rather long song in
four-part harmony, composed in a language unknown to all those who
have fought, and what's more thoroughly stuffed with barbarisms." Voltaire was not the only author to treat the victory ceremonies as an integral part of war–and most authors did not treat them as deserving of
satire. Thus Johann Christian Lünig deemed victory ceremonies to be a
fundamental aspect of the Kriegsmanier, the "proper manner" of civilized European warfare, and devoted dozens of pages to them. For example, he reported at some length on the English ceremonies following
the defeat of Louis at Blenheim:

> On the 14th of January, 1705, on an early Wednesday morning, a de-
> tachment of the Royal Bodyguard, along with Mounted Grenadiers
> and one of the two regiments of Foot Guards presented themselves
> at the Tower to collect the [captured] standards and flags. . . . They
> then marched in the following order [described at length]. . . . This
> magnificent procession passed through the streets of the Strand and
> Pall Mall, and before the royal palace of St. James and the park,
> where the Queen observed the processional from the room of Mylord
> FitzHarding. There followed a thirty gun salute. . . . They passed

through King Street to Westminster, where the standards and flags were hung in memory of the victory.[15]

The hanging of captured flags was always central to these ceremonies, and so was the singing of a "Te Deum," a hymn of thanks to God for victory, as, for example, at a Russian victory celebration in 1714, also described by Lünig in lavish detail: "On Sunday the 12th (23rd) of September, a *Te Deum Laudamus* was sung at public services in the renovated church . . . followed that evening by stately fireworks."[16] As for Chotusitz, German military men would still be describing its *Te Deum*, which began with a triple salvo by all the artillery of Berlin, as late as 1884.[17]

Voltaire may have found these public celebrations of victory risible, but they were an integral part of eighteenth-century princely war-making. Nor is this surprising: war-making was deeply associated with princely legitimacy, and princely legitimacy was founded in part on public commemorations of victory.

This too was significant for Malplaquet. The French, whatever strategic benefit they may have gotten from the battle, counted as the losers. That meant that the government of Louis XIV, which always invested heavily in victory propaganda, could not order that a *Te Deum* be sung: "Louis XIV was not able to celebrate a *Te Deum* for a combat, however glorious it may have been, that ended in the abandonment of the field of battle." Nevertheless the government made a game effort to draw some propaganda advantage: "[Louis] had the flags taken to Notre Dame, as would have been done after a victory, except for six of them, which were accorded to Villars."[18] As a contemporary newssheet explained, "[B]ecause it is important to capture the eyes and attention of the vulgar by means of sensible objects, fourteen flags and eight standards were carried in triumph to the church of Notre Dame."[19]

What is most striking about this odd propaganda half-measure is the fact that King Louis felt so much bound by the standard rule defining victory. Louis XIV was a prince of dazzling ceremony, who financed a stable of sculptors and painters producing costly and imposing victory images intended "to capture the eyes and attention of the vulgar"— to display his *gloire*, his military magnificence. Such was his style of government, and one would have thought that he had ample grounds for a full-scale victory celebration after Malplaquet. Moreover Malplaquet arrived at a moment when he was under extreme propaganda pressure and felt compelled to seek novel, almost desperate ways of rallying public support.[20] Yet even Louis XIV, in these desperate circumstances, could not ignore the established rule of victory: "the abandonment of the field of battle" counted as a loss, and no *Te Deum* would be sung.[21]

Te Deum ceremonies mattered. Victory was not just about hunting down and slaughtering the enemy; in fact vigorous pursuit of the defeated enemy was a very rare event. Victory was about celebrating victory, about singing a *Te Deum*, ideally "followed that evening by stately fireworks." Like monarchs of the previous centuries and autocrats down to the present day, the princes of eighteenth-century Europe set great store by their capacity to project glory through ceremonies and monuments of victory. Only forcing the enemy to yield the field of battle was sufficient to confer that kind of glory. That was the rule of victory, and the example of Malplaquet shows that even Louis XIV had to live by it.

It is important to observe, finally, that the home front was not the only place where a "complete" victory had propaganda value. It had value in the field as well. Eighteenth-century authors emphasized that winning victories helped to motivate troops, while suffering defeats undermined their morale. Voltaire's own account of Malplaquet is an example. The battle had been in a very real sense a triumph for France, Voltaire remarked; "nevertheless, the word 'lost battle' weighs on the losers, and undermines their courage."[22] Being deemed the losers made troops wobble. This was a commonplace in discussions of military courage. The *Encyclopédie* of Diderot and D'Alembert, in its article on valor, distinguished among different forms of courage and defined *bravura* as the kind of courage peculiar to soldiers in war. Other kinds of courage could withstand adversity, the article observed, but "bravura is shaken by a defeat."[23] (The *Encyclopédie* elsewhere defined a lost battle as "one in which you abandon the field of battle to the enemy.")[24] Later in the century, the *Encyclopédie Méthodique* included boosting troop morale in a long list of the propaganda advantages of victory. Winning a battle, the authors explained, was a matter of winning over your own troops, as well as the broader public and neutral powers. This was achieved by presenting "proofs of victory":

If the success of a battle seems uncertain, drive home [*faire valoir*] all of the circumstances that are in your favor, in order to publicize the fact that victory has been declared for you, in order to sustain the courage of your troops, and in order to avoid the danger that the newly conquered country, or some prince who had hitherto maintained his neutrality, should go over to the other side. The reputation for having shown superiority makes recruiting easier in the country, and attracts a large number of deserters to your army.

Winning a battle does not mean losing fewer men than the enemy. The proofs of victory are to keep control of the field of battle for a longer time; to capture the baggage train or the artillery of the enemy; to gather your dead and the dead of the enemy; to show yourself ready to fight [*de présenter*] the day after the battle, when the enemy declines, and to capture more of their flags, standards and drums. If this last advantage is not in itself a proof of victory, it at least serves to illustrate victory.[25]

Amassing the proofs of victory was imperative. "Losing fewer men" than the other side was not such a proof, not even when, as at Malplaquet, you imposed gargantuan losses on the enemy, not even when the enemy suffered losses that were twice as heavy your own. Proof of victory had to do with carrying off enemy flags and standards to hang in your churches; above all, it had to do with gaining control of the field of battle. That, everybody agreed, was the rule.

But was it really a rule in the full sense of the word? Were there really rules in premodern warfare at all? Many scholars have expressed deep doubts about whether premodern war was truly a rule-governed activity.

We have already seen enough to understand why there might be doubts. After all, if the retreat rule were *really* a rule in the full sense, one might think, then commanders would have agreed that it had to be obeyed. If it were *really* a rule, discussions of the art of war would all have turned on the question of how to force the enemy to retreat. Yet that is not the case. Commanders like Frederick the Great and the Maréchal de Saxe did not believe that there was any rule restricting them to gaining control of the field of battle. They were entirely ready to break any such rule in order to annihilate the enemy if they had the chance. And they were not alone: a century and a half before Frederick and Saxe wrote, the early modern literature was already saying the same thing: While conquering the field of battle counted as victory, commanders should always seize the opportunity to annihilate the enemy if it presented itself.[26]

It is not just that military commanders did not feel any obligation to follow the supposed rule. Governments did not peacefully submit to it either. If the retreat rule were *really* a rule in the full sense, one might think, then we would expect all the parties to a conflict to accept the verdict of battle. Once one side was driven from the field of battle, it should have meekly acknowledged its defeat. Yet we know that that was not the case either. Frederick may have felt entitled to celebrate his victory at Chotusitz with a majestic triple artillery salvo, and the diplomats may have declared him the winner, but Maria Theresa never believed that the rules obliged her to accept the verdict of that battle. Similarly the diplomats at Utrecht may have weighed the possibility that the allied victory at Malplaquet meant that Louis had lost the war, but in fact the war did not end. The rule was not enough to force definitive surrender down the throat of Louis XIV, even if it prevented him from celebrating a *Te Deum*. Sometimes people acted as though there was a rule; sometimes they didn't. So what exactly does it mean to say that there was a rule of victory declaring the victor to be the side that gained control of the field of battle?

The puzzle runs deep, and it has led scholars to split sharply over the question of whether premodern warfare was a rule-governed activity. It is a puzzle that we can solve only if we reflect carefully on the nature of legal rules. Odd though it may sound, we cannot do satisfying military history without doing a bit of philosophy of law.

The puzzle can most usefully be described by contrasting the two leading anthropological models of war: the model of war as a game and the model of war as a hunt. Scholars who think of premodern warfare as rule-governed most commonly think of war in the way Johan Huizinga did, as an activity of *Homo Ludens*, Man the Gameplayer. Scholars who doubt that there were rules tend to think of war more in the way that Aristotle did, as an activity (in Walter Burkert's coinage) of *Homo Necans*, Man the Hunter.[27] The puzzle of whether there were really rules is authentically difficult to solve because on the face of it there is a case to be made for both views.

On the one hand, there is a great deal about premodern warfare that looks unmistakably game-like, not just in the eighteenth century but in earlier centuries as well. To begin with, it is a striking fact that humans sometimes literally do play games to resolve conflicts that could be resolved through war: One thinks of the deadly Mesoamerican ballgame, which served, according to scholars, as "a substitute and a symbol for war, [acting] to resolve conflicts between Maya cities, and between the Maya and other neighboring peoples."[28] Conversely, one thinks of the famous Guerra del Fútbol between El Salvador and Honduras in 1969, a shooting war linked to a qualifying match in the World Cup. For inhabitants of both countries the role of sports fan easily became the role of deadly belligerent.[29] The same close connection between games and war is found in the writings of eighteenth-century jurists like Vattel: "Some scholars have argued, on the basis of the proposition that sovereigns recognize no judge but God, that the pretenders to the crown, if their claim is uncertain, should either negotiate or contract among themselves, or choose arbiters, or even use a game of chance [*sors*], or finally settle their differences through armed force, while the subjects of the realm in question are by no means entitled to decide for themselves."[30] Negotiations, dice games, wars, trials: for Vattel these were, in principle, interchangeable means of settling great disputes between princes, and he was only one of many jurists to think so.

Moreover when we consider the long history of the practice of pitched battle, it can be hard to resist the impression that a battle was a kind of game. A pitched battle, unlike a raid, pits two armed teams against each other. This has the air of a lethal team sport rather than a hunt. The winner in pitched battles like Malplaquet and Chotusitz was the side that forced its opponent off the field, no matter how high the human cost. This surely has the sound of something like a sumo match or a football game: the goal was to capture and hold the field, and your victory counted as victory even if your lineup was cruelly decimated. Victory, once achieved, was to be celebrated by a *Te Deum* and fireworks. What could be more like a modern sporting event?

It is also noteworthy that a pitched battle takes place on a special field, just as so many organized sporting events do. The very word *pitch* is still used for sports fields, just as it was once used for battles. In both antiquity and the Middle Ages, as we have seen, it was common to name a particular pitch and particular day for the encounter. "At Grancey in 1434, for instance," as Maurice Keen writes, "it was stipulated that the two armies must face each other in 'the place above Guiot Rigoigne's house on the right hand side towards Sentenorges, where there are two trees.'"[31] Pitched battle also includes one of the most striking features of organized sport: a kind of game clock, traditionally (if fictitiously) supposed to run from dawn to dusk.[32]

The retreat rule in particular seems to belong to the culture of gaming. Many sports, after all, involve forcing one side down the field or off the field. In the Western world, the retreat rule had two independent roots, one traceable to the ancient Greeks, one to the Middle Ages. Hans van Wees describes "the formal procedure for establishing the winner of a battle" among the Greeks:

> By the time of the Peloponnesian war, the universally accepted criterion of victory was having control of the dead bodies strewn across the battlefield: whichever side asked the enemy permission to retrieve the stripped corpses of their men admitted defeat. The victors asserted control of the battlefield by attaching a set of captured arms and armor to a stake or tree as a *tropaion*, "trophy" (literally "turning point marker"), at the spot where the enemy had been routed. The rules were firm: the winner should always grant a truce for the recovery of the dead when requested, and the loser should always leave the enemy's trophy intact until it collapsed of its own accord, even if this meant tolerating a constant painful reminder of defeat just outside the city walls.[33]

Roman texts also described victory, in a variation on the theme, as gaining control of the enemy camp, the place where the best booty was to be found.[34] The medieval tradition too treated gaining control of the battlefield, called in German by the eerie name *Wallstatt*, "killing field," as the mark of victory. In medieval parlance, this was to "gain the field," to "win the field," "to exercise control over the killing field"[35]—as a chilling medieval text described victory around the year 1000, "[T]hey made themselves the masters in the place of death."[36] This medieval tradition called for the victor to spend a night or more on the field of battle or perhaps in the camp of the enemy who had fled.[37] In particular, later medieval law required, at least on paper, the so-called *sessio triduana*, the "three-day sit-down." In order to demonstrate property rights, it was sometimes required that the claimant spend three days and three nights on a given parcel. Similarly medieval sources demanded that the victor spend three days and three nights among the corpses on the conquered field of battle in order to prove his claim—an apt symbolic practice in a world in which war was understood to be a means of acquiring property.[38]

The retreat rule thus took various forms, but in one way or another it was something of a Western universal for centuries. To be sure, it was not completely untouched by doubt. Applying the retreat rule could be difficult, partly because feigned retreats were a standard tactic. Moreover there was always some occasional support for a rival rule, which we may call *the casualties rule*, according to which, the victorious side was the one with fewer casualties. These two rules stood in real tension with each other, since it was often the case that one side could compel the other side to retreat only at the cost of taking higher casualties. Malplaquet was one of many examples of the conflict; there were many battles which counted as a victory for one side under the retreat rule, but as a victory for the other side under the casualties rule—many examples of victories achieved only "at a terrible cost in blood."[39] A famous case from the literature of antiquity, involving the Argives and the Spartans, served as a standard topos for discussion in the early modern period: "Both the two sides . . . claimed the victory for themselves, the one side saying that of them more had remained alive, and the others declaring that these had fled away, whereas their own man had stood his ground and had stripped the corpses of the other party."[40]

The temptation for a loser like Louis at Malplaquet to invoke the casualties rule was strong. Moreover some Roman texts seemed clearly to favor a casualties rule, notably when it came to the interesting question of when commanders could celebrate a triumph.[41] And some authors, like Isidore of Seville, declared that victory could perhaps be won by either rule: "It is called 'victory' because it is obtained by force [*vi*], that is to say by manly prowess [*virtute*]. . . . A victory counts as certain because you have killed the enemy, or because you have taken booty [through capturing the field or his camp], or both."[42] There were always people ready to invoke the casualties rule, and there were always Roman texts that could be cited in support of it. Nevertheless the retreat rule remained overwhelmingly dominant.

In particular the retreat rule was invoked in one striking property law context: the law of booty. War, as we have seen, was a legitimate mode of the acquisition of property, and victorious troops had property rights in booty. It was standard practice to motivate troops by holding out the prospect of booty.[43] As a result, observes John Lynn, armies were followed by sutlers ready to provide ready cash for the goods that soldiers had seized.[44] But what sort of property counted as "booty"? Soldiers were not entitled to seize anything they pleased from any victim they might happen upon. They were supposed to be warriors, not bandits, and they could acquire legal title to their booty only if they seized it from a lawfully defeated enemy. Moreover it would be impossible to keep order among troops if they could scatter and start collecting booty at any time. It was essential that they be required to achieve a victory before they began to engage in plunder.

Accordingly the law of booty had to have a rule determining what counted as victory, and it used the standard one, defining victory as gaining control of the field of battle. Our earliest evidence comes from a 1393 compact among Swiss soldiers, determining when they could take booty. Only once the field was taken and the enemy had entirely fled would they be permitted to begin stripping the corpses and ransacking the enemy camp.[45] This rule established itself firmly in the Articles of War, the early modern body of law regulating military conduct.[46] The standard sixteenth-century formulation belonged to the Articles of War promulgated by Emperor Maximilian I. It was borrowed by every early modern version of the Articles and was still the law in the eighteenth century:

> CLXI. *Item*, No one, in battles or sieges, is to start plundering or laying
> claims, unless and until the battlefield and/or locale has been

conquered. Everyone is to remain in good order, on pain of
corporal punishment.

CLXII. Nor shall anyone leave the camp to take booty or for any other
reason, without the knowledge and consent of his captain.[47]

The rule permitting booty taking only once the enemy had retreated
was so well known that it gave rise to a standard scene in seventeenth-
century battle painting. The popular war artists Sebastiaan Vrancx and
Jan Martszen, for example, painted genre scenes of the taking of booty
after a battle.[48] Those paintings show soldiers stripping corpses in the
foreground, while in the far background the defeated enemy has run off
in headlong retreat.

In all these respects, the resemblance between pitched battles, deadly
though they were, and sporting events seems unmistakable, and it may not
be surprising that our ancestors did indeed sometimes describe battle as a
form of game—an "athletic contest," a "dicing game," or the like. As late as
the mid-nineteenth century, standard texts on international law still spoke
in gaming terms. In war, August Wilhelm Heffter, the leading author of
the period wrote, "chance makes everything a throw of dice, a game." Or,
as he put it in describing the right of booty, "[T]he warring parties enter,
as it were, into mutual agreement by which they put up any objects they are
carrying with them with them as stakes in the game of war."[49] Pushing
back into earlier periods, we find many revealing texts. It is striking, for
example, to open the late antique *Etymologies* of Isidore of Seville, a prime
repository of ancient knowledge in the Middle Ages. Isidore discusses war
(along with the rules of court procedure) in a single book entitled "De
Bello et Ludis" (On war and games).[50] Like many authors, Isidore (or perhaps his ancient editor) seems to have regarded battle (and trial) as self-
evidently related to gaming.

In light of all this it is no surprise that many eminent historians, especially historians of ancient Greece and the Middle Ages, have been drawn
to the gaming analogy in analyzing battle warfare. Jacqueline de Romilly
and Jean-Pierre Vernant, for example, maintain that classical Greek battle warfare was an *agon*, a kind of sporting competition, closely related
to the other competitive sports that played such a dominant role in classical Greek culture. Greek authors from Aeschylus onward spoke of battle
as an agon.[51] This suggests clearly enough, these scholars argue, that

classical Greek battle was close in spirit to the javelin-throwing contests and races of Greek athletic games, "two faces of the same social phenomenon."[52] "The ferocity of [Greek] battles," writes the historian T. J. Cornell, endorsing this view, "should not be allowed to conceal the ludic character of hoplite warfare."[53] Medievalists too have been strongly drawn to the game-playing interpretation. For example, Kurt-Georg Cram, whose 1955 *Iudicium Belli* (The judgment of war), remains one of the finest studies of medieval battle law, concludes that Huizinga was right: medieval battle warfare was essentially a ludic contest.[54]

All in all it may seem entirely natural to conclude that the pitched battles of the past were, at bottom, high-stakes sporting matches, a lethal "game of war," in Heffter's words, in which the winner was the side that conquered the field of battle, with the booty taken on the field as the stakes. Not only natural, but useful: calling battles "games" seems to promise solutions to problems that have bothered military historians of the eighteenth century such as Jeremy Black. As the chapter epigraph suggests, Black finds it puzzling that Frederick the Great "restricted himself to gaining control of the battlefield" instead of engaging in pursuit. He also notes that "Frederick usually lost more men than his enemies, even in the battles he won."[55] What kind of generalship was Frederick engaged in? Why would he accept heavier casualties and not make every effort to hunt down and kill the enemy? The solution to Black's puzzle is simple, one might think, once we acknowledge that eighteenth-century battles were essentially games with rules: the rule declared that the victor was the one who gained control of the battlefield, even if doing so required him to take heavier casualties. What made Frederick such a brilliant commander was precisely his capacity to capture the trophy of the field of battle, the killing field, even at high cost. War was simply a game, and Frederick was a brilliant coach.

Simple, and persuasive, as this answer may seem, though, it has been rejected by many thoughtful scholars in recent years. In fact contemporary military historians of most periods, including both ancient Greece and the Middle Ages, now express grave skepticism about the "myth . . . that campaigns and battles were conducted by a set of strict sportsmanlike rules."[56] The supposed rules, these scholars observe, were often ignored. And even when formal battles were fought, they were fought with a kind of murderousness remote from the spirit of gaming; in practice, battles often degenerated into something that looked a great deal like raiding; to the extent the purpose of rules was to keep war within humane limits, they manifestly failed. If Man the Gameplayer sometimes initiated wars, he quickly surrendered to the impulse to become the Man the Hunter.

Scholars find it easy to show, for example, that there was no fixed rule against pursuing the enemy. The question of pursuit seems particularly revealing. To be content simply with controlling the field of battle is, after all, to abide by a kind of game rule, whereas to pursue the defeated enemy off the field is to engage in a kind of hunting behavior. Yet in all periods pursuit sometimes took place. As the fine specialist in Greek law Adriaan Lanni writes, "[W]hen circumstances permitted a safe pursuit, victorious armies did chase down and kill their opponents with impunity."[57] The realities of warfare, she concludes, were about what the "circumstances permitted," not about following the rules of a sport. Lanni is not alone in saying this. Peter Krentz, a prominent critic of the agonistic interpretation of Greek warfare, argues that what looks like rule-governed behavior was in fact typically driven by "matters of tactics rather than conventions."[58] If commanders were content simply to take control of the field of battle, it was because it made good military sense to do so, not because they were following some rule. Van Wees similarly observes that "throughout the history of Greek warfare, agricultural devastation, assaults on settlements, ambushes, and surprise attacks were at least as common as pitched battles, and far more common than pitched battles of the most ritualized kind. . . . Ideally, [Greek warfare] was 'agonal,' that is, fought by a set of restrictive rules which made it seem like a game. In reality, a ferocious pursuit of profit and honor constantly strained against any such restrictions and frequently drove the Greeks to the most uninhibited, destructive kind of 'total' warfare."[59]

Similar views have been expressed about the Middle Ages. If warriors camped on the battlefield, it was not because they felt obligated to satisfy a rule of property law that required a "three-day sit-down," argues the medievalist Malte Prietzel. It was because they had "practical reasons." It was a matter of "tactics rather than conventions": they stayed on the battlefield because it took time to collect and apportion the booty.[60] The standard dictionary of legal history agrees: the three-day sit-down had nothing to do with obedience to the rules of property law. It was a purely practical measure, undertaken for purposes of plundering and dealing with the corpses.[61] In any case, Prietzel adds, there were also strategic considerations for camping on the field: at times the only way to capitalize on the success of a victory was to stay put.[62] More generally, medieval warfare was so notoriously barbaric that many scholars find it difficult or impossible to credit the claim that it was governed by rules. "The rules and practices of knighthood and chivalry," Stephen Neff writes, "did little in practice to mitigate the horrors of war. . . . For the most part, medieval warfare presented a shocking picture of horror and brutality."[63] We have seen how right Neff is.

Such views have become commonplaces. The consensus among most contemporary scholars is that battle warfare, however game-like it may appear at first blush, was in fact not governed by game-like rules at all. The same view dominates among historians of the eighteenth century. Black analyzes Frederick the Great's reluctance to pursue the enemy as a matter of "tactics rather than conventions." It is not that Frederick would have rejected the idea of hunting down the enemy; it is simply that it was impractical to do so. "His tightly disciplined troops," Black argues, "could not be unleashed in a headlong pursuit without the danger of the units becoming less coherent, or even disintegrating through desertion, as soon as they were out of sight of their superiors."[64] As Black sees it, the answer to the puzzle of why Frederick "restricted himself to gaining control of the field of battle" is thus not that he was acting in obedience to a rule of victory. The answer is that he was *re*acting to the pressures of the combat situation. It was really all about "practical reasons."

For most contemporary military historians, Clausewitz accordingly remains the best guide to the past. Warfare in general, and eighteenth-century battle warfare in particular, was an exercise in brute violence, whose natural aim was to annihilate the enemy. Rather than being a stylized gaming match, premodern war was an improvisatory butchery. In particular, there was no game-like rule that defined victory as gaining control of the field of battle. All commanders always understood that it was sound tactics to engage in pursuit of the defeated enemy, and of course pursuit of fleeing soldiers is much more like a hunt than it is like a game.

So which is it? Was the battle warfare of the past a rule-bound agon, or was it an improvisatory butchery? Was it a gaming match or a chaotic hunt for human prey? Did human warfare evolve from the behavior of *Homo Ludens* or the behavior of *Homo Necans*? The controversy can be settled only if we think carefully about the nature of law.

As the examples of Malplaquet and Chotusitz show, there were indeed rules in the eighteenth century, and the same was true of earlier periods as well. Premodern battle warfare often really was a rule-governed activity—or, perhaps better, in the words of Josiah Ober, a rule-*oriented* activity[65]—and we cannot grasp its meaning unless we acknowledge as much. The fact that Louis XIV was unable to celebrate a *Te Deum* after Malplaquet had nothing to do with the tactical pressures of the combat situation. Louis faced a very real propaganda dilemma, because there was an unambiguous and universally accepted rule that declared that the French were the losers—a rule so securely established that even the most ruthless of European monarchs, committed to the most imposing forms of propaganda, in the most urgent of circumstances, could not defy it. This example, alongside many others, makes it perfectly clear that there were rules and that the rules mattered.

Nevertheless to say that there were rules is not to say that the rules were always obeyed, and it is certainly not to say that war was a game. There *were* rules, but we must think of them not as rules of a game but as rules of *law*. We must further recognize that they were not, for the most part, humanitarian rules of the kind that dominate in the law of war today. They were rules of the jus victoriae, rules of the law of victory, rules that aimed to determine who the winner was and what the winner won by virtue of victory. We must understand that there was no tension between tactics and conventions. The fact that the rules served the tactical needs of commanders does not imply that they were not rules. Finally, we must understand that the fact that commanders were permitted to engage in trickery does not mean that there were not rewards for following the rules.

The proposition that battles were a form of gaming is indeed appealing, and it is no surprise that Huizinga and others should have embraced it. But it is deeply misleading. Battles were not games; their rules were rules of law. The difference is fundamental. Games are defined by scrupulous obedience to rules; law is not. If the players in a game cease to play by the rules, the game is at an end. If, for example, one tennis player abruptly draws a revolver and shoots the other, the frame of the game is broken, and all of the spectators present understand that they are no longer witnessing a tennis match. Once the rules cease to dictate the behavior of the players completely, we have left the realm of the game behind. Law is not like that. It is in the nature of legal rules that they are never uniformly obeyed. Even when someone draws a pistol and refuses to obey, the law remains the law. The test of whether a given rule is a valid rule of law cannot be whether or not that rule is uniformly obeyed. If that were the test, then tax law would not be law, criminal law would not be law, and so on.

This basic point was most powerfully made by a veteran of the horrors of the American Civil War, Oliver Wendell Holmes. Holmes, whose tough-minded attitude toward the law impresses all of his readers to this day, insisted that we must think of the law from the point of view of the bad man, not the good man. The good man tends to identify law with morality, and correspondingly he tends to think of the law as a set of imperative rules that must be obeyed. The bad man, by contrast, asks whether he is likely to profit or suffer by following the rules, and he may decide not to do so if he can predict that the courts are unlikely to punish him.[66]

The Holmesian "bad man" view of the law has an important implication, drawn in a variety of ways by contemporary legal scholars. We should think of the law as a system of *incentives*. The law works when it gives people good reasons to follow its rules, and it does not cease to be the law simply because some people, whether wisely or not, refuse to follow the rules. A rule of law counts as a rule of law, on the Holmesian view, because failure to comply with it carries risks, while compliance promises at least potential advantages. The fact that murders are committed does not mean that there is no rule against murder. It means that the law has not succeeded in creating incentives sufficient to discourage all murders.

We must think of the premodern rules of pitched battle as rules of law in this Holmesian sense. There were not rules of a battle game that were scrupulously followed—certainly not in the eighteenth century, and not in earlier periods either. Premodern military commanders were a class of Holmesian bad men if there ever was one. They could be induced to follow the rules only if they were given incentives to do so. Everybody understood that; no one thought that war could be made to comply perfectly with the rules of victory.

In fact it was a commonplace in the Western juristic tradition that it was acceptable to cheat, and when the calculus of incentives encouraged them to cheat, commanders certainly did so. It could hardly be otherwise. The pressures of the situation were extraordinary: the participants faced a terrifying risk of death, while at the same time the potential rewards of victory could be immense, both for commanders and for soldiers. As Bodin said, to go into battle was to "wager a Kingdom." Sudden panics were common, and episodes of berserk rage took place as well. Under such circumstances it is inconceivable that the participants should have tamely and uniformly obeyed the rules, and nobody expected them to do so. It was only in situations where the overwhelming pressures of the battlefield were not present that anyone expected anything like full compliance with the law of victory—situations like the staging of a *Te Deum*.

Nevertheless there *were* rules, even on the battlefield, and eighteenth-century war could be kept within civilized limits because belligerents *did* believe they had incentives to obey those rules some of the time, and even most of the time. In fact the incentives were powerful enough that in the eighteenth century there could be a kind of rule of law.

What incentives were those? In part the law of the eighteenth century was motivated by incentives of a familiar kind: the incentives of reciprocity. Scholars often argue that norms of reciprocity form the foundation of the law of war.[67] Combatants have an incentive to treat their opponents decently, in the hope that they will be treated decently in return. The norms of reciprocity are particularly useful for explaining the success of rules of the jus in bello, as eighteenth-century authors themselves observed. To quote Martens, there were tactics that were "equally destructive for both Powers and therefore senseless as a matter of policy."[68]

But there was more than reciprocity at work in the jus victoriae rules that established who counted as the lawful victor and what counted as lawful spoils and gains. The jus victoriae functions in part by declaring *what you win by winning*, and the incentives at work on eighteenth-century battlefields were of exactly that kind. First of all, there were material incentives. As we have seen, gaining control of the field of battle gave troops a legal right to their booty—a right enforceable in court and much discussed by jurists. It is obvious that this gave individual soldiers an incentive to fight for control of the field of battle—and an incentive to stop fighting once control of the field was secured, since at that point they could begin plundering and stripping corpses.

We have also seen that there were incentives for the commanders. Acquiring the proofs of victory tended to bring wavering powers over to your side, as the *Encyclopédie Méthodique* observed. And as the examples of both Malplaquet and Chotusitz suggest, gaining control of the field of battle made you, at least potentially, the winner in the world of diplomacy, raising the prospect of "procuring a Peace." Eighteenth-century diplomats understood that it was possible, and permissible, to fight a war of annihilation. *Ius belli infinitum*, as the lawyer and diplomat Martens said: in the law of war all is permitted. But in line with the Kriegsmanier of the age, they were prepared to negotiate in ways that gave effect to a technical victory signaled by gaining control of the field of battle after open confrontation. They did not think it was necessary to require proof of victory through utter annihilation.

That meant that gaining control of the field of battle might be quite enough for a commander like Frederick the Great. Why should a shrewd commander take the risk of pursuit when there was a good chance that he could gain what he sought through diplomacy, simply by forcing the enemy to flee? And in the eighteenth century the chances *were* good. That is exactly how the French court analyzed Chotusitz: Frederick, its internal memo declared, had won "a victory so complete that a peace would of necessity follow from it."[69] Frederick, the Holmesian bad man, made a calculation about his incentives and determined that he had good material incentives to follow the standard rule of victory. The only reason that calculation made any sense is because there *was* a rule, even though it was not a rule that Frederick, or any other commander in the heat of battle, was obliged to follow.

Nor were the immediate material incentives the only ones. As the tale of the *Te Deum* of Malplaquet suggests, forcing the enemy to flee, and thus counting as the victor, brought propaganda and morale benefits. Some of the benefits spoke to the most critical need of battle warfare: maintaining the morale and courage of troops. Pitched battles could be fought only if troops would stand their ground. Treating battle as a kind of game fought over control of the field encouraged team morale in war just as it does in sports. As Voltaire and the *Encyclopédie Méthodique* explained, "sustaining the courage of your troops" was achieved partly by leading them to think of themselves and their "teammates" as joining in a contest to win the field of battle. It offered them a meaningful chance at victory without requiring them to accept the increased risk of death that a battle of annihilation would have entailed.

But there were also important morale benefits that had nothing to do with the immediate tactical needs of the battlefield. As the example of Malplaquet dramatically shows, counting as the technical victor mattered for maintaining the pomp and ceremony of princely states, which profited immensely from any opportunity to celebrate a *Te Deum* or commission a victory monument, painting, tapestry, or sculpture. Those were opportunities that accrued to the side that drove the enemy from the field of battle. In turn, maintaining pomp and ceremony mattered for maintaining the political legitimacy of princely states, and as I have argued at length, eighteenth-century warfare was thoroughly bound up with the legitimacy of princely states. Eighteenth-century warfare was the product of a long-term monopolization of legitimate military violence by the sovereign dynasts of Europe, and victory bolstered their legitimacy. We cannot understand the forms of eighteenth-century warfare, including the dominance of the retreat rule, unless we see it within the grander political order founded on state legitimacy.

The Holmesian bad men of eighteenth-century warfare thus had practical jus victoriae incentives for sticking to the rule that gaining control of the field of battle counted as victory. Still, the incentives were merely incentives, and there was no obligation to respond to them. As a result eighteenth-century authors sometimes spoke in ways that seem exceedingly strange to us. For example, the *Encyclopédie* of Diderot and D'Alembert distinguished victory from success in ways that might have been calculated to baffle the modern strategist:

A lost battle is one in which the field of battle is abandoned to the enemy, with the dead and wounded. If the defeated army retreats in good order with its artillery and its baggage, the fruit of the battle is sometimes limited to having tested one's forces against the enemy, and to gaining the field of battle; but if the defeated army is obliged to abandon its cannon, and to retreat in disorder, it is no longer in condition to reappear before the enemy until it has made good its losses. In consequence the victor becomes master of the countryside, and is in a position to undertake sieges. It is this consequence that ordinarily decides the success of battles, of which it is not rare to see the two parties trying to claim the advantage.[70]

From the perspective of modern Clausewitzian analysis this passage seems strange to the point of incoherence. How can victory in battle and success in battle be two different things? What is there *but* success? Why even bother to define a lost battle as "one in which the field of battle is abandoned to the enemy" if the real measure of success had to do with other factors? Yet nobody in the eighteenth century had any difficulty seeing the difference between success and victory. Malplaquet is the classic example: it *was* a success for the French, but it was not a victory.

Other texts said similar things. Driving the enemy from the field counted as a legal victory, and if that was enough for a commander's purposes he might stop there. At the same time it might also be wise to "profit" from the occasion by pushing on to further actions, and nothing in the law could prevent him from trying to so profit.[71] As van Wees says of classical Greek warfare, there was a thing called victory, to be achieved through proofs, and to be "emphatically marked and commemorated." But that did not prevent the Greeks from also seeking to gain military advantage by inflicting "high casualties."[72]

The fact that the rules were not always obeyed does not imply that there were not rules. We must bear that basic truth carefully in mind if we are to understand premodern warfare. We must also bear carefully in mind the distinction between rules of humanitarian law and rules of the law of victory. The modern secondary literature does not distinguish between these two classes of rules, but in fact the controversy is largely a controversy over which of the two classes matters. Scholars who think that war was a game, like Huizinga, Cram, Romilly, and Vernant, are mostly concerned with rules of the jus victoriae. They put the accent on the procedural rules for determining victory, and what they argue is essentially correct, if it is understood as an argument about the rules of the jus victoriae. Even the harshest critics of the game-playing model, such as the Greek historians van Wees and Krentz, acknowledge that jus victoriae rules, and in particular the rule defining victory as gaining control of the field of battle, mattered. In that respect, the rules, as even van Wees acknowledges, were firm.

So if a scholar like van Wees can sometimes observe that the rules were firm, why do he and others protest so loudly against the proposition that war was rule-governed? The straightforward answer is that they tend to conceive of the law of war in modern humanitarian terms, as the law of constraints on warfare, understood as a pestilential evil. They tend to take it for granted that the most important question to ask about the past is whether warriors obeyed rules of the jus in bello— whether, in the words of Neff, warriors obeyed rules designed to "mitigate the horrors of war."[73] This is a tendency encouraged by the leading English-language book on the subject, the 1994 *Laws of War: Constraints on Warfare in the Western World*.[74] That book is a collection of learned and wide-ranging essays, many of whose authors understand, at least implicitly, that there is more to the law of war than the jus in bello. Nevertheless the very title of the book, and often its text, start from the assumption that the problem of the law of war is the problem of *constraining* warfare. It presents itself as a book about "the limitations that Western societies have imposed on themselves in their conduct of war."[75]

And when scholars ask whether there were humanitarian limitations on the conduct of premodern war, they make the unsurprising discovery that there were very few indeed. As van Wees observes, "[With] startling regularity . . . the victor insisted on the complete elimination of the defeated community, massacring of all adult men, enslaving their dependents, and annihilating the town."[76] International Humanitarian Law of the modern kind did not have much purchase in past centuries.

Yet to frame our questions as about limitations, constraints, the jus in bello, or humanitarian considerations is anachronistic. Our ancestors did not necessarily think of war in that way. To be sure, there have always been efforts to establish humanitarian rules, but jus in bello rules did not come to dominate in the law of war until the end of the nineteenth century at the earliest. Much of the time, our ancestors thought of war not as a horror but as a procedure for resolving legal disputes. Much of the time, correspondingly, the correct question to ask about the past is not whether warriors were obedient to jus in bello rules that imposed constraints on warfare. In general, as critics of the game-playing analogy have repeatedly shown, they were not. The correct question to ask is whether they were motivated to obey the rules of the jus victoriae.

But what about the argument that eighteenth-century commanders also had "practical reasons" for the decisions they made? What, for example, about Black's argument that pursuit created the "danger of the units becoming less coherent, or even disintegrating through desertion"? Even if it looks like commanders were following the rules, is it not possible that they were actually motivated, as so many historians insist, by such considerations—by tactics rather than by conventions? The answer is yes, in a sense. Of course commanders had practical reasons for obeying the rules. But it is essential to recognize that that does not mean the rules were not rules.

Here again, it is difficult to do good military history without working through a bit of the philosophy of law. The fact that we have practical reasons for following a rule does not imply that it is not a rule. To think otherwise is to adopt a very naïve conception of the law. When scholars suppose that commanders must have considered *either* tactics *or* conventions, they start from the assumption that something only counts as law if it is prohibitory, if it forbids us from doing what we want to do or instinctively tend to do. They think of all law as though it were criminal law, in the business of forbidding acts. And of course, some law *is* in the business of forbidding. This is notably true of the modern law of war, whose principal aim is to forbid warriors from engaging in criminal or near-criminal acts.

But thoughtful legal scholars recognize that most law is not prohibi-tory but facilitative. Most law creates a framework that allows us to coop-erate with others and to make our way in a world in which we must have some sense, in advance, of how others will conduct themselves. Max Weber gave us one of the most elegant statements of this point: the law organizes social action, allowing us to orient ourselves toward the pre-dictable behavior of others. We must be able to understand the meaning and judge the intent of the actions of those with whom we transact. The law makes it possible for us to do so by establishing frameworks for ac-tion.[77] For example, it would be impossible to enter into contracts unless the law dictated what kind of conduct constituted an offer and what kind of conduct constituted an acceptance. In defining certain kinds of con-duct as offer and acceptance, the object of the law is not to forbid us from doing something we desire to do. Its purpose is not to establish a con-vention that runs counter to our tactical interests. It acts to *further* our collective interest, facilitating the process of contracting by laying down mandatory ground rules—and without contracting we would live in a world of theft, barter, and raiding. If the law stymied our practical needs, it would fail of its purpose. Modern legal philosophers make similar points: most of the time, the law is not something that forbids us from act-ing. Most of the time the law facilitates our cooperation, so that we can achieve our practical ends.[78] As H. L. A. Hart, the pioneer of modern Anglo-American legal philosophy, puts it, much of the law is made up not just of duty-imposing rules but of "power-conferring" rules, "rules for determining who has, and how they may exercise, the power to form contracts, acquire and dispose of property, initiate lawsuits, marry," and so on.[79]

The same is true of the premodern law of victory. The retreat rule conferred upon commanders a kind of power: if they drove the enemy from the field of battle, they could declare victory. Rather than prohib-iting some form of quasi-criminal behavior, the law offered them an opportunity to profit, provided that they followed the rule. It is not an accident that Pufendorf regarded the law of war as a branch of contract law. It was in the interest of all the parties to accept conventions that defined victory in ways that stopped short of annihilation. Battles of an-nihilation are hugely risky, for both sides, for all ranks, and for society in general; so are raids. Far better for all involved to establish clear conventions that allow combatants to keep war within the limits of a combat wager. Far better to have a rule that spares everybody on both sides the dangers of a pursuit. Far better to have a rule that allows you to declare victory early on, while maintaining the coherence and the morale of your troops.

Of course the law of victory served the practical needs of the belligerents in the eighteenth century (and in earlier centuries). In particular there is plenty of evidence that Black is right: pursuit did create a danger of disintegration. Frederick said so himself.[80] It was in his interest to follow the retreat rule. But that does not mean that the retreat rule was not law. It means that it was law well-adapted to its purposes. As the Marquis de Valori explained, "the design [Frederick] had to make a peace" could be achieved without his taking the risk of pursuit.[81] That was true only because the law declared that conquering the field of battle counted as a victory, and while no commander was obligated to follow the rule, in the end they generally did. As a result, the law succeeded in encouraging a culture of limited warfare.

The law of victory was power-conferring law, law that steered conduct by offering incentives, while doing little to prohibit misconduct. Perhaps the most revealing way to illustrate how this form of law functioned is to examine the law of trickery. Krentz makes what may seem a sensible argument: there cannot have been rules in premodern warfare, since trickery was permitted.[82] Yet careful thinking about the nature of law paints a different picture.

It is especially revealing to contrast the treatment of trickery in the premodern law of war with the treatment of trickery in the premodern law of homicide. The law of war and the law of homicide were often closely related in premodern legal analysis. Both involved killing, and for that reason jurists, especially Christian ones, often saw both as raising the same sorts of problems. In particular both bodies of law turned, in part, on the distinction between killing by trickery and killing in open confrontation. Yet the two bodies of law treated the distinction in strikingly different ways.

Let us begin with homicide. The premodern law of homicide, unlike the modern law of homicide, did not necessarily condemn all forms of killing. It typically treated killing through trickery as a kind of foul crime, to be harshly penalized. Killing in open confrontation, by contrast, was not infrequently tolerated. Indeed it was often respected: killing a man openly, in direct confrontation in a public place, was not in itself a dishonorable act, at least as long as it stemmed from an honorable motive; those who committed open killings were often pardoned or otherwise left unmolested.[83] Consequently early criminal prohibitions on murder tended not to be outright prohibitions on killing but prohibitions on killing through trickery. (This very old attitude still survives in the wording of some American homicide statutes, which define first-degree murder as murder "by means of poison, or by lying in wait.") What the law reprobated was not killing, but sneaking. The same attitude colored thinking about dueling. Vattel simply presented the accepted wisdom when he declared that war permitted trickery, whereas dueling required "open" killing.

But war *did* permit trickery, and that is a revealing fact. If jurists had been fully able to subject war to their ordinary scheme of prohibitions, they would presumably have banned trickery outright. They did not. From the earliest date they declared trickery, considered reprehensible in ordinary forms of killing, to be permissible in the large-scale killing of war. In fact trickery figured prominently in the literary and legal traditions of Western warfare, as the classic example of Odysseus and the Trojan horse suggests. Gregory Nagy has interpreted the Homeric tradition precisely as a meditation on the contrast between Achilles, the "open" killer, and Odysseus, the trickster.[84] Both of their approaches were presumptively legitimate. "Homeric warriors happily deceived their enemies," Krentz writes. Nor does it end with Homer. "Classical warfare is full of deceptions. . . . A desperate, or daring commander might, like Peisistratos in 546, attack during the afternoon siesta (Hdt. 1.63). And if the risks could be minimized, even a Lakedaimonian king might attack a camp during a meal."[85] The Greeks even celebrated a festival called the *Apatouria*, which honored a piece of combat trickery.[86] The traditional toleration of trickery influenced just war thinking. "If the war is just, " wrote Augustine, "the question of justice is unaffected by whether it is fought openly or through trickery."[87] The same tradition produced a large body of military literature on ruses or "stratagems," as they were called.[88] As for the Roman jurists, they had a tradition of calling trickery in war *dolus bonus*, "good trickery," by contrast with the "bad trickery" in other sorts of legal transactions.[89]

To be sure, trickery was sometimes frowned upon. "A victory won through trickery," said Isidore, "is shameful."[90] Nevertheless trickery in at least some forms remained routinely accepted in early modern warfare. It could hardly be otherwise in a Western tradition that included texts like Joshua 8. As a 1692 dissertation writer observed, "GOD himself ordered Joshua to set traps for the people of Ai, *Jos. 8:2*, and told David to attack the Philistines from behind, *2. Sam. 5: 23*."[91] If God himself endorsed trickery of all sorts—including, let us note, coming up on the enemy from behind (what in Napoleonic warfare would be called "la manoeuvre sur les derrières")—how could man reject it?

These attitudes were entirely alive in the law of the eighteenth century. Wolff, for example, declared that it was appropriate, and indeed imperative, to use stratagems—though not, as the jurists always declared, to the extent of perfidy. It was essential that commanders keep their word once given.[92] Vattel's passage on the questions deserves to be quoted again:

> Some nations (even the Romans) for a long time professed to despise every kind of artifice, surprise, or stratagem in war; and others went so far as to send notice of the time and place they had chosen for battle. In this conduct there was more generosity than prudence. Such behavior would, indeed, be very laudable, if, as in the frenzy of duels, the only business was to display personal courage. But in war the object is to defend our country, and by force to prosecute our rights which are unjustly withheld from us: and the surest means of obtaining this are also the most commendable provided they be not unlawful and odious in themselves.[93]

Vattel was certainly aiming to bring a measure of civilization to his discussion, condemning practices that were "unlawful and odious,"[94] but in essence his treatment of trickery differed little from what was said in earlier centuries.

As the toleration of trickery suggests, the strategy of the law in controlling warfare was different from the strategy of the law in controlling homicide. Rather than *prohibiting* trickery, the law set out to *encourage* honorable, open warfare. Thus eighteenth-century jurists, like the ancients,[95] always insisted that it was "more glorious and honest" to fight an open battle; and the example of Chotusitz and many other battles shows that an open victory did in fact count for more. If the jurists did not follow the law of homicide in prohibiting trickery, they did follow the law of homicide in attempting to facilitate open confrontation.

So it was that Vattel declared that even though trickery was acceptable, "when plain and open courage can secure the victory . . . it procures to the state a greater and more permanent advantage."[96] Many other authors said the same thing—for example, de Réal: "Open force is without a doubt the most natural, most noble, and most legitimate means of doing harm to the enemy, but artifice is not illicit in war."[97] As so often, it is in the world of eighteenth-century diplomacy that we can really trace the effects of this preference for open confrontation. As we saw in the case of Chotusitz, diplomats were prepared to move to the stage of a final and binding treaty settlement on the basis of an open victory that consisted only in driving the enemy off the field. Though the hold of the rules was never fully secure, capturing the field of battle counted as "the incontestable Trophy of Victory," and the civilization of the eighteenth century was prepared to accept that.

There *were* rules in eighteenth-century war. Indeed in the last analysis there was a kind of rule of law. This may seem a paradoxical claim. Invading a neighbor without warning in order to "maintain rights" is, to our minds, inherently lawless, and by most standard definitions, eighteenth-century warfare displayed anything but rule of law. This is not just because trickery was permitted. Eighteenth-century wars were wars of "self-help," in the language of lawyers: they were violent actions, undertaken unilaterally by princes, without the sanction of any court. As Pufendorf put it, a prince, being subject to the jurisdiction of no court, could make war simply "on the basis of his own judgment . . . avenging injuries by his own power [and] claiming rights due to him by the use of violence."[98]

Can any such system, any system founded on a unilateral right of violent self-help, really be said to have a rule of law? Kant certainly did not think so. It was outrageous, he wrote in 1795, that princes should regard themselves as the judges of their own causes and therefore permit themselves to enforce their rights through the devastation of war.[99] Only some sort of league of nations, he maintained, could bring the rule of law to the world of war.

Kant is by no means the only figure who would deny that eighteenth-century war can be regarded as having a rule of law. International relations realists would say much the same thing. Hans Morgenthau insists in his standard text that "when nation [is set] against nation in deadly conflict," it is because there is no consensus about the law and no court to resolve matters.[100] The very fact that the parties resort to force rather than to a court with effective jurisdiction demonstrates that the law has failed. Force and law are profoundly opposed, two utterly contrary ways of managing human affairs. From the point of view of modern international relations, just as from the point of view of Kantian philosophy, there was nothing that qualified as a rule of law in the practice of eighteenth-century warfare.

Nor is it easy to claim that there was a rule of law in eighteenth-century warfare under the definitions of modern international law. To be sure, modern international lawyers reject the proposition that there must be a court with effective supranational jurisdiction before we can speak of international *law*. Even in the absence of supranational sovereigns, they maintain, international affairs may be governed by something called "international customary law." But they hold that international customary law can be said to exist only in certain limited circumstances: "By definition, a customary rule must have two distinct elements: (1) a material element defined by *systematic practice* over time; and (2) a psychological element, the *opinio juris* or evidence that states regard the practice as a legal obligation."[101] Eighteenth-century warfare certainly satisfied the first of these two conditions. As we have seen, the restraint of eighteenth-century warfare was very much a "systematic practice," and a startlingly successful one. But it would hardly be easy to claim that it satisfied the second.

After all, commanders like Frederick the Great vocally denied that they had any obligation to conduct limited warfare. They expressly disclaimed any *opinio juris*. Nor is this true only of battlefield commanders. The same was true of a sovereign like Maria Theresa. Even after agreeing to the Peace of Breslau, she remained entirely unwilling to accept the verdict of Chotusitz, and she fought for decades to undo the consequences of her defeat. Within a few years, she renewed the conflict in Silesia; fifteen years later, she initiated the Seven Years War in the hope of undoing the Peace.[102] To be sure, eighteenth-century jurists objected to the sort of attitude she displayed. Like modern lawyers, they insisted that a legal claim that had been settled by victory and incorporated in a peace treaty could never be reopened.[103] "It is breaking the peace to start a war again over the same subject," declared Wolff.[104] "The effect of a treaty is to put an end to the war and abolish the subject," said Vattel.[105] Nevertheless subsequent wars, like the Seven Years War, could and did break out, and so it is hard to characterize these declarations of the jurists as anything but impotent preaching.

It would also be difficult to argue that there was a rule of law by the measure of modern legal sociology. Sociologists insist that there is only rule of law if the losing parties accept the adverse results of a decision. As Tom Tyler puts it in his classic book, *Why People Obey the Law*, "A judge's ruling means little if the parties to the dispute feel they can ignore it."[106] It is only if the parties submit, and cease fighting, that the law has succeeded. But of course, Maria Theresa did not submit.

Yet for all that, when we step back and consider the big picture of eighteenth-century continental war, it is impossible to mistake what we see: something that does indeed look very much like a rule of law. There is obvious truth in the description of the eighteenth century given by Eric Robson: "Though there were great wars, devastation and unnecessary bloodshed were kept in check by strict adherence to the rules, customs and laws of war, the accepted code of the eighteenth-century war game."[107] Eighteenth-century commanders really did play by the rules, even if they consistently denied that they were obligated to do so. There really was a systematic practice of civilized warfare, and one that lawyers have not ceased admiring since. If our standard definitions of "rule of law" do not capture the practice of eighteenth-century warfare, it must be because there is something amiss in our standard definitions.

So how should we describe the eighteenth-century rule of law in war that so manifestly existed?

First of all, we should describe it in classic Weberian terms: there was rule of law in eighteenth-century warfare because there was a well-established culture of legitimate princely authority, associated with a firm monopolization of violence. Societies with a culture of established authority are often societies at relative peace. Eighteenth-century warfare was fought in a culture of established sovereign authority, first and foremost princely authority. It was fought in a world in which established states of unquestioned legitimacy had succeeded in stamping out private violence. To be sure, there was more than one prince, and princes sometimes jostled for primacy and position. That is why, as a matter of law, they fought wars. Nevertheless the legitimacy of dynastic monarchy was mostly secure until the end of the century. Indeed the very forms and law of war embodied and symbolized the legitimate authority. That is why it is so important to insist that (princely) war was categorically different from (aristocratic) dueling.

Moreover even if eighteenth-century commanders and sovereigns admitted to no *opinio iuris*, in practice the law succeeded in establishing a system of incentives such that they did comply in the aggregate. No, Frederick was not obligated to restrict himself to gaining the field of battle, but the law of victory gave him an incentive to stop once he had won what his contemporaries deemed a complete victory, sufficient to procure a peace. That meant that he could decline to press on with the more dangerous and destructive warfare of annihilation. In particular it meant that he had no need to fight risky wars of devastation in order to achieve diplomatic recognition of his conquest. The accepted rules—*les idées communes*, as Mauvillon put it—permitted him to succeed without requiring a Sherman-like March to the Sea or a Moltke-like campaign of siege and burning. Those rules did not dictate Frederick's conduct. He could have acted differently, as his French allies angrily observed.

But the rules gave him reason enough to contain himself within the norms of limited battle warfare.

By the same token, though Maria Theresa challenged his victory, she too followed the rules of the law of victory in doing so. It was victory in the open confrontation of pitched battle that promised the sort of legal results that could be enshrined in a treaty. As a result, the Seven Years War, Maria Theresa's greatest effort at undoing the loss of Silesia, continued to take the form of battle warfare, and Frederick's success in fighting off her challenge was a success in the fighting of pitched battles. (It is striking that during the Seven Years War, Frederick was not deemed a loser despite the fact that his capital, Berlin, was occupied by his opponents more than once. Even the loss of his capital city was not what mattered. Battlefield victory was.) The rules did not dictate the conduct of war, but they did shape both the conduct of war and the consequences. In that sense too there was something that it is entirely right to call rule of law.

Not least, the eighteenth-century law of victory succeeded in resolving conflicts and establishing rights. The culture of limited battle warfare of the eighteenth century ultimately yielded remarkably durable legal results. The legal and diplomatic culture that produced treaties like the Treaty of Breslau was a culture that produced many enduring peaces—many more than subsequent periods would produce. The bottom line is that the battles of the eighteenth century, while in principle always subject to challenge, in practice *did* prove decisive—not only at Chotusitz but at clashes like Yorktown.

And that, finally, suggests a larger conclusion: decisions made by law prove more decisive than decisions made by force, whatever Clausewitz may have believed to the contrary. This was a truth in the eighteenth century, and it is a truth that we can still witness today. One need consider only the breakup of the Soviet Union. Soviet military conquests proved completely evanescent after fifty years. But Soviet legal decisions, such as the decision to maintain nominally independent states in Belarus and Georgia, and the decision to cede the Crimea to Ukraine, are proving remarkably, almost weirdly durable. Law lasts; force does not. The law of battles introduced an admixture of law into the world of eighteenth-century force—enough of an admixture that the results of victory had, in the aggregate, considerable staying power.

That said, the law of victory was not enough to transform warfare into a wholly controlled or wholly decisive business in the eighteenth century. Such is always the fate of international law and of the law of war in particular. But the law of victory was quite enough to make eighteenth-century warfare *more* controlled and *more* decisive than what came either before or after, and that is what counts.

CHAPTER 6

The Death of Pitched Battle

There is a fine, invisible thread connecting the success that we as-
cribe to luck and the genius of the commander. . . . For that reason, luck in war seems to have a much nobler nature than luck in
gambling.

Clausewitz, *Vom Kriege*

T HE SUN OF THE 1ST SEPTEMBER," reported the *Quarterly Review* in
October 1870, "rose on perhaps the greatest event of modern
history."

> To describe the battle of Sedan is beyond our province; and the
> daily papers have supplied the public with all the thrilling incidents
> of which their intrepid correspondents were the observers. It must
> suffice to say that the Germans enveloped the French position on all
> sides. . . . The battle had commenced at five in the morning, and at
> five in the afternoon the apparition of a French general waving a flag
> on the summit of the parapet of Sedan announced to the Germans
> their astonishing victory. . . . The Emperor, who during four hours
> appears to have courted death in the thickest press of the battle, sent
> an aide-de-camp to the King of Prussia with the note following:—
> "My brother, having failed to die at the head of my troops, I lay my
> sword at the feet of Your Majesty.—NAPOLÉON."[1]

The *Quarterly Review* was by no means the only European journal to
declare the Battle of Sedan "the greatest event of modern history." Many
reports used similar phrases: "one of the most decisive and momentous

victories in universal history"[2] and the like. Even King Wilhelm I of Prussia, a man who generally had a pedestrian way with words, was quoted in the German newspapers pronouncing the battle a "world-historical act."[3] September 2, "Sedan Day," would be feted for two generations thereafter as the founding day of the German Second Empire. Where Americans dated their founding moment to July 4, the date of the promulgation of a legal document, and the French dated their founding moment to July 14, the date of a popular insurrection in the streets of Paris, the Germans of the Second Empire would date their founding moment to the occasion of a pitched battle: the day when their "world-historical" battlefield victory forced the surrender of Napoleon III.

It was a textbook victory, one that represented an almost unparalleled triumph of battlefield tactics. Sedan is one of the rare examples in military history of a successful encirclement: as all Germans knew, Moltke, in the words of the Prussian novelist Theodor Fontane, "drew the great circle around Sedan."[4] Encirclement can yield a type of utter military victory that is impossible to achieve by frontal assault. That was the kind of victory achieved by Hannibal over the Romans at the most famous battle of encirclement, Cannae, and it was the kind of victory that Moltke achieved as well. Indeed the surrender of the entire French army at Sedan, along with the surrender of other French forces, ultimately left more than 300,000 prisoners of war in German hands.[5] Frederick the Great himself had never achieved victory on any such scale, and Moltke's tactics would remain the model for German strategists for decades.

Yet this "world-historical act" proved incapable of ending the Franco-Prussian War. Exemplary though the Prussian victory was, its verdict was not accepted by the French populace. News of the defeat was met by angry demonstrations in Paris, which the police struggled to quell. There were angry speeches in the Chamber of Deputies too, where the republican leader Jules Favre demanded a *résistance à l'outrance*, a resistance without limits. Within days Emperor Napoleon III was declared deposed, and a French republic had been declared; over the next months, forces of popular resistance were organized, among them the notorious *franc-tireurs*, French irregular snipers.[6] The battlefield victory at Sedan gave way to months of frustrating, bitter, and nasty irregular warfare, and the Prussians found themselves engaged in an ugly, amorphous conflict in which they had to treat the enemy as criminals while abandoning what they thought of as honorable forms of combat.[7] Instead of winning the war on the battlefield, they were obliged to win it through counterinsurgency and the bombardment of French cities.

Sedan was a model tactical victory, but it failed to terminate its war. Something similar happened in the American Civil War, fought several years earlier. American battles were not the high displays of military art seen in Europe in the period. There was no Prussian army and no Moltke in America; the victories of the Civil War were not textbook demonstrations. Instead they were pounding frontal clashes, better remembered today for the suffering of their soldiers than for the genius of their generals.

Nevertheless there *were* victories. But as was the case in the Franco-Prussian War, these victories did not have the effects that memories of the eighteenth century suggested they should have had. To begin with, battlefield victory, to the disappointment of the Confederacy, no longer brought the kind of diplomatic success it brought in the tidy age of Frederick the Great. A victory in the open confrontation of an eighteenth-century battle could be translated into a diplomatic triumph; such was the experience at Denain and Chotusitz. Such, for that matter, was the experience in the eighteenth-century beginnings of modern American history. It was victory in the Battle of Saratoga that brought the turning point in the early fortunes of American Revolution, achieving French recognition of American independence in 1777. It was victory at Yorktown in 1781 that brought decisive independence,[8] given diplomatic effect in the Treaty of Paris in 1783.

When the American Civil War began, there was every expectation that victory in battle would still have the same consequences. "[T]he secessionists of 1776," as James McPherson writes, "got what they hoped for after the battle of Saratoga: French recognition of the fledgling United States." "The secessionists of 1861" hoped for the same: diplomatic recognition was "the principal goal of Confederate foreign policy," and victory on the battlefield was expected to achieve it. Yet as McPherson writes in his essay "The Saratoga That Wasn't," one Confederate battlefield victory after another failed to achieve the hoped-for effect. The Second Battle of Bull Run in particular was a sparkling victory that once might have earned recognition, but now no longer carried the diplomatic day.[9] Contrary to the expectations on both sides, the rules had changed since 1781.

Nor of course was it only British and French diplomats who refused to accept the verdict of battle. The same proved true of the Americans themselves. When the war began, the universal expectation was that pitched battle would decide it—that, again in McPherson's words, the conflict would be resolved through "prompt, signal [and] decisive" battles.[10] So it was that the opening engagement of the war at First Bull Run attracted a characteristic mid-nineteenth-century phenomenon: battle tourists eager to witness history in the making.

Battle tourists appeared at every mid-nineteenth-century conflict from the Crimean War on. They often arrived in fine dress, in coaches, with servants and picnic baskets. In an age when pitched battles were regarded as "world-historical events," people wanted to be present to see them. Henri Dunant, for example, the founder of the Red Cross, started out as just such a battle tourist. He came to Solferino in order to witness history in the making, and his account of the battle began in the ordinary rip-snorting fashion of a battle tourist memoir. Only some fifteen pages into his text did Dunant begin to notice, and bewail, the horrors of the battlefield. The Battle of Sedan too was heavily attended by battle tourists, many of whom volunteered to serve as Red Cross nurses in order to witness the great event.

In the American Civil War, too, battle tourists arrived in numbers, expecting to watch a world-historical pitched battle settle the dispute between the North and the South.[11] Of course, they were disappointed. Contrary to the expectations of Washington and Richmond society, no quick and decisive resolution was achieved through open confrontation on the battlefield. Instead, like the Franco-Prussian War, the Civil War degenerated into a war of raiding and ravaging, an American *guerre à l'outrance*.

Irregular warfare took the American stage just as it took the European stage. Already in April 1862, the Confederate Congress took an unprecedented step, passing the Partisan Ranger Act, which authorized the issuance of commissions to Southerners who engaged in irregular warfare. To the anger of Northern military men, these commissions gave Confederate irregulars the status of formal combatants under the law of war, thus immunizing them from treatment as criminals.[12] As a result, the North faced a war of raids. The North too took to irregular warfare, of course, and in the end the American conflict, like the Franco-Prussian conflict, could be decided only by Sherman's campaign of devastation.

The Franco-Prussian War and the American Civil War are the two most famous examples of a phenomenon that surprised and pained contemporaries. Despite the expectations of battle tourists, despite the widespread conviction that great battles were world-historical events, despite the brilliance of Prussian tactics, wars could no longer be resolved through pitched battle.

The American Civil War and the Franco-Prussian War thus marked the end of classic battle warfare. This was a development for which contemporaries were unprepared. If the demise of battle warfare came as a surprise to contemporaries, though, historians can see that it had been coming since the late eighteenth century.

We can detect the beginning of the decline of eighteenth-century battle warfare in the American Revolution. It is true that the Americans ultimately won their independence through orderly eighteenth-century battle (and orderly eighteenth-century siege) at Saratoga and Yorktown, and the Founding Fathers were vocal about their commitment to the civilized law of war of the eighteenth century.[13] Nevertheless much of the time the American rebels, who were, after all, amateurs facing disciplined British troops, avoided formal battle. Instead they pioneered what, by the early nineteenth century, would become notorious as the *guerrilla*, the "little war." That is to say, they avoided the kind of open confrontation encouraged by the eighteenth-century law of war, preferring instead to revert to the sort of raiding that had predominated in the warfare of previous centuries.

The style of irregular warfare adopted by America's farmer rebels shocked and angered the British. As a British official complained, the Americans "avoid facing you in the open field." "Never," wrote another British officer, "had the British Army so ungenerous an enemy to oppose: they send their riflemen five or six at a time who conceal themselves behind trees etc till an opportunity presents itself of taking a shot at our advance sentries, which done they immediately retreat. What an unfair method of carrying on a war!"[14] From the point of view of eighteenth-century civilization, hiding behind a bush and shooting enemy soldiers, as the Americans did and as the French franc-tireurs would do, was not proper war at all. It was something dangerously close to murder. The Americans were only the first to engage in this revival of raiding; guerrillas of this kind would be fought in the Napoleonic period, most famously in Spain. A guerrilla would also be fought in the least-remembered of American military actions, the Mexican-American War of 1846–1848.[15]

The brushfires of guerrilla thus began burning in the late eighteenth century, and it is fair to say that the culture of battle warfare was already breaking down. But the breakdown was not immediately obvious to contemporaries, and it is essential to recognize that the emergence of the little war did not instantaneously transform warfare. On the contrary, the mysterious truth about the nineteenth century is that pitched battle did not vanish for a full three generations after the outbreak of the American Revolution.

Right down until the American Civil War and the Franco-Prussian War pitched battles, and to some extent sieges, continued to be the great deciding events. This was true of the Napoleonic Wars and even of a chaotic conflict like the Crimean War. It was true of battles like Magenta and Solferino, which pitted Napoleon III against the Austrians in the late 1850s in the conflict over Italian unification. Perhaps most strikingly, it was true of the Seven Weeks War between Austria and Prussia, contemporaneous with the American Civil War but decided in a dramatically different way. The Seven Weeks War was precisely the sort of conflict that the society folk of Richmond and Washington expected in 1861: a quick and clean war, resolved by "prompt, signal [and] decisive" battles.[16] In particular it was a war resolved by the last of the fully decisive battles in Western history: Königgrätz, fought in Bohemia, only a short distance from Chotusitz, in 1866. Unlike Gettysburg or Sedan, Königgrätz produced a verdict that was fully accepted by the defeated Austrians.

But if Königgrätz was possible in Central Europe, it was not possible in America or France. In these Atlantic countries it became clear that "the era of decisive battles," as Keegan writes, "was drawing to a close."[17] The problem, then, is ultimately a problem about mid-nineteenth century

America and France. What happened to cause battle warfare to collapse in the Atlantic world of the 1860s and 1870s?

Let us begin with what did not happen. The collapse of pitched battle was not the result either of technological change or of a supposed decline of aristocratic dueling culture.

It may seem natural to suppose that the technological advances of the nineteenth century were the underlying cause of the collapse of classic battle warfare. After all, there are few periods in human history during which the transformative social consequences of technological change have been felt as profoundly as in the nineteenth century. Yet technological change cannot account for the failure of pitched battle in the mid-nineteenth century. A truly transformative technological change would have made it impossible to stage the open confrontation of classic pitched battle at all. Such was the consequence of the mass introduction of the machine gun in World War I, which drove troops on the Western Front into the trenches, making open confrontation a physical impossibility. But the technological changes that had accumulated by the mid-nineteenth century did not yet have such dramatic effects.

For a long time, military historians ascribed the transformation of war in the mid-nineteenth century to a major shift in weaponry, the transition from muskets to rifles. Rifles had existed since the sixteenth century as hunting weapons, but prior to the nineteenth century they were difficult to employ in battle, since their rifled barrels could only be loaded slowly. The American rebels made use of their hunting rifles in the Revolution as part of the uncivilized guerrilla warfare that shocked the British, but rifles did not yet establish themselves in regular armies. The mass introduction of rifles into warfare was made possible by two technological advances. The first was the invention of the minié ball, a soft lead projectile that would pass quickly and easily down a rifled barrel and that came into use with the Crimean War. The second was the development of breech loading of the kind still used in modern firearms. One such breech-loader, the Prussian needle gun, proved critical to victory in the Seven Weeks War; another, the French chassepot, significantly superior to the needle gun, was in use by the late 1860s. Americans did not possess weapons of European sophistication during the Civil War; nevertheless they too used rifled weapons in battle as the conflict evolved.

The period when battle warfare lost its decisiveness was thus the first age of the usable rifle, and it may seem natural to suppose that it was rifling that caused the great transformation. Yet in recent years American Civil War historians such as Paddy Griffith, Brent Nosworthy, and Earl Hess have rejected this argument.[18] The use of rifles, they have shown, did not change the basic pattern of Civil War battle tactics. Despite technological advances in rifling, combatants continued to confront each other much as their predecessors had done in the age of muskets, and battles were not more lethal than eighteenth-century battles had been. The troops were not driven into the trenches in the way they would be in World War I,[19] and the classic pattern of open confrontation did not vanish. Hess wisely concludes that the Civil War was the grinding affair it was not because of the technological advance represented by rifling but because of the "political determination on the part of civilians and government alike to see the endeavor through to its bitter conclusion."[20] The problem was not that battles could not physically be staged; the problem was that, once staged, they failed to resolve their war.

Rifles may seem like transformative technical innovations, but close study of American Civil War battles suggests that politics, not technology, is what mattered. The same is clearly true of continental European warfare. Prussian and French troops carried the most superbly effective rifles of the day, but their possession of those weapons did not prevent them from staging "prompt, signal" pitched battles at Solferino, König-grätz, or Sedan. Like the Americans in the Civil War, they did not find themselves condemned to fighting trench warfare; it is manifestly false to claim that pitched battles had become technologically impossible. At Sedan as in the American Civil War, the shift lay, to echo Hess's words, "in the political determination on the part of civilians and government alike to see the endeavor through to its bitter conclusion."[21] What was at stake was not the technology, the mechanics of the violence, but the politics, the perception of what victory signified, and whether a battlefield defeat was enough to justify surrender.

The same can be said of other technological and quasi-technological shifts. Railroads came into use for the movement of troops and made a major contribution to the war efforts of the Union army and of the Prussians. But railroads did not make battles like Gettysburg or Königgrätz impossible. Neither did the increase in the size of the forces engaged. The latter is the shift to which Keegan has most recently pointed in his own military history of the American Civil War. "The era of decisive battles [drew] to a close," Keegan writes, because combatants "enlarg[ed] the size of their armies to a point at which it became difficult, if not impossible, to dispose of them in a single passage of fighting."[22] Yet at Sedan the Prussians *did* dispose of the French army in a single passage of fighting. Similar things can be said of Solferino, Magenta, and Königgrätz, just as similar things can be said of the Napoleonic battles at Austerlitz and Leipzig. The size of the armies involved did not make it technologically impossible to fight the battles of the nineteenth century. On the contrary, much of what made Sedan such an "astonishing victory" was the sheer size of the French forces that surrendered. Pitched battles like Gettysburg and Sedan did not fail because it had become technologically impossible to fight them; they failed because the general population would no longer accept their verdict.

Technology cannot explain the shift. Neither can the familiar argument that the transformation of the mid-nineteenth century resulted from the breakdown of aristocratic chivalry. Scholars, as we have seen, are accustomed to claiming that the restrained warfare of the eighteenth century was chivalric warfare, a form of aristocratic dueling, governed by aristocratic class consciousness. As Schmitt wrote in 1961, warfare could remain contained only "as long as war continued to contain something of the idea of a duel with open weapons and a chivalric ethos."[23]

Yet we have seen that to call the battle warfare of the eighteenth century a form of aristocratic dueling is to obscure the most important legal fact about it: the right to make war was reserved to sovereigns. An eighteenth-century battle was not a duel but the last surviving form of trial by combat, and nobles, far from playing the role of the heroes of civilized warfare, were the villains in every eighteenth-century legal account. That is only part of the story, though; when we turn to the nineteenth century, we find the very opposite of a collapse of the dueling ethos. The ironic truth is that the nineteenth century, far from being the period when the chivalric, dueling idea of war went into decline, was the period when that idea was born and triumphed.

The notion that restrained warfare is a form of chivalric or aristocratic dueling is a characteristic product of the Age of Romanticism, of the early nineteenth-century passion for the romance of the Middle Ages. It is an expression in law of the same fantasy world of chivalry to be found in the novels of Sir Walter Scott, the troubadour paintings of Ingres and Delacroix, and medieval romance operas like Wagner's *Tannhäuser* and *Lohengrin*. It first took hold in the reaction against the persecution of aristocrats in the French Revolution, and it gained adherents throughout the early decades of the century as military men and lawyers were drawn into the general cult of medieval chivalry just as *littérateurs*, painters, and composers were. Statesmen were drawn in too, and they began to offer the point of honor as a justification for war in a way that their eighteenth-century predecessors never did.

As we saw earlier, eighteenth-century jurists generally took a jaundiced view of medieval nobles, and they did not spend time praising the supposed beauties of chivalric warfare. There were inklings of a different view among figures like Robertson and Gibbon, but they had no obvious impact on thinking about the law. It was only in 1795, in the midst of the reaction against the French Revolution, that a technical work on law first appeared promoting the now familiar idea of the noble, chivalric law of war. This was the *Enquiry into the Foundation and History of the Law of Nations in Europe, from the Time of the Greeks and Romans to the Age of Grotius*, by a colorful lawyer and sometime novelist named Robert Plumer Ward.

Ward was a man who had a terrifying direct experience of the French Revolution. In 1790, after completing his legal studies, the young Ward went to France in search of a cure for an ailing knee. Far from finding a cure, as his biographer reports, he barely escaped death in the Terror: "It happened, unfortunately for him, that another 'Ward,' of about the same age and personal appearance, had incurred the suspicion of the republican party at a moment when suspicion lost all its doubts, and death followed close upon the heels of certainty. To use his own words, 'I was arrested for having the same name, and the same coloured coat and waistcoat as another Ward, guilty of treason; was ordered without trial to Paris, to be guillotined; and only escaped by their catching the real traitor.'" One does not know whether the story of Ward's close call, published in 1850, influenced *A Tale of Two Cities*, published by rival novelist Dickens nine years later. At any rate, upon returning to England, the young Ward became an impassioned opponent of the Revolution, bringing himself to the attention of Prime Minister Pitt and Lord Eldon in 1794 by denouncing a supposed republican plot.[24] In the summer of 1795 he composed his *Enquiry*, with its long chapter on "the influence of chivalry." The inspiration for Ward's chapter was clear enough from a passage in which he lavished praise on the ideals of French medieval chivalry: "A man, writing in these times, cannot but advert to the sad change which the manners and maxims of war of this once generous people [i.e., the French] have almost in a moment undergone. Some future investigator of our subject will possibly in other centuries have to remark, that at the close of eighteenth century, when the Convention of France had boasted that it had got the start of the rest of Europe by 2000 years in refinement and knowledge, it passed a decree by which every English and Hanoverian prisoner should be put to death."[25] This lucky English escapee from the guillotine, like many others in the middle years of the 1790s, saw the destruction of the ancien régime as a murderous folly, and as many others would do in subsequent decades, Ward became an idealizer of the "manners and maxims" of the medieval nobility.

To be sure, like the eighteenth-century authors who preceded him, Ward had to acknowledge the brutality of war, and life, in the Middle Ages. Scholars had amply demonstrated that medieval nobles were a thuggish class. But this did not prevent Ward from touting the "influence of chivalry" on the law of war. As we have seen, previous eighteenth-century authors all understood the diminution of violence since the Middle Ages to be the product of a sovereign monopolization of violence: princes had gradually put an end to the private wars of the nobility and so brought a civilized peace to Europe. Ward had little patience with that eighteenth-century view of the law of war. The truth, he insisted, was that the civilization of warfare sprang not from the efforts of kings but from within the maligned nobility itself. "CHIVALRY," he wrote, had "often before been the subject of criticism," but its "effect upon the laws of the world" had been unappreciated. To be sure, it arose in a period that mixed brutality and knightly honor. The Middle Ages had been the best of times and the worst of times:

It was the lot of these ages [i.e., the Middle Ages] . . . to be witness to the greatest inconsistencies at the same time; for at the same time, the most horrid and barbarous injustice, and the most heroic and disinterested acts of generosity, are for ever arresting our attention. The little progress which the *European* people had made in morality, the savage manners of those they sprang from, and the laxity of the various governments, gave loose . . . to the indulgence of every sort of passion. Above all, the universal independence of the Barons, under the feudal system, took away all restraint from those who were at once strong and willing enough to invade the peace of mankind. A man of brutal manners, and narrowness of soul, who dwelt within the walls of a fortress, whence he could sally forth at pleasure to the annoyance of his neighbours, and which afforded him a retreat from superiour force, or a secure deposit for his plunder, had every temptation to play the tyrant and the robber. Sovereigns and magistrates had long attempted in vain to repress these mischiefs.[26]

Efforts by "sovereigns and magistrates" to end baronial violence thus failed to end noble violence. Like every other eighteenth-century author, Ward knew that truth. Nevertheless he insisted that another factor had come into play, the noble point of honor of the high Middle Ages:

The miserable state of society during these ages, and the atrocities that were daily committed, produced a POINT OF HONOUR. . . . Men saw the necessity for reformation; the common modes had been tried in vain; and it was necessary to kindle *enthusiasm*, to effect a cure. By working therefore, though in a different way, upon the same warlike passions which caused the mischief, and raising the fervour of the mind, through every motive of religious devotion and every worldly prejudice; Europe at length raised within itself a spirit the very opposite to that of which it complained. Accordingly, if men were found, on the one hand, who gave way perpetually to their avarice, revenge, ambition, or lust; there were numbers, on the other, who placed the *point of honour* not only in abstaining personally from these, but in opposing and exterminating all those who did not.

It was thence that the laws of CHIVALRY arose; which have so often excited our interest in the numerous legends, and our admiration in the bold flights of poetry to which they gave birth.

I shall leave the regular account of the particulars of this remarkable Institution to those who have made it the immediate subject of many a learned and pleasing disquisition . . . and shall merely examine them [*sic*] according as they appeared to have influence on the law of nations. Such influence, as may be supposed, (considering the military spirit of the Institution) may be traced in more direct and regular steps than any other; and indeed, as long as it lasted, it will be found to have been the cause of considerable improvements in the mode of carrying on war. . . .

[The knight] was expected to be accomplished in all the gentler and more humane virtues of honour, courtesy, fidelity to his word, and kindness to the vanquished. . . . [The training of young knights] ensured the production and support of a vast body of the military all over the world; whose duty was to soften the horrors, as well to shine amidst the dangers, of war.[27]

The echo of Edmund Burke's defense of the nobility in this once famous passage sounds clearly enough.[28] In persecuting the Second and First Estates of the ancien régime, Burke declared, the French Revolution was setting out to demolish the pillars of European civilization. Ward saw it the same way: the revolutionaries were destroying the "foundations" of the civilized practice of war, which lay, not in royal efforts to curb the "brutal manners" of the nobility, but in the refined souls of the nobles themselves, determined to "soften the horrors" of war.

No prerevolutionary lawyer had ever offered anything quite like Ward's paean to medieval chivalry. But it fit the new tone of antirevolutionary, pro-nobility Europe, and over the next decades it slowly established itself in the general wisdom on the law of war. Its progress was slow, though. At first authors tended to identify chivalry as simply one of several factors behind the progress that had marked the development of the European law of war up until the disaster of the French Revolution.[29] The move from condemning medieval nobles to idealizing them was too radical a change to take place all at once. Even Romantic-era poets came slowly to the idealization of medieval chivalry. Thus Sir Walter Scott himself, the author who did more to burnish the reputation of chivalry than any other, was sufficiently well informed that he had to admit in 1828 that knights had a profit motive:

> A successful war had . . . peculiar advantages to those chivalrous adventurers. The knights, or nobles, who were overcome in battle, and compelled to yield themselves to the more fortunate among the victors, "rescue or no rescue," were obliged to purchase their liberty at such sum as might be agreed on. The conditions of these bargains were well understood, and the prisoner, according to his rank and wealth, adjusted with his captor the price of his enfranchisement. On this subject, so much generosity prevailed among the French and English in particular, that the victorious party frequently did not carry their prisoners off the field, but freely dismissed them, under the sole condition, that they should meet the captors afterwards, at a time and place fixed, and settle the terms of their ransom. To fail in such an appointment would have been, on the part of the captive knight, held most unworthy and dishonourable, and he would have exposed himself to the scorn of the ladies, minstrels, and heralds, to stand high in whose praise was the especial object of every true son of chivalry.[30]

The romance of ladies, minstrels, and true sons of chivalry still had to share the stage with the banality of ransom in the early nineteenth century. Other poets too could not ignore the sinister side in chivalry. The most notable example is that surpassingly strange meditation on the simultaneous bestiality and chivalry of aristocratic officers, Heinrich von Kleist's 1808 *Marquise von O*. This is the tale of a chivalrous aristocratic officer of the Napoleonic period who saves a noblewoman threatened by gang rape by common soldiers, only to yield to the temptation to rape her himself after she passes out.[31] (Kleist's strange novella ends happily when the lady and the officer finally marry, after the latter comes back to his chivalric senses.)

Kleist's novella was composed in a world in which the image of the warrior nobility was undergoing a disorienting change. Similarly in the literature of the law, the belief in the virtues of chivalry did not at first come entirely easily. In the immediate aftermath of the Napoleonic wars, jurists certainly found fine things to say about chivalry, but only within limits. In 1817, for example, Theodor Schmalz could praise the "poetry" of "knightly gallantry" which, along with religion and commerce, had "softened the crudity of the age and of war" in the High Middle Ages. But Schmalz, like Kleist, felt obliged to add that "of course, human culture is not always able to control the passions."[32] Schmalz was not alone in hedging his praise for chivalry. It remained difficult for lawyers to avoid the truth, so securely established by eighteenth-century scholarship, that medieval knights were principally in it for booty and ransom.[33]

Nevertheless as the Romantic movement gathered steam the darker side of medieval knighthood was eventually submerged. By the 1820s idealizations of chivalry had become common coin in the semipopular scholarly literature of works like Charles Mill's *History of Chivalry, or Knighthood and Its Times*:

> In the kingdoms which sprang from the ruins of the Roman empire, every king, baron and person of estate was a knight; and therefore the whole face of Europe was overspread with chivalry. Considered in this aspect, the knighthood and the feudalism of Europe were synonymous and coexistent. But there was a chivalry within this chivalry; a moral and personal knighthood; not the well-ordered assemblage of the instruments of ambition, but a military barrier against oppression and tyranny, a corrective of feudal despotism and injustice. Something like this description of knighthood may be said to have existed in all ages and countries.[34]

"In all ages and countries:" This is the romanticized concept of timeless military chivalry we still find in our law of war literature today. In the high Romantic era of the 1830s and 1840s many jurists repeated the view that, as an author put it in 1834, "in chivalric war, much humanity was displayed."[35] By 1832, for example, James Kent, the eminent New York jurist and one of the makers of American law, was offering the same

picture of the history of the law that would still be found a century later in
the writings of Schmitt and so many others: "The influence of chivalry had
a very beneficial effect upon the laws of war. It introduced declarations
of war by heralds, and to attack an enemy by surprise was deemed cow-
ardly and dishonourable. It dictated humane treatment to the vanquished,
courtesy to enemies, and the virtues of fidelity, honour, and magnanimity
in every species of warfare."[36] No sign of the booty-hunting, ransom-
exacting knight. No sign of the vicious baron "of brutal manners, and
narrowness of soul, who dwelt within the walls of a fortress," who was
still haunting the writings of Ward in 1795. No sign of kings either; Kent
saw war strictly from the point of view of the knights, without any interest in the conflict between monarchy and nobility that his predecessors
thought fundamental. This was the dominant tone of the 1830s and after.
In 1830 we find passages like this one, from the first number of the German
Journal of the Art, Science and History of War: "Instances of knightly
single combat [*Zweikämpfe*] were to be witnessed at Jena and Heilsberg.
Such scenes warm the heart of the historian, since they speak volumes
about how the old chivalric spirit still sparks up in the cavalry from time
to time."[37] By the 1840s the strong view of the civilizing role of chivalry
had taken firm root. In 1843 Karl Theodor Pütter could present the history of the law of war this way, citing Ward:

> As is often observed, a chivalric law of battle and war existed in the
> Middle Ages, which applied first and foremost to the knightly class.
> By means of this law, war was in some measure regulated and tamed,
> since princes and knights alike were bound by the rules of the chi-
> valric order. . . . This benefited both the country and the ordinary
> folk. . . . It was the custom and duty of a knight never to attack a de-
> fenseless person, or to attack without fair warning; and from the
> general principles of the territorial peace emerged the *declaration of
> war*, which is still observed by Christian princes down to this day.[38]

The same view could be found in a standard legal dictionary article titled
"The Law of War" in 1845: "The knightly class principally provided a
happy foretaste of the future order of things. . . . It is in the knighthood
that there first appeared combat without hatred, or any interest in annihi-

lating the enemy, combat founded in respect for the enemy. Knights fought for honor, and out of a thirst for great deeds, and had no need for hatred."[39] From the time of passages like this one onward, the literature took the same unwaveringly Romantic line still to be found in our own day.

The chivalric conception of restrained warfare was thus first born in the poetic mists of the Romantic era, and the same is true of the dueling conception. It was during these same years that statesmen began routinely to offer the point of honor as the leading justification for war.

Eighteenth-century wars, as we have seen, were ordinarily justified under theories that assumed that war was a means of acquiring property. In justifying them, jurists drew on centuries-old principles of just war theory, which always assumed that the "justice" of war involved the application of property law principles. Occasionally jurists spoke of the possibility that the point of honor might justify a war, and there were certainly some examples. But eighteenth-century warfare was frankly acquisitive, and the large goal of war was to enhance the *gloire* of the monarchs who mounted them. Correspondingly the manifestos of continental wars ordinarily rehearsed carefully stated legal claims under the law of dynastic succession. Wars were made on the say-so, as Voltaire mockingly observed, of genealogists. As for ordinary soldiers, just war theory and the practice of war alike assumed that their prime and wholly permissible motivation in battle was to take booty.

In the nineteenth century this understanding of the justice of war essentially collapsed; war ceased to be justified by reference to principles of property law. The old law of booty, though it did not entirely vanish, went into a notable decline. Nineteenth-century jurists continued to hold, though with some uneasiness, that it was perfectly legitimate to strip the corpses of the defeated enemy on the battlefield.[40] Under the law of the French *Code Civil*, first promulgated in 1804, booty taking continued to count as one of the legitimate modes of the acquisition of property.[41] Indeed French soldiers of the Napoleonic period were notorious for their booty taking. (Hegel was one of the victims, after the battle of Jena.)[42] Nevertheless jurists came to see the private property of noncombatants as sacrosanct. The shift was slow, but it came, notably in 1871, in the wake of the Franco-Prussian War, when the highest French court held that the principle of the sanctity of private property, proven by John Locke, was incompatible with the taking of booty from noncombatants.[43] The 1870s marked the sharp turning point: booty taking was no longer to be tolerated, at least in land wars. In a century in which the protection of private property reigned supreme among legal values, booty law could survive only in greatly diminished form.

Meanwhile the principle of dynastic succession, badly weakened by the events of 1789–1815, lost its purchase as well. The Congress of Vienna abandoned any form of strict dynastic succession as the foundation of territorial claims. In later decades, arguments from dynastic succession were still occasionally voiced, especially in Central European wars like the Danish War of 1864 and the Seven Weeks War of 1866.[44] Central Europe was a deeply conservative region, and some of the old forms hung on there. Nevertheless dynastic succession no longer stood at that foundation of the law of nineteenth-century war, as it had a century before.

As the idea of war as a legitimate mode of the acquisition of property faded, new forms of justification took the stage. Some of these involved reactionary interventionism under the leadership of Klemens von Metternich and fellow statesmen of the Concert of Europe in the early part of the nineteenth century. By midcentury some involved the imperative of national unification. And some, strikingly, involved the classic duelists' justification: the point of honor.

We find the point of honor coming to the fore as a justification in the same Romantic decades in which the cult of chivalry triumphed in the legal literature. Thus in 1841 the English were justifying the opening of the First Opium War in dueling language: "The only objects which Her Majesty desires to obtain are satisfaction for the injuries to which Her subjects have been exposed and for the insults which have been offered to Her Crown, and the establishment of peaceful and friendly commercial relations with China. . . . Her Majesty desires no acquisition of territory, nor any advantages for Her own subjects which should not equally be shared by other nations."[45] Of course, this was poppycock: the Opium Wars were patently fought for British trade advantage. In the eighteenth century, the British might not have been ashamed to say so; by the 1840s, however, they felt obliged to appeal to the dueling ethic in justifying their war. It had somehow become indecent to admit that wars were fought for gain rather than for "satisfaction for insults." Similarly in the run-up to the Crimean War in the mid-1850s, the French and English both spoke of "national honor," just as French engagement in the Second War of Italian Independence was justified by Napoléon III with the invocation of "the honor and the interests of France."[46] Interests played a role, but by the 1850s it was common to invoke honor as well, and first.

The most remarkable case, though, is the "world-historical" Franco-Prussian War itself. The origins of that war are indeed among the oddest, and to the modern eye most trivial, ever to have given rise to a major conflict. The story begins in 1868, when an uprising left the Spanish throne vacant. Two years later, in 1870, Leopold, Prince of Hohenzollern-Sigmaringen, presented himself as a candidate for the vacant throne. Spain was in France's backyard, and it had been ruled by Bourbons for a century and half. Consequently Leopold's candidacy was taken, as Howard recounts the history, as "an insult to France," and the government of Napoléon III demanded not only that it be withdrawn but that King Wilhelm make a commitment that Prussia would never advance such a candidacy again.

In the eighteenth century, this dispute would have produced manifestos sounding in the law of dynastic succession. The mid-nineteenth century, though, had become a chivalric, aristocratic age, and the entire dispute was perceived and presented as an affair of honor. Napoleon III's peremptory demand that Prussia abandon all future candidacies was communicated to Wilhelm by the French ambassador, the Count de Benedetti. Wilhelm, unsurprisingly, refused to enter into any such commitment. The immediate *casus belli* arose when Bismarck, in a famously shrewd stroke of manipulation, published a version of the encounter between Wilhelm and Benedetti calculated to inflame the rage of the French public: " 'His majesty the King,' concluded Bismarck's version, 'thereupon decided not to receive the French Ambassador again, and sent to tell him through the aide-de-camp on duty that his Majesty had nothing further to communicate to the Ambassador.' This, [Bismarck] assured his friends, would have the effect of a red rag on the Gallic bull."[47] Bismarck calculated correctly. His account was indeed taken as "an affront to the Emperor and to France."[48] As an official French statement explained, "[T]he insult to our dignity lay ultimately in the intentional publicity given to the refusal to receive our ambassador."[49] War followed, disastrously for France.

Nothing of the kind ever happened in the hardheaded, more calculating and acquisitive eighteenth century. The fact is that the greatest of point of honor wars was not some eighteenth-century conflict but the Franco-Prussian War of 1870; and the greatest of duel battles was Sedan, the last, and politically the least successful, "fateful day of open confrontation" in the history of Europe. It was only in the 1840s and 1850s that scholars routinely linked chivalry and restraint in their analysis of the law of war; it was in the same period that states began routinely to justify their wars by appealing to the point of honor. The chivalric, dueling conception of war reached its zenith not during the Enlightenment age of battle warfare but during the very decades when battle warfare was nearing its collapse.[50]

As this suggests, the proposition that the decline of classic warfare in the nineteenth century was the result of a decline in the chivalric or dueling ethos is little short of perverse as a matter of historical interpretation. The truth lies elsewhere: the restrained battle warfare of the eighteenth century had always been linked with the success of monarchical legitimacy. When we consider the evidence attentively, we discover an unsurprising truth: the nineteenth-century decline of pitched battle warfare followed the decline in the legitimacy of monarchical forms of government. Such is the straightforward answer to the mystery of why battle warfare survived for three generations after the first emergence of the guerrilla in the American Revolution: it survived as long as the legitimacy of monarchical government remained intact.

The decline in the monarchical form of government, it is important to emphasize, came only slowly during the decades after 1800 or so. There was no sudden and utter overthrow of either monarchy or battle warfare with the French Revolution. Just as the guerrilla developed only gradually from the late eighteenth century onward, so the monarchical form of government, and along with it the practice of battle warfare, hung on for two and a half generations.

The facts are familiar. The overall picture of continental government from 1800 to 1870 was one of a strong return to monarchical, or as the case might be imperial, forms. After 1800 monarchical government enjoyed an unmistakable revival in Europe, which can reasonably be dated to 1801. That was the year when Napoleon's France, still technically a republic, arranged the establishment of a new kingdom of Etruria, ruled by a Bourbon, no less.[51] In the subsequent years, after transforming himself from First Consul into Emperor, Napoleon replaced the various "sister republics" established in the first decade of Revolutionary Europe with kingdoms, notably ones ruled by his own family members, while himself marrying a Habsburg in the effort to claim a place for the Bonapartes among the dynastic houses of Europe.

Napoleon brought back monarchy, and after 1814 the establishment of monarchies remained the rule, not only in France and the reconstituted Netherlands but also in newly established polities like Belgium and Greece, for both of which German kings were found in the 1830s. Indeed the post-Napoleonic period was significantly *less* republican than the eighteenth century had been; two of the three great premodern republics, the Netherlands and Venice, had been subjected to monarchical rule, and only Switzerland remained. The French Second Republic of 1848 survived less than five years before giving way the plebiscitary Second Empire of Napoleon III. Italy, when it was unified, was unified under a monarch. Only with the (troubled) establishment of the French Third Republic in 1870 did an important and successful new republic emerge on the continent. The period from 1800 to 1870 was very much an age of revived monarchical legitimacy.

European monarchy did not by any means fade away in the seventy years after 1800, and neither did battle warfare. The persistence of battle warfare deserves to be emphasized since one has a natural tendency to assume that the French Revolution overthrew all the military traditions of the eighteenth century. That is the underlying assumption of Bell's *First Total War*, for example, just as it is the underlying assumption of a classic like Basil Liddell Hart's *Ghost of Napoleon*.[52] And it is certainly true that Napoleonic warfare was fought on a far grander scale than eighteenth-century warfare. It is also certainly true that the guerrilla began to emerge in Europe, especially in Spain and Italy. It is true that in the postrevolutionary world there were events like the Greek revolt, movements like the *carbonari*, and the revolutions of 1848, and that popular movements in general brought forms of violence that did not resemble the forms of classic warfare. But it is also true that when monarchies and empires went to war, they continued to fight pitched battles; and victory in battle continued to shape the diplomatic outcomes of war between monarchical states until 1870. In that sense, the rise of "total" war after 1792 did not completely transform the decision-making structures of warfare. The conservatism in European forms of government after 1800 was also a conservatism in the forms of war, and just as 1870 is the date that conventionally marks the beginning of the modern period in European art and culture, it is the date that best marks the beginning of the modern period in European war.

Thus Napoleon's epic battles after 1800 at Austerlitz, Jena, Borodino, Leipzig, and Waterloo were all pitched battles between emperors and kings, and the rhetoric surrounding them remained an insistent rhetoric of the clash of empires and kingdoms.[53] The same was true of later wars between continental monarchical states. The European great powers maintained a general peace among themselves in the generation after 1815. But when war arrived again in the mid-nineteenth century, it still had not entirely departed from eighteenth-century forms. Even when the empires and kingdoms of mid-nineteenth-century Europe had begun to justify their wars in the name of national unification, they continued to resolve them through pitched battle, just as their monarchical predecessors had done in the previous century. The great trial by combat between princes was still the characteristic European form of war, even after rifles and railroads had come on the scene.

Solferino, the battle that settled the Second Italian War of Independence in 1859, is one example. Today Solferino is best remembered as the battle whose horrors inspired Dunant to found the Red Cross, or perhaps for having given its name to the Paris street that houses the headquarters of the Socialist Party. But in its own day it was seen differently: Solferino was famous not only for being a battle fought by two empires (France and Austria-Hungary) and one kingdom (Sardinia) but also for being a battle at which the monarchs of all three powers were present. Even Dunant was impressed. In the opening sections of his memoir, he was moved to describe "the admirable calm and self-possession of the Chief of the House of Hapsburg" and the noble sight of Emperor Napoleon, who "was to be seen wherever his presence seemed to be needed."[54] In particular Solferino was famous for the princely presence and attitude of Emperor Franz Joseph; the emperor, as Hew Strachan writes, "himself took command. . . . [With] the withdrawal of the defeated side (the Austrians) guaranteed, [he] caught the spirit of the *ancien régime* exactly: he concluded, 'I have lost a battle. I pay with a province.'"[55] The spirit of the ancien régime indeed.

Königgrätz is another example, a particularly revealing example because of the air of eighteenth-century legal rhetoric that still lingered about warfare in conservative Central Europe. The Seven Weeks War was fought over the question of whether Prussia or Austria would be the dominant power in the German confederation. German commentators perceived it to be a war of national unification, just like the Second War of Italian Independence. Thus Johann Caspar Bluntschli, the leading European scholar of international law, insisted that modern wars, of which the Seven Weeks War was his prime case, could be justified by reference to the "necessity of the creation of a new evolving legal entity" through national unification.[56]

And yet, Bluntschli observed, in 1866 many Germans took the "infantile" view that wars could be justified only by rights of dynastic inheritance.[57] So indeed they did: the technical causes of the war in fact still involved the classic sorts of questions in dynastic succession.[58] In Central Europe, dynastic succession retained its hold, and battle warfare continued to be possible even in the age of national unification.

Not least, Sedan was a monarchical battle, pitting an emperor against a king in the last of the great monarchical trials by combat. Napoléon III presented his defeat that way when he laid his sword at the feet of his "brother," the king of Prussia. Even more revealingly, French politicians perceived it that way. When the verdict of Sedan was rejected, it was rejected, as all French schoolchildren still learn, because it was a defeat for the *emperor*, not a defeat for France. Victories in major pitched battles were ordinarily victories for emperors and kings, and defeats were defeats for emperors and kings as well. In that regard, nothing had changed since the eighteenth century.

In other ways too monarchical warfare of the nineteenth century continued to assume the legitimacy of eighteenth-century norms. In particular the retreat rule lingered, at least in practice if not in military theory. As we have seen, the application of the retreat rule was fundamental to the practice of eighteenth-century battle warfare. Forcing the enemy to retreat brought a technical victory on the eighteenth-century battlefield, and technical victory could carry powerful diplomatic and propaganda benefits.

In the aftermath of the Napoleonic wars, military strategists began to reject the retreat rule, which they regarded as incompatible with the demands of modern strategy. This rejection was only one aspect of a larger phenomenon: military strategists of the early nineteenth century were no longer willing to accept the old norms of the rule of law. Early nineteenth-century military writers showed a uniform disdain for the legal traditions of the eighteenth century. Jomini, for example, pioneered the cynical view of the wars of the eighteenth century, and in particular those of Louis XIV and Frederick the Great:

> There present themselves unfortunately, in our day, so many rights contestable and contested, that the greater part of wars, although founded in appearance upon inheritances, testaments and marriages, are in reality no more than wars of convenience. The question of the Spanish succession under Louis XIV, was the most natural in law, since it reposed on a solemn testament supported by family ties, and by the general wish of the Spanish nation; nevertheless it was one of the most contested by all Europe; it produced a general coalition against the legitimate legatee.
>
> Frederick II, profiting by a war of Austria against France, evokes old parchments, enters Silesia by main force, and seizes upon the rich province, which doubles the strength of the Prussian monarchy. . . .

> In such a war, there are no rules to give; *to know how to wait and to profit is everything.*[59]

This cynical account of Frederick's invasion, and of the nature of war, has become a commonplace. But Jomini may well have been the first to offer it, and it reflected a larger contempt for the legal traditions of the eighteenth century that he shared with his contemporaries among the military writers.

The most important of those contemporaries was, of course, Clausewitz, who abandoned the legal approach to war in his own distinctive way. Clausewitz was a man steeped in the literature of war, and many of the themes of the old legal literature reappeared in his work. Indeed there are moments when the doctrines of *On War* sound like nothing other than military recastings of the familiar legal doctrines of the early modern world. As we have seen, early modern law permitted trickery, so-called stratagems, but encouraged commanders to risk open confrontation in battle. "Open force is without a doubt the most natural, most noble, and most legitimate means of doing harm to the enemy," as a typical juristic statement ran, "but artifice is not illicit in war."[60] Clausewitz knew these traditions well, and he cited them. But he reframed the old legal question of the permissibility of *stratagems* in his new language of *strategy*. He presented his views in his chapter titled "Trickery":

> At first glance it may seem that "strategy" takes its name from "trickery" for good reason, and that "trickery" remains that best way to describe the essential character of strategy despite all the changes, real and apparent, in the overall structure of war since the time of the Greeks. . . .
>
> Nevertheless, however much we feel a certain need to regard those engaged in war as engaged in a competition to outdo each other in giving sly blows, cleverness, and trickery, we must concede that such qualities have been little in evidence in history, and have rarely made much of a mark amidst the mass of relations and circumstances. . . .
>
> Measures like deploying for battle in such a way as to fool the enemy require a considerable expenditure of time and power, and of

course, the greater the impression to be made, the greater the expen-
diture in these respects. . . . The truth is that it is dangerous to de-
tach large forces for long merely in order to make a false impression,
since there is always the danger that it will fail of its purpose, while
depriving the commander of those forces at the decisive point.[61]

Clausewitz thus framed his discussion as a response to the old legal literature on stratagems; and in the end, he reached the same conclusion
his predecessors among the jurists had reached: open confrontation in
battle was best.

Of course, he reached that conclusion for different reasons. Nevertheless it is hard to suppress the suspicion that he had not quite overcome
the assumptions and prejudices of the eighteenth-century jurists. In particular one suspects that his indebtedness to the old teachings of the law
may help explain one of his most notorious errors. Clausewitz is famous
for exaggerating the extent to which his model Napoleon favored open
confrontation. As French critics of Clausewitz have demonstrated, Napoleon in fact made heavy use of *la manoeuvre sur les derrières*, the "trick"
of attacking from behind.[62] Clausewitz proved unable to recognize that
fact. Was this because, for all his innovativeness, his thinking remained
so deeply shaped by the traditional categories and assumptions of the
law? Perhaps Clausewitz, for all his contempt for the law, was ultimately
unable to shake himself free of the traditional juristic attitudes. Like
Isidore of Seville, perhaps, he still thought of victory through trickery as
"shameful" and was reluctant to acknowledge that his hero Napoleon
had engaged in anything but open confrontation.

At any rate, although he knew the old law of stratagems, Clausewitz
refused to employ the old forms of juristic analysis. He no longer drew his
arguments from moral theology, from reflections on the Book of Joshua,
or from the legal calculus of diplomacy. Instead he took the venerable juristic problems and transformed them aggressively into problems of strategy. His framework of analysis may have come from the law, but he was
unwilling to think like a lawyer.

On the contrary he showed active hostility toward the law. This
was notably true of his conception of how open confrontation should be
conducted: through the *Vernichtungsschlacht*, the battle of annihilation.

Vernichtung, annihilation, was a standard term among early nineteenth-century jurists, but they always spoke of Vernichtung as something utterly incompatible with civilized, law-bound, warfare. As early nineteenth-century editions of Martens's standard legal text declared, "[T]he legitimate goal of war is never to exterminate the enemy. Instead it is to oblige him to accept a peace that satisfies our demands."[63] Another standard legal text put the same point this way in 1830: "The art of war is never, as the vulgar believe, the art of annihilation. It is the art of paralyzing the forces of the enemy."[64] For the leading German authors August Wilhelm Heffter and Johann Caspar Bluntschli, the refusal to seek the enemy's annihilation was the mark of civilized warfare: only against uncivilized tribes and "savages" was annihilation permissible. Civilized European powers should never engage in such conduct.[65]

Yet Clausewitz, like Jomini a man determined to discard legal pieties, insisted on the primacy, indeed the necessity, of annihilation. Where the lawyers held that only savages should be annihilated, Clausewitz insisted that civilized Europeans should be annihilated as well. Like another veteran of the Napoleonic Wars, the positivist legal thinker John Austin, Clausewitz had no patience with the traditional norms of lawful authority. The comparison of Clausewitz with Austin is a striking one. Austin, a radical skeptic of the great legal traditions of the West, famously declared in 1832 that law was nothing but commands backed by the threat of the infliction of an evil.[66] Clausewitz, who died a year earlier, saw the world in just the same way: war too was simply commands backed by the threat of the infliction of an evil.

Rejecting the old legal traditions as they did, these early nineteenth-century military authors also inevitably rejected the retreat rule. That rule, which had conduced to tame warfare in the eighteenth century, seemed unacceptably timid to both Jomini and Clausewitz; both insisted on the imperative of pursuit. "Victory," Clausewitz wrote, "does not consist in merely taking control of the field of battle, but in the destruction of the physical and moral force of the enemy . . . and this is achieved principally through pursuit once the battle has been won."[67] Accordingly when they discussed retreat, they discussed it not as a technical form of defeat but as a complex tactical problem.[68] Conversely, when they interpreted military history, they interpreted it as proving the importance of pursuit. Thus it is in the writings of Jomini that we first find the myth that Frederick the Great had engaged in vigorous pursuit.[69] Clausewitz especially lionized Napoleon's efforts at pursuit at battles like Austerlitz.[70] Other military authors shared their view; the Prussian officer Wilhelm von Willisen, for example, wrote in 1840 that a mere "tactical" victory on the battlefield was "of little significance." After all, "the victor on the battlefield ordinarily loses as many, or more, men as the vanquished." The real meaning of victory had to be sought elsewhere.[71]

Accordingly if we were to read only the writings of Jomini, Clausewitz, and other military strategists of the time, we would assume that the retreat rule had been cast upon the strategic rubbish heap once Napoleon appeared on the scene—that, like other aspects of the tame warfare of the eighteenth century, it disappeared in the age of "the first total war," while the art of war became the art of pursuit. Yet once again it is essential to look carefully at the practice of monarchical states. In point of fact, victory in the monarchical battles of the nineteenth century was still commonly decided according to the retreat rule.

This is true to some extent even of Napoleon. Of course, some of the greatest victories of the great general involved pursuit. But he did not hesitate to invoke the retreat rule when it served his purposes. Napoleon was too canny to restrict himself to the use of overwhelming force if submitting to the law of victory could further his ends, and he remained quite prepared to claim victory according to the eighteenth-century rules when he could do so. This was the case at critical battles like Marengo and Wagram.[72] Perhaps most strikingly, it was true of Borodino, a technical victory over the Russian army in September 1812. After he had driven the Russians from the field of battle, Napoleon failed to pursue them. This did not prevent him from proclaiming a traditional victory by the traditional rules.[73]

Whatever Jomini and Clausewitz may have said of him, Napoleon never systematically abandoned the retreat rule. The same remained the case in later imperial battles. Magenta, Solferino, and Königgrätz were all battles won without pursuit. They were all monarchical battles won, in the eyes of their contemporaries, by the traditional retreat rule.

When monarchs went to war, the battle warfare of the eighteenth century was not yet dead. By contrast, where popular movements played the leading role, classic pitched battle failed. In particular, wars involving republics consistently degenerated into more chaotic violence.

After 1800 republics were not much to be seen in Europe. But in the Americas there were republics, and they fought messy wars. The Mexican-American War, the first Western war staged between two republics in centuries, collapsed into an ugly guerrilla. The same thing happened in the American Civil War. And when a new European republic emerged in France in 1870, it was accompanied by the collapse of battle warfare there too. As soon as the formal announcement of the defeat at Sedan was made to the Chambre des Députés in Paris, Favre demanded resistance *à l'outrance*, war without limits, and *guerre à l'outrance* was indeed what the new republic fought, just as the republics at war in America five years earlier had done.

Republics fought what by eighteenth-century standards looked like dirty wars. This may seem troubling or ironic. How can it be that republics lost the capacity to fight in civilized ways? Kant, after all, maintained that republics would never fight wars at all, at least against other republics.[74] Modern followers of Kant, such as Michael Doyle, have tried to revive his claims, arguing that democracies are inherently unwarlike.[75] One might assume, moreover, that war would come less naturally to republics than to monarchies. War-making in the eighteenth century, after all, was undertaken in the interests of princely glory. Wouldn't that suggest that republics, when they fought wars at all, should fight tamer wars?

Yet it is not surprising that warfare in republics was not tame. Almost all human warfare in almost all times and places has been ferocious. The interlude of relative calm in the eighteenth century came during an exceptional moment of princely success in monopolizing violence. When the basic underpinnings of monarchical sovereign war-making gave way, it was entirely natural that human warfare should revert to the sort of ugliness that has always characterized it.

The monarchical monopoly of violence in the eighteenth century was indeed an exceptional interlude; when it broke down, war ran off the rails. Part of the problem was that the diplomatic practices of the eighteenth century could not easily accommodate the new republics. There was a sign of this in the aftermath of Valmy, the startling French victory over invading Prussian forces in 1792. On the morning of the day that Valmy was fought, Louis XVI was technically still on the throne, and after their defeat the Prussians were at first willing to negotiate a diplomatic settlement in standard eighteenth-century fashion. On that same day, however, the French monarchy was abolished by the Convention, and when word of this reached the Prussians, their government, already fearing the spread of revolutionary republicanism, refused to treat.[76] When a republic sat on the other side of the negotiating table, it was difficult to stand by the diplomatic norms of the eighteenth century.

But the larger reasons for the decline of eighteenth-century military practice among the new republics were straightforward. The institutions that had kept monarchical warfare within contained limits collapsed. Republican conflicts could not be analyzed within the tidy limits of the law of dynastic succession; instead they had to be justified according to more open-ended, and therefore more dangerous, norms. They were about struggles over republican legitimacy, not about property rights.

Moreover the single most important institutional development of the monarchical warfare could not survive the rise of republics; this was, as everybody recognized in the eighteenth century, the establishment of the professional standing army. Princely warfare could be kept under control because it was fought by a paid, uniformed, trained soldiery. As Martens explained in 1789, the eighteenth-century Kriegsmanier had been observed "above all since the introduction of regular troops." Republican warfare necessarily tended to spin out of control because it was no longer fought by the small professional standing armies of the eighteenth century, the regular troops in royal livery. To say this is only to repeat the obvious. It is common coin among military historians that the transformation of armies was fundamental to the transformation of the forms of war, and the amateur character of republican armed forces, especially in the early years of the Atlantic revolutions, is a commonplace as well. As Congress declared in 1778, America was "[w]ithout arms, without ammunition, without cloathing, without ships, without money, without officers skilled in war; with no other reliance but the bravery of our people, and the justice of our cause."[77] No amateur force could fight according to the orderly forms of the Kriegsmanier that monarchs had imposed on their soldiers. The same was true in revolutionary Europe. Europeans perceived the warfare of the First French Republic as dangerous precisely because it was amateur warfare. As the eminent classicist

C. G. Heyne said in 1794, in a speech that made its way into the literature of international law, internecine wars, wars of unbridled extermina-
tion, happened when "whole populations clashed" instead of "disciplined
soldiers, fighting for pay."[78] The French revolutionaries themselves said
much the same on the occasion of the *levée en masse* in 1793: republican
warfare was warfare of "nations against armies."[79] Everybody understood that at the time, and everybody has understood it since.

Unsurprisingly, the doctrines of the law of war did not change all that
much during the mostly monarchical age that was the first two-thirds of
the nineteenth century. The largest doctrinal changes came only after the
break caused by the American Civil War and the Franco-Prussian War. It
was then that the new problems of widespread guerrilla led two lawyers,
the German American Francis Lieber and the Swiss German Johann
Caspar Bluntschli, to formulate seminal doctrines on the problems of irregular warfare and the occupation of hostile territories.[80] Before that
point, though, nineteenth-century legal texts generally continued to repeat
the basic doctrines of the eighteenth-century law of victory.

Nevertheless there was one deep and arguably ominous shift that pre-
dated the 1860s. This was the decline of the idea of battle as a tacit contract of chance and the rise of the conception on display at Sedan: the
conception of battle as a world-historical event.

As we saw earlier, in the eighteenth century battle was regarded as the
creature of a tacit contract akin to contracts of games of chance. Under
this analysis, whose roots reached far back into the Middle Ages and
antiquity, the parties were deemed to be bound by the verdict of a pitched
battle because they had agreed to submit their fortunes to the chance of
arms. Battles were a form of sors, a wager, a decision-making procedure
founded in luck. In the technical language of the pre-nineteenth-century
world, to stage a battle was to allow a dispute to be settled by the eventus, the event of a chance proceeding. Political thinkers and lawyers
like Machiavelli and Grotius pondered the implications of this doctrine, which implied that Fortune could decide the fate of kingdoms,
while Montesquieu rejected the proposition that "Fortune could rule the
world," insisting that there were always deeper forces at work. "All

seeming 'accidents,'" Montesquieu insisted, "are the result of deeper causes."[81]

The success of battle warfare in the eighteenth century was thus tied up with a larger conception of the shape of human history; classic battle warfare depended on the willingness to believe that "Fortune could rule the world." In the nineteenth century, by contrast, a new conception of history established itself, according to which historical events were the products of deep laws of necessity or destiny. This is the Romantic conception of history that we find in Herder, Michelet, Quinet, Hegel, Marx, and other writers. It is a conception of history that inevitably brought with it the end of the theory of battle as a tacit contract of chance.

August Wilhelm Heffter, the leading international law scholar of the first part of the nineteenth century, described the breakdown of the older approach. In many ways, Heffter still saw war in the way his eighteenth-century predecessors did. Victory, he thought, was the product of chance: "Chance makes everything a throw of dice, a game." When it came to booty in particular, he continued to think in classic contract of chance terms. Nevertheless he had to acknowledge that the old chance of arms theory of war had died in the latter part of the eighteenth century:

> For the greater part of the eighteenth century, European diplomacy was a matter of political calculation, designed to eliminate every superiority in strength that might have endangered the balance of power— unless the chance of arms or the complexity of circumstances left one party helplessly at the mercy of another. . . . However this spirit of moderation perished over a period that began in the North with the partitions of Poland and in the West with the triumphs of the Revolution. From now on the victor dictated treaties. . . . Changes in territorial rights were accomplished simply with a legislative decree or a proclamation.[82]

For Heffter, the decline of the peaceable approach to war that accepted the chance of arms had come with the rise of cynical power politics. Unlike Jomini, however, Heffter did not date the shift to the time of Louis XIV or Frederick's invasion of Silesia. He rightly regarded the wars of most of the eighteenth century as tame. The shift, as he understood, really dated to the end of the century, the era of the revolutionary wars and the partitions of Poland (1772, 1793, and 1795), great seizures of territory which could not be justified by the classic law of dynastic succession.

Other texts suggest that the decline of the old approach was associated with the rise of nationalist sentiment in the 1780s. As late as 1789 a text like the *Encyclopédie Méthodique* was still declaring that battles were governed by "tacit conventions that have the character of a contract of a game of chance."[83] But around the same time, in 1785, Johann Gottfried Herder, the pioneer of nationalist history, was attacking the doctrine of the tacit contract of chance in the second volume of his *Ideas toward a Philosophy of the History of Mankind*. "Our jurists [*Staatslehrer*]," he wrote, attributed the validity of conquest and the legitimacy of dynasties "to a tacit contract," but in fact the contract simply ratified the right of the stronger, and the teachings of the jurists amounted to allowing violence to take the place of law.[84] Other authors of the mid-1780s expressed similar doubts,[85] and on the whole the doctrine seems to have died a rapid death.

The tacit contract of chance theory could not survive in the nineteenth century. Occasionally nineteenth-century writers adopted the old way of speaking. For example, an 1841 commentary on the French law against dueling presented war, in a way typical of the age, as a form of dueling; it described both dueling and war as surrenders to the chance of arms:

> The form of homicide that is authorized by natural law is the homicide of war, an immense duel of peoples, multiplied to horrific proportions. . . .
>
> War gave birth to the duel. . . . In war, one finds reciprocal aggression and defense; one finds rights subjected to the hazard of combat.[86]

Most texts, however, rejected the chance of arms theory of war. In fact some advanced thinkers rejected war entirely precisely on the grounds that it subjected human affairs to chance. That was the view expressed, for example, by *La Phalange*, the organ of the utopian socialist Charles Fourier.[87] In general, when later nineteenth-century texts mentioned this old doctrine, it was principally to discard it as inadequate to the momentousness of war.[88]

The same shift in attitude can be found among early nineteenth-century military writers, who abandoned the old legal approach to the role of chance in warfare. As Gat has shown, the hope that there could be a dependable science of war had been growing since the eighteenth century.[89] Some early nineteenth-century writers accordingly expressed the hope that chance could be eliminated, or at least minimized, through the use of scientific techniques. For example, Carl von Decker, in his *Basic Principles of Practical Strategy*, published in 1828, explained, "The sooner in the campaign it comes to battle, the less room is left for chance. Frederick II and Napoleon always kept this rule in view."[90] Jomini spoke in similar terms:

> As for the superior ability of generals, no one can deny that it is one of the most certain guarantees of victory. . . . To be sure, great commanders have been defeated by mediocre men on many occasions; but the exception does not make the rule. A misunderstood order or a chance event may hand over to the enemy camp the best-laid possibilities for success prepared by an able general. . . . That is one of the hazards that there is no way of foreseeing or avoiding. Yet would it be just, for that reason, to deny the influence of principles and science in ordinary circumstances? . . . Even if it were the case that the number of battles won through able maneuvers did not exceed the number won through chance events, that would prove absolutely nothing against my assertion.[91]

Even these authors did not think that chance could be wholly eliminated, though. Instead, as Gat has elegantly demonstrated, the tendency of the early nineteenth century was different. In line with the enthusiasms of the Romantic era, military authors tended to see chance as a factor that could be mastered by "genius." Brilliant commanders showed their brilliance by seizing chance opportunities.

Clausewitz was the supremely important author to think in such terms. As always, the themes of the early modern legal literature still sounded through his work. It is a famous fact that Clausewitz remained obsessed with the inevitability of chance, just as early modern jurists had been obsessed with it. But chance was no longer the basis of a legal doctrine for Clausewitz. Instead it was a subject for philosophical rumination:

> All actions in war aim at probable, not certain, success; and where there is no certainty, we must leave matters to Fate or Luck, whichever term one prefers. To be sure, we may insist that there should be as little chance as possible, or rather that chance play as little a role as possible in some particular situation—that is to say, that we may insist that chance play as little a role as possible *in some particular situation*, but not that one should always prefer the situation in which uncertainty is minimized; that would be a monstrous violation of basic principles. Such is the lesson of all our theoretical views. There are situations in which the greatest daring is the greatest wisdom.

Thus far, Clausewitz's thoughts were little different from the thoughts of Frederick the Great or the eighteenth-century jurists. War was a great gamble, and when all went well it favored the bold. But Clausewitz was simply no longer willing to accept the gambling ethos that had ruled in the previous century; as he continued in the same passage, he struggled to find a way to deny that gambling was what was really going on:

> Now in everything which is left to fate by the actor, his personal merit seems to play no role, and the same is true of his responsibility; nevertheless we cannot suppress an inward desire to applaud him whenever his aims are achieved, and we feel a kind of uneasiness of spirit when his aims are not achieved. . . .
>
> It is unmistakably the case that the mental gratification we feel when he succeeds, and the uneasiness we feel when he fails, rest on the obscure feeling that there is a fine, invisible thread connecting the success that we ascribe to luck and the genius of the man. . . . For that reason, luck in war seems to have a much nobler nature than luck in gambling.[92]

Luck still governed war. In this Clausewitz, once again, did not see matters fundamentally differently from his juristic predecessors. But, Romantic that he was, he could not overcome the *dunkles Gefühl*, the "obscure feeling," that there was more at work than chance.

At any rate, the classic tacit contract of change doctrine essentially vanished among both jurists and strategists. With its decline came an idea of battle that fit better within the "obscure feelings" of the Romantic era: the idea of battle as, in the words of King Wilhelm in 1870, a world-historical event. Where victory in battle had once been regarded as an eventus, an indeterminate outcome of chance occurrences, the nineteenth century came to regard it as an event, a moment in the large drama of human history.[93] This was the idea we find in authors such as Creasy: the idea of the Great Battles of World History, of battles as Great Events that reflected Historical Destiny and/or the great clash of Historical Forces.[94]

This dominant nineteenth-century conception of battle had a long history behind it. The lawyerly conception of battle as a procedure for asserting rights always coexisted with the millenarian conception of battle as a way of making history. As we have seen, the millenarian conception played an especially large role in the cultural traditions of Christianity, which celebrated the Battle of Milvian Bridge and the Battle of Clavijo.

In the old civilization of the eighteenth century this grandiose millenarian conception of battles was relatively absent. Authors certainly spoke of memorable or great battles, but the conception of battles we find in the literature that has grown up since Creasy's *Fifteen Decisive Battles of the World* was much less prominent than it would become in the nineteenth century. Even battles like Marathon and Tours, which nineteenth- and twentieth-century historians alike would describe as pivotal moments in the shaping of Western history, did not attract quite the same sort of excited commentary in the more sober eighteenth century. Perhaps the most striking example of the decline of the "great turning point" conception of battle is to be found in the treatment of the Battle of Milvian Bridge. By the end of the seventeenth-century wars of religion, learned authors were already dismissing the proposition that God had in any way intervened at Milvian Bridge, and Enlightenment authors such as Gibbon found the very idea a subject simply for ostentatious skepticism.[95]

Gibbon is a particularly striking witness for the skepticism of the eighteenth-century Enlightenment when it came to supposedly great historic battles. He was in some ways a proto-Romantic, and at some points he was willing to allow that a battle like Tours might possibly have had great historic consequences.[96] At other times, though, his native Enlightenment skepticism welled up, and he became acerbic about the supposed importance of battles. Take his account of the Battle of Adrianople, the Gothic victory often described as the strategic disaster that caused the fall of the Roman Empire. Gibbon expressed scorn for the proposition that any single military event could have such consequences. He saw larger forces at work. In particular, he saw a broader failure of Roman nerve: "The fabric of a mighty state, which has been reared by the labours of successive ages, could not be overturned by the misfortune of a single day, if the fatal power of the imagination did not exaggerate the real measure of the calamity."[97]

It was part of the Enlightenment skepticism of a man like Gibbon to doubt the proposition that battles were world-historical events. In the nineteenth century, by contrast, the old millenarian tradition reasserted itself. As the chance of arms theory of battle declined, the idea of a battle as a world-historical event, a kind of climax in sacred or semisacred history, gained ground. The rise to prominence of this grandiose conception can be dated, once again, to the 1830s, notably among the followers of Hegel.

There is an often repeated but apocryphal legend that Hegel himself believed that history had ended with the Battle of Jena in 1806. (This is a legend most recently retold by Francis Fukuyama.)[98] Hegel did not say anything of the kind, but after his death some of his followers did,[99] and from the 1830s onward many Hegelians began to speak in such terms. By the 1850s books on great battles were being published at a rapid clip in every European country, first and foremost among them Creasy's much-imitated *Fifteen Decisive Battles*. Monuments were being erected on the great battlefields of Europe—or at least on the spots that people guessed might be the right ones. Tourist guides to all of those sites were published in numbers. It belonged to the culture of the day that Prussians could regard their crisp victory at Königgrätz (July 3, 1866) as clear evidence that the Almighty willed the creation of a unified German nation.[100] Conversely, it belonged to the same culture of the day that vanquished Confederate officers, as Cynthia Nicoletti has recently demonstrated, could believe that their loss in the American Civil War represented the judgment of God.[101]

Pitched battle, in short, lost its eighteenth-century juristic significance. No longer a wager turning on dynastic succession and property claims, it began to represent something much grander. It began to represent what Germans thought they had witnessed at Sedan: the verdict of history.

Conclusion

IN THE AFTERMATH OF WORLD WAR I, many yearned for a return to the contained warfare of the eighteenth century, that "last and most beautiful creation of the old civilization destroyed by the French Revolution."[1] Especially during the ominous and anxious decade of the 1930s, authors such as the American military historian Hoffman Nickerson spoke longingly of the lost orderliness of the eighteenth-century world.[2] By far the most famous of these interwar laments was produced by Basil Liddell Hart. In his 1934 book *The Ghost of Napoleon*, Liddell Hart launched a bitter and controversial attack on all of the strategic innovations that arrived with Napoleonic warfare.[3] Most especially he attacked Clausewitz. As he put it in 1931, "[S]ince the late eighteenth century the nations have been enslaved by a military doctrine—the doctrine of a fight to the finish—from which, once committed to war, they were helpless to shake free."[4]

What indeed made the "beautiful creation" of eighteenth-century limited warfare possible and why are we "helpless to shake free" from uncontained warfare today? Liddell Hart believed that the answer was to be found in the history of strategy; he thought that it was a "military doctrine," Clausewitz's doctrine of annihilation, that had cut the struts out from under the eighteenth-century civilization of warfare. He is not alone. Many others have tried to explain the rise of modern war by studying the history of strategy, and in particular by pondering the strategic doctrines of Clausewitz and the dramatic campaigns of Napoleon.

But the history of strategy offers at best only the beginnings of an answer. The deeper and better answer has to do with eighteenth-century political culture. Eighteenth-century war was not like modern war. Instead of being a desperate last resort to be used only in self-defense or in the face of humanitarian emergencies, eighteenth-century war was simply a political tool of legitimate monarchs. It was an accepted legal procedure, used for the advancement of sovereign ambitions. That means that by the measure of the modern law of war, the eighteenth century seems primitive and even barbaric. Since the 1920s, lawyers have firmly renounced the proposition that a war could count as a legal procedure;[5] and the modern law of war utterly rejects the sorts of princely wars of aggressive aggrandizement fought by Frederick the Great.[6] Yet the eighteenth century managed to maintain model standards of containment. Therein lies the paradox, and it should trouble us.

The best starting point for explaining the paradox of eighteenth-century war is to be found, oddly enough, in the writings of Clausewitz himself. In fact it is to be found in the maxim for which Clausewitz is most notorious today: "War is the continuation of politics by other means." To modern ears this formula sounds shockingly cynical, the epitome of the hard, amoral approach to war. But Clausewitz scholars have demonstrated that it was in fact one of his most conservative pronouncements, produced at a moment when he too, late in life, was seeking the key to understanding limited warfare,[7] and, shocking though it sounds to us, it captured the essence of what kept eighteenth-century warfare within bounds. Limited warfare, the beautiful creation of the eighteenth century, was possible because war was simply an instrument of ordinary politics.

Today we think of wars as horrific undertakings, and we countenance them only if they are fought in the name of very great causes or in cases of extreme necessity. The idea that a state might casually initiate a war for mere political advantage strikes us as an appalling violation of fundamental jus ad bellum norms. One does not sow death in order to gain the upper hand over one's political rivals.

But in the old civilization of the eighteenth century nobody would have found Clausewitz's familiar maxim shocking. Making a war certainly meant condemning many soldiers to death in battle. But, deadly though it was, war was an accepted, conventional means of achieving conventional political goals. The eighteenth century was the age of "cabinet wars," of wars initiated through ordinary political deliberation for ordinary political ends. These eighteenth-century cabinet wars did indeed function as "a continuation of politics," and in more senses than one. Harold Lasswell famously defined *politics* as "who gets what, when and how,"[8] and in part eighteenth-century warfare was political because it fit that definition. It was an unapologetically acquisitive enterprise, intended to sort out the conflicting claims of rival princes and incidentally to reward soldiers with booty.

But there is manifestly more to politics than Lasswell's definition, and more in ways that matter for thinking about the character of eighteenth-century war. Politics is certainly about deciding who gets what, when, and how; but decisions count as conventionally political only if they are made in settings where the basic terms of governmental legitimacy are fixed.[9] We can have conventional politics in contemporary Washington or Paris or Berlin because our fundamental forms of government are securely established. No one challenges the basic legitimacy of modern democracy. If that were not the case, we would have not conventional politics but revolution.

Eighteenth-century warfare belonged to the world of conventional politics in that sense; it did its distributive work without raising any revolutionary challenges to the basic legitimacy of eighteenth-century monarchical forms of government.[10] Eighteenth-century wars never aimed at "regime change," to use modern American parlance. The rival powers engaged in eighteenth-century cabinet wars had no interest in upsetting the legitimate constitution of dynastic power in European society. Even Frederick the Great, despite his modern reputation to the contrary, did not challenge the established legal order of his age.

In fact far from challenging the legitimacy of existing government, eighteenth-century warfare reinforced it. The authority to make public war, like the authority to order public executions, lay at the foundation of princely legitimacy. Going to war was a normal and necessary political activity for eighteenth-century sovereigns: it proclaimed to the world that they, and they alone, retained the right to resolve their legal disputes through the chance of arms rather than submitting to the jurisdiction of an ordinary court.

Figures like Voltaire, and especially Kant, had nothing but contempt for the military-political culture of the monarchical eighteenth century. Kant in particular believed that the eighteenth-century world required radical reformation. He expressed disdain for the work of the jurists; Pufendorf and Vattel, he wrote, were "peddlers of false comfort."[11] They had failed in the true task of the law, which was to reject radically the fatal proposition that a war could count as a legal procedure. They had failed to pursue the only real path of peace, which was to establish republics in place of monarchies and to create international institutions to resolve international conflicts by law.[12] Only in a world of republican government and collective deliberation in a United Nations would the evils of war end.

Lawyers have been understandably stirred by Kant's vision ever since. But the promise of his theory has yet to be realized, and as the American republic laboriously disengages from two long, awful, and doubtfully successful wars, it is important to ask whether Kant was right about the eighteenth-century traditions he rejected. Were Pufendorf and Vattel really just "peddlers of false comfort"? It is true that they were not modern humanitarians. It is true that they were willing to sanction acts like Frederick the Great's invasion of Silesia, which to us look like instances of egregious criminal aggression. It is true that they assumed the legitimacy of monarchical government and tolerated war-making as an expression of monarchical legitimacy—though Vattel, in fairness, had more courage to dissent from eighteenth-century orthodoxy than most. But it is also true that they lived in a century that enjoyed the blessings of a style of contained warfare whose disappearance Liddell Hart and many others have bemoaned ever since World War I. Was there something of value in the eighteenth-century monarchical culture that Kant missed?

There was. The uncomfortable truth is that the very features of eighteenth-century warfare that Kant rejected most indignantly were fundamental to the culture of eighteenth-century restraint. The eighteenth-century law of war was not primarily about protecting individual human rights. It was about showing respect for the legitimacy and sovereignty of (monarchical) states. That seemed awful to Kant, and it may still sound awful to us. But because the wars of the eighteenth century symbolized the lawful rule of eighteenth-century sovereigns, they were fought in lawful ways. Sovereign monarchs counted as sovereign because they had managed to control the use of violence in their societies, and when they resorted to violence themselves, they did so in demonstratively controlled ways. It was the very fact that war-making was a ritual expression of lawful sovereign power that encouraged it to remain within ritualized limits. It was *because* princes found staging slaughters to be a routine and untroubling expression of their unchallenged sovereignty that the killing in their wars could be conducted in a spirit of restraint.

Jurists like Pufendorf and Vattel worked to encourage that spirit of restraint. The fundamental strategy of eighteenth-century law was not to forbid sovereign criminality but to reward civilized sovereign behavior. The jurists encouraged the practice of civilized warfare by giving legal effect to civilized victories. They were in no position to impose any obligation on sovereigns to fight contained pitched battles or courteous sieges, but they could deem a victory achieved through open confrontation to be worthy of enhanced diplomatic respect. They were in no position to eliminate the "ferocity and cupidity" of monarchical warfare, but they could hold that sovereigns acquired property rights only if they made their wars on the basis of some legal pretext, however specious. When the jurists pursued this strategy, they were working within a tradition that extended back to Saint Augustine, and their doctrines were more than just false comfort. In the end, they helped to create a civilized culture of state legitimacy. The very fact that war counted as a legal procedure meant that it could be fought in a procedurally orderly way. If eighteenth-century rulers had fought unbridled wars, if they had fought what the jurists condemned as "wild beast wars," their claim to be lawful sovereigns would have been weakened. If they had used the methods of a Genghis Khan in pursuing their political ends, they would not have enjoyed the kind of ceremonious legitimacy that a Louis XIV or a Frederick II enjoyed. If they had fought to the finish, they would have appeared on the European stage as barbarians.

Eighteenth-century war was limited war because it was a lawful activity for lawful sovereigns in a world in which the law of war was founded on systematic deference to the prerogatives of state sovereignty and a commitment to rewarding civilized behavior without requiring it. The lessons of eighteenth-century warfare are difficult for us to learn today because we have become idealists of a kind that they never were. We are the children of Kant, and we viscerally reject the notion that war can be used as a means of maintaining sovereign rights or a way of reinforcing or displaying sovereign legitimacy. We are no longer able to accept the proposition that an enterprise that causes so much suffering could be just a matter of the bald pursuit of property claims. We certainly do not think people should die just to dramatize the glory and legitimacy of rulers. "Waging wars for the glory of one's country," as Martha Finnemore writes, "is no longer honored or even respectable in contemporary politics."[13] Certainly as lawyers we no longer have any desire to be deferential to sovereigns, especially undemocratic ones.

But the painful paradox is that the deferential law of eighteenth-century law was considerably more effective than anything we have found since. Since the eighteenth century we have witnessed the gradual decline of the rule of sovereigns of the classic monarchical type, and the gradual rise of the rule of modern ideas of justice. We have witnessed the collapse of the conception of war as a form of civil justice, founded in property law, and the triumph of a conception of war as an act undertaken only in desperate necessity. This transformation has taken place for noble reasons, but it has resulted in sprawling and amorphous wars and it has come at a high cost in human lives. We may well believe that the cost is acceptable, but we should acknowledge that we are paying it.

The military civilization of the eighteenth century, it must be emphasized, was not the product of aristocratic culture. It is true enough the eighteenth-century armies were officered by an "international aristocracy,"[14] as so many historians and lawyers have emphasized. It is true enough the European nobility profited socially from its association with the apparatus of war. It is true enough that wars were fought under the banner of a Kriegsmanier, of "manners" of war that, like so many of the manners of Europe, were cultivated with special diligence by the courtly nobility. Nevertheless to describe eighteenth-century battle wars as aristocratic is to misconstrue their legal significance hopelessly, and it is to miss all the lessons we can learn from studying them. War was a civilized business in the eighteenth century not because of the behavior of its officers in the field, not because of its jus in bello, but because war was an accepted legal procedure, intimately bound up with the settled political legitimacy of eighteenth-century monarchical states.

All that is very remote from our world. Yet remote as the monarchical culture of the eighteenth century is, there are lessons to be learned from it—more than one.

The first is that it is a mistake to focus too much on chivalry or on the jus in bello. There is no necessary connection between chivalry and contained warfare. The nightmare wars of the twentieth century boasted many examples of chivalric conduct. In World War I in particular there was a deep commitment to chivalry on all sides—a commitment that did nothing to contain the war. Even Nazi officers were sometimes known to act in chivalrous ways. To put the emphasis on chivalry—on the mores of the combatants, on the jus in bello—is to ignore what matters most. War is not just a series of acts of violence, and we will never build a fully effective law of war if we focus only on the acts of violence that are regulated by the jus in bello. War is a complex political activity with complex political meaning, and it can hope to be kept within limits only if its aims are more or less the aims of conventional politics—only if it poses no basic, revolutionary questions about the organization of society and the legitimacy of states. Wars enter their most dangerous territory not when they lose touch with chivalry but when they aim to remake the world.

That suggests a second lesson: great risks for the law of war arise when we commit ourselves to grand campaigns in the name of good government, campaigns for regime change. The curse of modern warfare, and of the modern law of war, is not that we have abandoned chivalry on the field of battle. The curse of modern warfare, and of the modern law of war, is that ever since 1863 and 1870 our wars have consistently ended up raising basic, revolutionary questions about the organization of society and the legitimacy of states. We want to go to war only when there is something foul or evil or aggressive about the regime we fight. In America in particular we want to fight only "good wars." Most especially we want to fight good wars that begin in self-defense and end in the revolutionary cause of spreading democracy through the world. Yet "good wars" easily become bad wars.

The consequence is that we face another paradox in the law of war, a paradox that we face in other areas of the law as well. This paradox arises whenever we try to found our law too much on the dictates of high morality. It arises, for example, in criminal law. We may tell ourselves that the machinery of criminal law is so awful that it should be used only in cases where a truly foul or evil act has been committed. The immense weight of government, we may say, should be brought to bear only on true evildoers, on persons who are deserving of the deepest blame. Taking that view helps us to steel ourselves for the dirty work of the law. It affords us what I have elsewhere called "moral comfort"; it helps us convince ourselves that we are doing awful things only in obedience to the highest moral imperatives.[15] Yet once we commit our criminal justice system to the fight against evil, we risk seeing it go into dangerous overdrive. It is no easy task to put the brakes on the fight against evil. The American criminal justice system has gone into just that kind of dangerous overdrive since the 1970s, in my view. The proposition that criminal law should be founded exclusively on the morality of just blame began in an American effort to limit the criminal law, but it has ended forty years later in a limitless exercise of state power.

The law of war is prey to the same paradox. Fighting wars only in the name of high morality sounds like the right thing to do, just as punishing crime in the name of high morality sounds like the right thing to do. Doing everything we can to rid the world of evil states sounds far better than deferring to the prerogatives of sovereigns. Founding our law of war on a highly developed jus ad bellum, informed by a strong commitment to the struggle against criminality and evil, affords us substantial moral comfort. Beginning wars only in self-defense or humanitarian intervention and fighting them for democracy once they have begun seems to put us on the side of the angels.

But fighting in the name of high morality easily degenerates into hard and bitter fighting. Huizinga understood this. Wars against "devils, heathens [or] heretics," he wrote, can never be fought in a limited way.[16] Schmitt understood it too. He was wrong to believe that medieval just war theory was about good and evil, but he was right about the consequences of framing war as a matter of good and evil more broadly: "Treating the enemy as a criminal runs parallel with the increased use of weapons of annihilation and the displacement of war beyond the field of battle."[17] Grotius fell victim to the dangers of this paradox when he held that "if the matter in question is worth fighting a war over" it would be "vain and impious" not to "deploy all of one's forces."[18] Just wars, that is to say, must be unlimited wars. That is exactly how the wars of religion were fought in Grotius's age, of course.

High morality is an exceedingly treacherous foundation for the law of war. The largest lesson of the eighteenth century is that it may be better that war should simply be a way of deciding who gets what, when, and how.

Of course, we cannot go back to the eighteenth century. The warfare of the eighteenth century was the product of peculiar and transitory circumstances. It came during a passing moment when legitimate monarchs triumphed after centuries of struggle with the armed nobility, and it was destined to last only as long as sole monarchical legitimacy lasted. It rested on a brutal disregard for the value of human life that we are no longer prepared to accept. And while the technology of war still permitted classic pitched battle warfare in the 1870s, it certainly no longer does. Nevertheless reflecting on the eighteenth century can help us as we weigh our modern dilemmas.

First of all, reflecting on the eighteenth century can remind us how much the problems of war remain bound up with problems of state legitimacy. To be sure, war-making and political legitimacy no longer stand in the same relationship that they stood in during the eighteenth century, at least among the wealthy democracies of the West. It is no longer necessary to make war in order to symbolize and reinforce state legitimacy. Modern Western states maintain their legitimacy in other ways: they offer the promise of prosperity, and they submit to elections. States founded on prosperity and consent have no imperative need of military glory to command obedience, any more than they have need of public executions. The nature of war abroad has inevitably changed because the nature of legitimation at home has changed.

Yet it is essential to recognize that the link between war-making and legitimacy has not been severed. Our regimes may no longer need to make war in order to bolster their legitimacy, but every government at war still seeks to bring home victory in order to win elections, and the fact that we fight for democracy abroad does something to reinforce the legitimacy of democracy at home. Moreover outside the wealthy West the relationship between war and legitimacy still bears a closer resemblance to its eighteenth-century form. When states claim the right to build nuclear weapons, for example, they are not just maneuvering for strategic advantage; they are insisting on their own fully legitimate sovereignty. And of course terrorist organizations too claim the legitimate right to make war. Like Grotius, determined to defend the legitimacy of the Dutch Republic in the midst of monarchies, modern terrorists insist that private war is permissible.

It is obvious enough that these are phenomena that we cannot understand if we think only about strategy. Military might is not just about strategy. Claims to legitimacy are at stake as well, just as they were in the eighteenth century. If we remember our own past, we may be able to muster some wisdom about how to deal with the present. The dynamic of legitimacy matters for thinking about nuclear proliferation, for example. It will not always be possible to disarm dangerous states, but we must remember that what counts for states is not just the strategic value of their arms but the symbolic value. France and Britain do not keep their nuclear arms because they expect ever to use them; they keep nuclear arms in order to proclaim their sovereignty to the world. Like the old nobility, they insist on their right to bear arms. Perhaps the best we can hope for, in the long run, is to encourage other states to take the same attitude. Perhaps the best we can hope for is the kind of solution that eighteenth-century monarchs managed: they forbade their nobilities to make private war, but they never denied them their right to bear arms. This was a formula that permitted those monarchs to maintain a high standard of peace.[19]

If we remember our past we can also maintain a clearer view of the risks in any foreign policy that raises symbolic doubts about the sovereignty of other states. The desire to denounce evil states is one we all feel powerfully, and in the world we live in it is inevitable that much of our foreign policy will aim at undermining evil states. Recent international law reflects the depth of that desire. Over the past decade, lawyers have promoted the norm of the "responsibility to protect," which would oblige the international community to use coercive measures against evil regimes.[20]

Yet we must bear in mind the costs and dangers of such projects. Every move we make that seems to question the sovereignty of other states creates a bit more incentive for those states to prove their sovereignty through violence. Sometimes it may be wise to display respect toward heavily armed sovereigns, however much we detest them. If we undermine their legitimacy they may lash out. The urge to run thugs out of power is always strong; but sometimes there is nothing worse than a failed state. Sometimes the most important thing is to establish a government that can maintain a monopoly of legitimate violence and put an end to a disastrous chaos. That certainly does not mean we should always tolerate thugs. What it means is that flexible diplomacy may be a better way of dealing with disreputable sovereigns than obligatory legal norms. Political leaders and diplomats must make hard choices—choices that may require them to depart from the strictest standards of high morality, while keeping an eye on the possibilities for long-term improvement.

Challenging the legitimacy of states in the name of justice carries terrible risks. That presents a delicate and difficult conundrum for our diplomats. It is not a good thing if the humanitarian tone of our international law makes the work of those diplomats even more difficult.

There is another critical feature of eighteenth-century warfare from which we can still learn something: its acquisitive character. Following a tradition that reached back into remote antiquity, eighteenth-century jurists and commanders understood war to be a means of acquiring property—a legitimate mode of the acquisition of crowns, territories, and booty. Even Christian just war theory assumed that war was a legitimate acquisitive enterprise. It was jus victoriae, law that specified the spoils to which victors were entitled.

This is an attitude that we are completely unwilling to embrace today. Since the mid-nineteenth century it has come to seem utterly unacceptable that wars should be fought for acquisitive gain. Indeed the sharpest charge that critics of modern wars raise, especially critics on the left, is that those wars are fought for acquisitive gain. The common refrain of opponents of the American War in Iraq, for example, was that it was a war fought not in self-defense, not for democracy, but for oil.

Yet in the eighteenth century no one felt any embarrassment about fighting wars for gain. This may sound shocking today, but here again we face a paradox: acquisitive wars, wars fought according to the banal calculus of gain, are wars that can (at least potentially) be fought within civilized limits. That is what the eighteenth-century experience shows. When we are simply out to make a profit, we do what we can to minimize our losses. Our willingness to make sacrifices is limited, and we are open to compromise. A thought experiment about the war in Iraq helps make the point. Suppose we *had* invaded Iraq solely to take control of its oil. Suppose that all of the forces engaged in the war had all had the same aim of controlling the oil of Iraq. Suppose that our law were the law of victory, declaring that the victor would be entitled to claim the oil of Iraq as spoils. As the fighting began to spin out of control, as losses on all sides began to mount, we might all have been willing to sit down at the table and cut a deal. There is no point in absorbing limitless losses in the pursuit of profit.

Acquisitive wars can be tame wars. To be sure, they are not necessarily so. One need think only of the monstrous wars over oil and diamonds fought in Africa today. It takes more than a mere profit-making mentality to keep war within bounds. Nevertheless acquisitive wars *can* be tame. They can potentially belong to the world of what eighteenth-century philosophers called *doux commerce*.[21] They can be wars that have the "sweetness" of commerce, wars informed by the willingness of the merchant to avoid unnecessary conflict in order to consolidate his gains. Twentieth-century caricatures always showed fat cigar-smoking capitalists plotting to trigger wars, but a moment always arrives when fat capitalists are ready to make peace.

The Battle of Chotusitz and its aftermath make for a fine example. Frederick the Great and Maria Theresa went into the battle calculating risks of profit and loss. Frederick in particular decided to accept the chance of arms, the hazard of a general affair, because he believed that the potential for gain was high enough to justify the risk he took. Once Frederick had driven the Austrians from the field of battle, both rivals made a calculation that it was wise to call a halt. Given their relative positions—including, of course, Maria Theresa's need to deploy her resources in the struggle against other powers—they were willing to sit down at the table and cut a deal. This was possible only because both Hohenzollerns and Habsburgs were engaged in a calculus of gains and losses.

Of course, there is something shocking in the mounting of such a calculating, acquisitive war. No one today would be in favor of permitting wars to be initiated for acquisitive goals. The acquisitive enterprises of these dynasts visited death upon thousands of their own subjects. On the field of Chotusitz alone, three thousand human beings perished, and thousands more suffered injuries that blighted their lives, all in order to gain a chunk of territory for the house of Hohenzollern. Nevertheless Chotusitz was an incident in a war that was successfully contained within the confines of the battlefield. In the words of Henry Maine, eighteenth-century wars were wars of a "ferocity and cupidity" that was sanctioned by the law of victory. But by making its concession to human cupidity and turning a jaundiced eye on human ferocity, the law found a way, as Maine wrote, to "command obedience to a rule."[22]

No one today, I repeat, would favor permitting wars to be initiated for acquisitive gain, and there are some wars, like the war against Hitler, that must be fought to the finish. But there are other wars in which we grow weary and want to make peace. If we still need the modern jus ad bellum, we also need a modern jus victoriae that will permit bargains between sovereigns in order to achieve peace. The best way to make a lasting peace may be to broker a deal in which everybody gains some material advantage so that everybody can claim a piece of victory. It is not a good thing if the humanitarian tone of our international law prevents us from cutting deals.

That does not mean that we should always bargain our way out of trouble. Appeasement is obviously sometimes a foolish strategy. But establishing democracies is sometimes a foolish strategy too. It is well to remember that one of the factors that favored Hitler's rise to power was the establishment of a republic in Weimar Germany that never enjoyed secure public legitimacy. The point is not that we should always choose one strategy over the other; the point is only that we should keep our options open. We should not allow our idealism to foreclose the option of bargaining our way out of trouble when it is *not* foolish to do so.

The frank acquisitiveness of war was only part of what explains the mentality of the dynasts at Chotusitz. It was also critically important that both Hohenzollerns and Habsburgs accepted the proposition that chance could decide human affairs. They did not believe that the outcome of great battles had to be the result of historical destiny. Their war was not yet what war became in the nineteenth century of Creasy: the Handmaiden of History. Their battles were not yet world-historical acts. An eighteenth-century pitched battle was an enforceable gamble accepted by risk takers in a world in which regimes could prosper and fail without any sense that their fortunes reflected the true drive or deep meaning of History. The ups and downs of the great dynastic houses of Europe bore, to that extent, a resemblance to the ups and downs of the great merchant houses of Europe: both were determined partly by sporadically random currents in a flow of history that had no necessary single strong direction. They could be the result of gambles of the kind Frederick the Great was famous for taking.

That attitude too is lost to us. Since at least the 1830s, if not the 1790s, wars have become struggles over the true course of history—over what forms of government and social organization will rule in the millennium toward which we suppose humanity to be marching. They have become the sort of conflicts that Creasy thought he could identify: Marathon, the battle that supposedly saved Western civilization, or Tours, the battle that supposedly kept Europe alive against the onslaught of Islam. Since the 1830s the tendency to see wars in that sort of millenarian light has taken firm hold. Our wars have become much less like gambles and much more like crusades.

Of course, some things have changed since the 1830s. In that era Westerners still imagined that wars would be fought in the form of pitched battles. Indeed the prevailing nineteenth-century philosophy of the history of war was a Great Event philosophy, a philosophy that imagined that a single battle could shape the course of human events for centuries. We no longer see the world that way. Weber condemned the notion that battles like Marathon were world-historical events as fantasies, founded on a failure to think clearly about history.[23] Thoughtful philosophers of history today agree. They generally think in terms of what Fernand Braudel called the *longue durée*: they believe that the real forces at work in history are long-term structural developments that have little or nothing to do with the everyday human experience of epiphenomenal events like pitched battles. And of course our wars no longer take the form of pitched battles at all.

Nevertheless the idea that wars are fought over world-historical stakes has by no means died. We remain prey to the belief that victory *proves* something about the course of history. World War II in particular seemed, to some of the victorious Allies, to prove that Western liberalism was destined to triumph, while to others it seemed just as clearly to prove the same thing about communism. Undoubtedly if the war had come out differently, it would have seemed to prove the inevitability of fascism. Of course, any such belief is nonsense. Braudel and Montesquieu were right: there are much larger economic and social forces at work. If those forces mean that Germany will dominate the continent of Europe, for example, from the point of view of economic history it does not ultimately matter who won World War I or II. Yet the horror and violence of war overwhelm our modern senses so much that we continue to look for great ultimate millennial meaning in the fact of victory or defeat.

The inevitable consequence is that we find it difficult to bring our wars to any generally accepted conclusion. If the world-historical meaning of Allied victory in World War I or World War II is that history intends Western democracy to triumph everywhere, then of course the wars cannot end until Western democracy triumphs everywhere. If the aim of the War in Iraq, latterly, is to bring the triumph of democracy to the Middle East, then of course the war can never end until democracy has triumphed in the Middle East. There is no law of victory to specify any lesser prize. There is no room to negotiate an end to the war because the expectations of the victor have become too absolute to permit a compromise.

Modern victors believe they are riding the wave of history, and it follows that they claim limitless rights. The American law of war developed a term for such a claim as World War II wound to its end: *unconditional surrender*, which began as a strategic doctrine but was transformed into a legal doctrine. After the war the Americans (like the Soviets) invoked unconditional surrender in order to claim the right to remake the societies of their defeated enemies. Inventing the doctrine of unconditional surrender required some juristic ingenuity. Classical international law would have permitted the victors to transform the society of a vanquished country only if they annexed that country or extinguished it.[24] The victorious Allies had no desire to annex or extinguish the Axis states, but they did desire to transform their societies. Unconditional surrender was the doctrine devised by the U.S. State Department, under heavy political pressure from the White House, to meet that need.[25] By virtue of unconditional surrender Americans declared their power to remodel Germany and Japan as Western democracies, while allowing them to continue to exist. (The Soviets, of course, made similar claims of their own.) It is the same doctrine of unconditional surrender that we applied, in effect, in Iraq.[26]

We want to believe that we are fighting in the service of History, and correspondingly unconditional surrender has emerged as our modern jus victoriae. Indeed unconditional surrender is all that modern American law possesses by way of a jus victoriae. It seems to us to have glorious antecedents in World War II, but lawyers have been very unsure about how it can be justified, and it is time that we recognize it makes for very poor legal doctrine. There were deep and important reasons for remodeling German and Japanese society after the war (though the effort was not always well-conceived and certainly not always successful). But it is by no means clear that the practices of World War II are the practices we should still be following today. If the doctrine of unconditional surrender is the only kind of jus victoriae we have, our law is dangerously impoverished. The value of the law, most of the time, does not lie in vindicating high ideals like democracy. It lies in creating a framework for negotiation. Good law makes peace. Most of the time that means allowing the parties to find a way to accommodate each other. Good law guarantees basic entitlements that the parties can then bargain over. That is how the classic jus victoriae worked: it accorded rights to victors in such a way that deals could be cut.

We need a law of victory that can help us cut deals and end wars without insisting that every victory must end in a great triumph for the historic cause of democracy. Of course, that *is* how wars end in practice, even today; diplomats do cut deals. The world has not gone entirely mad since the eighteenth century. The problem is that the modern law of war does too little to help the process along. On the contrary, the law threatens to make the process more difficult. Since the late nineteenth century, lawyers have become more and more firmly wedded to their idealistic work. They want to combat the horror of war through the jus in bello and the jus ad bellum, and more recently by creating an international criminal law and a humanitarian jus post bellum. They are eager to stand for high morality, to join a crusade for ultimate justice.

There is nothing wrong with humanitarian work, of course; humanitarian work is noble and important. And there *are* evils that must be put down because they are evil. Hitler is the incontestable example. Nevertheless some measure of thoughtful jus victoriae is essential for smoothing the process of most peacemaking. Life teaches all of us that the impulse to do justice is often at war with the need to make peace. If there is nothing wrong with humanitarian work, there would also be nothing necessarily wrong with finding ways to give victors a profitable reward for their victory so that they can return home in some kind of triumph, even if they have not succeeded in building a democracy and vindicating justice everywhere they have put their boots on the ground.

Wars will end more easily if the combatants can all be given something, even if that something is commercial concessions, access to oil, or cooperation in international policing. Wars will end more easily if we can cut deals, and to cut deals you need entitlements that you can trade away. Too much high morality makes it too hard to dicker. The law of war might save more lives if, instead of insisting that wars should be fought only to establish the millennium, it contributed its mite to making deal cutting a little easier. That does not mean that wars should be initiated for gain. We still need a proper jus ad bellum, and it is entirely right that the modern jus ad bellum should be founded in some conception of the right of self-defense, and perhaps in the necessity of humanitarian intervention. But all of our experience shows that wars, once begun, acquire new purposes. We need a jus victoriae to specify those purposes in such a way as to coax our wars to end with as little destructiveness as possible. We need law that defines victory in such way as to permit a brokered peace.

A law of war that awarded victors commercial concessions and oil in order to allow them to go home claiming victory may sound utterly repugnant. But to pretend that such interests have played no role in our wars is to make law for a fantasy world, and to admit that they have played a role is to add something to our repertoire of possibilities for making wars less awful. Good law is made for the world in which we live. It would be better if there were no wars at all. Who could possibly deny that? But there *are* wars, and the job of lawyers is not to create a perfect world; it is to patch together arrangements we can live with. Wars enter their most dangerous territory when they aim to remake the world, and the same is true of lawyers.

Notes

Acknowledgments

Index

Notes

INTRODUCTION

1. Sebastian Vrancx and Jan Brueghel the Younger, "The Aftermath of a Battle," Musée des Beaux-Arts de Liège. On Vrancx and his "plundering pictures," see David Kunzle, *From Criminal to Courtier: The Soldier in Netherlandish Art, 1550–1672* (Leiden, Netherlands: Brill, 2003), 293–297.

2. Henri Dunant, *A Memory of Solferino*, trans. anon. (Washington: American National Red Cross, 1939), 36–40.

3. See Chapter 2.

4. I have slightly altered the dramatic translation of Megasthenes, Indika, in *Ancient India as Described by Megasthenes and Arrian*, ed. J. W. McCrindle (Bombay: Education Society, 1877), 33. The text is preserved in *Diodorus of Sicily*, trans. C. H. Oldfather (Cambridge, MA: Harvard University Press, 1979), 2:8 (Diod. 2.36.7).

5. At least, Waterloo is remembered as a one-day battle. Thoughtful military historians might regard it as having lasted three days. Nevertheless, the narrative that has established itself is of a one-day conflict. The place of such conventional narratives is discussed in Chapter 1.

6. Jean Guilaine and Jean Zammit, *Le sentier de la guerre: Visages de la violence préhistorique* (Paris: Seuil, 2001), 51.

7. See the essays in Carsten Stahn and Jann K. Kleffner, eds., *Jus Post Bellum: Towards a Law of Transition from Conflict to Peace* (The Hague: Asser, 2008).

8. John Keegan, *The American Civil War: A Military History* (New York: Vintage, 2009), 235.

9. See, e.g., Robert Kolb and Richard Hyde, *An Introduction to the International Law of Armed Conflicts* (Oxford, UK: Hart, 2008), 9–10, 15. Ryan Goodman notes that

the distinctions between the two categories tends to break down in a world in which the same humanitarian assumptions underlie both. See Goodman, "Controlling the Recourse to War by Modifying *Jus in Bello*," *Yearbook of International Humanitarian Law* 12 (2009): 53–84.

10. See, e.g., Yoram Dinstein, *The Conduct of Hostilities under the Law of International Armed Conflict* (Cambridge: Cambridge University Press., 2004), 1–3; A. P. V. Rogers, *Law on the Battlefield*, 2nd ed. (Manchester: Manchester University Press, 2004), 3–7.

11. Dunant himself was not a modern humanitarian, of course. His aim was to care for the wounded, not to treat war as essentially evil. My point is only to emphasize that modern lawyers—and modern observers generally—share his sense of horror.

12. *Trial of the Major War Criminals before the International Military Tribunal, Nuremberg, 14 November 1945–1 October 1946* (Buffalo: Hein, 1995), 1: 186.

13. This is a phrase found occasionally in the pre-modern literature. See, e.g., Stephen C. Neff, *War and the Law of Nations, A General History* (Cambridge: Cambridge University Press, 2005), 66. It is also sometimes invoked among scholars who aim to create a humanitarian *jus post bellum*. See esp. Neff, "Conflict Termination and Peace-Making in the Law of Nations," in *Jus Post Bellum*, ed. Stahn and Kleffner, 77–92. For a critique of the use of the search for historical sources for a *jus post bellum*, see Gregory Lewkowicz, "*Jus post bellum*: Vieille ancienne ou nouvelle branche du droit," at http://www.philodroit.be/IMG/pdf/Lewkowicz_-_Jus_post_bellum.pdf.; and, for reflections by a learned scholar, see Randall Lesaffer, "Alberico Gentili's *Jus Post Bellum* and Early Modern Peace Treaties," in *The Roman Foundations of the Law of Nations: Alberico Gentili and the Justice of Empire*, ed. Benedict Kingsbury and Benjamin Straumann (New York: Oxford University Press, 2010), 210–240. I am adopting the term *jus victoriae* for my own purposes and in ways different from its most common pre-modern usage.

14. The key document, the Kellogg-Briand Pact of 1928, condemned "the recourse to war for the solution of international controversies." General Treaty for the Renunciation of War as an Instrument of National Policy, Art. I, in *League of Nations Treaty Series* 94 (1929): 63.

15. Brian Orend, "*Jus Post Bellum*: A Just War Perspective," in *Jus Post Bellum*, ed. Stahn and Kleffner, 38.

16. Immanuel Kant, "Zum ewigen Frieden," in Kant, *Über den Gemeinspruch: das Mag in der Theorie richtig sein, taugt aber nicht für die Praxis/Zum ewigen Frieden: Ein philosophischer Entwurf*, ed. Heiner F. Klemme (Hamburg: Meiner, 1992), 66.

17. See Robert Kolb, "Sur l'origine du couple terminologique *ius ad bellum/ius in bello*," *Revue internationale de la Croix Rouge* 79 (1997): 593–602. The distinction was certainly implicit in the earlier literature, but it was only clearly laid out in Kant's 1797 *Rechtslehre*. Immanuel Kant, *Metaphysische Anfangsgründe der Rechtslehre*, ed. Bernd Ludwig (Hamburg: Meiner, 1986), 164 (Pt. II, §53).

18. E.g., Jean-Mathieu Mattéi, *Histoire du droit de la Guerre, 1700-1819: Introduction à l'histoire du droit international* (Aix-en-Provence: Presses Universitaires d'Aix-Marseille, 2006), 30 and often.

19. "Force," as the political scientist Martha Finnemore wisely writes, "is viewed as legitimate only as a last resort, and only for defensive or humanitarian purposes. The

irony is that the diminished normative value has not brought any obvious decrease in the frequency or use of force. The twentieth century was one of the bloodiest on record." Finnemore, *The Purpose of Intervention: Changing Beliefs about the Use of Force* (Ithaca, NY: Cornell University Press, 2003), 19.

20. Eric Robson, "The Armed Forces and the Art of War," in *The New Cambridge Modern History*, ed. G. R. Potter and G. R. Elton, vol. 7: *The Old Regime, 1713–63*, ed. J. O. Lindsay (Cambridge: Cambridge University Press, 1979), 165.

21. Russell F. Weigley, *The Age of Battles: The Quest for Decisive Warfare from Breitenfeld to Waterloo* (Bloomington: Indiana University Press, 1991), 168.

22. David A. Bell, *The First Total War: Napoleon's Europe and the Birth of Warfare as We Know It* (Boston: Houghton Mifflin, 2007), 5.

23. Guglielmo Ferrero, "L'évolution de la guerre depuis trois siècles," *Revue internationale de la Croix-Rouge* 13 (1931), 183.

24. Carl Schmitt, *Theorie des Partisanen: Zwischenbemerkung zum Begriff des Politischen* (Berlin: Duncker & Humblot, 1963), 17.

25. Henry Stimson, "The Pact of Paris: Three Years of Development," *Foreign Affairs* 11 (1932) (Special Suppl.), iv.

26. Bell, *First Total War*, 50. Compare, e.g., R. R. Palmer, "Frederick the Great, Guibert, Bülow: From Dynastic to National War," in *Makers of Modern Strategy: From Machiavelli to the Nuclear Age*, ed. Peter Paret, with Gordon A. Craig and Felix Gilbert (Princeton, NJ: Princeton University Press, 1986), 91–119.

27. Michael Howard, "Constraints on Warfare," in *The Laws of War: Constraints on Warfare in the Western World*, ed. Michael Howard, George J. Andreopoulos, and Mark R. Shulman (New Haven, CT: Yale University Press, 1994), 4.

28. Geoffrey Best, *War and Law since 1945* (Oxford, UK: Clarendon, 1994), 17.

29. Neff, *War and the Law of Nations*, 57, 91, 186.

30. For unilateral and bilateral theories, see ibid., 163; and esp. the learned exposition in Peter Haggenmacher, *Grotius et la doctrine de la guerre juste* (Paris: Presses Universitaires de France, 1983), 279–311.

31. Bell, *First Total War*, 50.

32. See Barbara Ziereis, "Kriegsgeschichte im Spielfilmformat: Der erste Weltkrieg im Tonspielfilm der Weimarer Republik," in *Krieg und Militär im Film des 20. Jahrhunderts*, ed. Bernhard Chiari, Matthias Rogg, and Wolfgang Schmidt (Munich: Oldenbourg, 2003), 305.

33. Carl von Clausewitz, *On War*, ed. and trans. Michael Howard and Peter Paret (Princeton, NJ: Princeton University Press, 1976), 75.

34. Roger Chickering, introduction to *War in an Age of Revolution, 1775–1815*, ed. Roger Chickering and Stig Förster (Cambridge: Cambridge University Press, 2010), 5.

35. Schmitt, *Theorie des Partisanen*, 17. Bell's interesting account sees the transition as a transition from aristocratic culture to militarism, *First Total War*, 13 and often.

36. Emer Vattel, *Law of Nations*, trans. Joseph Chitty (London: Sweet, 1834), 374 (Bk. III, Chap. 10, §178). For a law of war text paying some attention to the importance of the doctrine of public war—though while devoting far more space to chivalry—see Leslie Green, *The Contemporary Law of Armed Conflict*, 3rd ed. (Manchester: Manchester University Press, 2008), 29–33, 35–36.

37. For these formulae, see Chapter 3.
38. Jean-Jacques Rousseau, "Jugement sur la paix perpétuelle de l'Abbé Saint-Pierre," in *Rousseau: Oeuvres complètes* (Paris: Gallimard, 1959), 3:594.
39. Johan Huizinga, *Homo Ludens: A Study of the Play Element in Culture* (Boston: Beacon, 1950).

1. WHY BATTLES MATTER

Epigraph: Vegetius, *Epitoma rei militaris*, ed. M. D. Reeve (Oxford: Clarendon, 2004), 91 (3.11.1): "ad . . . incertum et ad fatalem diem nationibus ac populis. . . . Nam in euentu aperti Martis uictoriae plenitudo consistit."

1. Christopher Allmand, "War and the Non-Combatant in the Middle Ages," in *Medieval Warfare: A History*, ed. Maurice Keen (New York: Oxford University Press, 1999), 260–261.
2. See, e.g., Aldo A. Settia, *Rapine, assedi, battaglie: La guerra nel Medioevo* (Rome: Laterza, 2002).
3. Allmand, "War and the Non-Combatant in the Middle Ages," 260–261.
4. Aristotle, *Politics*, trans. H. Rackham (Cambridge, MA: Harvard University Press, 1977), 30 (1255b, 37–39).
5. Leopold Pospisil, *Anthropology of Law: A Comparative Study* (New York: Harper and Row, 1971), 9.
6. Lawrence H. Keeley, *War before Civilization: The Myth of the Peaceful Savage* (New York: Oxford University Press, 1996), 22–24.
7. Napoleon A. Chagnon, *Yanomamo: The Fierce People*, 3rd ed. (New York: Holt, Rinehart and Winston, 1983).
8. Leo Frobenius, *Menschenjagden und Zweikämpfe* (Jena, Germany: Thüringer, 1902).
9. Azar Gat, *War in Human Civilization* (New York: Oxford University Press, 2006), 117.
10. Keeley, *War before Civilization*, 65–67.
11. Ibid., 88.
12. Frobenius, *Menschenjagden und Zweikämpfe*.
13. Keeley, *War before Civilization*, 59–60.
14. Jean Guilaine and Jean Zammit, *Le sentier de la guerre: Visages de la violence préhistorique* (Paris: Seuil, 2001), 51.
15. Mark Edward Lewis, *Sanctioned Violence in Early China* (Albany: State University of New York Press, 1990), 23–26, 38.
16. Discussion and citation to further literature in John A. Lynn, *Battle: A History of Combat and Culture* (Boulder, CO: Westview, 2003), 55–56; Stephen C. Neff, *War and the Law of Nations: A General History* (Cambridge: Cambridge University Press, 2005), 14–17, 23.
17. For the famous flower wars, in an account with a generally sober skepticism about the overall character of Aztec warfare, see Ross Hassig, *Aztec Warfare: Imperial*

Expansion and Political Control (Norman: University of Oklahoma Press, 1988), 54. For a broader account of ancient ritualized warfare, see Neff, *War and the Law of Nations*, 20–29.

18. Arnaldo Momigliano, "Some Observations on the Causes of War in Ancient Historiography," in *Studies in Historiography* (New York: Harper and Row, 1966), 120.

19. Hans van Wees, *Greek Warfare: Myths and Realities* (London: Duckworth, 2004), 124.

20. Demosthenes, "Third Philippic," in *Demosthenes*, trans. J. H. Vince (Cambridge, MA: Harvard University Press, 1970), 1:250 (9.48).

21. Van Wees, *Greek Warfare*, 134.

22. *Thucydides*, trans. C. F. Smith (Cambridge, MA: Harvard University Press, 1977), 3:78-80 (5.41.2); cf. *Herodotus*, trans. A. Godley (Cambridge, MA: Harvard University Press, 1981), 1:102-104 (1.82).

23. W. Kendrick Pritchett, *The Greek State at War* (Berkeley: University of California Press, 1974), 2:14.

24. *Herodotus*, trans. Godley, 2:2 (5.1.) To be sure, this passage is about a conflict in Thrace. Nevertheless, I cite it to illustrate a larger set of assumptions.

25. Jacqueline de Romilly, "Guerre et paix entre cités," in *Problèmes de la guerre en Grèce ancienne*, ed. J.-P. Vernant (The Hague: Mouton, 1968), 211.

26. Van Wees, *Greek Warfare*, 117, 126.

27. Peter Krentz, "Deception in Archaic and Classical Greek Warfare," in *War and Violence in Ancient Greece*, ed. Hans van Wees (London: Duckworth, 2000), 168, 170.

28. Keeley, *War before Civilization*, 174.

29. See, e.g., William V. Harris, *War and Imperialism in Republican Rome, 327–70 B.C.* (Oxford: Clarendon, 1979), 51–53.

30. See, e.g., Kurt-Georg Cram, *Iudicium belli: Zum Rechtscharakter des Krieges im deutschen Mittelalter* (Munich: Böhlau, 1955), 89; M. H. Keen, *The Laws of War in the Late Middle Ages* (London: Routledge & K. Paul, 1965).

31. Wilhelm Erben, *Die Schlacht bei Mühldorf: 28. September 1322*, Veröffentlichungen des Historischen Seminars der Universität Graz 1 (Graz: Leuschner and Lubensky, 1923).

32. See the discussion below, Chapter 5.

33. See the admirable statement of this point by David Whetham, *Just Wars and Moral Victories: Surprise, Deception and the Normative Framework of European War in the Later Middle Ages* (Leiden: Brill, 2009); Wolfgang Schild, "Schlacht als Rechtsentscheid," in *Schlachtfelder: Codierung von Gewalt im medialen Wandel*, ed. Steffen Martus, Marina Münkler, and Werner Röcke (Berlin: Akademie, 2003), 147–168; and classically the works of Keen and Cram.

34. Dante, *Dante's "Monarchia,"* trans. Richard Kay (Toronto: Pontifical Institute of Medieval Studies, 1998), 164 (2.9) "Quod per duellum acquiritur, de iure acquiritur. Nam ubicumque iudicium deficit, vel ignorantie tenebris involutum vel propter presidium iudicis non habere, ne iustitia derelicta remaneat recurrendum est ad Illum qui tantum eam dilexit ut quod ipsa exigebat, de proprio sanguine ipse moriendo supplevit." This represents the classic medieval concept of the recourse to God in cases in which human *ignorantia* made human justice impossible.

35. Frederick H. Russell, *The Just War in the Middle Ages* (Cambridge: Cambridge University Press, 1975), 25.

36. Georges Duby, *Le dimanche de Bouvines: 27 Juillet 1214* (Paris: Gallimard, 2005), emphasizes the fact that Bouvines took place on a Sunday. As Erben has shown, this was not uncommon. See Wilhelm Erben, *Kriegsgeschichte des Mittelalters*, Beiheft 16 der Historischen Zeitschrift (Munich: Oldenbourg, 1929), 89.

37. *Rudolfi Fuldensis Annales* in *Monumenta Germaniae Historica (Scriptores)* (Leipzig: Hiersemann, 1925), 1:363.

38. Werner Goez, "Über Fürstenzweikämpfe im Spätmittelalter," *Archiv für Kulturgeschichte* 49, no. 2 (1967): 159; Jonathan Sumption, *The Hundred Years War*, vol. 2: *Trial by Fire* (Philadelphia: University of Pennsylvania Press, 2001), 33-34.

39. Whetham, *Just Wars*, 7-14, summarized the development of the historiography.

40. Allmand, "War and the Non-Combatant," 260-261; cf., e.g., Settia, *Rapine, assedi, battaglie*, 4.

41. Justine Firnhaber-Baker, "Guerram Publice et Palam Faciendo: Local War and Royal Authority in Late Medieval France" (PhD diss., Harvard University, 2007), 53-54. My thanks to Professor Firnhaber-Baker for making her work available to me.

42. Gat, *War in Human Civilization*, 129.

43. See Chapter 6.

44. Jehuda L. Wallach, *The Dogma of the Battle of Annihilation: The Theories of Clausewitz and Schlieffen and Their Impact on the German Conduct of the Two World Wars* (Westport, CT: Greenwood, 1986).

45. See, e.g., Victor David Hanson, *Carnage and Culture: Landmark Battles in the Rise of Western Power* (New York: Doubleday, 2001), 440-441.

46. This was Henry Hallam's once famous *View of the State of Europe during the Middle Ages* (1818; New York: Colonial Press, 1899), 2:8 n. 0.

47. Edward Shepherd Creasy, *The Fifteen Decisive Battles of the World: From Marathon to Waterloo*, 29th ed. (London: Bentley, 1879), ix.

48. For discussion of the famous controversy between Eduard Meyer and Max Weber over the significance of Marathon, see Fritz Ringer, *Max Weber: An Intellectual Biography* (Chicago: University of Chicago Press, 2004), 81-82. See further the discussion in Chapter 6.

49. Richard Holmes and Martin Marix Evans, eds., *Battlefield: Decisive Conflicts in History* (New York: Oxford University Press, 2006), 7; Paul K. Davis, *100 Decisive Battles: From Ancient Times to the Present* (New York: Oxford University Press, 1999), 1.

50. Davis, *100 Decisive Battles*, 105. In fairness to Davis, his discussion is a piece of more carefully hedged hypothetical history than this one quote implies. Nevertheless his writing is typical of a literature that assumes that, all other things being equal, battles always determine the course of history in the same way.

51. Ibid., 138.

52. Montesquieu, *Considérations sur les causes de la grandeur des Romains et de leur décadence* (Paris: Hachette, 1945), 103.

53. J. F. Verbruggen, *The Art of Warfare in Western Europe during the Middle Ages: From the Eighth Century to 1340*, trans. Sumner Willard and S. C. M. Southern (Amsterdam, NY: North-Holland, 1977), 9.

54. Lynn, *Battle*.

55. John Keegan, *The Face of Battle* (New York: Penguin, 1978), 28.

56. Joseph de Maistre, *Les soirées de Saint-Pétersbourg: Septième entretien* (Paris: La Colombe, 1960), 227: "C'est l'imagination qui perd les batailles."

57. Hanson, *Carnage and Culture*, 7.

58. *Intruction militaire du Roi de Prusse pour ses généraux* (Frankfurt: n.p., 1761), 137 (Art. XXXIII).

59. See the discussion in the Conclusion.

60. Keegan, *Face of Battle*, at, e.g., 46.

61. Hervé Drévillon, *Batailles: Scènes de guerre de la table ronde aux tranchées* (Paris: Seuil, 2007), 253–296.

62. Caesar, *The Gallic War*, trans. H. J. Edwards (Cambridge, MA: Harvard University Press, 2006), 38 (1.26).

63. Tom R. Tyler, *Why People Obey the Law* (Princeton, NJ: Princeton University Press, 2006).

64. *Livy*, trans. F. G. Moore (Cambridge, MA: Harvard University Press, 1971), 8: 484 (30.32): "Roma an Carthago iura gentibus daret ante crastinam noctem scituros."

65. Pospisil, *Anthropology of Law*, 9.

2. ACCEPTING THE WAGER OF BATTLE

Epigraph: Éléazar Mauvillon, *Histoire de la dernière guerre de Bohème* (Amsterdam: La Compagnie, 1701 [1745]), 2:1.

1. Michael Howard, "Constraints on Warfare," in *The Laws of War: Constraints on Warfare in the Western World*, ed. Michael Howard, George J. Andreopoulos, and Mark R. Shulman (New Haven, CT: Yale University Press, 1994), 5–6.

2. The haunting closing lines of Charles Baudelaire's "La cloche fêlée," from *Les fleurs du mal* (Paris: Poulet-Malassis et de Broise, 1857), 137: "le râle épais d'un blessé qu'on oublie / Au bord d'un lac de sang, sous un grand tas de morts / Et qui meurt, sans bouger, dans d'immenses efforts." These lines echo the equally famous but (to our ears) shockingly comical account of the survival of the title character on the field of Eylau in Balzac's *Le Colonel Chabert* (1832), whose head pops out from among the corpses "like a mushroom." See *Oeuvres de H. de Balzac* (Brussels: Meline, Cans, 1837), 3:349. In the comparison of the two works, we can take the measure of the shift in European attitudes toward the horror of war over that critical quarter century.

3. Robert Darnton, *The Great Cat Massacre and Other Episodes in French Cultural History* (New York: Basic, 1984), 77–78.

4. See, e.g., Pieter Spierenburg, *The Spectacle of Suffering: Executions and the Evolution of Repression, from a Preindutstrial Metropolis to the European Experience* (Cambridge: Cambridge University Press, 1984).

272 Notes to Pages 51–57

5. Most famously illustrated in Jacques Callot's series of prints *Les grandes misères de la guerre* (1633).

6. Samuel, Freiherr von Pufendorf, *De jure naturae et gentium libri octo* (Buffalo, NY: Hein, 1995), 521–522 (bk. V, chap. 9, § 3); see also 901–904 (bk. VIII, chap. 8).

7. Stephen C. Neff, *War and the Law of Nations: A General History* (Cambridge: Cambridge University Press, 2005), 138. I have benefited from Neff's account on 131–158, but I dissent from his verdict that the wager theory can be properly characterized as a "dueling" theory.

8. August Wilhelm Heffter, *Das europäische Völkerrecht der Gegenwart*, 3rd ed. (Berlin: Schroeder, 1855), 203.

9. Pufendorf, *De jure naturae et gentium*, 521–522 (bk. V, chap. 9, § 3).

10. Mauvillon, *Histoire de la dernière guerre de Bohème*, 2:1.

11. "Manifeste du Roi contre la cour de Dresde, Berlin, l'an 1745," in *Preussische Staatsschriften aus der Regierungszeit König Friedrichs II (1740–1745)*, ed. Reinhold Koser (Berlin: Duncker, 1877), 695.

12. Azar Gat, *War in Human Civilization* (New York: Oxford University Press, 2006), 129.

13. Jean Bodin, *Les six livres de la République* (Paris: Fayard, 1986), 5:152.

14. Jean-Jacques Rousseau, "Jugement sur la paix perpétuelle de l'Abbé Saint-Pierre," in *Rousseau: Oeuvres complètes* (Paris: Gallimard, 1959), 3:594.

15. *Trial of the Major War Criminals before the International Military Tribunal, Nuremberg, 14 November 1945–1 October 1946* (Buffalo: Hein, 1995), 22:464.

16. Eric Robson, "The Armed Forces and the Art of War," in *The New Cambridge Modern History*, ed. G. R. Potter and G. R. Elton, vol. 7: *The Old Regime, 1713–63*, ed. J. O. Lindsay (Cambridge: Cambridge University Press, 1979), 165.

17. I take the quote from Edward Gibbon's description of the idealized pre-Enlightenment of the Age of the Antonines: *The History of the Decline and Fall of the Roman Empire*, ed. J. B. Bury (London: Methuen, 1909), 1:86.

18. Kalevi J. Holsti, *Peace and War: Armed Conflicts and International Order, 1648–1989* (Cambridge: Cambridge University Press, 1991), 64.

19. Robson, "The Armed Forces and the Art of War," 165.

20. See, e.g., Armstrong Starkey, *War in the Age of Enlightenment, 1700–1789* (Westport, CT: Greenwood, 2003), 6.

21. Russell F. Weigley, *The Age of Battles: The Quest for Decisive Warfare from Breitenfeld to Waterloo* (Bloomington: Indiana University Press, 1991), 168.

22. Michael Howard, *War in European History*, rev. ed. (New York: Oxford University Press, 2009), 60.

23. For the defense of this traditional view against the claims of Martin van Creveld, see John A. Lynn, "The History of Logistics and Supplying War," in *Feeding Mars: Logistics in Western Warfare from the Middle Ages to the Present* (Boulder, CO: Westview, 1993), 17–18.

24. Emer de Vattel, *The Law of Nations; or, Principles of the Law of Nature, Applied to the Conduct and Affairs of Nations and Sovereigns*, trans. Joseph Chitty (London: Sweet, 1834), 365–366 (bk. III, chap. 9, §165). For the broader juristic discussion of the substitution of contributions for pillage, see Jean-Mathieu Mattéi, *Histoire du*

droit de la guerre, 1700–1819: Introduction à l'histoire du droit international (Aix-en-Provence: Presses Universitaires d'Aix-Marseille, 2006), 2:768–772.

25. Adam Smith, *Lectures on Justice, Police, Revenue and Arms Delivered in the University of Glasgow, Reported by a Student in 1763*, ed. Edwin Cannan (Oxford: Clarendon, 1896), 273.

26. See, e.g., Gat, *War in Human Civilization*, 464–465, summarizing much literature.

27. Randall Lesaffer, "Siege Warfare in the Early Modern Age: A Study on the Customary Laws of War," in *The Nature of Customary Law*, ed. Amanda Perreau-Saussine and James Bernard Murphy (Cambridge: Cambridge University Press, 2007), 176–202; Fred Anderson, *Crucible of War: The Seven Years' War and the Fate of Empire in British North America, 1754–1766* (New York: Vintage, 2000), 253. For an eighteenth-century description of orderly surrender upon siege, see Johann Christian Lünig, *Theatrum ceremoniale historico-politicum, oder Historisch- und politischer Schau-Platz aller Ceremonien* (Leipzig: Weidmann, 1719–1720), 2:1258–1259.

28. [M. M.], *Nouveau dictionnaire historique des sièges et batailles mémorables, et des combats maritimes les plus fameux, de tous les peuples du monde, anciens et modernes, jusqu'à nos jours*, 6 vols. (Paris: Gilbert, 1809).

29. John A. Lynn, *Battle: A History of Combat and Culture* (Boulder, CO: Westview, 2003), 144.

30. For a detailed survey, see David Chandler, *The Art of Warfare in the Age of Marlborough* (London: Batsford, 1976). The problems were, of course, much more complex than my text indicates. For infantry practices, see [Jean-Lambert-Alphonse] Colin, *L'infanterie au XVIIIe siècle: La tactique* (Paris: Berger-Levrault, 1907), 31–32, 35–36.

31. *Intruction militaire du Roi de Prusse pour ses généraux* (Frankfurt: n.p., 1761), 137 (art. XXXIII).

32. Maurice, comte de Saxe, *Les rêveries* (Paris: H. Charles-Lavauzelle, 1895), 119.

33. Gibbon, *History of the Decline and Fall of the Roman Empire*, 4:178. This famous passage, read in context, does not contend that eighteenth-century warfare was indecisive in the modern sense. What Gibbon wrote was that the wars of his time were "undecisive" because they did not permit any single power to dominate Europe. His statement was about balance-of-power politics, not about the conduct of warfare.

34. See, e.g., Dennis Showalter, *The Wars of Frederick the Great* (London: Longman, 1996), 1–2. John Lynn famously coined the phrase *war as process*. See Lynn, "International Rivalry and Warfare, 1700–1815," in *The Short Oxford History of Europe: Eighteenth-Century Europe*, ed. T. C. W. Blanning (New York: Oxford University Press, 2000), 178–217. See also Jeremy Black, *European Warfare, 1660–1815* (New Haven, CT: Yale University Press, 1994), 67–87.

35. Howard, *War in European History*, 70–71; in the legal literature, Neff, *War and the Law of Nations*, 88.

36. See, e.g., François Eugène de Vault and Jean Jacques Germain, Baron Pelet, eds., *Mémoires militaires relatifs à la succession d'Espagne sous Louis XIV* (Paris: Imprimerie Royale, 1835–1862), 10:63.

37. Carl von Clausewitz, *Vom Kriege: Hinterlassenes Werk des Generals Carl von Clausewitz* (Bonn: Dümmler, 1980), Nachricht, 182–183.

38. Ibid., 191 (bk. I, chap. 1), 467–468 (bk. IV, chap. 11).
39. Victor David Hanson, *Carnage and Culture: Landmark Battles in the Rise of Western Power* (New York: Doubleday, 2001), 8, 24.
40. Black, *European Warfare*, 70.
41. Weigley, *Age of Battles*, 537–538.
42. Black, *European Warfare*, 74.
43. Black is cautious in his claims and not entirely willing to abandon the prevailing view. He concedes that there could be ultimate indecisiveness in the eighteenth century, owing to a politically determined "inability of states to exploit fully their military potential." Ibid., 85.
44. Ibid.
45. Ian Brownlie, *International Law and the Use of Force by States* (Oxford: Clarendon, 1963), 17.
46. Sharon Korman, *The Right of Conquest: The Acquisition of Territory by Force in International Law and Practice* (New York: Oxford University Press, 1996), 68–72.
47. Gerhard Ritter, *Frederick the Great: A Historical Profile*, trans. Peter Paret (Berkeley: University of California Press, 1968), 80–81.
48. See especially Gerhard Ritter, *Staatskunst und Kriegshandwerk: Das Problem des "Militarismus" in Deutschland* (Munich: Oldenbourg, 1954), 1:42–45. For discussion of Ritter's intentions in 1936, and the ambiguous reception of his book, see Christoph Cornelißen, *Gerhard Ritter: Geschichtswissenschaft und Politik im 20. Jahrhundert* (Düsseldorf: Droste, 2001), 502–503.
49. Even the superbly well-informed account of Theodor Schieder, *Frederick the Great*, trans. S. Berkeley and H. Scott (London: Longman, 2000), 90–98, includes the judgment that Frederick "demonstrated that legal claims mattered less to him than military action." Ibid., 98. Other relatively sober accounts certainly can be found. See, e.g., Jürgen Ziechmann, *Fridericianische Encyclopédie* (Bremen: Hauschild, 2011), 180–181. Historians are of course aware of Frederick's claims in the law of dynastic succession, and especially in Germany they recite them. It is the larger context of the law of war, which I present in Chapters 3 and 4, that has been forgotten.
50. Korman, *Right of Conquest*, 72, citing Lord Acton, *Lectures on Modern History*, ed. John Neville Figgis and Reginald Vere Laurence (London: Macmillan, 1926), 291.
51. See Thomas Carlyle's effort in *History of Frederick II of Prussia, Called Frederick the Great* (Leipzig: Tauchnitz, 1862), 6:161 to dismiss Frederick's insistence that he was simply claiming his rights. Elsewhere Carlyle's account is generally quite solid.
52. Nathan Ausubel, *Superman: The Life of Frederick the Great* (New York: Washburn, 1931).
53. Antoine Henri, baron de Jomini, *Summary of the Art of War or, A New Analytical Compend of the Principal Combinations of Strategy, of Grand Tactics and of Military Policy*, trans. O. F. Winship and E. E. McLean (New York: Putnam, 1854), 27.
54. See, e.g., Robert T. Foley, *German Strategy and the Path to Verdun: Erich von Falkenhayn and the Development of Attrition, 1870–1916* (Cambridge: Cambridge University Press, 2005), 41–45.

55. Korman, *Right of Conquest*, 72 n. 28.

56. For a general account see, e.g., Reed Browning, *The War of the Austrian Succession* (New York: St. Martin's Press, 1993).

57. Mattéi, *Histoire du droit de la guerre*, 71, 823–1068; Frederik Dhondt, "From Contract to Treaty: The Legal Transformation of the Spanish Succession, 1659–1713," *Journal of the History of International Law* 13 (2011): 347–375.

58. See Showalter, *Wars of Frederick the Great*, 45–51.

59. Preussen. Grosser Generalstab, *Der erste schlesische Krieg* (Berlin: Mittler, 1890–1893), 3:254. Part of the Austrian forces retreated to Horka, 5 kilometers south of Chotusitz, though other elements retreated further. Showalter, *Wars of Frederick the Great*, 59–61 gives a thoughtful account.

60. "Nous étions cette fois [i.e., à Mollwitz] trop heureux de n'être pas battus pour pousser au delà de notre ambition. A Czaslau, je suivis, autant que je pus, les ennemis avec mon infanterie sans vouloir la débander. À la vérité, si ma cavalerie n'eût pas été dans le désordre que je vous ai dépeint tantôt, je l'eusse poussée en avant, mais les têtes n'étoient pas assez rassises pour leur confier une pareille besogne." Frederick in conversation with the Comte de Gisors, Camille-Félix-Michel Rousset, in *Le Comte de Gisors: 1732–1758* (Paris: Didier, 1868), 106. Frederick further excused his failure to pursue the enemy by saying that he, unlike the French, could not take too many risks, because with his few resources he was not "en état de supporter de grandes pertes." Ibid.

The Marquis de Valori, a diplomat deeply involved in the events, described Frederick's failure to annihilate in this way: "A Czaslau, il fut en quelque façon surpris, sachant cependant que les ennemis devaient l'attaquer et faire la paix s'ils étaient battus. Ce fut, en effet, la suite qu'eut cette bataille, où il fit la même faute qu'à Molwitz en ne suivant point sa victoire, quoiqu'il eût promis à Schmettaw qui lui en démontra la facilité et l'utilité. Le dessein où il était de faire la paix, lui fit croire qu'il n'avait pas besoin d'achever de battre ses ennemis, et en cela il se méprit beaucoup." *Mémoires des négociations du marquis de Valori* (Paris: Didot, 1820), 1:259–260. A similar report was given by Frederick's staff officer Carl von Schmettau, who "counseled Frederick to make a lively pursuit of the enemy." Frederick, it is reported, replied that Schmettau was right—but added, "[I]ch will sie nicht so weit herunter bringen." *Lebensgeschichte des Grafen von Schmettau* (Berlin: Himburg, 1806), 2:222.

61. Belleisle, letter from Kuttenberg, June 4, 1742, in Ministère des Affaires Étrangères, Archives Diplomatiques, Correspondance Politique (Prusse), 122:13, La Courneuve, France.

62. Valori, June 6, 1742, in Ministère des Affaires Étrangères, Archives Diplomatiques, Correspondance Politique (Prusse), 122:26, La Courneuve, France.

63. Mauvillon, *Histoire de la dernière guerre de Bohème*, 2:105.

64. See *Politische Correspondenz Friedrichs des Grossen*, ed. J. H. Droysen (Berlin: Duncker & Humblot, 1879), 2:164–175.

65. *Mémoires du duc de Luynes sur la cour de Louis XV* (Paris: Firmin Didot, 1860) 4:149.

66. Draft letter to Frederick, June 1, 1742, in Ministère des Affaires Étrangères, Archives Diplomatiques, Correspondance Politique (Prusse), 122:2, La Courneuve, France.

67. Christophe de Koch, *Abrégé de l'histoire des traités de paix entre les puissances de l'Europe depuis la Paix de Westphalie* (Basel: Decker, 1796), 2:54: "victoire complette."

68. Voltaire, lettre 1505 (to Frederick the Great), in *Oeuvres Complètes de Voltaire*, vol. 36: *Correspondance IV* (Paris: Garnier, 1880), 128–129; Samuel Johnson, letter 17 (to the Reverend Dr. Taylor), in *Letters of Samuel Johnson, LL.D.*, ed. George Birkbeck Hill (New York: Harper, 1892), 1:13. Johnson observed that the victory had cost Frederick twice as many men as the Austrians, but he expressed no doubt that it was a victory.

69. Weigley, *Age of Battles*, 173.

70. Vattel, *Law of Nations*, 374–375 (bk. III, chap. 10, §178); cf. Pufendorf, *De jure naturae et gentium*, 521–523 (bk. V, chap. 9, § 3).

71. *Mémoires des négociations du marquis de Valori*, 1:259–260.

72. Draft of letter to Valori, May 27, 1742, Ministère des Affaires Étrangères, Archives Diplomatiques, Correspondance Politique (Prusse), 121:438, La Courneuve, France.

73. Abbé de Mably, *The Principles of Negotiations; or, An Intoduction to the Public Law of Europe Founded on Treaties, Etc.* (London: Rivington & Fletcher, 1758), 3.

74. Marquise du Chatelet au Roi de Prusse, June 2, 1742, in *Lettres de la Marquise du Chatelet*, ed. Eugène Asse (Paris: Charpentier, 1878), 435.

75. R. R. Palmer, *A History of the Modern World*, 3rd ed. (New York: Knopf, 1961), 126; Derek Croxton, *Peacemaking in Early Modern Europe: Cardinal Mazarin and the Congress of Westphalia, 1643–1648* (Selinsgrove, PA: Susquehanna University Press, 1999), 24–25.

76. See, e.g., Charles Giraud, *Le Traité d'Utrecht* (Paris: Plon,1847), 102.

77. Letter to Podewils, May 26, 1742, in *Politische Correspondenz Friedrichs des Grossen*, 2:179.

78. *Les principes généraux de la guerre*, chap. 26: "Pourquoi et comment on livre bataille," in *Oeuvres de Frédéric le Grand*, ed. J. D. E. Preuss (Berlin: Decker, 1856), 28:93.

79. For her aims, see the account in Alfred Ritter von Arneth, *Geschichte Maria Theresia's* (Vienna: Braumüller, 1875), 6:121–125.

80. Pufendorf, *De jure naturae et gentium*, 521–522 (bk. V, chap. 9, § 3); see also 901–904 (bk. VIII, chap. 8).

81. Ibid. Cf. especially 903 (bk. VIII, chap. 8, §5).

82. Gaspard de Réal de Curban, *La science du gouvernement, ouvrage de morale, de droit et de politique* (Paris: Libraires Associés, 1764), 5:621.

83. For the rejection of a defense of duress more generally in eighteenth-century law, see Mattéi, *Histoire du droit de la guerre*, 954–956.

84. Johann Ludwig Klüber, *Europäisches Völkerrecht* (Stuttgart: Cotta, 1821), 1:414 (§256): "der durch das Schicksal der Waffen entstandene Verlust" conveys full title on the victor, but (as Klüber emphasizes) only once peace is agreed upon.

85. *Encyclopédie méthodique par ordre des matières* (Paris: Panckoucke, 1789) 29:3, 43: "une espèce de convention tacite qui tient du contrat des jeux de hasard."

86. See *Oxford Latin Dictionary*, s.v. "anceps."

87. See, e.g., Vault and Pelet, *Militaires relatifs à la succession d'Espagne sous Louis XIV*, 11:48.

88. In Edward Barrington de Fonblanque, *Political and Military Episodes in the Latter Half of the Eighteenth Century, derived from the Life and Correspondence of the Right Hon. John Burgoyne, General, Statesman, Dramatist* (London: Macmillan, 1876), 477.

89. François-Alexandre Aubert de La Chesnaye des Bois, *Dictionnaire militaire portatif, contenant tous les termes propres à la guerre* (Paris: Duchesne, 1758), 459.

90. "Manifeste du Roi contre la cour de Dresde, Berlin, l'an 1745," 695.

91. Frederick, Letter 809 to the Maréchal de Belleisle, June 18, 1742, in *Politische Correspondenz Friedrichs des Grossen*, 206.

92. "Histoire de mon Temps," in *Oeuvres de Frédéric le Grand*, 2:82.

93. Johannes Gronovius, Jean Barbeyrac, Heinrich Cocceji, and Samuel Cocceji, commentary in *Hugonis Grotii de iure belli ac pacis libri tres, cum annotatis auctoris, nec non J. F. Gronovii Notis & J. Barbeyracii animadversionibus commentariis insuper locupletissimis Henr. l. b.. de Cocceii . . . Insertis quoque Observationibus Samuelis l. b. de Cocceii* (Lausanne: Bousquet, 1752) 4:369 (Heinrich and Samuel Cocceji). For the Spanish Neo-Scholastics, e.g., Vitoria: until victory came, he declared, "res est in periculo," chance rules. Discussed in Peter Haggenmacher, *Grotius et la doctrine de la guerre juste* (Paris: Presses Universitaires de France, 1983), 275.

94. St. Thomas Aquinas, *Summa Theologiae: Latin Text and English Translation* (New York: McGraw-Hill, n.d.), 40:64 (2a 2ae q. 95, 8); Samuel Cocceji, commentary in *Hugonis Grotii de iure belli ac pacis*, 4:369.

95. See, e.g., Vault and Pelet, *Mémoires militaires relatifs à la succession de L'Espagne*, 10:63: "[L]'événement d'un combat est toujours incertain"; de La Chesnaye des Bois, *Dictionnaire miltiaire portatif*, 459.

96. For the contractual analysis in Roffredus and other early treatise writers, see Marco Cavina, *Il duello giudiziario per punto d'onore: Genesi, apogeo e crisi nell'elaborazione dottrinale italiana* (Turin: Giappichelli, 2003), 53. The contractual analysis was also chewed over among the Spanish Neo-Scholastics, who considered it from the point of view of both internal and external fora. See the discussion of Suarez and Lessius in Haggenmacher, *Grotius et la doctrine de la guerre juste*, 293–294; and Josef Soder, *Francisco Suárez und das Völkerrecht: Grundgedanken zu Staat, Recht und internationalen Beziehungen* (Frankfurt: Metzner, 1973), 308–309.

97. For a classic nineteenth-century discussion, rich in comparative material, see Bernhard Mathiass, *Die Entwicklung des römischen Schiedsgerichts* (Rostock: Stiller, 1888), 7–18; and further Karl von Amira, *Nordgermanisches Obligationenrecht* (Leipzig: Veit, 1892), bk. 2, vol. 1:249–256. For medieval *Zweikämpfe* as legal *Kampfwette*, see Udo Friedrich, "Die 'symbolische Ordnung' des Zweikampfs im Mittelalter," in *Gewalt im Mittelalter: Realitäten, Imaginationen*, ed. Manuel Braun and Cornelia Herberichs (Munich: Fink, 2005), 154.

98. I have made this argument at length in James Q. Whitman, *The Origins of Reasonable Doubt: Theological Roots of the Criminal Trial* (New Haven, CT: Yale University Press, 2008), 14–16.

99. John Keegan, *The Face of Battle* (New York: Penguin, 1978), 28.

100. "Commodum eius esse debet, cuius periculum est." This is the conventional formula, drawn from the classical texts.

101. Kurt-Georg Cram, *Iudicium belli: Zum Rechtscharakter des Krieges im deutschen Mittelalter* (Münster: Böhlau, 1955), 108.

102. In making this argument I take sides in what is now an old, and perhaps forgotten, debate. Older German scholars argued the medieval war was a *Kampfwette*. See especially Cram, *Iudicium belli*; and Karl Gotthelf Jakob Weinhold, "Beiträge zu den deutschen Kriegsalterthümern," *Sitzungsberichte der Königlich Preussischen Akademie der Wissenschaften zu Berlin*, Philos.-hist. Cl. (1891, no. 2): 543–567. These scholars tended to see the legal forms they identified as survivals of ancient "Germanic" practices. Postwar scholars, understandably uncomfortable with that sort of Germanizing analysis, attacked them. See especially Franz Pietzcker, "Die Schlacht bei Fontenoy," *Zeitschrift der Savigny-Stiftung für Rechtsgeschichte* (Germ) 81 (1964): 318–340. It is not my intention in the least to endorse the supposed "Germanic" roots of these practices. The question, rather, is whether the combat wager is a widespread human phenomenon, in war as in other legal activities. It is. It is entirely comprehensible that in the wake of 1933–1945 scholars would want to distance themselves from scholarly nationalism. But it would be very wrong to abandon the insights of classic German scholarship simply because they appealed, for the wrong reasons, to the Nazis.

103. Cf. Haggenmacher, *Grotius et la doctrine de la guerre juste*, 433–437.

104. *Herodotus*, trans. A. Godley (Cambridge, MA: Harvard University Press, 1982), 2:2 (5.1.).

105. *Livy*, trans. B. O. Foster (Cambridge, MA: Harvard University Press, 1976), 1:82 (1.24). I have slightly altered Foster's English translation on p. 83.

106. Ibid., 78 (1.23): "[E]ventus tamen belli minus miserabilem dimicationem fecit, quod nec acie certatum est et tectis modo dirutis alterius urbis duo populi in unum confusi sunt."

107. Aquinas, *Summa Theologiae*, 40:64 (2a 2ae q. 95, 8).

108. Dante, *Dante's "Monarchia,"* trans. Richard Kay (Toronto: Pontifical Institute of Medieval Studies, 1998), 164 (2.9).

109. Although they certainly were acceptable in those circumstances. See Aquinas, *Summa Theologiae*, 40:64 (2a 2ae q. 95, 8); and for the orthodoxy of this view, see Cavina, *Duello giudiziario per punto d'onore*, 43 n. 143.

110. I have taken the translation of *nationibus ac populis* as "nations" from a contemporary French translation: Vegetius, *De re militari libri quinque, cum selectis notis G. Stevvechii et P. Scriverii, nec non ad codicum manuscriptorum fidem notis perpetuis criticis emendati, addita versione gallica* (Nürnberg: Raspe, 1767), 300.

111. Raimundo Montecuccoli, "Della battaglia," in *Opere*, ed. Giuseppe Grassi (Milan: Silvestri, 1831), 1:258.

112. See the discussion by Maureen Slattery, "King Louis XI: Chivalry's Villain or Anti-Hero," *Fifteenth Century Studies* 23 (1997), 59; and, for the later influence,

Heinrich Rantzau, *Commentarius bellicus* (Frankfurt: Apud Zachariam Palthenium, 1595), 169.

113. Bodin, *Six livres de la République*, 5:152: "Il ne faut pas mettre un Royaume au hazard d'une victoire."

114. "Apologie de Raimond Sebond," in *Essais de Michel de Montaigne* (N.p.: Imprimerie Nationale, 1998), 2:226–227 (bk. 2, chap. 12).

115. Rantzau, *Commentarius bellicus*, 169.

116. Niccolò Machiavelli, *Discorsi sopra la prima deca di Tito Livio, seguiti dalle considerazioni intorno ai discorsi del Machiavelli di Francesco Guicciardini*, ed. Corrado Vivanti (Turin: Einaudi, 1997), 61.

117. Alciato, "De Singulari Certamine," in *Tractatus universi iuris* (Venice: n.p., 1584) 12:293v (3, §8) [293r–308v]. François Hotman in particular endorsed the contractual analysis that would dominate in the eighteenth century: *De feudis commentatio tripertita* (Lyon: Apud Iohannem Lertotium, 1573), "Disputatio de iure feudali," cap. XLV, 123, describing arranged battles in contractual terms as a "duorum pluriumve concertatio . . . ut ex . . . eventu de re ambigua diiudicetur."

118. Machiavelli, *Discorsi sopra la prima deca di Tito Livio*, 362; cf. Francesco Guicciardini, *Storia d'Italia*, ed. G. Rossini (Naples: Unione Tipografica-Editrice Torinese, 1874), 1: 230 (bk. 2, chap. 5): "[I]n tutte le azioni umane, e nelle guerre massimamente, bisogna spesso accomodare il consiglio alla necessità, né, per desiderio di ottenere quella parte che è troppo difficile e quasi impossibile, esporre il tutto a manifestissimo pericolo."

119. Cf. the discussion of Haggenmacher, *Grotius et la doctrine de la guerre juste*, 293–294, presenting nuanced treatments in both internal and external fora.

120. Balthasar Ayala, *De iure et officiis bellicis et disciplina militari libri III*, ed. John Westlake (Washington: Carnegie Institution, 1912), 28v–29r (bk. I, chap. 3, §11).

121. Ibid., 29 (bk. I, chap. 3, §13).

122. For a brief discussion see Fritz Helge Voß, *Ius belli: Zum völkerrechtlichen Kriegsrecht in Europa in der sog. Spanischen Epoche der Völkerrechtsgeischte* (Baden-Baden: Nomos, 2007), 175–176.

123. "La guerre fait péricliter tout un État," as the French version of Grotius had it. *Droit de la paix et de la guerre de M. Grotius*, trans. Antoine de Courtin (Amsterdam: Wolfgang, 1688), 97 (bk. 1, chap. 3).

124. See the discussion in Chapter 5.

125. Grotius, *De iure belli ac pacis* (repr. Buffalo, NY: Hein, 1995), 583–584 (bk. 3, chap. 20, §§42–43).

126. Ibid., 583 (bk. 3, chap. 20, §42).

127. Ibid., 4:336 (bk. 3, chap. 20, §43).

128. Ibid.

129. See Franciscus Zypaeus, *Notitia juris belgici* (Antwerp: Verdussen, 1665), 119.

130. Gronovius, Barbeyrac, Cocceji, and Cocceji, commentary in *Hugonis Grotii de iure belli ac pacis*, 4:368–369 (Heinrich and Samuel Cocceji).

131. Montesquieu, *Considérations sur les causes de la grandeur des Romains et de leur décadence* (Paris: Hachette, 1945), 103.

132. See, e.g., Gibbon, *The History of the Decline and Fall of the Roman Empire*, 4:126: "Such is the empire of Fortune. . . . A bloody and complete victory has sometimes yielded no more than the possession of the field; and the loss of ten thousand men has sometimes been sufficient to destroy, in a single day, the work of ages." Nevertheless see also his discussion of the battles of Adrianople and Tours, discussed in Chapter 6.
133. "Manifeste du Roi contre la cour de Dresde, Berlin, l'an 1745," 695.

3. LAYING JUST CLAIM TO THE PROFITS OF WAR

Epigraph: Aristotle, *The Nicomachean Ethics*, trans. H. Rackham (Cambridge, MA: Harvard University Press, 1982), 486–488 (8.9.5.1160A).

1. *Oeuvres de Frédéric le Grand*, ed. J. D. E. Preuss (Berlin: Imprimerie Royale, 1846), 2:81–82. For a detailed account of the battle, see Dennis Showalter, *The Wars of Frederick the Great* (New York: Longman, 1996), 45–51.
2. Lawrence H. Keeley, *War before Civilization: The Myth of the Peaceful Savage* (New York: Oxford University Press, 1996), 65–67.
3. Azar Gat, *War in Human Civilization* (New York: Oxford University Press, 2006), 117.
4. Peter Krentz, "Deception in Archaic and Classical Greek Warfare," in *War and Violence in Ancient Greece*, ed. Hans van Wees (London: Duckworth, 2000), 168, 170.
5. The Latin formula *ius belli infinitum* appears in the first German edition (Georg Friedrich von Martens, *Einleitung in das positive europäische Völkerrecht auf Verträge und Herkommen gegründet* (Göttingen: Dieterich, 1796), 304 [§265]) and in later French editions, but not in the first French edition: *Précis du droit des gens moderne de l'Europe, fondé sur les traités et l'usage* (Göttingen: Dieterich, 1789) 1:339–340 (§231).
6. Adam Ferguson, *An Essay on the History of Civil Society*, 2nd ed. (London: Millar & Caddell, 1768), 307, 306. I have reversed the order of the two passages quoted.
7. Georg Friedrich von Martens, *Précis du droit des gens moderne de l'Europe, fondé sur les traités et l'usage*, 3rd ed. (Göttingen: Dieterich, 1821), 461 (§270).
8. *Mémoires des négociations du Marquis de Valori* (Paris: Didot, 1820), 1:259–260.
9. Stephen C. Neff, *War and the Law of Nations: A General History* (Cambridge: Cambridge University Press, 2005), 29.
10. Carl Schmitt, *Der Nomos der Erde im Völkerrecht des* Jus Publicum Europaeum, 4th ed. (Berlin: Duncker & Humblot, 1997), 298.
11. Alexis Blane and Benedict Kingsbury, "Punishment and the *Ius Post Bellum*," in *The Roman Foundations of the Law of Nations: Alberico Gentili and the Justice of Empire*, ed. Benedict Kingsbury and Benjamin Straumann (New York: Oxford University Press, 2010), 263.
12. For larger European Enlightenment context, see Peter Haggenmacher, "Mutations du concept de guerre juste de Grotius à Kant," *Cahiers de philosophie politique et juridique* 10 (1986): 105–125.

13. Schmitt, *Der Nomos der Erde im Völkerrecht des* Jus Publicum Europaeum, 138.

14. For this commonplace, see, e.g., Steven P. Lee, *Ethics and War: An Introduction* (Cambridge: Cambridge University Press, 2012), 61.

15. Neff, *War and the Law of Nations*, 99–100, correctly tracing the doctrine to older theology of doubt.

16. Cf., e.g., Wilhelm G. Grewe, *Epochen der Völkerrechtsgeschichte* (Baden-Baden: Nomos, 1984), 248; Neff, *War and the Law of Nations*, 92.

17. David A. Bell, *The First Total War: Napoleon's Europe and the Birth of Warfare as We Know It* (New York: Mariner, 2007), 50–51.

18. Carl Schmitt, *Theorie des Partisanen: Zwischenbemerkung zum Begriff des Politischen* (Berlin: Duncker & Humblot, 1963), 17.

19. The roots of international law in the Roman law of property are traced in Randall Lesaffer, "Argument from Roman Law in International Law," *European Journal of International Law* 16 (2005): 25–58. The Roman property law roots of international law have attracted considerable attention from students of European imperial expansion in the early modern period. Alongside Lesaffer's article, see Lauren Benton and Benjamin Straumann, "Acquiring Empire by Law: From Roman Doctrine to Early Modern Practice," *Law and History Review* 28 (2010): 1–38. I do not discuss imperial wars in this book, but my argument can be understood to show that European continental wars and imperial wars were closely related in their assumption that private law property norms were fundamental to the analysis of war.

20. Note that the Treaty of Breslau expressly protected the rights of Silesian Catholics. For contemporary awareness of the religious dimension, see the demonstrative reprint of the provisions of the Treaty guaranteeing Catholic rights in Anon., "Schlesische Nachrichten von dem zu Breslau geschlossenen Frieden," *Acta Historico-Ecclesiastica oder gesammelte Nachrichten von den neuesten Kirchen-Geschichten* 6, number 31 (1742): 697–700.

21. Michael Walzer, *Just and Unjust Wars: A Moral Argument with Historical Allusions*, 4th ed. (New York: Basic, 2006), 21.

22. Richard J. Regan, *Just War: Principles and Cases* (Washington: Catholic University of America Press, 1996), 17.

23. Robert Hoag, "The Recourse to War as Punishment," *Studies in the History of Ethics*, June 2006, http://www.historyofethics.org/022006/022006Hoag.shtml. This conventional view can also be found in David Luban's interesting essay "War as Punishment," *Philosophy and Public Affairs* 39 (2011): 299–330.

24. Regan, *Just War*, 17–18.

25. My debt to Peter Haggenmacher's masterpiece, *Grotius et la doctrine de la guerre juste* (Paris: Presses Universitaires de France, 1983), will be clear throughout this chapter.

26. François Gény, one of the pioneers of modern legal thought, is a particularly important example.

27. Alfred Vanderpol, *La doctrine scolastique du droit de guerre* (Paris: Pedone, 1919), 300–320, discussing 2a 2ae 40, 1: "ut . . . illi qui impugnantur propter aliquam culpam impugnationem mereantur." For a careful study of Aquinas's thought extending beyond this famous passage and placing him in the context of the wars of his time,

see Gerhard Beestermöller, *Thomas von Aquin und der gerechte Krieg: Friedensethik im theologischen Kontext der Summa Theologiae* (Cologne: Bachem, 1990). It is worth adding that Vanderpol, whatever his failings, had real gifts as a scholar. His book remains well worth reading.

28. For medieval authors, see Frederick H. Russell, *The Just War in the Middle Ages* (Cambridge: Cambridge University Press, 1975), 172; Raymond de Peñaforte, discussed in Haggenmacher, *Grotius et la doctrine de la guerre juste*, 263; Honoré Bonet, *The Tree of Battles*, ed. and trans. G. W. Coopland (Cambridge, MA: Harvard University Press, 1949), 157–158. Sixteenth-century theologians are discussed in Jean-Mathieu Mattéi, *Histoire du droit de la guerre, 1700–1819: Introduction à l'histoire du droit international* (Aix-en-Provence: Presses Universitaires d'Aix-Marseille, 2006), 302–303 n. 829; Haggenmacher, *Grotius et la doctrine de la guerre juste*, 244 (on Cajetan).

29. Alberico Gentili, *De iure belli libri tres* (repr. Buffalo, NY: Hein, 1995), 1:150–151 (bk. I, chap. 20): "ulcisci iniurias, & punire nocentes, & ius suum vindicare . . . Neque enim hic est bellum, nisi pars quaedam iustitiae, quae punire crimina velit."

30. Hugo Grotius, *De jure belli ac pacis libri tres* (repr. Buffalo, NY: Hein, 1995), 101 (bk. 2, chap. 1, §2): "Plerique bellorum tres statuunt causas justas, defensionem, recuperationem rerum, & punitionem." The tendency to think of war as punishment came, in some ways, wholly naturally to just war casuists. As I have shown elsewhere, the basic theology of killing that underlay just war theory applied not only to soldiers but also to judges in criminal matters. Since criminal judges presided over executions, they resembled soldiers, from the point of view of theology. Both judges and soldiers were obliged to kill, and so both were subject to the same just war rules of conscience. See James Q. Whitman, *The Origins of Reasonable Doubt: Theological Roots of the Criminal Trial* (New Haven, CT: Yale University Press, 2008). The analogy between the judge and the soldier certainly suggests that making war was like punishing criminals; for Gentili, for example, it seemed obvious that the punishment function of war grew out of the close analogy between the soldier and the judge: "Non tamen magistratus exerit gladium nisi ex gravissima causa." Gentili, *De iure belli*, 1:150–151 (bk. I, chap. 20). The continuation of the passage, though, pressed beyond the analogy to judging: "& medici non nisi gravissimis morbis remedia gravissima afferunt."

31. Discussion in, e.g., Haggenmacher, *Grotius et la doctrine de la guerre juste*, 189–193.

32. Isidore of Seville, *Etym.* 18.1.2: "De Bellis," in *Isidorus Hispalensis, Etymologiae XVIII*, ed. J. Cantó Llorca (Paris: Belles Lettres, 2007), 48.

33. See the superb discussion in Haggenmacher, *Grotius et la doctrine de la guerre juste*, 203–223.

34. Aristotle, *Nicomachean Ethics*, 486–488 (8.9.5.1160A).

35. Cicero, *De Officiis*, trans. W. Miller (Cambridge, MA: Harvard University Press, 1975), 22 (1.21).

36. See Malcolm Davies, *The Greek Epic Cycle*, 2nd ed. (Bristol: Bristol Classical, 2001), 47, 74–75.

37. Qur'an, 8:41–44.

38. Max Weber, *Wirtschaft und Gesellschaft: Grundriss der verstehenden Soziologie* (Tübingen: Mohr, 1972), 587.

39. Economic historians certainly no longer accept all of Weber's claims about the ancient economy, but there is no doubt that he brilliantly captured the spirit of the legal texts that were his principal sources. For a defense of the centrality of profit making through war in the ancient economy, see M. M. Austin, "Hellenistic Kings, War and the Economy," *Classical Quarterly*, n.s. 36 (1986): 450–466. My thanks to Joseph Manning for pointing me to this text.

40. *The Institutes of Gaius*, ed. and trans. F. de Zulueta (Oxford: Clarendon, 1946), 238 (4.16): "maxime enim sua esse credebant, quae ex hostibus cepissent."

41. J. Rufus Fears, "The Theology of Victory at Rome: Approaches and Problems," in *Aufstieg und Niedergang der römischen Welt: Geschichte und Kultur Roms im Spiegel der neueren Forschung* series 2, volume 17, part 2 (Berlin: De Gruyter, 1981): 771.

42. For "spear-won" property, see Walter Schmitthenner, "Über eine Formveränderung der Monarchie seit Alex. d. Gr.," *Saeculum* 19 (1968): 32–46. It would be wrong to deny the difficulty in interpreting these sources. The Homeric tradition clearly shaped perceptions of the actions of figures like Alexander, and we must read these texts critically. Nevertheless the strength of the cultural tradition is palpable.

43. Compare Rudolf von Jhering's observations on the connection between *Krieg* and *kriegen*: *Scherz und Ernst in der Jurisprudenz*, ed. Max Leitner (Vienna: Linde, 2009), 129.

44. Haggenmacher, *Grotius et la doctrine de la guerre juste*, 409–426.

45. Augustine, *Contra Faustum manichaeum,* Corpus scriptorum ecclesiasticorum latinorum 25 (Prague: Tempsky, 1891), 672 (chap. 22, para. 74): "[N]ec bella per Moysen gesta miretur aut horreat, quia et in illis divina secutus imperia non saeviens, sed oboediens fuit, nec deus, cum iubebat ista, saeviebat, sed digna dignis retribuebat dignosque terrebat. qui enim culpatur in bello? . . . [N]ocendi cupiditas, ulciscendi crudelitas, inplacatus atque implacabilis animus, feritas rebellandi, libido dominandi et si qua similia, haec sunt, quae in bellis iure culpantur, quae plerumque ut etiam iure puniantur, adversus violentiam resistentium sive deo sive aliquo legitimo imperio iubente gerenda ipsa bella suscipiuntur a bonis." It is important to recognize that Augustine's concern in this famous passage is with the state of mind of those engaged with war, who are to act as ministers of God and not out of their own passion. That is, his concern is a moral theological one, belonging fundamentally to the law of conscience.

46. See Thomas Elßner, *Josua und seine Kriege in jüdischer und christlicher Rezeptionsgeschichte* (Stuttgart: Kohlhammer, 2008). Book of Wisdom, 10:2: Righteous may seize booty.

47. For this and other interpretive strategies among earlier Church Fathers, see Roland H. Bainton, *Christian Attitudes toward War and Peace: A Historical Survey and Critical Re-evaluation* (New York: Abingdon, 1960), 82.

48. C. 23, 2, 2: "Iusta autem bella solent diffiniri, quae ulciscuntur iniurias, sic gens et civitas, petenda est, quae vel vindicare neglexerit quod a suis improbe factum est, vel reddere quod per inurias ablatum est. Sed et hoc genus belli sine dubio iustum est, quod Deus inperat, qui novit quid cuique fieri debeat." From Augustine, Quaestiones in Heptateuchum 6 (Quaestiones in Jesum Nave), X, in *Patrologiae Cursus Completus*, ed. J.-P. Migne (Turnhout: Brepols, 1985) 34:781. Augustine continued,

"In quo bello ductor exercitus, vel ipse populus, non tam auctor, quam minister judicandus est." It is important to read the entire passage. In his emphasis on the necessity that the Christian act as "minister," he was once again putting the focus on conscience and salvation. See further the discussion in Whitman, *Origins of Reasonable Doubt*, 38–40. Augustine's commentary on Joshua entered canon law with changes noted in Haggenmacher, *Grotius et la doctrine de la guerre juste*, 157.

49. Much of our interpretation of just war theory rests on misleading translations of the term *injuria*. See, e.g., Bainton, *Christian Attitudes toward War and Peace*, 96; Russell, *Just War in the Middle Ages*, 18. As Russell rightly observes, Augustine also emphasized the idea that the goal of war is peace (16–17). There is nothing in that idea, of course, that implies that the purpose of war is the punishment of evil. Settling civil disputes also makes peace.

50. I have modified the English Standard Version here, substituting the Latin of the Vulgate: "serviet tibi sub tributo."

51. Henry Sumner Maine, *Ancient Law: Its Connection with the Early History of Society, and Its Relation to Modern Ideas* (London: Murray, 1861), 247–248. Maine was speaking of the Roman rules, but his observations apply superbly to the Canon rules that developed from them.

52. Cicero, *De Officiis*, 38 (1.36): "[N]ullum bellum esse iustum, nisi quod aut rebus repetitis geratur aut denuntiatum ante et indictum."

53. Literature in Haggenmacher, *Grotius et la doctrine de la guerre juste*, 231.

54. *Livy*, trans. F. G. Moore (Cambridge, MA: Harvard University Press, 1971), 1:116–118 (1.32.12–14).

55. This from Servius' commentary on the Aeneid. *Servii Grammatici in Vergilii Carmina Commentarii*, ed. G. Thilo and H. Hagen (Leipzig: Teubner, 1884), 2:313–314 (9.52).

56. For discussion of these texts from a point of view different from my own, see Clifford Ando, "Empire and the Laws of War: A Roman Archeology," in Kingsbury and Straumann, *Roman Foundations of the Law of Nations*, 30–52.

57. For example, Gaius in *Digest of Justinian*, ed. T. Mommsen and P. Krueger, trans. A. Watson et al. (Philadelphia: University of Pennsylvania, 1985), 4:488 (D.41.5.7): "Item quae ex hostibus capiuntur, iure gentium statim capientium fiunt . . . adeo quidem, ut et liberi homines in servitutem deducantur: qui tamen, si evaserint hostium potestatem, recipiunt pristinam libertatum."

58. Isidore of Seville, Etym. 18.1.2: "De Bellis," in *Isidorus Hispalensis, Etymologiae XVIII*, 48.

59. Haggenmacher, *Grotius et la doctrine de la guerre juste*, 157, 255–268, 161 on glossa ordinaria; cf. Mattéi, *Histoire du droit de la guerre*, 302.

60. Baldus de Ubaldis, *In primum, secundum & tertium cod. lib.* (Venice: n.p., 1586), 228v (ad Cod., 3, 31, 2. n. 77). For a detailed discussion of civilian texts, with their emphasis on property claims, see Luisa Bussi, "Il problema della guerra nella prima civilistica," in *A Ennio Cortese*, ed. Domenico Maffei, Italo Barocchi, Mario Caravale, Emanuele Conte, and Ugo Petronio (Rome: Cigno, 2001), 124–135.

61. Raphael Fulgosius, *In primam pandectarum partem commentaria*, ad Dig. 1.1.5, quoted and discussed in Haggenmacher, *Grotius et la doctrine de la guerre juste*,

285–286 n. 1351. The relevant passage of the Digest can be found in *Digest of Justinian*, ed. Mommsen and Krueger, 1:2.

62. "In iusto autem bello quod fit ex edicto principis, & liberi homines capti servi fiunt, & in eorum dominium res transeunt occupare." Henri de Suze (Hostiensis), *In secundem decretalium librum commentaria* (Venice: Apud Iuntas, 1581), 136. See further the discussion of Haggenmacher, *Grotius et la doctrine de la Guerre Juste*, 259.

63. Grotius, *De jure belli ac pacis*, 101 (bk. 2, chap. 1, §1): "Causa justa belli suscipiendi nulla esse alia potest nisi injuria"; Samuel Rachel, *De iure naturae et gentium dissertationes*, ed. Ludwig von Bar (Washington, DC: Carnegie Institution, 1916), 271 (chap. XL); Samuel, Freiherr von Pufendorf, *De jure naturae et gentium libri octo* (repr. Buffalo, NY: Hein, 1995), 6 (bk. I, chap. 1, §8): "Bellum . . . est status injurias violentas mutuo inferentium & propulsantium, aut quae sibi debentur vi extorquere nitentium."

64. See Haggenmacher, *Grotius et la doctrine de la guerre just*, 171–173 on Vitoria.

65. Isidore, Etym. 18.2.8 "De Bellis" in *Isidorus Hispalensis, Etymologiae XVIII*, 68–70.

66. Gratian Decretum, Distinctio Prima, C. X. "Quid sit ius militare," available at http://geschichte.digitale-sammlungen.de/decretum-gratiani/kapitel/dc_chapter_0 _0014.

67. "[C]um habet iustum bellum & non exercet illud, nisi contra nocentes, & non habet intentionem corruptam, quidquid capit ab hostibus suum est, nec tenetur resitutere." Raymond of Peñafort, *Summa de paenitentia*, ed. Xavier Ochoa and Aloisio Diez (Rome: Commentario pro Religiosis, 1976), lib. II, tit. 5, sec. 17, col. 485.

68. Johannes Teutonicus Glossa ordinaria to C. 23, q. 7, pr., v. *nunc* autem: "Non solum heretici, sed omnes hostes licite possunt spoliari rebus suis, dummoddo bellum sit iustum," quoted in Russell, *Just War in the Middle Ages*, 163 n. 106. In his forthcoming book *Surrender*, the manuscript of which he kindly shared with me, John Lynn observes that early modern authorities cited Matthew 12:1–7 in support of the right to pillage. Lynn, Surrender, chap. 1 (manuscript on file with author).

69. Bartolus of Sassoferrato, *Commentaria in partem digesti novi* (Basel: Ex Officina Episopiana, 1588), 639 (ad Dig. 49.15.28). The relevant passage of the Digest can be found in *Digest of Justinian*, ed. Mommsen and Krueger, 4:892.

70. Haggenmacher, *Grotius et la doctrine de la guerre juste*, 288–292; Mattéi, *Histoire du droit de la guerre*, 752–755.

71. Balthazar Ayala, *De iure et officiis bellicis et disciplina militari libri III*, ed. John Westlake (Washington, DC: Carnegie Institution, 1912), 32v–54r (bk. I, chap. 5); Hugo Grotius, *De jure praedae commentarius*, ed. R. Fruin (The Hague: Nijhoff, 1868) (posthumously published manuscript).

72. Paul Hazard, *La crise de la conscience européenne (1680–1715)* (Paris: Boivin, 1935).

73. Carl L. Becker, *The Heavenly City of the Eighteenth-Century Philosophers* (New Haven, CT: Yale University Press, 1932).

74. Bell, *First Total War*, 50–51; Schmitt, *Der Nomos der Erde im Völkerrecht des Jus Publicum Europaeum*, 138.

75. Mattéi, *Histoire du droit de la guerre*, 404. Mattéi sees an incipient crisis of just war theorizing in the writings of Bynkershoek and Moser but does not see the definitive decline until the nineteenth century (320–325).

76. Discussion ibid., 359–361, 374–379.

77. Ibid., 374–390; Joachim von Elbe, "Die Wiederherstellung der Gleichgewichtsordnung," *Zeitschrift für Ausländisches und Öffentliches Recht und Völkerrecht* 4 (1934): 226–260.

78. See the discussion in Johannes Kunisch, *Friedrich der Grosse: Der König und seine Zeit* (Munich: Beck, 2004), 185–192.

79. Emer de Vattel, *Le droit des gens, ou, Principes de la loi naturelle, appliqués à la conduite & aux affaires des nations & des souverains*, ed. Paul Pradier-Fodéré (Paris: Guillaumin, 1863), 3:36 (bk. III, chap. 13, §162).

80. Robert Joseph Pothier, *Traité du domaine de propriété* (Paris: Debure, 1772), 88–89, §§87–88.

81. Vattel, *Droit des gens*, 3:74 (bk. III, chap. 13, §193): "La guerre fondée sur la justice est donc un moyen légitime d'acquérir suivant la loi naturelle."

82. Mattéi, *Histoire du droit de la guerre*, 330–332.

83. Christian Wolff, *Principes du droit de la nature et des gens*, ed. Jean-Henri-Samuel Formey (Amsterdam: Rey, 1758), 258 (bk. 9, chap. 1, §§3 and 4); 300 (bk. 9, chap. 8, §19).

84. Mattéi, *Histoire du droit de la guerre*, 251, observes of this Wolff passage that war thus involves legitimate acquisition "d'ordre patrimoniale, acquisitions par achat ou par héritage."

85. Vattel, *Droit des gens*, 3:35 (bk. III, chap. 9, §160); further discussion and quotes in Mattéi, *Histoire du droit de la guerre*, 1001–1003.

86. *Droit Public de France, Ouvrage Posthume de M. L'Abbé de Fleury, composé pour l'éducation des Princes*, ed. J. P. Daragon (Paris: La veuve Pierres, 1769), 2:289–293. For another statement of this eighteenth-century commonplace, framed in the language of moral theology, see Jacques Joseph Duguet, *Institution d'un prince, ou Traité des qualitez, des vertus, et des devoirs d'un souverain, Seconde partie: Des devoirs du prince par rapport au gouvernement temporel* (Leiden: Verbeek, 1739), 497.

87. For an example of refined problems, see, e.g., Pufendorf, *De jure naturae et gentium*, 893–894 (bk. 8, chap. 6, §22).

88. The rights in question—what were called "perfect rights"—were defined by Vattel, *Droits des gens*, 4 (bk. II, chap. 5, §66) as "rights not to suffer an injustice"; cf. Martens, *Einleitung in das positive europäische Völkerrecht*, 297 (bk. 8, chap. 3, §260): "jede Verletzung einer vollkommnen Pflicht."

89. *Droit Public de France, Ouvrage Posthume de M. L'Abbé de Fleury*, 2:292–293.

90. Arthur Nussbaum, *A Concise History of the Law of Nations* (New York: Macmillan, 1954), 166, 177.

91. Sharon Korman, *The Right of Conquest: The Acquisition of Territory by Force in International Law and Practice* (Oxford: Clarendon, 1996), 70.

92. Mattéi, *Histoire du droit de la guerre*, 994–998, treating conquest as a matter of mere force.

93. Johann Jakob Moser, *Grundsäze des europäischen Völker-Rechts in Kriegs-Zeiten* (Tübingen: Cotta, 1752), 4 (bk. 1, chap. 2, §§1ff.).

94. Vattel, *Droit des gens*, 1:229 (bk. I, chap. 5, §66).

95. Vattel tried more broadly to limit the use of war, though he remained within the thought-world of his time. See, e.g., *Droits des gens*, 2:378 (bk. III, chap. 3, §38): "La victoire suit ordinarement la force et la prudence, plutôt que le bon droit. Ce serait une mauvaise règle de décision; mais c'est un moyen efficace, pour contraindre celui qui se refuse aux voies de la justice et il devient juste dans les mains du prince qui l'emploie à propos et pour un sujet légitime."

96. Martens, *Einleitung in das positive europäische Völkerrecht*, 82–83 (bk. 3, chap. 2, §68).

97. For Vattel's repetition of the standard theology of conscience, see Vattel, *Droits des gens*, 2:378–379 (bk. III, chap. 3, §40).

98. Gerhard Ritter, *Frederick the Great: A Historical Profile*, trans. P. Paret (Berkeley: University of California Press, 1968), 80–81. Ritter's account is of course not the only one. I cite it because of its influence in the literature of international law. I return to this question below.

99. Richard Rolt, *An Impartial Representation of the Conduct of the Several Powers of Europe Engaged in the Late General War* (London: Longman, 1749), 1:192–198.

100. *Scots Magazine* 3 (March 1741): 121–124.

101. *Die neue Europäische Fama, welche den gegenwärtigen Zustand der vornehmsten Höfe entdecket* 61 (1740): 599, 888–889 and often.

102. Nussbaum, *Concise History of the Law of Nations*, 177.

103. In part, this may have been because the Habsburgs had not fulfilled their own obligations vis-à-vis Frederick William, though that fact was probably little known at the time. See the discussion in Kunisch, *Friedrich der Grosse*, 163.

104. *Die neue Europäische Fama, welche den gegenwärtigen Zustand der vornehmsten Höfe entdecket* 61 (1740): 888–889.

105. For contemporary examples of how seriously these questions were taken in cases not involving the Pragmatic Sanction, see, e.g., Johann Carl König, *Selecta juris publici novissima: Zum Behuf der Reichs-Historie und der Staatsrechten* (Marburg: Möller, 1745), 8:415; *Genealogisch-Historische Nachrichten von den allerneuesten Begebenheiten, welche sich an den Europäischen Höfen zutragen* (Leipzig: Heinsius, 1741), 21:1013. My aim, I should emphasize, is not to argue that Frederick was necessarily in the right, but that the question was an entirely serious and open one.

106. *Droit Public de France, Ouvrage Posthume de M. L'Abbé de Fleury*, 2:292–293.

107. Hermann Lorenz von Kannegießer, *Actenmäßige und rechtliche Gegeninformation* (n.p.: n.p., 1741), e.g., 37.

108. Vattel, *Droit des gens*, 2:339 (bk. III, chap. 1, §3): "la conservations de ses droits."

109. Isidore of Seville, Etym. 18.1.2: "De Bellis," in *Isidorus Hispalensis, Etymologiae XVIII*, 48.

110. Ibid.

111. *Droit Public de France, Ouvrage Posthume de M. L'Abbé de Fleury*, 2:289–293.

112. Martens, *Einleitung in das positive europäische Völkerrecht*, 299 (bk. 8, chap. 3, §261), 300 (§262).

113. Vattel, *Droit des gens*, 3:1 (bk. III, chap. 8, §136).

114. Wolff, *Principes du droit de la nature et des gens*, 3:297.

115. J.-M. Gérard de Rayneval, *Institutions du droit de nature et des gens*, new ed. (Paris: Durand, 1851) 1:13: "[L]a guerre *defensive* est donc celle que soutient un état injustement attaqué, soit par les armes, *soit dans ses droits*." This passage does not appear in the 1803 edition of Rayneval's work, but his editor notes that this mid-nineteenth-century edition is taken from autograph corrections of his text (i). For another example, see Theodor Schmalz, *Das europäische Völker-Recht* (Berlin: Duncker and Humblot, 1817), 220 (bk. VI, chap. 2); and generally the discussion in Mattéi, *Histoire du droit de la guerre*, 125–132.

116. "Réfutation du Prince de Machiavel," in *Oeuvres de Frédéric le Grand*, 8:332–333.

117. Vattel, *Droit des gens*, 2:405 (bk. II, chap. 4, §58).

118. Martens, *Einleitung in das positive europäische Völkerrecht*, 300 (bk. 8, chap. 3, §262). This was indeed the practice early on in the century.

119. Moser, *Grundsäze des europäischen Völker-Rechts in Kriegs-Zeiten*, 91–92 (bk. 2, chap. 3, §§12, 13, 16).

120. See Johann Christian Lünig, *Theatrum ceremoniale historico-politicum, oder Historisch- und politischer Schau-Platz aller Ceremonien* (Leipzig: Weidmann, 1719–1720), 2:1233. The question was bound up with the tradition of the use of heralds, as Lünig explained. For the sake of brevity, I do not describe that tradition here. For the background in the law of the seventeenth century, see the excellent study of Randall Lesaffer, "Defensive Warfare, Prevention and Hegemony: The Justifications for the Franco-Spanish War of 1635," *Journal of the History of International Law* 8 (2006): 91–123, 141–179.

121. "Patent wegen des Ein-Marsches S. königlichen Maiestät in Preussen Troupen in das Herzogthumb Schlesien, 1 Dec. 1740," in *Preussische Staatsschriften aus der Regierungszeit König Friedrichs II*, ed. Reinhold Koser and Otto Krauske (Berlin: Duncker, 1877), 1:69–70. Neff's judgment: "The only statement that can confidently be made is that it was common—though far from universal—for states to give some kind of more or less clear signal to the enemy, to the home population and to the world at large." Neff, *War and the Law of Nations*, 110.

122. Moser, *Grundsäze des europäischen Völker-Rechts in Kriegs-Zeiten*, 91 (bk. 2, chap. 3, §14).

123. Kannegießer, *Actenmäßige und rechtliche Gegeninformation*, 4.

124. Jean Rousset de Missy, *Recueil historique d'actes, négociations, mémoires et traitez: Depuis la Paix d'Utrecht jusqu'au Second Congrès de Cambray inclusivement* 15 (The Hague: Gosse, 1742): 253ff.; *Journal historique sur les matières du tems*, January 1741, 457.

125. I have slightly altered the translation in Antoine Henri, baron de Jomini, *Summary of the Art of War, or, A New Analytical Compend of the Principal Combinations of Strategy, of Grand Tactics and of Military Policy*, trans. O. F. Winship and E. E. McLean (New York: Putnam, 1854), 27.

126. Korman, *Right of Conquest*, 68–69.

127. Kunisch, *Friedrich der Grosse*, 166. Kunisch's thoughtful and learned account culminates in a quasi-defense of Frederick, borrowed from Macaulay, on the grounds that his raison d'état calculations were sound (191–192).

128. For Ritter's intentions, and the ambiguous reception of his book, see Christoph Cornelißen, *Gerhard Ritter: Geschichtswissenschaft und Politik im 20. Jahrhundert* (Düsseldorf: Droste, 2001), 269-271; Gregory Weeks, "Gerhard Ritter," in *Encyclopedia of Historians and Historical Writing*, ed. Kelly Boyd (Chicago: Fitzroy Dearborn, 1999), 2:997.

129. Ritter, *Frederick the Great*, 82. For the contemporary recognition of the link between Ritter's account of Friedrich's "ice cold cynicism" and the politics of Hitler, see Cornelißen, Ritter, 276.

130. The most dramatic detail in Ritter's account turns on Frederick's "cynical and arrogant" marginal comment to a memo of Podewils: "Bravo, das ist die Arbeit eines trefflichen Charlatans!" Yet we must remember that Podewils *opposed* the invasion of Silesia! Kunisch, *Friedrich der Grosse*, 171. Whatever Frederick meant by his comment, it cannot have been intended as cynical praise for some lawyer's carefully crafted argument in favor of his cause. In the postwar years, Ritter himself retreated somewhat from his earlier portrait of Frederick. See especially Ritter, *Staatskunst und Kriegshandwerk. Das Problem des "Militarismus" in Deutschland* (Munich: Oldenbourg, 1954), 1:42-45; and the discussion in Cornelißen, *Ritter*, 502-503.

131. Wolff, *Principes du droit de la nature et des gens*, 295 (bk. 9, chap 7, §§3, 4).

132. *Droit Public de France, Ouvrage Posthume de M. L'Abbé de Fleury*, 2:297.

133. Charles François Lefèvre de la Maillardière, *Précis du droit des gens, de la guèrre, de la paix, et des ambassades* (Paris: Quillau, 1775), 92.

134. Vattel, *Droit des gens*, 2:373 (bk. III, chap. 3, §32); 3:74 (bk. III, chap. 13, §193). Vattel was certainly not entirely comfortable with this doctrine. As he put it elsewhere, "[I]l faut que des motifs honnêtes et louables concourent avec les raisons justificatives pour lui [l'État] faire entreprendre la guerre" (2:372 [bk. III, chap. 3, §29]). At the same time, there was an air of impotent pleading to his account. As he put it in the following paragraph, "Si une guerre injuste enrichit l'État . . . elle le rend odieux aux autres nations" (372 [§30]). No doubt he would have preferred not to endorse such "unjust" enrichment by a state, but he could not deny its lawful character.

135. My translation of *leidige Tröster*. Immanuel Kant, "Zum ewigen Frieden," in *Über den Gemeinspruch: Das mag in der Theorie Richtig Sein, taugt aber nicht für die Praxis/Zum ewigen Frieden: Ein philosophischer Entwurf*, ed. Heiner F. Klemme (Hamburg: Meiner, 1992), 65. Of course, Kant included Grotius on the roster.

136. Ryan Goodman and Derek Jinks, "How to Influence States: Socialization and Human Rights Law," *Duke Law Journal* 54, no. 3 (2004): 621-703.

137. See the judgment of Theodor Schieder, *Frederick the Great*, trans. S. Berkeley and H. Scott (London: Longman, 2000), 98.

138. "Patent wegen des Ein-Marsches S. Königlichen Maiestät in Preussen Troupen in das Herzogthumb Schlesien," 1:69-70.

139. Gabriel-Honoré de Riquetti, comte de Mirabeau, *De la monarchie prussienne* (London: n.p., 1788): 1:67: "[C]ette guerre et cette conquête furent justes autant que la guerre et les conquêtes peuvent l'être."

140. Vattel, *Droit des gens*, 3:74 (bk. III, chap. 13, §193).

4. THE MONARCHICAL MONOPOLIZATION OF MILITARY VIOLENCE

Epigraph: Emer de Vattel, *The Law of Nations; or, Principles of the Law of Nature, Applied to the Conduct and Affairs of Nations and Sovereigns*, trans. Joseph Chitty (London: Sweet, 1834), 374–375 (bk. 3, chap. 10, §178).

1. "Guerre," in *Dictionnaire Philosophique*, in *The Complete Works of Voltaire*, ed. Ulla Kölving et al. (New York: Oxford University Press, 1994), 23:187–190.

2. Geoffrey Best, *War and Law since 1945* (Oxford: Clarendon, 1994), 17.

3. Michael Howard, "Constraints on Warfare," in *The Laws of War: Constraints on Warfare in the Western World*, ed. Michael Howard, George J. Andreopoulos, and Mark R. Shulman (New Haven, CT: Yale University Press, 1994), 4.

4. Vattel, *Law of Nations*, 374–375 (bk. 3, chap. 10, §178). I have adopted Chitty's translation of "manie."

5. Emer de Vattel, *Le droit des gens, ou, Principes de la loi naturelle, appliqués à la conduite & aux affaires des nations & des souverains*, ed. Paul Pradier-Fodéré (Paris: Guillaumin, 1863), 2:333 (bk. 2, chap. 18, §333).

6. Montesquieu, *De l'esprit des lois* (Paris: Garnier-Flammarion, 1979), 1:158 (bk. IV, chap. 2).

7. Jonathan Dewald, *The European Nobility, 1400–1800* (Cambridge: Cambridge University Press, 1996), 146.

8. General survey of the early modern tradition in Peter Haggenmacher, *Grotius et la doctrine de la guerre juste* (Paris: Presses Universitaires de France, 1983), 91–148.

9. Samuel, Freiherr de Pufendorf, *De jure naturae et gentium libri octo* (repr. Buffalo, NY: Hein, 1995), 885 (bk. VIII, chap. 6, §8).

10. M. H. Keen, *The Laws of War in the Late Middle Ages* (London: Routledge & K. Paul, 1965), 72–77.

11. Juan López, "De bello & Bellatoribus," in *Tractatus illustrium in utraque tum Pontificii, tum Caesarei iuris facultate iurisconsultorum [Tractatus universi iuris]*, bk. XVI (Venice: n.p., 1584), 321r col. 1, 322v col. 1.

12. Alberico Gentili, *De iure belli libri tres* (repr. Buffalo, NY: Hein, 1995), 1:22, 30–31 (bk. I, chap. 3): "Principes bellum gerunt"; 1:34 (bk. I, chap. 4): "Latrones bellum non gerunt."

13. Hugo Grotius, *De jure belli ac pacis libri tres* (repr. Buffalo, NY: Hein, 1995), 46 (bk. 1, chap. 3, §2). Discussion in Peter Haggenmacher, *Grotius et la doctrine de la guerre juste*, 144–146; Jean-Mathieu Mattéi, *Histoire du droit de la guerre, 1700–1819: Introduction à l'histoire du droit international* (Aix-en-Provence: Presses Universitaires d'Aix-Marseille, 2006), 145.

14. Richard Zouche, *Iuris et iudicii fecialis sive iuris inter gentes, et quaestionum de eodem explicatio* (repr. Buffalo, NY: Hein, 1995), 30 (part I, §6).

15. Textor, *Synopsis iuris gentium*, ed. Ludwig von Bar (Washington: Carnegie Institution, 1916), "De Bello," 2 (chap. XVI, §6): war is "status licitae offensionis hostilis ex justa causa inter potestates regias vel quasi publice auctoritate indictus." We should also see Bynkershoek's elegant Roman solution in the same light: Cornelis van Bynk-

ershoek, *Quaestionum juris publici libri duo* (Leiden: Kerckhem, 1737), 2: "Bellum est eorum qui suae potestatis sunt, juris sui persequendi ergo, concertatio per vim vel dolum."

16. Vattel, *Droit des gens*, 2:4 (bk. II, chap. 3, §38). On this see Emmanuelle Jouannet, *Emer de Vattel et l'émergence doctrinale du droit international classique* (Paris: Pedone, 1998), 337–339; and for the originality of Vattel, see Francesco Mancuso, *Diritto, stato, sovranità: Il pensiero politico-giuridico di Emer de Vattel tra assolutismo e rivoluzione* (Naples: Edizioni Scientifiche Italiane, 2002), 112–118. For other special cases of nonprincely states, see Mattéi, *Histoire du droit de la guerre*, 146–165, discussing the peculiar cases of English parliamentarism, Poland, the Holy Roman Empire, and the American and French Revolutions.

17. Johan Huizinga, *Homo Ludens: A Study of the Play Element in Culture* (Boston: Beacon, 1950), 102. The standard English translation makes the odd decision to render *strijd* as "strife" rather than "combat."

18. Wolfgang Schild, "Schlacht als Rechtsentscheid," in *Schlachtfelder: Codierung von Gewalt im medialen Wandel*, ed. Steffen Martus, Marina Münkler, and Werner Röcke (Berlin: Akademie, 2003), 151.

19. Achatz von Mueller, "Schauspiele der Gewalt," in *Das Duell: Der tödliche Kampf um die Ehre*, ed. Uwe Schultz (Frankfurt: Insel, 1996), 16–17.

20. Stephen C. Neff, *War and the Law of Nations: A General History* (Cambridge: Cambridge University Press, 2005), 74.

21. Justine Firnhaber-Baker, "Guerram Publice et Palam Faciendo: Local War and Royal Authority in Late Medieval France" (PhD diss., Harvard University, 2007), 53–54.

22. Keen, *Laws of War in the Late Middle Ages*, 191.

23. Lynn, draft book manuscript entitled *Surrender*, chap. 1 (copy of manuscript on file with author). But see the cautious assessment of Nicholas Wright, *Knights and Peasants: The Hundred Years War in the French Countryside* (Woodbridge, UK: Boydell, 1998), 63–79, emphasizing that peasants were not the only ones to suffer.

24. Norbert Elias, *The Civilizing Process*, trans. Edmund Jephcott (Oxford: Blackwell, 1994), 162.

25. Friedrich Nietzsche, "Zur Genealogie der Moral," in *Werke: Kritische Gesamtausgabe*, ed. Giorgio Colli and Mazzino Montinari (Munich: De Gruyter, 1968), Abteilung 6, Vol. 2: 289.

26. Arlette Jouanna, *Le devoir de révolte: La noblesse française et la gestation de l'état moderne, 1559–1661* (Paris: Fayard, 1989), 30–31, 384–388.

27. William Beik, *Absolutism and Society in Seventeenth-Century France: State Power and Provincial Aristocracy in Languedoc* (Cambridge: Cambridge University Press, 1985), 181–183; Brian Sandberg, *Warrior Pursuits: Noble Culture and Civil Conflict in Early Modern France* (Baltimore: Johns Hopkins University Press, 2010), 256.

28. Charles du Fresne, sieur du Cange, "Dissertation des guerres privées et du droit de guerre par coutume," in *Glossarium ad scriptores mediae et infimae latinitatis* (Frankfurt: Zunner, 1710), 7:121.

29. Jean-Baptiste de la Curne de Sainte-Palaye, *Mémoires sur l'ancienne chevalerie, considérée comme un établissement politique & militaire* (Paris: Duchesne, 1759), 2:47–48, 49. On La Curne de Sainte-Palaye and his Europe-wide influence, see Lionel Gossman, *Medievalism and the Ideologies of Enlightenment: The World and Work of La Curne de Sainte-Palaye* (Baltimore: Johns Hopkins University Press, 1968), 327–348.

30. Henri, comte de Boulainvilliers, *Essais sur la noblesse de la France* (Amsterdam: n.p., 1732), 132–133, 136–137.

31. Nannerl O. Keohane, *Philosophy and the State in France: The Renaissance to the Enlightenment* (Princeton, NJ: Princeton University Press, 1980), 346.

32. See, e.g., Jouanna, *Devoir de révolte*, 42–43, 51–52.

33. Philippe Contamine, "The Growth of State Control, Practices of War, 1300–1800: Ransom and Booty," in *War and Competition between States*, ed. Philippe Contamine (New York: Oxford University Press, 2000), 164.

34. Keen, *Laws of War in the Late Middle Ages*, 104. See Lynn, *Surrender*.

35. Keen, *Laws of War in the Late Middle Ages*; Kurt-Georg Cram, *Iudicium Belli: Zum Rechtscharakter des Krieges im deutschen Mittelalter* (Munich: Böhlau, 1955); Robert Stacey, "The Age of Chivalry," in Howard, Andreopoulos, and Shulman, *Laws of War*, 27–39.

36. See, e.g., Keen, *Laws of War in the Late Middle Ages*, 24–26.

37. This from *De la lecture des livres françois considérée comme amusement* (Paris: Moutard, 1780), 1:96, 99. This (extremely ironic) discussion of Christine de Pizan and Honoré Bonet is an unusual example of discussion of the later medieval literature in the eighteenth century. Nor is it surprising that eighteenth-century jurists noticed the prominence of ransom in medieval knightly warfare. In this respect at least, the law of their own eighteenth century was no different from that of the Middle Ages. As we saw in Chapter 3, eighteenth-century war, like medieval war, was fought primarily for gain, and the eighteenth-century law of war retained the right to hold prisoners for ransom. See, e.g., Georg Friedrich von Martens, *Einleitung in das positive europäische Völkerrecht auf Verträge und herkommen gegründet* (Göttingen: Dieterich, 1796), 310 (§ 270).

38. La Curne de Sainte-Palaye, *Mémoires sur l'ancienne chevalerie*, 1:311.

39. William Robertson, *The History of the Reign of Emperor Charles V, with a View of the Progress of Society in Europe, from the Subversion of the Roman Empire, to the Beginning of the Sixteenth Century* (London: Strahan, 1769), 1:70.

40. Edward Gibbon, *The History of the Decline and Fall of the Roman Empire*, ed. J. B. Bury (London: Methuen, 1914), 6:293–294, 3: 73.

41. Pufendorf, *De jure naturae et gentium*, 885 (bk. VIII, chap. 6, §8).

42. Cajetan, quoted and discussed in St. Robert Bellarmine, "Doctrina de Duello," in *Miscellenea iuridica Iustiniani et Gregorii IX legibus commemorandis* (Rome: Universitas Gregoriana, 1935), 156–157.

43. Quoted and discussed in Marco Cavina, *Il duello giudiziario per punto d'onore: Genesi, apogeo e crisi nell'elaborazione dottrinale italiana (sec. XIV–XVI)* (Turin: Giappichelli, 2003), 13.

44. François Billacois, *Le duel dans la société française des XVIe–XVIIe siècles: Essai de psychosociologie historique* (Paris: Editions de l'Ecole des Hautes Études en Sciences Sociales, 1986), 33–34. City dwellers, as free persons, also had the privilege—or, as they often viewed it, the burden—of trial by combat. Many cities sought exemptions from the practice. As this suggests, the history of trial by combat as a distinctly noble practice is complex—too complex, though, to be reviewed in detail here.

45. Nietzsche, "Genealogie der Moral," 277.

46. For a fuller account, see James Q. Whitman, *The Origins of Reasonable Doubt: Theological Roots of the Criminal Trial* (New Haven, CT: Yale University Press, 2008), 72–82.

47. Ibid., 77–79.

48. Well described in Haggenmacher, *Grotius et la doctrine de la guerre juste*, 427.

49. Note the remarkable discussion of Baldus, holding that "pugna aequiparatur torturae, quae non habet fieri nullis indiciis praecedentibus." "In Feudorum Usus [ad de Pace Tenenda, Fredericus]," F. 57 ra, in Cavina, *Duello giudiziario per punto d'onore*, 71–72 n. 47. For trial by combat used to resolve property disputes, see Giovanni da Legnano, *Tractus de bello, de represaliis et de duello*, ed. Thomas Erksine Holland, Classics of International Law 8 (Oxford: Carnegie Institution / Oxford University Press, 1917), 344–345, Latin on 443–444 (chap. 176).

50. Mathias Schmoeckel, "'Ein sonderbares Wunderwerck Gottes': Bermerkungen zum langsamen Rückgang der Ordale nach 1215," *Ius Commune* 26 (1999): 123–164.

51. Frederick I, Constitutio de Pace Tenenda, *Monumenta Germaniae Historica (Leges)* (Hanover: Hahn, 1837), 2:101–103; Paolo Piccolo, ed., *Liber Augustalis di Federico II di Hohenstaufen: Le costituzioni di Melfi, 1231* (Naples: Luciano, 2001); Paul Viollet, ed., *Les établissements de Saint Louis* (Paris: Renouard, 1881), 487–488: "[E]n lieu de batailles nous metons preuves de tesmoinz et de chartes"; Constitution of Mainz 1235, discussed in Hans Fehr, "Das Waffenrecht der Bauern im Mittelalter," *Zeitschrift der Savigny-Stiftung für Rechtsgeschichte* (Germ.) 35 (1914): 192–197.

52. Classic discussion in Henri Morel, "La fin de duel judicaire en France," *Revue historique du droit français et étranger* 42 (1964): 574–639.

53. See the discussion in Cavina, *Duello giudiziario per punto d'onore*, 68–69.

54. Morel, "Fin du duel judiciaire en France"; and the perceptive summary of the literature in Robert A. Nye, *Masculinity and Male Codes of Honor in Modern France* (Berkeley: University of California Press, 1998), 23–24.

55. Billacois, *Duel dans la société française*, 35.

56. Robert A. Schneider, "Swordplay and Statemaking," in *Statemaking and Social Movements: Essays in History and Theory*, ed. Charles Bright and Susan Harding (Ann Arbor: University of Michigan Press, 1984), 272–273.

57. Justine Firnhaber-Baker, "Seigneurial and Royal Power in Later Medieval Southern France," *Past and Present* 208 (2010): 1–40.

58. Jouanna, *Devoir de révolte*; Nye, *Masculinity and Male Codes of Honor in Modern France*, 24.

59. Billacois, *Duel dans la société française*, 209.

60. See the capacious investigation of the history in Cavina, *Duello giudiziario per punto d'onore.*

61. Georges Scelle, *Droit international public: Manuel élémentaire avec les textes essentiels* (Paris: Domat-Montschrestien, 1944), 636: the "guerre-duel (duel judiciaire) connue aussi en Droit interne médiéval, où la force prouve le Droit. . . . C'est une sorte d'ordalie." Cf. Jean Lagorgette, *Le rôle de la guerre: Étude de sociologie générale*, Thèse Dijon (Paris: Giard & Brière, 1906), 318–319. This is also the judgment, if only in passing, of the ever wise Peter Haggenmacher: "Mutations du concept de guerre juste de Grotius à Kant," *Cahiers de philosophie politique et juridique* 10 (1986): 122.

62. Textor, *Synopsis iuris gentium*, "De Bello," 11–12 (chap. XVII, §§10–12, 13). I have borrowed from the accompanying English translation on 171.

63. Discussion in Neff, *War and the Law of Nations*, 91.

64. See, e.g., Vattel, *Droit des gens*, 2:301 (bk. II, chap. 18, §324). Confusion was always possible since *injuria* was identical with the French term *injure*. The English term "insult" was similarly ambiguous.

65. See, e.g., Charles François Lefèvre de la Maillardière, *Précis du droit des gens, de la guèrre, de la paix, et des ambassades* (Paris: Quillau, 1775), 99, using the dueling language of insults. For the most part, though, even Maillardière gave a standard and unadventurous account of the law of war.

66. David A. Bell, *The First Total War: Napoleon's Europe and the Birth of Warfare as We Know It* (New York: Mariner, 2007), 50.

67. Pufendorf, *De jure naturae et gentium*, 885 (bk. VIII, chap. 6, §8).

68. Frederick II, "Réfutation du Prince de Machiavel," in *Oeuvres de Frédéric le Grand*, ed. J. D. E. Preuss (Berlin: Imprimerie Royale, 1846), 8:332.

69. Werner Goez, "Über Fürstenzweikämpfe im Spätmittelalter," *Archiv für Kulturgeschichte* 49, no. 2 (1967): 146–147; for ancient examples, see W. Kendrick Pritchett, *The Greek State at War* (Berkeley: University of California Press, 1974), 4:17–19, with further references.

70. Huizinga, *Homo Ludens*, 91–92.

71. "Pugna": Cavina, *Duello giudiziario per punto d'onore*, 7; Haggenmacher, *Grotius et la doctrine de la guerre juste*, 431–433.

72. Haggenmacher, *Grotius et la doctrine de la guerre juste*, 433–435.

73. This is again a practice that can be documented beyond this period. For antiquity, see J. J. Glück, "Reviling and Monomachy as Battle Preludes in Ancient Warfare," *Acta Classica* 7 (1964): 25–31; and the discussion in Pritchett, *Greek State at War*, 4:16.

74. Goez, "Über Fürstenzweikämpfe im Spätmittelalter," 150–153 and often.

75. Ibid., 151-152, 154.

76. Paris à Puteo, "Tractatus elegans et copiosus de re militari," in *Tractatus universi iuris* 16 (Venice: n.p., 1584): 407v–408r. But see also 425r, discussing seriously the possibility of personal combat between princes.

77. Huizinga, *Homo Ludens*, 92.

78. Goez, "Über Fürstenzweikämpfe im Spätmittelalter," 136–137.

79. The tendency to think of princely encounters as a ritual trial by combat ran very deep. One 1649 text went so far as to declare that every time princes met each other,

even for negotiation, their encounter was to be viewed as a duellum: it was a trial by combat to see which of the two princes could achieve victory by claiming ceremonial precedence. Diego de Saavedra Fajardo, *Idea principis christiano-politici, centum symbolis expressa* (Brussels: Jan Mommaert, 1649), 563: "Duellum propre est mutuum Principum conspectus & praesentia, in quo de caeremoniis decertatur, unoquoque poscente primas, & cum altero de victoria contendente."

80. Extensively treated in Cram, *Iudicium Belli*.

81. Ibid., 87, 103–105 and often; Wilhelm Erben, *Kriegsgeschichte des Mittelalters*, Beiheft 16 der Historischen Zeitschrift (Munich: Oldenbourg, 1929), 92–103.

82. Most famously in the contention between Charles of Anjou and Pedro III of Aragon over the control of Sicily. Their arranged battle was to pit one hundred knights from each side against each other at a field in Bordeaux, with King Edward I of England serving as judge. Early modern jurists, fascinated by this contest, reported that the pope approved this arrangement and that it took place as planned. Andrea Alciato, "De singulari certamine," in *Tractatus universi iuris* (Venice: n.p., 1584), 12:293r (chap. 3, §8); Balthazar Ayala, *De iure et officiis bellicis et disciplina militari libri III*, ed. John Westlake (Washington, DC: Carnegie Institution, 1912), 28v (bk. I, chap. 3, §11). On both counts they were wrong. Pope Martin IV in fact condemned the plan, declaring that the Church "did not tolerate trial by combat, whether it involves Princes and Noble Persons or private persons." See the reconstruction in Goez, "Über Fürstenzweikämpfe im Spätmittelalter," 157 n. 95.

83. See Cram, *Iudicium Belli*, 138, 173–175.

84. I have slightly altered the translation of J. Rawson Lumby in Francis Bacon, *Bacon's History of the Reign of King Henry VII* (Cambridge: Cambridge University Press, 1876), 5, 8.

85. Gentili, *De iure belli*, 1:600–615 (bk. III, chap. 15); Grotius, *De jure belli ac pacis*, 397 (bk. 2, chap. 23, §10), 583–584 (bk. 3, chap. 20, §43); Hotman, *De feudis commentatio tripertita* (Lyon: Apud Iohannem Lertotium, 1573), "Disputatio de iure feudali," cap. XLV, 123: battles a "duorum pluriumve concertatio . . . ut ex . . . eventu de re ambigua diiudicetur."

86. Pufendorf, *De jure naturae et gentium*, 903 (bk. VIII, chap. 8, §5).

87. Franz Schmier, *Jurisprudentia publica universalis*, 2nd ed. (Salzburg: Mayr, 1742), 342 (bk. IV, chap. I, sec. VIII, §III).

88. John Tillotson, *Sermons sur diverses matières importantes*, trans. Jean Barbeyrac (Amsterdam: Brandmüller, 1738), 5:197–198.

89. Anon., "Quelques Nouvelles de Littérature et autres Remarques curieuses," *Journal des Sçavans*, 1761:162–165. Gerdil considered and rejected the classic argument that princes could mount a monomachy in order to spare the blood of their fellow citizens. Like Machiavelli, he concluded that they must use "toutes les forces de l'État, dirgées avec sagesse" (163).

90. D. L. C., *Lettres politiques, historiques, et galantes* (Amsterdam: Aux Dépens de la Compagnie, 1742), 228–229.

91. Johann Joachim Schwabe, *Belustigungen des Verstands und des Witzes* (Leipzig: Breitkopf, 1742), 46.

92. Frederick II, "Réfutation du Prince de Machiavel," 8:332.

93. Bell, *First Total War*, 34.

94. Elias, *The Civilizing Process*, 162, 245–246.

95. Ibid., 189, 446–447.

96. Martens, *Einleitung in das positive europäische Völkerrecht*, 304 (§265).

97. Michael Howard, *War in European History*, rev. ed. (New York: Oxford, 2009), 60.

98. See, e.g., Mattéi, *Histoire du droit de la guerre*, 55. Discussion of the history of the term in Haggenmacher, *Grotius et la doctrine de la guerre juste*, 250 n. 1144.

99. See, e.g., Thomas Rahn, "Grenz-Situationen des Zeremoniells in der frühen Neuzeit," in *Die Grenze: Begriff und Inszenierung*, ed. Markus Bauer and Thomas Rahn (Berlin: Akademie, 1997), 178 n. 6.

100. Johann Christian Lünig, *Theatrum ceremoniale historico-politicum, oder Historisch- und politischer Schau-Platz aller Ceremonien* (Leipzig: Weidmann, 1719–1720), 1:1–2.

101. Ibid., 2:1233–1234.

102. *Kurtzgefaßte doch gründliche Nachricht von dem Kriegs-Ceremonial und sogenannten Kriegsmanier* (Leipzig: n.p., 1745), 33.

103. Samuel, Freiherr von Pufendorf, *Einleitung zu der Historie der vornehmsten Reiche und Staaten so jetziger Zeit in Europe sich befinden* (Frankfurt: Knochens, 1705), 705, 706. Pufendorf did credit them with skill in defending sieges, though.

104. Emer de Vattel, *Mémoirs politiques concernants la guerre* (Frankfurt: Aux Dépens de la Compagnie, 1758), pt. I, chap. II, §17, p. 17.

105. See, e.g., Paul Hay du Chastelet, *Politique militaire, ou Traité de la guerre*, new ed. (Paris: Jombert, 1758), 172. Hay du Chastelet was of course a seventeenth-century author, but the reprint of his book reflects his continuing authority.

106. John A. Lynn, *Giant of the Grand Siècle: The French Army, 1610–1715* (Cambridge: Cambridge University Press, 1997), 398.

107. Quoted in ibid., 400.

108. Roger Chickering, introduction to *War in an Age of Revolution, 1775–1815*, ed. Roger Chickering and Stig Förster (Cambridge: Cambridge University Press, 2010), 5.

109. Augustine, in *Il "De libero arbitrio" di S. Agostino*, ed. Franco de Capitani (Milan: Vita e Pensiero, 1987), 246.

110. David Whetham, *Just Wars and Moral Victories: Surprise, Deception and the Normative Framework of European Law in the Later Middle Ages* (Leiden: Brill, 2009), 12.

111. *Mercure historique et politique*, March 1689, 245–246.

5. WERE THERE REALLY RULES?

Epigraph: Jeremy Black, "Eighteenth-Century Warfare Reconsidered," *War in History* 1 (1994): 222.

1. André Corvisier, *La Bataille de Malplaquet, 1709: L'effondrement de la France évité* (Paris: Economica, 1997).

2. Frederick Dhondt, "From Contract to Treaty: The Legal Transformation of the Spanish Succession, 1659–1713," *Journal of the History of International Law* 13 (2011): 347–375.

3. John A. Lynn, *The Wars of Louis XIV, 1667–1714* (London: Longman, 1999), 326–327.

4. Corvisier, *Bataille de Malplaquet*, 121–124.

5. *Letters and Dispatches of John Churchill of Marlborough*, ed. Sir George Murray (London: Murray, 1844), 4:593.

6. Fagel and the Comte d'Albemarle, both quoted in Corvisier, *Bataille de Malplaquet*, 98.

7. Charles-Théodore Beauvais, *Victoires, conquêtes, désastres, revers et guerres civiles des Français* (Paris: Panckoucke, 1823), 481.

8. *Les délices des Pais-Bas*, new ed. (Bruxelles: Foppens, 1726), 64. Cf. "Lettre d'un Officier des Alliés," in *La clef du cabinet des princes de l'Europe, ou Recueil historique & politique sur les matières du temps* (n.p.: Jacques le Sincère, 1709), vol. 11 (October 1709), 330: "We forced them to abandon the field of battle, but this was the only trophy that was left to us at the price of so much blood."

9. Lynn, *Wars of Louis XIV*, 334.

10. See, e.g., ibid., 334–335.

11. Frederick II, "Principes généraux," chap. 26 in *Oeuvres de Frédéric le Grand*, ed. J. D. E. Preuss (Berlin: Imprimerie Royale, 1846), 28:83.

12. *Lettres historiques, contenant ce qui se passe de plus important en Europe* (The Hague: Moetjens), vol. 37 (October 1709), 462.

13. "Extrait du régistre des résolutions de leurs hautes puissances du Dimanche 27. Juillet 1710," in Casimir Freschot, *Actes, mémoires et autres pièces authentiques concernants la Paix d'Utrecht* (Utrecht: Water & Poolsum, 1712–1713), 128. The taking of Mons and Douai were also listed among the victories that might have justified such a demand.

14. In a very large literature, see, e.g., J. Rufus Fears, "The Theology of Victory at Rome: Approaches and Problems," in *Aufstieg und Niedergang der römischen Welt: Geschichte und Kultur Roms im Spiegel der neueren Forschung* series 2, vol. 17, part 2 (Berlin: De Gruyter, 1981), 736–786; Michael McCormick, *Eternal Victory: Triumphal Rulership in Late Antiquity, Byzantium, and the Early Medieval West* (Cambridge: Cambridge University Press, 1986).

15. Johann Christian Lünig, *Theatrum ceremoniale historico-politicum, oder Historisch- und politischer Schau-Platz aller Ceremonien* (Leipzig: Weidmann, 1719–1720), 2:1281.

16. Ibid., 2:1287.

17. Gr. L. "Zur Erinnerung an König Friedrich II. im Feldzuge 1742," *Jahrbücher für die Armee und Marine* 50 (1884): 22.

18. I have slightly altered the text in Corvisier, *Bataille de Malplaquet*, 100.

19. *Lettres historiques*, 466.

20. Lynn, *Wars of Louis XIV*, 326–327.

21. Nor was this the only conflict over a *Te Deum* that grew out of the allied invasion of 1709. Tournai was the scene of another: As a French text reports, "[T]he city

of Tournai having surrendered to Prince Eugene and the Duke of Marlborough, it was demanded that M. de Beauveau, the Bishop of Tournai, order that a *Te Deum* be sung. This he firmly refused to do." *Recueil de pièces pour servir à l'histoire ecclésiastique à la fin du XVIIIe. siècle et au commencement du XIXe* (n.p.: n.p., 1823), 611. The brave bishop of Tournai resisted allied demands that he order the hymn. This did not convert Tournai into a victory for the French (the Austrians, for example, still sung a *Te Deum* over Tournai in Vienna [*Mercure historique et politique*, October 1709, 379]), but it did afford some propaganda satisfaction. M. de Beauveau would be celebrated as a kind of national hero for decades, his story taught in schools and recorded in popular chronicles of French history. *Nouvel abrégé chronologique de l'histoire de France* (Paris: Prault, 1744), 404; Jean-Baptiste Mailly, *Fastes juifs, romains et français, ou Eléments pour le cours d'histoire du collège Godran de Dijon* (Dijon: Frontin, 1782), 499; also *Journal du Marquis de Dangeau* (Paris: Didot, 1858), 3:106.

22. "Mais le nom de bataille perdue impose aux vaincus et les décourage." Voltaire, *Siècle de Louis XIV* (Paris: Hachette, 1888), 277.

23. Alexandre Masson, marquis de Pezay, "Valeur (Morale)," *Encyclopédie, ou Dictionnaire raisonné des sciences, des arts et des métiers*, ed. Denis Diderot and Jean le Rond d'Alembert (Neufchatel: Faulche, 1765), 16:820.

24. Anon., "Bataille," *Encyclopédie, ou Dictionnaire raisonné des sciences, des arts et des métiers*, ed. Denis Diderot and Jean le Rond d'Alembert, 3rd ed. (Geneva: Pellet, 1778–1779) 4:523.

25. *Encyclopédie méthodique: Art militaire* (Paris: Panckoucke, 1784), 1:286–287.

26. Everybody had always agreed that while it might sometimes be wise to allow the enemy to retreat unmolested, it might also sometimes be wise to pursue and destroy him. Thus sixteenth- and seventeenth-century authors often cited a Roman maxim, repeated down into the time of the American Revolution, that held that a sensible commander should "build a golden bridge" for the enemy, allowing him to retreat unimpeded. But that did not stop them from declaring that it was always good policy to engage in pursuit if at all possible. See Achilles Tarducci, "Turca vincibilis in Ungaria," reprinted in Hermann Conring, "De bello contra Turcas prudenter gerendo libri varii," in *Opera* (Braunschweig: Meyer, 1730), 5:1012–1013. Tarducci's text here was borrowed from Christoph Besold, *De arte iureque belli* (Strasbourg: Zetzner, 1624), 172, who in turn borrowed it from the Italian of Lodovico Guicciardini, *Delle cose più memorabili seguite in Europa* (Antwerp: Silvio, 1565), 189. For the continued use of the proverb "build a golden bridge" in the era of the American Revolution, see Robert Middlekauff, *The Glorious Cause: The American Revolution, 1763–1789*, rev. ed. (New York: Oxford University Press, 2005), 427.

27. Walter Burkert, *Homo Necans: The Anthropology of Ancient Greek Sacrificial Ritual and Myth*, trans. Peter Bing (Berkeley: University of California Press, 1983); and for the background in hunting, see Walter Burkert, *Creation of the Sacred: Tracks of Biology in Early Religions* (Cambridge, MA: Harvard University Press, 1996).

28. Eric Taladoire and Benoit Colsenet, "'Bois ton sang, Beaumanoir': The Political and Conflictual Aspects of the Ballgame in the Northern Chiapas Area," in *The Meso-american Ballgame*, ed. Vernon L. Scarborough and David R. Wilcox (Tucson: University of Arizona Press, 1991), 174.

29. Ryszard Kapuscinski, *The Soccer War*, trans. William Brand (New York: Vintage, 1992).

30. Emer de Vattel, *Le droit des gens, ou, Principes de la loi naturelle, appliqués à la conduite & aux affaires des nations & des souverains*, ed. Paul Pradier-Fodéré (Paris: Guillaumin, 1863), 1:229 (bk. I, chap. 5, §66).

31. M. H. Keen, *The Laws of War in the Late Middle Ages* (London: Routledge & K. Paul, 1965), 129.

32. In fact premodern battles seldom if ever ran from dawn to dusk. Most estimates suggest that they lasted a couple of hours at most; nobody could continue fighting for longer than that. Interesting observations in Kurt Raaflaub, "Homerische Krieger, Protohopliten und die Polis: Schritte zur Lösung alter Probleme," in *Krieg, Gesellschaft, Institutionen: Beiträge zu einer vergleichenden Kriegsgeschichte*, ed. Burkhard Meißner, Oliver Schmitt, and Michael Sommer (Berlin: Akademie, 2005), 231–232, especially 238. For the column of Trajan and his forum at Rome, where Aurora and Hesperus are depicted as the symbols of times of day in which those victories were achieved, see W. Kendrick Pritchett, *The Greek State at War* (Berkeley: University of California Press, 1974), 4:46 n. 147; Vegetius, *Epitoma rei militaris*, ed. M. D. Reeve (Oxford: Clarendon, 2004), 91 (3.11.1), 85,(3.9.2) (two or three hours). For the proposition that a battle must be completed in one day, see Paris à Puteo, "Tractatus elegans et copiosus de re militari," in *Tractatus universi iuris* 16 (Venice: n.p., 1584): 396v, with citations to earlier medieval jurists. For the one-day requirement in duels, François Billacois, *Le duel dans la société française des XVIe–XVIIe siècles: Essai de psychosociologie historique* (Paris: Editions de l'Ecole des Hautes Études en Sciences Sociales, 1986), 28–29.

33. Hans van Wees, *Greek Warfare: Myths and Realities* (London: Duckworth, 2005), 136. Cf. Plutarch, "Life of Nicias," in *Plutarch's Lives*, ed. B. Perrin (Cambridge, MA: Harvard University Press, 1967), 3:228 (Nic. 6.5).

34. *Livy*, ed. E. Sage and A. Schlesinger (Cambridge, MA: Harvard University Press, 1979), 12:154 (40.50.4).

35. These and more phrases in Malte Prietzel, *Kriegführung im Mittelalter: Handlungen, Erinnerungen, Bedeutungen* (Paderborn, Germany: Schöningh, 2006), 158 nn. 172–173.

36. Ibid., 153.

37. Generally ibid., 150–173.

38. In practice there are only few clearly documented cases. Prietzel, *Kriegführung im Mittelalter*, 164–168. For the early modern rule, see, e.g., Besold, *De arte iureque belli*, 172–173, quoting Martin du Bellay, *Mémoires*, in *Collection complète des mémoires rélatifs à l'histoire de France* (Paris: Foucault, 1821), 13:473: "Saepe receptus, der Abzug/oder Auffbruch/speciem habet fugae, quique recipiunt se in tutiora loca, animo decertandi carent. Communement gens qui se retirent, ne sont coustemiers

a tenir bataille; ainsique font ceux qui marchent en avant." Gentili offered a particularly striking analysis of the rule at the end of the sixteenth century. Why, he
asked, was it the case that the proof of victory involved having control of the
corpses on the field? The answer was typical of premodern law, which established
a ritual for determining who was the status-superior and who was the status-
inferior. Status-inferiors were required to come to the home of their superiors, bow
down, and beg favors. The rule of victory, Gentili held, took the same form: the
loser had been proven to be the status-inferior. That meant that he had to come to
the victor, bow down, and beg the favor of the return of his dead. Alberico Gentili,
De iure belli libri tres (repr. Buffalo, NY: Hein, 1995), 1:603 (bk. III, chap. 15): "Sed
& rationis est, ut, qui rogat, inferior censeatur, & victus." For the background in
legal reasoning, see James Q. Whitman, "The Seigneurs Descend to the Rank of
Creditors: The Abolition of Respect, 1790," *Yale Journal of Law and Humanities*
6 (1994): 249–283.

39. "Rex adepta cum multo suorum cruore victoria," quoted in Prietzel, *Kriegführung
im Mittelalter*, 157 n. 171. The Battle of Fornovo in 1495 offers another example.

40. Hdt. 1.82.6, trans G. C. Macaulay, in Herodotus, *The Histories*, ed. Donald Lateiner
(repr. New York: Barnes and Noble, 2004), 31.

41. Valerius Maximus, *Memorable Sayings and Doings*, ed. D. R. Schackleton Bailey
(Cambridge, MA: Harvard University Press, 2000), 1:200 (2.8): "ne quis trium-
pharet nisi qui quinque milia hostium una acie cecedisset" and the subsequent
discussion in his heading "de iure triumphandi." There is much dispute about
whether these rules really applied in practice. See Mary Beard, *The Roman Triumph* (Cambridge, MA: Belknap Press of Harvard University Press, 2007),
210. What matters for my purposes here is that they provided some authority for a
casualties rule.

42. Isidore, Etym. 18.2.1, "De Bellis," in *Isidorus Hispalensis, Etymologiae XVIII*, ed. J.
Cantó Llorca (Paris: Belles Lettres, 2007), 60–61. This passage deserves longer
commentary. I take *exspoliatio* here to refer to capture of the enemy camp according
to the standard Roman rule.

43. Robert Joseph Pothier, *Traité du droit de domaine de propriété* (Paris: Debure,
1772), 88–89 (§§87–88).

44. John A. Lynn II, *Women, Armies and Warfare in Early Modern Europe* (Cambridge:
Cambridge University Press, 2008), 149 and often. Of course, the best booty was
gained by sacking cities, not by winning pitched battles. Most battlefield booty
involved stripping the corpses of ordinary soldiers. Even dead soldiers had cash
on them, though, since the safest place to keep your cash was on your person, and
at least one early modern illustration of booty taking shows victorious soldiers
splitting a hefty take in coins. Moreover there were times when even battle booty
could sometimes be extraordinarily rich. Princes, typically eager to display magnificence, often brought immense finery to their battle camp. As a result, the camp
of a defeated prince could hold treasures, for example, the famous *Burgunderbeute*, the Burgundian booty seized from the camp of Charles the Bold after his
defeat by the Swiss at the Battle of Grandson in 1476, a magnificent collection of

riches that was celebrated in Swiss chronicles and that later made its way piece-meal into Swiss museums. See *Die Burgunderbeute und Werke burgundischer Hofkunst* (Bern: Historisches Museum, 1969). All of that awaited soldiers as long as it counted as booty.

45. See Bernhard Settler, "Der Sempacher Brief von 1393: Ein Verkanntes Dokument aus der älteren Schweizergeschichte," *Schweizerische Zeitschrift für Geschichte* 35 (1985): 1–20. For the law in this period see also the discussion in the Lynn draft manuscript entitled *Surrender*, chap. 1 (copy of manuscript on file with author).

46. For a survey of the law of booty, see Fritz Redlich, *De Praeda Militari: Looting and Booty, 1500–1815* (Wiesbaden: Steiner, 1955), and the still useful dissertation of Axel Franz Julius Benedix, *De praeda inde ab antiquitate ad usque nostram aetatem bello terrestri legitime parta* (Bratislava: Raabe, 1874). Also see Fritz Helge Voß, *Ius belli: Zum völkerrechtlichen Kriegsrecht in Europa in der sog. Spanischen Epoche der Völkerrechtsgeischte* (Baden-Baden: Nomos, 2007), 177–206. For the history of these field regulations, see Max Jähns, *Geschichte der Kriegswissenschaften, vornehmlich in Deutschland*, 3 vols. (repr. Hildesheim: Olms, 1966), 1:208–209, 759–763.

47. Quoted from Johann Christian Lünig, *Corpus iuris militaris* (Leipzig: Lanckisch, 1723) 1:71.

48. Sebastian Vrancx and Jan Brueghel the Younger, *The Aftermath of a Battle*, Musée des Beaux-Arts de Liège. For an example from Martszen, see http://www.sothebys .com/en/catalogues/ecatalogue.html/2010/old-master-and-british-paintings-day -sale-l10034#/r=/en/ecat.fhtml.L10034.html+r.m=/en/ecat.lot.L10034.html/169/, now in a private collection in New York.

49. August Wilhelm Heffter, *Das europäische Völkerrecht der Gegenwart*, 3rd ed. (Berlin: Schroeder, 1855), 203, 237: "Zufälligkeiten würfeln ihn [den Krieg] oft zusammen und machen ihn meist zu einem Spiel, dessen Schwankungen nie zuvor zu berechnen sind. . . . [D]ie kriegführenden Theile geben gleichsam wechselseitig dem Spiel des Krieges dasjenige preis, was sie bei ihrem Zusammentreffen bei sich führen."

50. Isidore, Etym. bk. 18, "De Bello et Ludis," in *Isidorus Hispalensis, Etymologiae XVIII.*

51. Aeschylus, *Eumenides*, ed. H. Lloyd-Jones (Cambridge, MA: Harvard University Press, 1963), 2:358 (913–915). See, e.g., Pierre Ducrey, "Aspects juridiques de la victoire et du traitement des vaincus," in *Problèmes de la guerre en Grèce ancienne*, ed. Jean-Pierre Vernant (The Hague: Mouton, 1968), 232.

52. Jean-Pierre Vernant, introduction to *Problèmes de la guerre en Grèce ancienne*, 21; cf. Raoul Lonis, *Guerre et réligion en Grèce à l'époque classique: Recherches sur les rites, les dieux, l'idéologie de la victoire* (Paris: Belles Lettres, 1979), 25–40.

53. T. J. Cornell, "On War and Games in the Ancient World," in *War and Games*, Studies in the Nature of War 3, ed. T. J. Cornell and T. B. Allen (San Francisco: Boydell, 2002), 45.

54. Kurt-Georg Cram, *Iudicium Belli: Zum Rechtscharakter des Krieges im deutschen Mittelalter* (Munich: Böhlau, 1955), 15, 181–182.

55. Black, "Eighteenth-Century Warfare Reconsidered," 222–223. Text also in Jeremy Black, *European Warfare, 1660–1815* (New Haven, CT: Yale University Press, 1994), 75.

56. Van Wees, *Greek Warfare*, 1. For similar views from a well-informed specialist in International law, see Peter Malanczuk, *Akehurst's Introduction to Modern International Law*, 7th ed. (London: Routledge, 1997), 307–308, treating eighteenth-century war as governed by the political dynamic rather than by law.

57. Adriaan Lanni, "The Laws of War in Ancient Greece," *Law and History Review* 26 (2008): 486.

58. Peter Krentz, "Fighting by the Rules: The Invention of the Hoplite Agôn," *Hesperia* 71 (2002): 25; van Wees, *Greek Warfare*, 134–135, and his somewhat more cautious statement on 150.

59. Van Wees, *Greek Warfare*, 117.

60. Prietzel, *Kriegführung im Mittelalter*, 168.

61. Werner Ogris, "Sessio triduana," in *Handwörterbuch zur deutschen Rechtsgeschichte* (Berlin: Schmidt, 1964–1988), 4:1649.

62. Prietzel, *Kriegführung im Mittelalter*, 162–163, on battle of Montlhéry, 1465.

63. Stephen C. Neff, *War and the Law of Nations: A General History* (Cambridge: Cambridge University Press, 2005), 74.

64. Black, "Eighteenth-Century Warfare Reconsidered," 222.

65. Josiah Ober, "Classical Greek Times," in *The Laws of War: Constraints on Warfare in the Western World*, ed. Michael Howard, George J. Andreopoulos, and Mark R. Shulman (New Haven, CT: Yale University Press, 1994), 25.

66. Oliver Wendell Holmes Jr., "The Path of the Law," *Harvard Law Review* 10 (1897): 457–478.

67. See, e.g., James D. Morrow, "When Do States Follow the Laws of War?," *American Political Science Review* 101 (2007): 559–572.

68. Georg Friedrich von Martens, *Précis du droit des gens moderne de l'Europe, fondé sur les traités et l'usage* (Göttingen: Dieterich, 1789) 1:339–340 (§231).

69. Draft of letter to Valori, May 27, 1742, Ministère des Affaires Étrangères, Archives Diplomatiques, Correspondance Politique (Prusse), 121:438, La Courneuve, France.

70. Anon., "Bataille," *Encyclopédie, ou Dictionnaire raisonné des sciences, des arts et des métiers*, ed. Denis Diderot and Jean le Rond d'Alembert, 3rd ed. (Geneva: Pellet, 1778–1779) 4:523.

71. *Dictionnaire militaire portatif* (Paris: Gissey, 1758), 3:15 (s.v. "occasion").

72. Van Wees, *Greek Warfare*, 124.

73. Neff, *War and the Law of Nations*, 74.

74. Howard, Andreopoulos, and Shulman, *The Laws of War*.

75. Michael Howard, "Constraints on Warfare," ibid., 1.

76. Van Wees, *Greek Warfare*, 126.

77. Max Weber, *Wirtschaft und Gesellschaft: Die Wirtschaft und die gesellschaftlichen Ordnungen und Mächte*, vol. 3: *Recht*, ed. Werner Gephart and Siegfried Hermes, in *Max Weber Gesamtausgabe* (Tübingen: Mohr, 2010), 22–23: 196: "Nicht jedes (objektive) 'Rech' ist . . . 'garantiertes' Recht. Wir wollen von Recht . . . auch überall

da sprechen, wo die Bedeutung der Geltung einer Norm darin besteht: daß die Art der Orientierung des Handelns an ihr überhaupt irgendwelche 'Rechtsfolgen' hat. Das heißt: wo irgendwelche andren Normen gelten, welche an die 'Befolgung' oder 'Verletzung' jener ersten bestimmte, ihrerseits durch Rechtszwang garantierte Chancen eines Einverständnishandelns knüpfen." Of course, Weber was not speaking of eighteenth-century war, where the "durch Rechtszwang garantierte Chancen" were not to be seen. Nevertheless the victory rules described in the text did establish norms that were the basis of "Einverständnisverhandeln."

78. See especially Scott Shapiro, *Legality* (Cambridge, MA: Harvard University Press, 2011).

79. Quoted in ibid., 40.

80. "A Czaslau, je suivis, autant que je pus, les ennemis avec mon infanterie sans vouloir la débander. À la vérité, si ma cavalerie n'eût pas été dans le désordre que je vous ai dépeint tantôt, je l'eusse poussée en avant, mais les têtes n'étoient pas assez rassises pour leur confier une pareille besogne." Frederick in conversation with the Comte de Gisors, Camille-Félix-Michel Rousset, *Le Comte de Gisors: 1732–1758* (Paris: Didier, 1868), 106.

81. *Mémoires des négociations du Marquis de Valori* (Paris: Didot, 1820), 1:259–260.

82. Peter Krentz, "Deception in Archaic and Classical Greek Warfare," in *War and Violence in Ancient Greece*, ed. Hans van Wees (London: Duckworth, 2000), 167–200.

83. See the remarks of Pieter Spierenburg, *A History of Murder: Personal Violence in Europe from the Middle Ages to the Present* (Cambridge: Polity, 2008), 38. The topic deserves more discussion than I can give it here.

84. Gregory Nagy, *Best of the Achaeans*, rev. ed. (Baltimore: Johns Hopkins University Press, 1999), 40.

85. Krentz, "Fighting by the Rules," 28.

86. See Toepfler, "Apaturia," in *Paulys Realencyclopädie der classischen Altertumswissenschaft*, ed. Georg Wissowa (Stuttgart: Drückenmiller, 1894), vol. 1, 2: cols. 2672–2680.

87. Augustine, Quaestiones in Heptateuchum 6 (Quaestiones in Jesum Nave), X, in *Patrologiae Cursus Completus*, ed. J.-P. Migne (Turnhout: Brepols, 1985) 34:781.

88. For a much-reprinted eighteenth-century version, see *Polyaenus' Stratagems of War*, trans. Richard Shepherd (London: Nicol, 1793).

89. See the discussion of Everett L. Wheeler, *Stratagem and the Vocabulary of Military Trickery* (Leiden: Brill, 1988), 93–100.

90. Isidore, Etym. 18.2.1, in *Isidorus Hispalensis, Etymologiae XVIII*.

91. Jacobus Zetzkius, *De jure belli* (Duisburg: Franco Sas, 1692), 12–13.

92. See, e.g., Christian Wolff, *Principes du droit de la nature et des gens*, ed. Jean-Henri-Samuel Formey (Amsterdam: Rey, 1758), 300 (bk. VIII, §18). For a broader survey of the law of stratagems, see Jean-Mathieu Mattéi, *Histoire du droit de la guerre, 1700–1819: Introduction à l'histoire du droit international* (Aix-en-Provence: Presses Universitaires d'Aix-Marseille, 2006), 789–795.

93. Emer de Vattel, *The Law of Nations; or, Principles of the Law of Nature, Applied to the Conduct and Affairs of Nations and Sovereigns*, trans. Joseph Chitty (London: Sweet, 1834), 374 (bk. III, chap. 10, §178).

94. I leave the details aside, but it is worth noting that of the two classic forms of trickery, lying in wait and poisoning, it was first and foremost poisoning that was condemned by classic law. It may be worth noting that poisoning was the classic means of killing used by women.

95. Demosthenes, "Third Philippic," in Demosthenes, ed. J. H. Vince (Cambridge, MA: Harvard University Press, 1970), 1:250 (9.48); Polybius, *The Histories*, trans. W. Paton, F. Walbank and C. Habicht (Cambridge, MA: Harvard Univerity Press, 2011), 4:460 (13.3.2–6).

96. Vattel, *Law of Nations*, 374 (bk. III, chap. 10, §178). Contrast with Cicero, *De Officiis*, ed. W. Miller (Cambridge, MA: Harvard University Press, 1975), 360 (3:87).

97. Gaspard de Réal de Curban, *La science du gouvernement, ouvrage de morale, de droit et de politique* (Paris: Libraires Associés, 1764), 5:436.

98. Samuel, Freiherr de Pufendorf, *De jure naturae et gentium libri octo* (repr. Buffalo, NY: Hein, 1995), 885 (bk. 8, chap. 6, §8).

99. Immanuel Kant, "Zum ewigen Frieden," in *Über den Gemeinspruch: Das mag in der Theorie Richtig Sein, taugt aber nicht für die Praxis / Zum ewigen Frieden: Ein philosophischer Entwurf*, ed. Heiner F. Klemme (Hamburg: Meiner, 1992), 64–68.

100. Hans J. Morgenthau, *Politics among Nations: The Struggle for Power and Peace*, 5th ed. (New York: Knopf, 1978), 431.

101. Gerhard von Glahn and James Larry Taulbee, *Law among Nations: An Introduction to Public International Law*, 8th ed. (New York: Pearson/Longman, 2007), 63.

102. Alfred Ritter von Arneth, *Geschichte Maria Theresia's* (Vienna: Braumüller, 1863–1879), 6:121–125.

103. The principle *ne bis in idem*, "no double jeopardy," applied in war just as it did in other areas of the law. Discussion in Mattéi, *Histoire du droit de la guerre*, 990–992.

104. Wolff, *Principes du droit de la nature et des gens*, 304 (bk. IX, §9).

105. Vattel, *Droit des gens*, 3:188 (bk. IV, chap. 2, §19); cf. de Réal, *Science du gouvernement* 5:620: prince may not reclaim rights abandoned by "an express or tacit act."

106. Tom R. Tyler, *Why People Obey the Law* (Princeton, NJ: Princeton University Press, 2006), 19.

107. Eric Robson, "The Armed Forces and the Art of War," in *The New Cambridge Modern History*, ed. G. R. Potter and G. R. Elton, vol. 7: *The Old Regime, 1713–63*, ed. J. O. Lindsay (Cambridge: Cambridge University Press, 1979), 165.

6. THE DEATH OF PITCHED BATTLE

Epigraph: Carl von Clausewitz, *Vom Kriege: Hinterlassenes Werk des Generals Carl von Clausewitz* (Bonn: Dümmler, 1980), 330 (bk. II, chap. 5).

1. *Quarterly Review* 129 (October 1870): 235.

2. Joseph Thomas, *Universal Pronouncing Dictionary of Biography and Mythology* (Boston: Lippincott, 1870), 2:1275.

3. Letter to Queen Augusta of September 3, 1870, quoted in *Landeshuter Zeitung*, September 11, 1870, 947.

4. Theodor Fontane, *Irrungen wirrungen: Berliner Roman*, 4th ed. (Berlin: Fontane, 1896), 69: "um Sedan herum den großen Zirkel gezogen."

5. See Johann Caspar Bluntschli, "Völkerrechtliche Betrachtungen über den französich-deutschen Krieg," *Jahrbuch für Gesetzgebung, Verwaltung und Rechtspflege des Deutschen Reiches* 1 (1871): 296.

6. Whether the *franc-tireurs* were really irregulars was a matter of some legal ambiguity. The same is true of confederates fighting under the Partisan Ranger Act. It was precisely the resulting problems that preoccupied Francis Lieber and Johann Caspar Bluntschli, discussed later in this chapter. Nevertheless, to spare the reader too much involved discussion, I use the term "irregular."

7. Franz Herre, *Moltke: Der Mann und sein Jahrhundert* (Stuttgart: Deutsche Verlags-Anstalt, 1984), 305–307.

8. Yorktown was a siege, of course, but a characteristically orderly eighteenth-century one.

9. James McPherson, "The Saratoga That Wasn't: Confederate Recognition and the Effect of Antietam Abroad," in *Inside the Confederate Nation: Essays in Honor of Emory M. Thomas*, ed. Lesley J. Gordon and John C. Inscoe (Baton Rouge: Louisiana State University Press, 2005), 97, 102, 104. Howard Jones, in *Abraham Lincoln and a New Birth of Freedom: The Union and Slavery in the Diplomacy of the Civil War* (Lincoln: University of Nebraska Press, 1999), 105–106, argues that the British were simply disappointed by the failure of the Confederates to achieve a "climactic victory." I register my skepticism that any victory would have sufficed.

10. James M. McPherson, *This Mighty Scourge: Perspectives on the Civil War* (New York: Oxford University Press, 2007), 67.

11. See, e.g., William C. Davis, *Battle at Bull Run: A History of the First Major Campaign of the Civil War* (Baton Rouge: Louisiana State University Press, 1977), 239.

12. John Fabian Witt, *Lincoln's Code: The Laws of War in American History* (New York: Free Press, 2012), chap. 6; Stephen C. Neff, *Justice in Blue and Gray: A Legal History of the Civil War* (Cambridge, MA: Harvard University Press, 2010), 76–78. Again I leave to one side the vexed legal question of whether "irregular" is the appropriate term.

13. See the treatment of Witt, *Lincoln's Code*, chap. 1.

14. George Germain and William Carter, quoted and discussed in Eric Robson, *The American Revolution in Its Political and Military Aspects, 1763–1783* (Hamden, CT: Archon, 1965), 96, 100.

15. Witt, *Lincoln's Code*, chap. 4.

16. McPherson, *This Mighty Scourge*, 67.

17. John Keegan, *The American Civil War: A Military History* (New York: Vintage, 2009), 234–235.

18. Paddy Griffith, *Battle Tactics of the Civil War* (New Haven, CT: Yale University Press, 1987); Brent Nosworthy, *The Bloody Crucible of Courage: Fighting Methods and Combat Experience of the Civil War* (New York: Carroll & Graf, 2003); Earl

J. Hess, *The Rifle Musket in Civil War Combat: Reality and Myth* (Lawrence: University of Kansas Press, 2008).

19. Americans certainly did entrench themselves at times, as at Petersberg, but they managed to mount pitched battles as well.

20. Hess, *Rifle Musket in Civil War Combat*, 207.

21. Ibid.

22. Keegan, *The American Civil War*, 234–235.

23. Carl Schmitt, *Theorie des Partisanen: Zwischenbemerkung zum Begriff des Politischen* (Berlin: Duncker & Humblot, 1963), 17.

24. Edmund Phipps, *Memoirs and the Political and Literary Life of Robert Plumer Ward, Esq.* (London: Murray, 1850), 1:8–9, 14–15.

25. Robert Ward, *Enquiry into the Foundation and History of the Law of Nations in Europe, from the Time of the Greeks and Romans to the Age of Grotius* (London: Strahan, 1795), 2:172.

26. Ibid., 2:155–156.

27. Ibid., 2:157–159, 159–160.

28. Edmund Burke, *Reflections on the Revolution in France*, ed. L. G. Mitchell (New York: Oxford University Press, 1993), 78–79.

29. By 1798 it was common to read passages like this, still under the spell of Scottish Enlightenment history: "The gradations of civil society are marked by the peculiar characters of the wars which have distinguished its progress; and which may be divided into wars of chivalry; wars of conquest; wars of religion; wars of the balance of power; and wars of commerce. But we are now actually arriving at the wars of the rights of men; the fury of which will be best repressed by opposing to it the barrier of the rights of nations." Anon., "National Affairs," *Analytical Review*, 1798, 92–93. Cf. James Mackintosh, *A Discourse on the Study of the Law of Nature and Nations* (London: Caddell, 1799), 14, ascribing the improvements in European "manners" to, "above all, that general mildness of character and manners which arose from the combined and progressive influence of chivalry, of commerce, of learning, and of religion."

30. *The Miscellaneous Prose Works of Sir Walter Scott, Bart.*, vol. 28, *Tales of a Grandfather* (Edinburgh: Cadell, 1850), 36.

31. Available at http://www.kleist.org/texte/DieMarquisevonOL.pdf.

32. Theodor Schmalz, *Das europäische Völker-Recht in acht Büchern* (Berlin: Duncker & Humblot, 1817), 36.

33. G. F. Martens's standard international law text, for example, betrayed no influence of the chivalric idea, either in its first version in 1796 or in later editions through the 1830s. Martens was quite well aware, as La Curne de Sainte-Palaye had been, that medieval knights went to war for profit, and he said so. Georg Friedrich von Martens, *Einleitung in das positive europäische Völkerrecht auf Verträge und herkommen gegründet* (Göttingen: Dieterich, 1796), 310–311 (§270). Some jurists did try to insist, like Scott, that chivalry had at least tempered the profit motive. In 1844, for example, August Wilhelm Heffter insisted that knights were encouraged to spare their captives not only "by the prospect of ransom" but also because of their "chivalric sensibility." August Wilhelm Heffter, *Das europäische Völkerrecht der Gegenwart*

(Berlin: Schroeder, 1844), 214 (§127); cf. also §119. For similar discussions, see Georg Friedrich von Martens, *Précis du droit des gens moderne de l'Europe*, ed. Charles Vergé (Paris: Guillaumin, 1858), 2:237; Adolf Trendelenburg, *Naturrecht auf dem Grunde der Ethik* (Leipzig: Hirzel, 1860), 533.

34. Charles Mills, *The History of Chivalry, or Knighthood and Its Times* (London: Longman Hurst, 1825), 3.

35. J. W. Barber, *An Account of the Most Important and Interesting Religious Events, Which Have Transpired from the Commencement of the Christian Era to the Present Time* (New Haven, CT: L. H. Young, 1834), 123: a knight's "valour was connected with modesty, and both were, in the highest degree conspicuous. In chivalric war, much humanity was displayed; though in contentions of a different kind, it was unhappily suppressed. As a knight fought for the church, he was intolerant. . . . His sense of honour was keen, and his independence was consistent with discipline and submission."

36. James Kent, *Commentaries on American Law*, 2nd ed. (New York: Halsted, 1832), 11.

37. Anon., "Abriß der Geschichte der Kavallerie in Europa seit Einführung des Feuergewehrs (Fortsetzung)," *Zeitschrift für Kunst, Wissenschaft und Geschichte des Krieges* 1 (1830): 125. This sort of thing required some recasting of the eighteenth-century tradition. When Royer-Collard published his 1830 edition of Vattel, for example, he attached to it a translation of Mackintosh, which of course included a celebration of chivalry, otherwise absent from the greatest of Enlightenment international law texts. Emer de Vattel, *Le droit des gens, ou Principes de la loi naturelle appliquée à la conduite des affaires des nations et des souverains*, ed. Paul Royer-Collard (Paris: Aillaud, 1830).

38. Karl Theodor Pütter, *Beiträge zur Völker-rechts Geschichte und Wissenschaft* (Leipzig: Wienbrack, 1843), 92.

39. B., "Kriegsrecht," in *Rechtslexikon für Juristen aller teutschen Staaten*, ed. Julius Weiske (Leipzig: Wigand, 1845), 6:219.

40. August Wilhelm Heffter, *Das europäishe Völkerrecht der Gegenwart*, 3rd ed. (Berlin: Schroeder, 1855), 237 (§135). Even Bluntschli, who detested booty taking, had to concede its occasional legality until the large-scale legal shift of the 1870s. Contrast Johann Caspar Bluntschli, *Das moderne Völkerrecht der civilisirten Staten* (Nördlingen: Beck, 1866), e.g., 358 (§657) with Bluntschli, *Das Beuterecht im Krieg und das Seebeuterecht insbesondere: Eine völkerrechtliche Untersuchung* (Nördlingen: Beck, 1878).

41. This was understood to derive from public law. Claude Étienne Delvincourt, *Cours de Code Napoléon* (Paris: Gueffier, 1813), 1:175; for the subsequent era, see Alexandre Duranton, *Cours de droit français suivant le code civil*, 4th ed. (Paris: Thorel, 1844), 4:271; Jean Charles Florent Demolombe, *Cours de code civil* (Paris: Durand, 1857), 13:98–99.

42. For a description, see Hans Friedrich Fulda, *Georg Wilhelm Friedrich Hegel* (Munich: Beck, 2003), 270.

43. Excerpted and discussed in Paul Pradier-Fodéré, *Commentaire sur le code de justice militaire* (Paris: Dumaine, 1873), 595–597; Bluntschli, *Beuterecht im Krieg und das Seebeuterecht insbesondere*. Pradier-Fodéré was particularly impressed by Chief

Justice Marshall's opinion in *Brown v. United States*, 12 U.S. 110 (1814). Pradier-Fodéré, *Commentaire sur le code de justice militaire*, 599.

44. See the realist survey in Kalevi J. Holsti, *Peace and War: Armed Conflicts and International Order, 1648–1989* (Cambridge: Cambridge University Press, 1991), 140–141. Holsti's aims, I should emphasize, are different from mine: he is concerned with appraising the causes of wars in a way that range well beyond the legal justifications that are my subject.

45. Stanley to the Board of Control, December 31, 1841, quoted and discussed in Peter Ward Fay, *The Opium War, 1840–1842* (Chapel Hill: University of North Carolina Press, 1997), 340.

46. Orlando Figes, *The Crimean War: A History* (New York: Holt, 2010), 111, 159; *Rélation de la guerre d'Italie, depuis le départ des troupes jusqu'à leur rentrée triomphale, le 14 août 1859* (Paris: Gustave Havard, 1859), 56.

47. Michael Howard, *The Franco-Prussian War: The German Invasion of France, 1870–1871* (repr. London: Routledge, 2006), 55.

48. For a contemporary account, see G. Martiny de Riez, *Histoire illustrée de la guerre de 1870–1871* (Laon, France: Deneuville, 1871), 26.

49. *Journal officiel de l'Empire Français* (July 31, 1870).

50. It is true that creating republican armies meant eliminating, at least for a period, the aristocratic domination of the officer corps. It is also true that in the nineteenth century this meant a gradual—*very* gradual—severing of the ties between aristocratic culture and the officer corps in France. Undoubtedly there was a slow republicanization of the culture of the French army over the course of the nineteenth century, and especially in the years immediately before 1914. But it is at best forced to point to the revolutionary-era experience as evidence that an aristocratic military culture had collapsed before 1870. The case is even weaker when it comes to Prussia. The officer corps of European powers, even of Britain, remained heavily, even predominantly aristocratic throughout the nineteenth century. See, e.g., John H. Kautsky, *The Politics of Aristocratic Empires* (Chapel Hill: University of North Carolina Press, 1982), 363.

51. William Doyle, *The Oxford History of the French Revolution* (New York: Oxford University Press, 1989), 379–380.

52. Liddell Hart, *The Ghost of Napoleon* (New Haven, CT: Yale University Press, 1934).

53. Among innumerable examples, see, e.g., Charles Hubert Millevoye, *La bataille d'Austerlitz: Poëme* (Paris: Renouard, 1806), 29, 43.

54. Henri Dunant, *A Memory of Solferino*, trans. anon. (Washington, DC: American National Red Cross, 1939), 31, 32.

55. Hew Strachan, *European Armies and the Conduct of War* (London: Allen & Unwin, 1983), 71.

56. Bluntschli, *Das moderne Völkerrecht der civilisirten Staten*, 291 (§517): "notwendige neue Rechtsbildung" justifies war.

57. Ibid.: "eine eher kindliche als juristische Ansicht."

58. See the account in Wilhelm Rüstow, *Der Krieg von 1866 in Deutschland und Italien, politisch-militärisch beschrieben* (Zürich: Schultheß, 1866), 3, 13.

59. I have slightly altered the translation in Antoine Henri, baron de Jomini, *Summary of the Art of War or, A New Analytical Compend of the Principal Combinations of Strategy, of Grand Tactics and of Military Policy*, trans. O. F. Winship and E. E. McLean (New York: Putnam, 1854), 27.

60. Gaspard de Réal de Curban, *La science du gouvernement, ouvrage de morale, de droit et de politique* (Paris: Libraries Associés, 1764), 5:436.

61. Clausewitz, *Vom Kriege*, 385–386 (bk. 3, chap. 10).

62. For the classic attack on Clausewitz, see Hubert Camon, *La guerre Napoléonienne: Les systèmes d'opérations, théorie et technique* (Paris: Economica, 1997), 34–35, and the discussion in Azar Gat, *The Origins of Military Thought from the Enlightenment to Clausewitz* (New York: Oxford University Press, 1989), 208–209.

63. Georg Friedrich von Martens, *Précis du droit des gens moderne de l'Europe, fondé sur les traités et l'usage*, 3rd ed. (Göttingen: Dieterich,1821), 461 (§270).

64. Silvestre Pinheiro-Ferreira, *Précis d'un cours de droit public: Interne et externe* (Paris: Rey et Gravier, 1830), 2:85.

65. Bluntschli, *Das moderne Völkerrecht der civilisirten Staten* 298 (§535); Heffter, *Das europäische Völkerrecht der Gegenwart*, 229 (§130), though admitting that *Vernichtung* may sometimes de facto occur (192 [§107]).

66. John Austin, *The Province of Jurisprudence Determined* (London: Murray, 1832), 6–8.

67. Clausewitz, *Vom Kriege*, "Nachricht," 182–183.

68. Antoine Henri, baron de Jomini, *Précis de l'art de la guerre, ou, Nouveau tableau analytique des principales combinaisons de la stratégie, de la grande tactique et de la politique militaire*, new ed. (Paris: Anselin, 1838), 2:106–133; Clausewitz, *Vom Kriege*, 486–488 (bk. IV, chap. 13).

69. See his account of Chotusitz in Antoine Henri, baron de Jomini, *Histoire critique et militaire des guerres de Frédéric II*, 3rd ed. (Paris: Magimel, Anselin et Pochard, 1818), 20–21.

70. Clausewitz, *Vom Kriege*, 884 (bk. 7, chap. 7, "Die Offensivschlacht").

71. Wilhelm von Willisen, *Theorie des großen Krieges* (Berlin: Duncker & Humblot, 1840), 1:92.

72. Jérémie Benoit and Bernard Chevallier, *Marengo: Une victoire politique* (Paris: Réunion des Musées Nationaux, 2000), 122; *Nouvelles littéraires et politiques* 128 (July 1809).

73. Eighteenth bulletin of the *Grande Armée*, Mojaïsk, September 12, 1812, in J. David Markham, *Imperial Glory: The Bulletins of Napoleon's Grande Armée, 1805–1814* (London: Greenhill, 2003), 297.

74. Immanuel Kant, "Zum ewigen Frieden," in *Über den Gemeinspruch: Das mag in der Theorie Richtig Sein, taugt aber nicht für die Praxis / Zum ewigen Frieden: Ein philosophischer Entwurf*, ed. Heiner F. Klemme (Hamburg: Meiner, 1992), 61–62.

75. Michael W. Doyle, "Kant, Liberal Legacies, and Foreign Affairs," *Philosophy and Public Affairs* 12 (1983): 205–235, 323–353.

76. Kurt Heidrich, *Preussen im Kampfe gegen die französische Revolution bis zur zweiten Teilung Polens* (Stuttgart: Cotta, 1908), 332.

77. Quoted in *Scots Magazine* 40 (August 1778): 421.

78. Christian Gottlob Heyne, *De bellis internecinis eorumque caussis et eventis*, in *Opuscula academica* (Göttingen: Diitrich, 1796), 4:472–473.

79. Isnard, Address to the Nation, in *The Political State of Europe for the Year 1793* (London: Jordan, 1793), 269–270.

80. Johann Caspar Bluntschli, *Das moderne Völkerrecht der civilisirten Staten* (Nördlingen: Beck, 1872), 320 (§570a); Francis Lieber, *Instructions for the Government of Armies of the United States, in the Field* (New York: Van Nostrand, 1863), 21–22 (§82). For their relations see Betsy Röben, *Johann Caspar Bluntschli, Francis Lieber und das moderne Völkerrecht, 1861–1881* (Baden-Baden: Nomos, 2003). Röben paints a more humanitarian picture of Lieber than does Witt, *Lincoln's Code*, chaps. 7 and 8.

81. Montesquieu, *Considérations sur les causes de la grandeur des romains et de leur décadence* (Paris: Hachette, 1945), 103.

82. Heffter, *Das europäische Völkerrecht der Gegenwart*, 203 (§113), 236 (§136), 20–21 (§9).

83. *Encyclopédie méthodique par ordre des matières* (Paris: Panckoucke, 1789), 29:3, 43: "une espèce de convention tacite qui tient du contrat des jeux de hasard."

84. Johann Gottfried Herder, *Ideen zur Philosophie der Geschichte der Menschheit* (Riga: Hartknoch, 1785), 2:253 (IV, "Die Regierungen sind festgestellte Ordnungen").

85. See, e.g., *Deutsche Encyclopädie oder allgemeines Real-Wörterbuch aller Künste und Wissenschaften* (Frankfurt: Varrentrapp und Wenner, 1785), 10:535, s.v. "Friede."

86. Dufour, *Commentaire législatif de la loi du 8 Janvier 1841 sur le duel* (n.p., n.d.), 15.

87. *La Phalange*, June 24, 1842, 1228.

88. Joseph-Marie Portalis, *De la guerre, considérée dans ses Rapports avec les Destinées du genre humain, les droits de nations et la nature humaine* (Paris: n.p., 1856), 8 (the author was the son of the famous jurist); Jean Lagorgette, *Le rôle de la guerre: Étude de sociologie générale* (Paris: Giard & Brière, 1906), 165.

89. Gat, *The Origins of Military Thought*.

90. Carl von Decker, *Grundzüge der praktischen Strategie* Bibliothek für Offiziere, Bd. 7 (Berlin: Herbig, 1828), 191.

91. Jomini, *Précis de l'art de la guerre, ou, Nouveau tableau analytique*, 1:101–103.

92. Clausewitz, *Vom Kriege*, 330 (bk. II, chap. 5).

93. Lynn's wonderful formulation, "war as event," is meant differently, but it captures this great cultural shift magnificently. John Lynn, "International Rivalry and Warfare, 1700–1815," in *The Short Oxford History of Europe: Eighteenth-Century Europe*, ed. T. C. W. Blanning (New York: Oxford University Press, 2000), 178–217.

94. See Weber's assault on the nineteenth-century fascination with Marathon (Eduard Meyer) and Tagliacozzo (Karl Hampe) in Max Weber, "Objektive Möglichkeit und adäquate Verursachung in der historischen Kulturbetrachtung," in *Gesammelte Aufsätze zur Wissenschaftslehre* (Tübingen: Mohr, 1922), 273–275.

95. See Gibbon's discussion and references to Godefroy in Edward Gibbon, *The History of the Decline and Fall of the Roman Empire*, ed. J. B. Bury (London: Methuen, 1914), 2:323–324 (chap. 20).

96. Ibid., 5:266 (chap. 49): Tours "perhaps" saved Europe from "the Mahometan yoke"; and more assertively in the well-known passage at 6:16–19 (chap. 52).

97. Ibid., 2:599 (chap. 26).

98. Francis Fukuyama, *The End of History and the Last Man* (New York: Free Press, 1992), 64. Fukuyama presumably borrowed here from Alexandre Kojève, *Introduction to the Reading of Hegel*, trans. James H. Nichols Jr. (New York: Basic, 1969), 44.

99. Hegel himself simply noted that he had finished his *Phänomenologie* at the time of the battle, "amid the cannon thunder." The more grandiose interpretation emerged in the 1830s, after his death. For a description of its emergence among his followers, see G. J. P. J. Bolland, "Zur Neuen Ausgabe," in *Georg Wilh. Friedr. Hegels Phänomenologie des Geistes*, ed. Bolland (Leiden: Adriani, 1907), xxvi–xxvii. For an early example, see Friedrich Kapp, *Georg Wilhelm Friedrich Hegel als Gymnasial-Rektor* (Minden: Essmann, 1835), 1.

100. Frank Becker, *Bilder von Krieg und Nation: Die Einigungskriege in der bürgerlichen Öffentlichkeit Deutschlands, 1864–1913* (Munich: Oldenbourg, 2001), 132.

101. Cynthia Nicoletti, "The American Civil War as a Trial by Battle," *Law and History Review* 28 (2010): 71–110.

CONCLUSION

1. Guglielmo Ferrero, "L'évolution de la guerre depuis trois siècles," *Revue internationale de la Croix-Rouge* 13 (1931): 183.

2. Hoffman Nickerson, "War, Democracy and Peace," *Criterion* 14 (1935): 351–363. This fine essay anticipates some of the claims of this book.

3. Liddell Hart, *The Ghost of Napoleon* (New Haven, CT: Yale University Press, 1934).

4. Liddell Hart, *Thoughts on War* (Staplehurst, UK: Spellmount, 1999), 42–43.

5. Kellog-Briand Pact of 1928, General Treaty for the Renunciation of War as an Instrument of National Policy, Art. I, in *League of Nations Treaty Series* 94 (1929): 63.

6. See most recently the Kampala amendment to the Rome Statute, discussed in Jennifer Trahan, "The Rome Statute's Amendment on the Crime of Aggression: Negotiations at the Kampala Review Conference," *International Criminal Law Review* 11 (2011): 49–104.

7. Discussion with further citations in, e.g., Beatrice Heuser, *Reading Clausewitz* (London: Pimlico, 2002), 30–33. For wise remarks on the implication of this teaching by a great student of Clausewitz, see Raymond Aron, *Sur Clausewitz* (Brussels: Éditions Complexe, 1987), 103.

8. Harold D. Lasswell, *Politics: Who Gets What, When, How* (New York: P. Smith, 1950).

9. Lasswell himself was prepared to view elite ascendancy through any means, including revolutionary and military violence, as political. See notably his discussion of Clausewitz in ibid., 55–61.

10. Scholars sometimes interpret the proposition that war should be a "continuation of politics" to mean that the military should be subject to civilian control. That would be a highly inapposite way of describing the eighteenth century.

11. My translation of *leidige Tröster*. Immanuel Kant, "Zum ewigen Frieden," in *Über den Gemeinspruch: Das mag in der Theorie Richtig Sein, taugt aber nicht für die*

Praxis / Zum ewigen Frieden: Ein philosophischer Entwurf, ed. Heiner F. Klemme (Hamburg: Meiner, 1992), 65.

12. Ibid., 64–68.

13. Martha Finnemore, *The Purpose of Intervention: Changing Beliefs about the Use of Force* (Ithaca, NY: Cornell University Press, 2003), 19.

14. Michael Howard, "Constraints on Warfare," in *The Laws of War: Constraints on Warfare in the Western World*, ed. Michael Howard, George J. Andreopoulos, and Mark R. Shulman (New Haven, CT: Yale University Press, 1994), 4.

15. James Q. Whitman, *The Origins of Reasonable Doubt: Theological Roots of the Criminal Trial* (New Haven, CT: Yale University Press, 2008).

16. Johan Huizinga, *Homo Ludens: A Study of the Play Element in Culture* (Boston: Beacon, 1950), 90.

17. Carl Schmitt, *Der Nomos der Erde im Völkerrecht des* Jus Publicum Europaeum, 4th ed. (Berlin: Duncker & Humblot, 1997), 298.

18. Hugo Grotius, *De iure belli ac pacis libri tres, cum annotatis auctoris, nec non J. F. Gronovii Notis & J. Barbeyracii animadversionibus commentariis insuper locupletissimis Henr. l. b.. de Cocceii . . . Insertis quoque Observationibus Samuelis l. b. de Cocceii* (Lausanne: Bousquet, 1752), 4:336 (bk. 3, chap. 20, §43).

19. Ryan Goodman and Derek Jinks write of the "socialization" of states through the mechanisms not only of coercion and persuasion but also of acculturation. Goodman and Jinks, "How to Influence States: Socialization and Human Rights Law," *Duke Law Journal* 54 (2004): 621–703, also summarizing much other literature. In a sense, my argument here is also one about socialization. I think it is important to emphasize, though, that the logic of maintaining state legitimacy can make states more dangerous actors in the process of socialization than modern individuals are. Because the right to use violence is a question of existential significance for sovereigns, they cannot be "socialized" out of the use of violence in the same way individuals can be. That means that the work of socializing states must confront peculiar risks and difficulties.

20. For the still "aspirational" character of the responsibility to protect, see Anthony Aust, *Handbook of International Law* (Cambridge: Cambridge University Press, 2010), 214.

21. For reflections by a leading modern specialist in international trade, see Robert Howse, "Montesquieu on Commerce, Conquest, War and Peace," *Brooklyn Journal of International Law* 31 (2006): 693–708.

22. Henry Sumner Maine, *Ancient Law: Its Connection with the Early History of Society, and Its Relation to Modern Ideas* (London: Murray, 1861), 247–248.

23. Max Weber, "Objektive Möglichkeit und adäquate Verursachung in der historischen Kulturbetrachtung," in *Gesammelte Aufsätze zur Wissenschaftslehre* (Tübingen: Mohr, 1922), 273–275.

24. For an excellent account, see Eyal Benvenisti, *The International Law of Occupation* (Princeton, NJ: Princeton University Press, 1993), 92–97. The key question, finessed by the victors in 1945 but still troubling to lawyers, was whether unconditional surrender was a form of the classic doctrine of *debellatio*, and whether *debellatio* could be appropriately invoked.

25. The pressures emanating from the White House and the resulting discomfort of planners with knowledge of the law are vividly described in "The Reminiscences of Hugh Borton," Columbia University Oral History Research Office, 1958, 14–15.

26. For efforts of legal scholars to grapple with the problems created by the American traditions of unconditional surrender/*debellatio* and the situation in Iraq, see Melissa Patterson, "Who's Got the Title, or, The Remnants of *Debellatio* in Post-Invasion Iraq," *Harvard International Law Journal* 47 (2006): 467–488; Adam Roberts, "Transformative Military Occupation," *American Journal of International Law* 100 (2006): 580–622. For a survey of the law as seen by international lawyers, see Yutaka Arai-Takahashi, *The Law of Occupation: Continuity and Change of International Humanitarian Law, and Its Interaction with International Human Rights Law* (Leiden, Netherlands: Nijhoff, 2009).

Acknowledgments

My work on this book was supported by a fellowship from the John Simon Guggenheim Foundation, for which I express my deep gratitude. An early version of my research was presented as the Fulton Lecture in Legal History at the University of Chicago Law School. My warm thanks to my friends at Chicago and to the Fulton family. I also benefited immensely from the opportunity to present my work to French colleagues as a visiting fellow at the Institut Michel Villey at the Université de Paris II.

Two superb scholars gave much time to critical readings of my drafts: John Lynn, a prince among military historians, and Gabriella Blum, the sharpest and most inventive of students of the law of war. I owe a great deal to both of them. Gracious invitations permitted me to present my work at seminars at Tel Aviv University, The Hebrew University, New York University Law School, Columbia Law School, and Harvard Law School.

There are too many friends and colleagues at Yale Law School to thank individually, but as so often I owe special thanks to Bruce Ackerman for his attentive and critical reading and to John Witt, my fellow wanderer in the laws of war. Justine Firnhaber-Baker and Cynthia

Nicoletti kindly provided me with copies of their unpublished work. Among many others from whose interventions and comments I have profited I would especially like to thank William Ewald, George Fletcher, R. H. Helmholz, Randall Lesaffer, Sara McDougall, Laurent Mayali, William Ian Miller, Samuel Moyn, Stephen Neff, Scott Shapiro, and Robert Sloane.

Index

just war theory, property rights and,
95–132; counsel of conscience and,
103–104; eighteenth-century traditions,
113–119; Frederick the Great's "manner
of war" and, 95–97; Frederick the
Great's seizure of Silesia and, 119–132;
medieval and early modern tradition,
100–113; role in conventional account of
eighteenth-century warfare, 97–99;
treating war as a form of punishment,
100–103
jus victoriae, 10–12; Frederick's Mollwitz
and Chotusitz victories and, 70–76;
monarchical power and, 15–21;
republicanism and decline of monarchical power, 21–24; rules of war and
incentives, 189–194; use of term, 266n13

Kant, Immanuel, 11, 129, 202, 235, 248
Keegan, John, 8, 39–40, 43–44, 82–83, 212,
215
Keeley, Lawrence, 28, 29, 32, 95
Keen, Maurice, 142, 145, 182
Kent, James, 221–222
Kingsbury, Benedict, 97–98
Kleist, Heinrich von, 220
Königgrätz, Battle of, 22, 212–213, 229
Korman, Sharon, 67–69, 117, 126
Krentz, Peter, 32, 187, 195, 198–199
Kriegsmanier (manner of war), 96,
162–169, 176, 236

la Curne de Sainte-Palaye, Jean-Baptiste
de, 144, 146
Lanni, Adriaan, 187
Lasswell, Harold, 247
*Laws of War: Constraints on the Warfare
in the Western World* (Howard), 195
legal significance, of victory, 46, 47
legitimacy: modern war and, 253–255;
princely authority and rules of war,
204–206; reinforced through practice of
eighteenth-century warfare, 245–251;
violence and, 169–171
Leopold, Prince of Hohenzollern-
Sigmaringen, 225

Lewis, Mark, 30
Liddell Hart, Basil, 227, 245, 248
Lieber, Francis, 237
Livy, 46, 80, 84–85
Locke, John, 224
López, Juan, 139
Louis XIV, King of France, 162, 167, 170,
172–178, 180, 189, 230–231
Lünig, Johann Christian, 164–167, 176, 177
Lynn, John, 39, 142, 166–167, 184

Machiavelli, Niccolò, 53, 83–84, 86–88,
90, 91, 237
Maine, Henry, 109, 127, 257
Malplaquet, Battle of, 58, 172–179, 183–184,
189
Marathon, Battle of, 38
Maria Theresa, of Austria, 69, 73, 76,
121–122, 180, 203, 205, 256–257
Marlborough, Duke of, 173, 175
Marquise von O (Kleist), 220
Martens, Georg Friedrich, 96, 97, 118, 123,
125, 162–163, 191, 192, 233, 306n33
Martszen, Jan, 185
Mattéi, Jean-Mathieu, 114
Maurice, comte de Saxe, 59, 61, 179–180
Mauvillon, Marquis de, 72, 204
Maximilian I, 184–185
McPherson, James, 209, 210
medieval era, warfare in, 3–4, 33–35
Memoirs on the Chivalry of the Past (la
Curne de Sainte-Palaye), 144
military violence, monarchical monopolization of, 133–171; battle warfare as
princely trial by combat, 153–160;
dueling and trial by combat contrasted,
147–153; Kriegsmanier and, 162–169;
noble combat and chivalry, 140–147;
princely struggle over right to make war,
133–140; relationship of violence and
legitimacy, 169–171
millenarian events, 53; modern warfare
and, 258–259; pitched battles seen as,
237–244; significance of victory and,
46–49
Mills, Charles, 221
Milvian Bridge, Battle of, 46–47, 242